THE CAMBRIDGE COMPAN

MW00335165

The Cambridge Companion to Kaz introduction to key aspects of the nove volume addresses Ishiguro's engageme humanity and personal responsibility, ... aesthetic value and political valency, with the vicissitudes of memory and historical documentation, and with questions of family, home, and homelessness. Focused through the personal experiences of some of the most memorable characters in contemporary fiction, Ishiguro's writing speaks to the major communitarian questions of our time – questions of nationalism and colonialism, race and ethnicity, migration, war, and cultural memory and social justice. The chapters attend to Ishiguro's highly readable novels while also ranging across his other creative output. Gathering together established and emerging scholars from the UK, Europe, the USA, and East Asia, the volume offers a survey of key works and themes while also moving critical discussion forward in new and challenging ways.

Andrew Bennett is Professor of English at the University of Bristol.

A complete list of books in the series is at the back of this book.

THE CAMBRIDGE
COMPANION TO
KAZUO ISHIGURO

EDITED BY
ANDREW BENNETT
University of Bristol

CAMBRIDGE
UNIVERSITY PRESS

CAMBRIDGE
UNIVERSITY PRESS

Shaftesbury Road, Cambridge CB2 8EA, United Kingdom

One Liberty Plaza, 20th Floor, New York, NY 10006, USA

477 Williamstown Road, Port Melbourne, VIC 3207, Australia

314–321, 3rd Floor, Plot 3, Splendor Forum, Jasola District Centre, New Delhi – 110025, India

103 Penang Road, #05–06/07, Visioncrest Commercial, Singapore 238467

Cambridge University Press is part of Cambridge University Press & Assessment, a department of the University of Cambridge.

We share the University's mission to contribute to society through the pursuit of education, learning and research at the highest international levels of excellence.

www.cambridge.org
Information on this title: www.cambridge.org/9781108830218

DOI: 10.1017/9781108909525

First published 2023

A catalogue record for this publication is available from the British Library.

Library of Congress Cataloging-in-Publication Data
Names: Bennett, Andrew, 1960 December 2- editor.
Title: The Cambridge companion to Kazuo Ishiguro / edited by Andrew Bennett, University of Bristol.
Description: Cambridge, United Kingdom ; New York, NY : Cambridge University Press, 2023. | Series: Cambridge companions to literature | Includes bibliographical references and index.
Identifiers: LCCN 2022044119 (print) | LCCN 2022044120 (ebook) | ISBN 9781108830218 (hardback) | ISBN 9781108822022 (paperback) | ISBN 9781108909525 (epub)
Subjects: LCSH: Ishiguro, Kazuo, 1954—Criticism and interpretation. | LCGFT: Literary criticism.
Classification: LCC PR6059.S5 Z53 2023 (print) | LCC PR6059.S5 (ebook) | DDC 823/.914-dc23/eng/20221101
LC record available at https://lccn.loc.gov/2022044119
LC ebook record available at https://lccn.loc.gov/2022044120

ISBN 978-1-108-83021-8 Hardback
ISBN 978-1-108-82202-2 Paperback

CONTENTS

CONTENTS

FIGURES

CONTRIBUTORS

DOUG BATTERSBY is a Marie Curie Global Fellow at Stanford University and the University of Bristol. He is the author of *Troubling Late Modernism: Ethics, Feeling, and the Novel Form* (2022) and essays on several modern and contemporary writers, including an article on Ishiguro published in *MFS: Modern Fiction Studies* (2021). His current book project explores representations of the heart in Victorian and modernist fiction.

ANDREW BENNETT is Professor of English at the University of Bristol. His most recent monograph is *Suicide Century: Literature and Suicide from James Joyce to David Foster Wallace* (2017). He has published widely on British Romantic literature and on twentieth-century and contemporary literature. He is co-author, with Nicholas Royle, of *An Introduction to Literature, Criticism and Theory* (6th ed., 2023) and *This Thing Called Literature: Reading, Thinking, Writing* (2nd ed., 2024). He contributed a chapter on *When We Were Orphans* to *Kazuo Ishiguro: New Insights* (2023), edited by Peter Sloane and Kristian Shaw.

STEPHEN BENSON is an associate professor in the School of Literature, Drama and Creative Writing at the University of East Anglia. He is the co-editor of *Creative Criticism: An Anthology and Guide* (2014) and *Writing the Field Recording: Sound, Word, Environment* (2018). His essay on music in the work of Ali Smith is included in the *Routledge Companion to Music and Modern Literature* (2022).

PETER BOXALL is Professor of English at the University of Sussex. He has written several books on the novel, including *The Value of the Novel* (2015) and *The Prosthetic Imagination* (2020). He is currently preparing a volume of collected essays, entitled *The Possibility of Literature*, and writing a book entitled *Fictions of the West*.

LAURA COLOMBINO is Full Professor of English at the University of Genova. Her focus is on the relationship between literature and other disciplines, namely the visual arts, architecture, and philosophy. She authored the books *Ford Madox Ford: Vision, Visuality and Writing* (2008) and *Spatial Politics in Contemporary*

London Literature: Writing Architecture and the Body (2013). She also co-edited *The Routledge Research Companion to Ford Madox Ford* (2018) and the special issue of *Textual Practice* on 'Narrating the (Non)Human: Ecologies, Consciousness and Myth' (2022). She sits on the editorial board of the Oxford University Press complete edition of Ford's works.

ROBERT EAGLESTONE is Professor of Contemporary Literature and Thought at Royal Holloway, University of London. He works on contemporary literature and literary theory, on contemporary philosophy and on holocaust and genocide. He is the author of eight books, including *The Broken Voice: Reading Post-Holocaust Literature* (2017) and *Truth and Wonder: A Literary Introduction to Plato and Aristotle* (2021), and the editor or co-editor of ten further books including *Brexit and Literature* (2018) and, with Daniel O'Gorman, *The Routledge Companion to Twenty First Century Literary Fiction* (2019).

VANESSA GUIGNERY is Professor of Contemporary English and Postcolonial Literature at the École Normale Supérieure de Lyon. She has published several books and essays on the work of Julian Barnes, including *The Fiction of Julian Barnes* (2006), *Conversations with Julian Barnes* (2009), co-edited with Ryan Roberts, and *Julian Barnes from the Margins* (2020). She is the author of monographs on Ben Okri's *The Famished Road* (2012), B. S. Johnson (2009), and Jonathan Coe (2015). She is currently writing a book on Kazuo Ishiguro's creative process through an examination of his archives preserved at the Harry Ransom Center in Austin, Texas.

REBECCA KARNI is a lecturer in the Department of Literary Arts and Studies at the Rhode Island School of Design. Her research interests are in contemporary global Anglophone, world, British, American, and Japanese literatures; transnational and comparative literary studies; the novel; narrative and literary theory; global film; and translation studies. Her publications include 'Made in Translation: Language, "Japaneseness", "Englishness", and "Global Culture" in Ishiguro' in *Comparative Literature Studies* and a forthcoming chapter, 'Ishiguro's Tempered Presentational Realism and Practice', in *Kazuo Ishiguro: New Insights*, edited by Peter Sloane and Kristian Shaw (2023).

LIANI LOCHNER is an associate professor of Anglophone Postcolonial Literature at Université Laval, Canada. Educated in South Africa and England, her research interests are in critical theory and world literature, and she has published related essays on a wide range of authors including Ishiguro, J. M. Coetzee, and Zoë Wicomb. Her chapters on *Never Let Me Go* have appeared in *Kazuo Ishiguro: New Critical Visions of the Novels*, edited by Barry Lewis and Sebastien Groes (2011), and *Kazuo Ishiguro in a Global Context*, edited by Cynthia Wong and Hülya Yıldız (2014).

ULRIKA MAUDE is Professor of Modern Literature at the University of Bristol, where she is also Director of the Centre for Health, Humanities and Science. She has published widely on modernism and on Samuel Beckett, including *Beckett, Technology and the Body* (2009) and the forthcoming *Samuel Beckett and Medicine*. She is co-editor of *Beckett and Phenomenology* (2009), *The Cambridge Companion to the Body in Literature* (2015), and *The Bloomsbury Companion to Modernist Literature* (2018).

PETER SLOANE is Senior Lecturer in English at the University of Buckingham. He is the author of the monographs *David Foster Wallace and the Body* (2019) and *Kazuo Ishiguro's Gestural Poetics* (2021), and the editor of the forthcoming collections *Kazuo Ishiguro: New Insights* (2023) and *ReFocus: The Films of Claire Denis* (2023). His current monograph project explores the experience of refugees in world literature and film.

IVAN STACY is an associate professor in the School of Foreign Languages and Literature at Beijing Normal University. He is the author of *The Complicit Text: Failures of Witnessing in Postwar Fiction* (Lexington 2021) and has published on complicity and the carnivalesque in the work of Ishiguro, W. G. Sebald, Thomas Pynchon, and China Miéville, as well as the American television series *The Wire*. Ivan has lived and taught in the UK, China, South Korea, Thailand, Libya, and Bhutan.

YOSHIKI TAJIRI is a professor at the University of Tokyo. He has published extensively on modernism in English literature, Samuel Beckett, J. M. Coetzee, Ishiguro, Yukio Mishima, and other authors. He has published *Samuel Beckett and the Prosthetic Body: The Organs and Senses in Modernism* (2007) and co-edited *Samuel Beckett and Pain* (2012), *Samuel Beckett and Trauma* (2018), *Reading Kazuo Ishiguro's 'Never Let Me Go'* (in Japanese, 2018), and *Kazuo Ishiguro and Japan* (in Japanese, 2020). He has also translated Ishiguro's 'A Family Supper' into Japanese.

JERRINE TAN was born and raised in Singapore. She received her BA in English and Economics from University of California, Berkeley and her MA and PhD in English from Brown University. She is Assistant Professor of English at City University Hong Kong. Her research interests include world literature and film, contemporary fiction, twentieth-century American literature, and gender and sexuality studies. Her academic essays have appeared or are forthcoming in *Modern Fiction Studies* and *Wasafiri* among other journals. She writes regularly for public-facing platforms such as *Literary Hub*, WIRED, *Los Angeles Review of Books*, *Brooklyn Rail*, and *Asian American Writers' Workshop*.

YUGIN TEO is Senior Lecturer in Communications and English at Bournemouth University. He is the author of *Kazuo Ishiguro and Memory* (2014) and his research on memory, care technologies in science fiction, and contemporary literature has been published in the journals *C21: Journal of 21st-Century Writings*, *Critique: Studies in Contemporary Fiction*, *Medical Humanities*, and a special issue of *Science Fiction Film and Television*. Together with Aris Mousoutzanis, he co-edited a special issue of *Science Fiction Studies* on nostalgia published in 2021. He is currently working on a chapter on controversies for a companion to literary media.

CYNTHIA F. WONG is Professor of English at the University of Colorado, Denver, where she teaches modern and contemporary world literature. She is the author of *Writers and Their Work: Kazuo Ishiguro* (3rd ed., 2019) and co-editor, with Brian Shaffer, of *Conversations with Kazuo Ishiguro* (2008) and with Hülya Yıldız of *Kazuo Ishiguro in a Global Context* (2015). She has published essays on Asian American authors Jhumpa Lahiri, Karen Tei Yamashita, Joy Kogawa, and Julie Otsuka.

ACKNOWLEDGEMENTS

It was a great pleasure to meet with many of the contributors to this volume at the Twenty-First Century Perspectives on Kazuo Ishiguro conference in Wolverhampton at the beginning of February 2020, just as the project was getting off the ground but also just before conferences and other in-person events suddenly stopped for many months. I also enjoyed meeting many of the contributors again in June 2021, but online this time at a workshop that we organized to share our initial thoughts on Ishiguro's new novel, *Klara and Sun*. First and foremost, I want to thank all of the contributors for their excellent chapters and for their good-humoured and graceful co-operation at all stages.

The volume was initiated at the suggestion of Bethany Thomas, my editor at Cambridge University Press, who offered wise and astute advice on the project as a whole and on individual chapters. She has been ably supported by others at Cambridge University Press, including especially George Paul Laver (editorial assistant) and Aiswarya Narayanan (project manager). I am also indebted to Penny Harper for her expert copy-editing, and to Ben Hickey for his great work in compiling the index.

Ulrika Maude has not only contributed a chapter to the book but lived with it as it evolved from an initial idea to a completed typescript: many, many are the occasions on which we have shared our interest in and love for Kazuo Ishiguro's work over the last few years, and neither the book as a whole nor my contributions to it would be what they are without her input – my warm thanks go to Ulrika for her ideas, her inspiration, and her continuing support.

Key sections of the Introduction began as part of a paper on 'The Author Oeuvre' that I presented at the launch of *The Cambridge Handbook of Literary Authorship* at the University of Ghent in October 2019: I would like to thank Gert Buelens for inviting me to speak and for starting me thinking about Ishiguro and the profession of authorship.

The images from Kazuo Ishiguro's manuscript notes in Chapter 6 are reproduced with kind permission from Kazuo Ishiguro and the Harry Ransom Center, The University of Texas at Austin.

CHRONOLOGY

1954   Born on 8 November in Nagasaki, Japan, to Shizuo Ishiguro and Shizuko (née Michida), a middle child with two sisters.

1960   The family move to Guilford in Surrey, UK, in April, when Shizuo, a research scientist, takes up a post at the National Institute of Oceanography in Wormley.

1966   Leaves Stoughton Primary School, Guildford.

1973   Graduates from Woking County Grammar School for Boys; undertakes various casual jobs on a gap year before university.

1974   Hitchhikes around the West Coast of the USA and British Columbia with a guitar, attempting to establish himself as a singer-songwriter as well as starting to draft stories. After returning to the UK, enrols on a degree in English and Philosophy at the University of Kent.

1975   Suspends studies at university for the academic year 1975–6, taking up a job as a community worker in Renfrew, near Glasgow.

1978   Graduates from the University of Kent.

1979   Works with homeless people for the Cyrenians charity in Notting Hill, London. Meets Lorna MacDougal.

1980   Graduates with an MA in Creative Writing from the University of East Anglia (taught by Malcolm Bradbury; mentored by Angela Carter). Works in Cardiff as a social worker. 'A Strange and Sometimes Sadness' is published in the literary magazine *Bananas*.

1981   Moves to Sydenham, South London, working with the homeless until taking up full-time writing in 1982. Three stories published by Faber in *Introduction 7: Stories by New Writers* ('A Strange and Sometimes Sadness'; 'Getting Poisoned'; 'Waiting for J'); 'A Family Supper' is published in *Quarto* magazine.

1982   *A Pale View of Hills* is published by Faber in the UK. Commissioned by Channel 4 to write two plays for television. Becomes a British subject.

1983 'A Family Supper' published by Penguin in *Firebird 2*; 'Summer after the War' published in the *Granta* 'Best of Young British Novelists' volume. *A Pale View of Hills* awarded Winifred Holtby Prize for fiction.

1984 Commissioned TV script, *A Profile of Arthur J. Mason*, is broadcast by Channel 4.

1986 Publishes *An Artist of the Floating World*, which wins the Whitbread Book of the Year award and is shortlisted for the Booker Prize. Publishes an Introduction to Penguin the translation of Yasunari Kawabata's *Snow Country* and *Thousand Cranes*. TV play *The Gourmet* is broadcast by Channel 4. Marries Lorna. Travels in East Asia (Singapore and Malaysia).

1989 Publishes *The Remains of the Day*, which wins the Booker Prize. Visits Japan for the first time since leaving the country in 1960. Elected Fellow of the Royal Society of Literature.

1992 Birth of daughter, Naomi.

1993 The film version of *The Remains of the Day* (dir. James Ivory with film script by Ruth Prawer-Jhabvala; starring Anthony Hopkins and Emma Thompson) is released and is nominated for eight Oscars, five Golden Globe awards, and six BAFTAS.

1995 Publishes *The Unconsoled*, which is shortlisted for the Booker Prize. Awarded the OBE for services to literature, and Italy's Premio Scanno prize.

1998 Awarded the Chevalier de l'Ordre des Arts et des Lettres by the French Government.

2000 Publishes *When We Were Orphans*, which is shortlisted for the Booker Prize and the Whitbread award.

2003 Contributes liner notes to the American jazz vocalist Stacey Kent's *In Love Again* CD.

2004 Release of *The Saddest Music in the World* (dir. Guy Madden), for which Ishiguro originally wrote the screenplay.

2005 Publishes *Never Let Me Go*, which is shortlisted for the Booker Prize.

2006 *The White Countess* (dir. James Ivory; starring Ralph Fiennes and Natasha Richardson), for which Ishiguro wrote the screenplay, is released in the UK.

2007 Shizuo Ishiguro dies. Begins collaboration with Stacey Kent: lyrics appear on four songs on her *Breakfast on the Morning Tram* CD.

2009 *Nocturnes: Five Stories of Music and Nightfall* is published and is shortlisted for the James Tait Black Memorial Prize.

2010 Film version of *Never Let Me Go* is released (dir. Mark Romanek, screenplay by Alex Garland; starring Carey Mulligan, Keira Knightley, and Andrew Garfield).

2011 Lyrics for 'Postcard Lovers' on Stacy Kent's CD *Dreamer in Concert*.

2013 Lyrics for three songs on Stacy Kent's CD *The Changing Lights*.

2015 *The Buried Giant* is published. Papers, including drafts, letters, and notes, are bought by the Harry Ransom Center at the University of Texas, Austin.

2017 Awarded the Nobel Prize in Literature. Lyrics for 'Bullet Train' on Stacy Kent's *I Know I Dream* CD.

2018 Awarded the Japanese Order of the Rising Sun.

2019 Awarded a British knighthood for services to literature. Shizuko Ishiguro dies.

2021 *Klara and the Sun* is published. Lyrics for three songs on Stacy Kent's *Songs from Other Places* CD.

2022 Release of *Living* (dir. Oliver Hermanus; starring Bill Nighy), for which Ishiguro wrote the screenplay based on Akira Kurosama's *Ikiru* (1952).

Major Publications in Date Order

1982 *A Pale View of Hills*
1986 *An Artist of the Floating World*
1989 *The Remains of the Day*
1995 *The Unconsoled*
2000 *When We Were Orphans*
2005 *Never Let Me Go*
2009 *Nocturnes: Five Stories of Music and Nightfall*
2015 *The Buried Giant*
2021 *Klara and the Sun*

ABBREVIATIONS

AFW   *An Artist of the Floating World*
BG   *The Buried Giant*
CKI   *Conversations with Kazuo Ishiguro*
KS   *Klara and the Sun*
N   *Nocturnes: Five Stories of Music and Nightfall*
NLMG   *Never Let Me Go*
PVH   *A Pale View of Hills*
RD   *The Remains of the Day*
TCE   *My Twentieth Century Evening and Other Small Breakthroughs*
U   *The Unconsoled*
WWWO   *When We Were Orphans*

ANDREW BENNETT

Introduction

Regularly cited as one of the most important novelists writing in English today, Kazuo Ishiguro is the author of eight novels, a short-story collection and several uncollected short stories, as well as song lyrics and scripts for the cinema and for television.[1] Beginning with *A Pale View of Hills* in 1982, Ishiguro's novels have consistently focused on the effect on individuals of larger cultural, political, and historical movements and dilemmas in ways that have captured the imagination of an international readership while also gaining enormous critical acclaim and forging for themselves a place in the contemporary literary canon. With Ishiguro's position in British and World literature confirmed by the opening of his personal archive at the Harry Ransom Center in Austin, Texas in 2017, and by awards such as the Nobel Prize in Literature in 2017, the Japanese Order of the Rising Sun in 2018, and a British knighthood for services to literature in 2019, this is undoubtedly the moment for a *Cambridge Companion* – a volume designed both to take stock of and to reconsider Ishiguro's remarkable body of work. While the chapters in the present volume are concerned most of all with his consistently profound, intriguing, and highly readable novels, they also range across Ishiguro's other creative output and draw on the many illuminating interviews that he has given over the last four decades.

Along with countless reviews and magazine and newspaper pieces, Ishiguro's work is the subject of several hundred academic book chapters and full-length scholarly journal articles, as well as a number of research monographs, essay collections, and student-oriented textbooks.[2] The present volume draws on this work by gathering together a range of established and emerging scholars from the UK, Europe, the USA, and East Asia. Offering a survey of the key works and themes while also moving critical discussion forward in new and challenging ways, *The Cambridge Companion to Kazuo Ishiguro* aims to offer an essential guide for both students and established academics. Wide-ranging in its engagement with Ishiguro's writings, the volume allows for key themes and questions to be fully addressed while also affording space for detailed discussion of specific works.

Ishiguro's novels and short stories focus in innovative ways on fundamental questions of humanity and personal responsibility, on aesthetic value and political valency, on the vicissitudes of memory and historical documentation, and on questions of family, home, and homelessness in relation to personal and social identity. His writing speaks in distinctive ways to some of the major communitarian questions of our time: nationalism and colonialism, race and ethnicity, migration, war, and cultural memory and social justice. And his novels and short stories do so by closely following the reconstruction in narrative form of the experiences of individuals who are, almost invariably, calamitously fallible because all-too-human (or in the case of clones or AI robots, all-too-human-like). But Ishiguro's consistent and variously charged thematic focus on the relationship between personal responsibility and – or *for* – social harm is also notable for its highly accomplished deployment of the inherent resources of language, narrative voice, and narrative structure. A supreme prose stylist whose work is notable for the ways it exploits the subtle, sometimes almost imperceptible rhetorical malfunctions and inarticulacies of narrators, for the expressive lapses in memory and in the moral rectitude of the individuals who people his stories and tell their tales, Ishiguro's novels are notable for the skill with which characterization and voice are intricately intertwined, and for the sophistication with which they challenge formal and generic preconceptions about the novel form itself.

Forever Flinching

Born in Nagasaki, Japan, in 1954, Ishiguro's family moved to England in 1960 when his father took up an initially temporary but soon permanent post as a research scientist at the National Institute of Oceanography in Surrey. In interviews about his life and work and through the themes and narrative techniques of the novels and stories, Ishiguro traces the condition of being caught between two or more worlds – a condition hinging on questions of belonging and home, on immigration and cultural displacement, on nationality and ethnic or racial difference, and, especially, on language itself as a non-transparent, non-'obvious' medium of communication. 'I wasn't a very English Englishman, and I wasn't a very Japanese Japanese either', Ishiguro memorably commented of his earlier self in a published conversation with the Japanese writer Kenzaburō Ōe in 1989 (*CKI* 58).

Ishiguro's migrant condition and the fact that English was the second language he learned to speak might account in part for the unique and often quietly surprising ways that his writing develops, and responds to, language. The precise, carefully poised, lucid prose of his novels is itself testament to the difficulty and complexity of saying what you mean and meaning what you say.[3] And his writing is intimately engaged with the hidden occlusions, obfuscations, and displacements that words allow a speaker: 'I'm interested in the way words hide meanings', he commented in a 1990 interview, with a keen eye on the paradox of a writer saying such a thing (CKI 71). Whether it is a clone who unquestioningly adopts the euphemistic language of discrimination in Never Let Me Go ('normals' for the privileged natural-born people in a society; 'completing' for the death of a clone whose vital organs have been harvested), or an AI robot who records the dystopian vocabulary of privilege and brutal social categorization and effective segregation in Klara and the Sun ('lifted', 'social interaction scores', 'substitutions', 'interaction meetings', 'continuation', 'slow fade'), Ishiguro's novels exploit the way the words we use both disclose and conceal ideas, actions, and circumstances, political as well as personal. But in other ways, too, and just through their often almost wilful blindness to their own condition and to the societies in which they live, Ishiguro's first-person narrators often conceal as much as they reveal about what they themselves often don't really know or understand in the narratives they tell us. That words can hide meaning is perhaps a given in relation to pretty much any literary work. But Ishiguro's novels are particularly attuned to the ways narrators conceal and camouflage meanings and do so not least from themselves. Language has this 'other function', Ishiguro comments in an interview, 'which is to conceal and suppress, to deceive one's self and to deceive others (CKI 51). Thus, he remarks, his most famous novel, The Remains of the Day, is 'written in the language of self-deception' (CKI 38). The major innovation involved in Ishiguro's mastery of narrative technique is arguably that it reminds us not just that we shouldn't necessarily trust narrators but that, as he puts it in another interview, there is a 'deep reason' why 'we all have to be unreliable narrators': 'most of us when we look at ourselves', he says, 'have to be rather unreliable in order to face ourselves' (CKI 139). And this sense of unreliability goes deep – into the structure and trajectory of Ishiguro's novels, and into our understanding, such as it is, of his characters. After all, with the exception of the occasionally personalized but predominantly third-person narrator of The Buried Giant, all of Ishiguro's narrators are also the protagonists of the stories they tell. It is prose that works through what John Self has recently characterized as a 'raw' and indeed 'almost demented' kind of narrative 'purity' that consistently refrains from offering any kind of authoritative commentary on a narrator-character's perspective, personality, ethical choices, actions, or voice.[4] Framed as they are by his narrators' occluded sense of themselves, the exigencies of Ishiguro's narratives mean that his language itself is, as he puts it, 'forever flinching from facing up to something' (*CKI* 23). And it is in relation to the varied ways in which people flinch from the truth in the words they use to think and talk about themselves that Ishiguro organizes his remarkable and quietly subversive, hauntingly evocative novels.

Turning Points

To introduce this volume and to offer an overview of Ishiguro's work, we might consider the overview of his life and work that the author himself offered on the occasion of his Nobel lecture in Stockholm on 7 December 2017.[5] *My Twentieth Century Evening and Other Small Breakthroughs* is notable as one of the few public statements that Ishiguro has made on his work outside of the many interviews he has given over the years. And as well as offering a commentary on his career and insights into his working life, the Nobel lecture amounts to something like an exemplary instantiation of modern authorship. Arranged in eight sections, the lecture is structured around a series of six moments – 'small breakthroughs' – in the author's professional or writerly life, the often 'small, scruffy moments' with their 'quiet, private sparks of revelation' that, he explains, are 'important turning points in a writer's career' (*TCE* 30). Ishiguro's lecture, in other words, is a kind of authorial memoir, a brief writer's life.[6]

The lecture begins with Ishiguro's arrival at the University of East Anglia in 1979 sporting a fashionably drooping moustache and shoulder-length hair to begin an MA in Creative Writing – the kind of endeavour that has become, over the intervening forty years, something of a rite of passage, a professional qualification, for a modern author.[7] Ishiguro remembers himself as a writer or writer-in-embryo: he has had a radio play rejected by the BBC and has otherwise only completed two short stories (which he judges to be 'not so good') and begun a third with the intriguing if perhaps somewhat unpromising theme of 'an adolescent who poisons his cat'.[8] Renting a room that is 'not unlike the classic writer's garret', the aspiring novelist sets out to 'transform' himself 'into a writer' (*TCE* 3–4). The breakthrough or 'turning point' in this section involves Ishiguro's realization that Japan could be the subject matter of his first novel – a surprising turn, he suggests, in an era before globalization, multiculturalism, the emergence of 'World Literature' as a category, and the marked public emphasis on minority ethnic narratives of more recent decades.

The second breakthrough or turning point comes after a brief flashback on Ishiguro's arrival in England in 1960 at the age of five and the consequent transformation of Japan for the boy into a matter of memory and imagination. Offering tantalizing and strategically placed personal biographical details, Ishiguro explains that it is now 1983 and that he is living in a modest rented flat in London with his wife, Lorna, and working on his second novel. Reading Proust, he ponders the difference between a screenplay and a novel and recognizes the capacity for prose fiction to express the 'richness' of 'inner movements impossible to capture on the screen' (*TCE* 16). The breakthrough comes as a new understanding of the novel's potential to explore what will become Ishiguro's major theme in novels from *An Artist of the Floating World* in 1986 to *The Buried Giant* in 2015: 'the many layers of self-deception and denial that shrouded any person's view of their own self and of their past' (*TCE* 17).[9] In a sense, the statement encapsulates the primary focus and force of Ishiguro's novels. Mostly written in the first person, each novel concerns the narrator's self-deception and denial as a governing narrative strategy and theme. The following breakthroughs may be seen as nuances on and developments of this central organizing thrust of Ishiguro's writing.

The third turning point revolves around *The Remains of the Day*, and Ishiguro's realization that narrative power can be generated through the collapse of a dam of emotional repression: the butler, Stevens, seems almost to be able to see that his whole life – and his sense of dignity, loyalty, duty, and professionalism – has been a kind of terrible error.[10] Like the Imperialist Japanese propaganda artist Masuji Ono in Ishiguro's previous novel, *An Artist of the Floating World*, Stevens's tragedy is in being a person who firmly believes that he is on the right side of history – always in Ishiguro a dangerous conceit – only to find later on that he really wasn't. The fourth breakthrough comes after a visit to Auschwitz in 1999, from which Ishiguro recalls realizing that while his work has often turned on the 'struggle' between forgetting and remembering for an individual, in the future he will need to focus on the necessity of amnesia for a whole community or nation (a theme that will be fully realized twenty-five years later in *The Buried Giant*) (*TCE* 25).[11] A further revelation has to do with a move from individualized, character-centered narratives to relationship-driven plots in his novel *Never Let Me Go* (*TCE* 29). The final breakthrough is a response to the 'dangerously increasing division' that he perceives in the rise of Trump, Brexit, and right-wing populism in Europe and across the world. Arguing that the post-war liberal-humanist consensus involving a progress narrative of increasing tolerance and freedom is in danger of being overtaken by 'Far Right ideologies and tribal nationalisms' (*TCE* 33), Ishiguro argues that the next generation of writers – a generation from which the then sixty-three-year-old writer excludes himself – will have to find 'a new idea, a great humane vision, around which to rally' (*TCE* 6).

The Parallel Person

Ishiguro's carefully curated overview of the turning points in his career, framed as they are within a series of intimate domestic scenes from a twentieth-century life, offers an exemplary presentation and indeed performance of authorship: this is what the author – or at least what a certain kind of highly successful and internationally esteemed contemporary author – looks like. Indeed, the Nobel lecture opens itself up to a reading in which 'Kazuo Ishiguro' becomes a character in a scene of his own writing. In this sense, Ishiguro is not only a privileged commentator on the body of writing that is ascribed to his name but himself something like a fictional character constructed out of that body of work – while also of course being an embodied human being who lives, breathes, is married to Lorna with whom he has a daughter and a house in North London, writes books, gives interviews: someone who does all the things that we might minimally expect a standardly functional human being to do, including eating, sleeping, breathing, thinking, deciding, talking, and moving and behaving in certain ways.

The key breakthrough or turning point that Ishiguro describes, I have suggested, is the recognition that 'many layers of self-deception and denial' may be said to 'shroud' a person's sense of 'their own self and of their past' and that these layers may themselves make the basis for a novel. On the one hand, the comment refers to a key thematic consideration in Ishiguro's work: each of his novels is concerned with, and in almost all cases narrated by, an individual whose view of themselves is partial, shrouded, self-deceiving, faulty. Ishiguro's novels, we might say, are about nothing other than this, at heart – about the fallible, ignorant, self-deceiving, amnesiac, uncertain narrator-protagonist coming up against the intractable forms of their own denial. On the other hand, the comment has to do with the individual who makes these books and who, *along with or on account of them*, constitutes the author, Kazuo Ishiguro. Standing on the podium in the Swedish Academy in Stockholm, reading from the lectern, is the author who is also a construct, a fiction of authorship – not only the originator or inventor of a certain body of work but in effect himself an invention of that work, part of what is fabricated, contrived, or assembled by it. It is significant, therefore, that there's a kind of quiet, urbane, outwardly modest, restrained, dignified, largely affectless, careful, considerate, and humane tenor in the rhetoric of Ishiguro's lecture and in its performance – and in the persona, the body language, the speech patterns, the intonation, the dress code that Ishiguro projects in his public appearances more generally. But it is a persona and person that is itself reflected in, or that reflects, the prose, the subject matter, and the narrative personae – the narrators and protagonists – of the novels.

It is perhaps no coincidence, therefore, that Ishiguro's novels consistently foreground the question of professional behaviour, ethics, and competence. Almost all of Ishiguro's novels focus, one way or another, on the entwining of the protagonist's identity with a profession – on a person's professional competence or excellence, and their pride in their work. Ishiguro's novels emphasize the skill of a Japanese water-colourist, the dignity of an English butler, the brilliance of a concert pianist, or the supposed genius of a famous detective. In the case of *Never Let Me Go*, it is the care and dedication that Kathy H., the narrator, offers her dying patients that is emphasized. Similarly, *The Buried Giant* plays imaginatively on the early-medieval myth (or cliché) of the values inherent to the figure of the warrior-knight, while *Klara and the Sun* is in part about the professional dedication, loyalty, and even pride that an AI robot takes in performing her duties. As some of these examples starkly indicate, however, Ishiguro is consistently concerned with the ways in which what seems to the narrator to constitute a redemptive dedication to and identification with their profession can also (and therefore) involve collusion with a terrible social and ethical harm. Rather than being a strategy that will resolve the finely calibrated discrimination, injustice, or inequity of a society, dedication to what one sees as one's professional duty can even, through collusion in or with societal norms, exacerbate the harm that one is attempting to diminish.

But as a critical element in the Ishigurian *oeuvre*, this consistent probing of the paradox of professional excellence opens up important questions for authorship itself. If one consistent element in Ishiguro's fiction involves the recognition that professional excellence can, by virtue of that very excellence, be harmful, then his novels also raise the question of what harm an *author* might unwittingly effect, since for a writer like Ishiguro – a writer lucky or talented enough to make a living from his work – authorship can truly be said to be a profession. The writer Kazuo Ishiguro, in other words, is deeply implicated in these meditations on professionalism. For more than two hundred years, after all, poets and novelists have been held up as exemplary beings, unacknowledged legislators, whose work has the potential to 'save' us within the terms of what Leo Bersani has memorably named the 'culture of redemption'.[12] But if the writer is not vatic, not a seer or prophet, if the writer is fallible, cognitively limited, ethically compromised, mortal, or just wrong – as Ishiguro variously acknowledges of himself in interviews – and if we nevertheless trust authors to offer us some kind of wisdom, knowledge, or truth, then the very act of writing novels, of being an author, is complicated and perhaps compromised or indeed deficient. Authorship is itself implicated in, collusive with, a system (the system of, or that relies upon, ignorance, fallibility, self-deceptive pride, political naivety) that it seeks to question or transcend.[13] And yet Ishiguro's recognition of this authorial condition is, we might say, at the same time a key dimension in his humane, ethical, and politically astute narrative vision.

Following the publication of his most famous novel, Ishiguro would regularly insist in interviews that 'we're all like butlers': we're all like butlers, he would say, because none of us 'know enough about what's going on out there'.[14] But his insistence on saying that we are all like Stevens – the butler in *The Remains of the Day* who looks back from 1956, the moment of the Suez crisis, to his time dutifully and unquestioningly managing an English country house for an aristocratic owner who embroils himself in fascist politics by negotiating with the Nazis in the lead-up to the Second World War – should also be interpreted as Ishiguro saying first of all of himself '*I am like Stevens, I am like a butler*'. There is no hard line, in this thinking, between the text and the author – the flesh-and-blood man whom you observe on the podium of the Swedish Academy in the online video or whose words you read on the pages of the printed lecture. Kazuo Ishiguro – at least the 'parallel person' that he has taken to referring to in interviews recently, the one who gets reviewed and who has received quite a remarkable number of 'gongs and things'[15] – is in part himself a construct of the novels that have made such a profound impact on Anglophone and indeed World literature over more than forty years, and that have forged for themselves a place in public consciousness and in an always emerging, ever developing, literary canon. And it might be said that it is the self-effacing professional modesty in Kazuo Ishiguro's recognition of the limitations of authorship that in the end allows for – that generates, indeed – the urgency and evocative affective power of the body of work that goes under his name.

Notes

1 Ishiguro 'now ranks among England's most distinguished contemporary novelists'; he is 'one of the most accomplished and celebrated writers of our time'; 'one of the world's most important contemporary writers'; 'generally considered to be one of the finest writers working today'; 'among the most celebrated writers in contemporary Britain' (Brian W. Shaffer, *Understanding Kazuo Ishiguro* (Columbia: University of South Carolina Press, 1998), p.1; Sebastian Groes and Barry Lewis, 'Introduction' to *Kazuo Ishiguro: New Critical Visions of the Novels* (London: Palgrave Macmillan, 2011), p.1; Matthew Beedham, *The Novels of Kazuo Ishiguro* (London: Palgrave Macmillan, 2010), p.10; Wai-Chew Sim, *Kazuo Ishiguro* (Abingdon: Routledge, 2010), p.1; Chu-chueh Cheng, *The Margin without Centre: Kazuo Ishiguro* (Oxford: Peter Lang, 2010), p.1). As Peter Sloane comments, 'few authors are greeted with, or are greeted with and *sustain*, the degree of international criticism and popular acclaim that Ishiguro has inspired' (*Kazuo Ishiguro's Gestural Poetics* (London: Bloomsbury, 2021), p.161).

2 For details of some of this work, see the Guide to Further Reading section at the end of this book.

3 Critics such as Vanessa Guignery and Adam Parkes have started to make clear the care and *difficulty* involved in producing these effects by their scrupulous examinations of the draft materials in the Ishiguro Archive at the Harry Ransom Center, University of Austin, Texas: see Guignery's chapter on 'The Ishiguro Archive', in this volume, and Parkes, 'Ishiguro's "<Strange> Rubbish": Style and Sympathy in Never Let Me Go', *Modern Fiction Studies* 67:1 (2021): 171–204.

4 John Self, review of *Klara and the Sun*, in *The Times*, 24 February 2021.

5 In addition to its publication as a book by Faber & Faber, *My Twentieth Century Evening and Other Small Breakthroughs* is available online on the Nobel Prize website in English and in Swedish, French, German, and Spanish translations, together with a video of the lecture: www.nobelprize.org/prizes/literature/2017/ishiguro/lecture/.

6 As Sloane points out, turning points are often highlighted in Ishiguro's novels themselves, not least by the use of the phrase 'turning points' (*Kazuo Ishiguro's Gestural Poetics*, pp.7–8); see also Ivan Stacy's discussion of turning points in Ishiguro's novels in Chapter 16, below, pp. 241–5.

7 See Jason Puskar, 'Institutions: Writing and Reading', in Ingo Berensmeyer et al., eds., *The Cambridge Handbook of Literary Authorship* (Cambridge: Cambridge University Press, 2019), p.438, on creative writing courses as preparing individuals 'not just to write better, but to *be* authors, to perform professionally'.

8 All three stories were published by Faber & Faber in 1981 in a volume of stories by 'New Writers', as 'A Strange and Sometimes Sadness' (first published in 1980), 'Getting Poisoned', and 'Waiting for J'.

9 This may be said to be a theme, retrospectively, even in his 1982 novel *A Pale View of Hills* – and then most recently in *Klara and the Sun* (2021).

10 See Guignery's discussion of the 'missed life theme' in Chapter 6 in this volume (pp.102).

11 See Ishiguro's comment that 'for that moment, unfortunately, I couldn't think how I'd do it' (*TWE* 25).

12 See Leo Bersani, *The Culture of Redemption* (Cambridge, MA: Harvard University Press, 1990).

13 In recent interviews, Ishiguro has even questioned the value of writing fiction as such. Speaking to *Wired* magazine in March 2021, for example, he notes how important science was during the Covid-19 pandemic but also how far politicians like Donald Trump have gone in subverting rational and truthful discourse. 'The idea is that the truth is what you wish to believe. Feel it emotionally strongly enough in your heart', he comments:

People like me have placed so much emphasis on the importance of emotional truth; I create things like novels that are supposed to kind of move people. And it has made me kind of pause a moment. Looking at these two completely opposed attitudes to coexisting in a massive way in our lives at the moment, I kind of wonder if I actually contributed to this idea of what you feel is the truth. (Will Knight, '*Klara and the Sun* Imagines a Social Schism Driven by AI', *Wired*, 8 March 2021: published online at www.wired.com/story/kazuo-ishiguro-interview/)

14 See *CKI* 87: 'Often we just don't know enough about what's going on out there and I felt that that's what we're like. We're like butlers.' See also p.101: 'What we do is we do a job, we work for an employer or organization or maybe some cause – political cause – and we just do a little thing. We hope that somebody up there, upstairs uses our little contribution in a good way.... In other words, we're rather like butlers.'

15 Bryan Appleyard, 'Kazuo Ishiguro Interview: "We Can Fly Too Close to the Sun"', *The Sunday Times*, 21 February 2021 (accessed online at www.thetimes.co.uk/article/kazuo-ishiguro-interview-we-can-fly-too-close-to-the-sun-t65x5s5xv).

PART I

Kazuo Ishiguro in the World

ANDREW BENNETT

Ishiguro and the Question of England

Surrey

In Ishiguro's first novel, *A Pale View of Hills*, the protagonist and narrator Etsuko recalls the events leading up to her departure from Nagasaki for England shortly after the Second World War. In the narrative present (three decades later), Keiko, Etsuko's daughter with her first, Japanese, husband has recently committed suicide. Etsuko's second daughter, Niki, lives in London but is visiting her mother, a widow who lives alone in a cottage in a village in one of the Southern counties of England (it is unnamed, but we might call it 'Surrey'). Niki is Etsuko's daughter by her second marriage, to the Englishman with whom she left Japan. As we learn in the novel's first paragraph, the 'vague echo of the East' that marks Niki's name is a compromise between her father's preference for a Japanese name and her mother's desire for something unequivocally English (*PVH* 9).

Etsuko's commitment to a certain sense of England and of Englishness is confirmed at the end of the novel: looking out at the view of the surrounding countryside from her garden, she comments to Niki that she 'enjoy[s] the quiet': 'I always think it's so truly like England out here', she says:

> When your father first brought me down here, Niki, I remember thinking how so truly like England everything looked. All these fields, and the house too. It was just the way I always imagined England would be and I was so pleased. (*PVH* 182)

The repetition of the phrase 'truly like' brings out a key concern in Ishiguro's work: the question of England, and of what it is 'truly like'. Looking out at England, or at a part of it, from a garden *in* England, what Etsuko sees is not so much England as something 'truly like' it. This sense that what you see when you look at England is something 'truly like' it – an ersatz England or simulacrum of the country, a 'mythical version of England', as he puts it in a 1989 interview, that is also England (*CKI* 45–6) – is a recurrent theme in

Ishiguro's writing from *A Pale View of Hills* onwards and is particularly prominent in four novels: *The Remains of the Day*, *When We Were Orphans*, *Never Let Me Go*, and *The Buried Giant*.[1]

This chapter will focus on the question of England as bringing together a number of related issues, including identity and ethnicity, nationhood, language, migration, belonging, and not belonging. Such themes resonate widely in the work of a writer who left Japan in 1960 at the age of five to live in the seemingly quintessentially 'English' home-counties town of Guildford, in Surrey (the birthplace, as it happens, of the seemingly quintessentially English writer P. G. Wodehouse), and who only returned to visit his birth country twenty-nine years later, in 1989.[2] *A Pale View of Hills* is about leaving Japan and about the difficulty of emigrating to a new country: the suicide of Keiko is presented as an eventual consequence of this national-cultural-linguistic hiatus – one that Ishiguro himself experienced (though as far as we can tell, seems to have survived happily) as a child and that is reconfigured in indirect ways in several of his novels. As Yoshiki Tajiri, Liani Lochner, Jerrine Tan, and Rebecca Karni forcefully bring out in their various contributions to the present volume, Ishiguro's novels – even, or especially, his early, so-called Japanese novels – have a complex relationship with Japan and with England, with his birth country and the country in which he grew up and in which he resides, having taken UK citizenship in 1982.

Ishiguro comments in a memorable moment from a 1989 interview that his move at an early age from Japan to England meant that he 'wasn't a very English Englishman' but was also not a 'very Japanese Japanese either' (*CKI* 58). In this chapter, however, I want to suggest that Ishiguro's first novel also inaugurates a series of narratives that articulate a specific sense of trauma or wounding in relation to the cross-cultural move, translation, or emigration that is also, at the same time, more general than that: Ishiguro's narratives are not only about the metaphorically exilic, ungrounded condition of the migrant but also (and therefore) about the human condition more generally. Like other locations in Ishiguro's writing, England in this sense is a specific place and at the same time, nowhere, everywhere, or anywhere.[3]

Ishiguro has often been at pains to distance himself from, to disavow or deny, the specificity of cultural and national allegiance as it obtrudes into the settings of his novels. In an interview from 2005, for example, he explains that while his first two novels have Japanese narrators and (largely) Japanese settings, he always felt that 'the Japanese element' was 'a relatively superficial part of my writing' and that it was used to 'orchestrate something else that I was more fundamentally interested in' (*CKI* 23). Partly for this reason, Ishiguro explains, his third novel, *The Remains of the Day*, makes the ultra-English country house its setting and the supposedly quintessentially English figure of the butler (a figure adopted and adapted, above all, from Jeeves in P. G. Wodehouse's novels) its narrator and protagonist. And yet in a 2008 interview in the *Paris Review*, Ishiguro explains that his first wholly UK-based novel in fact paradoxically constitutes a move *away* from England and Englishness and that he was 'very consciously trying to write for an international audience' by taking 'a myth of England that was known internationally' – the myth in this case being embodied in the figure of the English butler.[4] In other words, the apparent Englishness of Ishiguro's most 'English' novel itself involves a myth of Englishness that consists precisely in being 'truly like', but therefore not, English. The more English it is, the less English it paradoxically becomes. In another interview, Ishiguro comments that *The Remains of the Day* is an 'extra-English novel or, perhaps I should say, a super-English novel': it is 'more English than English', he remarks (*CKI* 73). Indeed, as he also comments, the Englishness of *The Remains of the Day* is not one that British people are likely to recognize, but is rather an Englishness that 'has been conjured up for the consumption of foreigners all around the world' (*CKI* 147). In other words, Ishiguro's version of Englishness is a hyper-Englishness that is precisely and for that reason not English. For Ishiguro – whose Japanese settings in the first two novels are dreams or fantasies as much as memories of a country that the author himself had not seen since he left the country as a young boy – culture, nationhood, and nationality are always already fictive, invented, constructed, always 'floating' (to adopt a telling word from the title of Ishiguro's second novel), and always fundamentally conceived of as what the political theorist Benedict Anderson calls an 'imagined community'.[5]

Norfolk

The first part of Ishiguro's second-most-famous novel, *Never Let Me Go*, is based on another quintessentially 'English' genre, the boarding school novel – a genre that goes back at least to Thomas Hughes's 1857 novel *Tom Brown's School Days*. In many ways, Ishiguro's novel exemplifies his doubly paradoxical concern with a sense of England and of Englishness that is both highly specific and (to use Ishiguro's own word) 'universal', as well as at the same time both quintessential and a copy or simulacrum of that supposed essence – fundamentally English while also *therefore* fundamentally not English.

The thirty-one-year-old narrator of *Never Let Me Go*, Kathy H., looks back on her life as it comes towards its preprogrammed end. As a clone, she has been specifically produced or generated to be farmed, as an adult, for body parts that will save the lives of non-clones ('normals', as they are called in the novel's sinisterly euphemistic lexicon). Characterized by pride in her achievements as a carer for other 'donors', there is something obtuse and even self-harmingly complacent about Kathy's account of an atrocity in which she is also a victim – the compulsory farming of 'clones' for body parts to allow non-clones ('normals') to live longer. Indeed, her pride in her work *is* – or is necessary for – her obtuse ethical position. This is, of course, an ethical obtuseness that Kathy shares with other Ishiguro protagonists, including most famously the butler (and narrator) Stevens in *The Remains of the Day*, as well as Ono in *An Artist of the Floating World* and Christopher Banks in *When We Were Orphans*. On account of her programming, and for all her programmed care for Josie, even Klara in *Klara and the Sun* is oblivious to or insouciant about the severely harmful – indeed, deadly – nature of the society that she is built to serve. While Ishiguro's stated aim in writing *Never Let Me Go* was to examine the response of individuals to their own mortality, critics have tended to focus on the ways in which the novel questions the limits of the human (and, relatedly, of humanity or humanism).[6] But with its particular if rather subtle and indirect emphasis on England, Ishiguro is also exploring what it means to be both part of and not part of a society or culture. For Ishiguro, I want to suggest, the relationship with one's 'imagined community' can itself be imagined as a life-and-death question.

Part One of *Never Let Me Go* is set in Hailsham, a fictional and stereo-typically English boarding school of the late-twentieth century.[7] As the reader is gradually made aware, the critical difference from the average English boarding school is that the children in this school are clones who, as adults, will gradually be robbed of their vital organs, which will be 'donated' to 'normals', resulting in the premature death of the clones in early adulthood. The novel pushes hard at aligning the closed micro-society of Hailsham with that of other fictional representations of English boarding schools, and their particular customs and rituals, their codes of honour and friendships, their architectural spaces, playing grounds, and rural surround-ings. And partly through the boarding-school *topos*, England is itself a thematic focus of the novel.

The word 'England' itself appears six times in *Never Let Me Go*, and is specifically connected to a somewhat nostalgic, idealized version of England's more rural counties. The most explicit expression of this sense of Englishness occurs towards the beginning of the novel:

> It was Miss Emily herself who taught us about the different counties of England. She'd pin up a big map over the blackboard, and next to it, set up an easel. And if she was talking about, say, Oxfordshire, she'd place on the

easel a large calendar with photos of the county. She had quite a collection of these picture calendars, and we got through most of the counties this way. She'd tap a spot on the map with her pointer, turn to the easel and reveal another picture. There'd be little villages with streams going through them, white monuments on hillsides, old churches beside fields; if she was telling us about a coastal place, there'd be beaches crowded with people, cliffs with seagulls. I suppose she wanted us to have a grasp of what was out there surrounding us, and it's amazing, even now, after all these miles I've covered as a carer, the extent to which my idea of the various counties is still set by these pictures Miss Emily put up on her easel. I'd be driving through Derbyshire, say, and catch myself looking for a particular village green with a mock-Tudor pub and a war memorial – and realise it's the image Miss Emily showed us the first time I ever heard of Derbyshire. (NLMG 64–5)

It is an idyllic England that Miss Emily reveals to the students, and one specifically designated by the more-or-less geographically contingent constructs of county boundaries. It is, of course, the idealized, ersatz version of England that you might find in a picture calendar – a genre that is itself a byword for romanticized or idealized representations of people, animals, and places: the photographic instantiation of nostalgia. And it is notable that it is these fantasies of England that Kathy looks for as she drives around England in her role as carer for successive donors in the later stages of their artificially induced sickness and premature death. The implication is that she only sees or recognizes England when the village that she is driving through reminds her of the idealized calendar image. The representation, the ersatz, the simulacrum, comes first. She knows she is in England when she sees a bit of it that looks like its idealized representation. And the passage also reminds us of the fact that the children-clones, and later the carers and donors that the clones become as adults, both belong to and are excluded from England. Miss Emily shows the children these images in order to give them a 'grasp' of 'what was out there surrounding us'. During their time in the carefully if intangibly policed boundaries of Hailsham, England is 'out there' literally, beyond the school's grounds, even while Hailsham is itself part of England. But there is a sense in which England goes on being 'out there' even after the clones leave the school, and later leave the teenage halfway house of 'The Cottages': rather than living in the actual English counties, Kathy looks for and indeed drives through fantasy counties and an imagined country or community of which she can never be a part.

The county of Norfolk is a particular, part-comic, part-tragic focus of the novel. As Kathy goes on to explain, Miss Emily's calendars have no photographs of Norfolk, which she describes vaguely, and in an 'afterthought', as 'very nice'. Miss Emily comments that Norfolk is the 'forgotten county':

'You see, because it's stuck out here on the east, on this hump jutting into the sea, it's not on the way to anywhere. People going north and south . . . bypass it altogether. For that reason, it's a peaceful corner of England, rather nice. But it's also something of a lost corner' (*NLMG* 65). Kathy explains that, from this moment on, the children begin to conceive of Norfolk as England's 'lost corner' and, through a kind of pun, by linguistic association with the 'Lost Corner' at Hailsham (the place where lost property is stored) they begin to think of Norfolk as the place where things that are lost might be found. Norfolk as the 'lost county' plays an important part in the England that Ishiguro therefore invokes and invents in the novel, which culminates in a dramatic scene of tormented, inchoate, undirected rage that takes place in that desolate county (250–1). Since the novel, and the children's lives, have overwhelmingly to do with loss – the loss that the children experience on account of having no parents, and the consequential loss that they experience on understanding that their lives will be prematurely cut short – Norfolk takes on a pivotal role in their conception of England. Norfolk is imagined as the site of loss but therefore also as the fantasy site of retrieval, as a place where one might be able to retrieve what has been lost.

But the novel is also about the idea that what is most profoundly 'lost' might be that which one never had. The clones suffer from the irredeemable loss of a mother who never existed: there is no possibility of retrieving their mothers because, as artificially generated clones, they were not gestated in or born out of the wombs of women. Norfolk, as the ambiguously titled 'lost county' of England – the place where everything lost will reappear and a place that is itself lost – becomes the geographical symbol of the illusion of an impossible (re)discovery of that which is experienced as lost even while it was never possessed in the first place. As a synecdoche for England, Norfolk can be seen as representing an impossible nationhood and place of (be)longing.

Logres

The Buried Giant, Ishiguro's next novel, is also centrally concerned with England, and concerned indeed further to disrupt the idea of it. The critical reception of the novel has largely been concerned with questions of memory and cultural trauma, with forgetting and atrocity, as general and non-specific questions in human communities and societies. Ishiguro refers in interviews to his concern with locating the novel's events in a way that will distance them from any particular or specific locale while offering recent historical instances of intercommunal violence in the former Yugoslavia, Rwanda, or South Africa as exemplifying the kind of place in which the novel could have been set, but wasn't. By setting the novel in an ancient and only indistinctly known or understood past, Ishiguro explains, he was able to distance the events from the limitations of a particular geopolitical site and location.[8] Setting the novel in sixth-century Britain focuses our attention not so much on a contemporary political circumstance and place as on the very source of ethnic and national identity – and therefore of heterogeneity, discord, and conflict – itself. And yet the location, the place in which the events take place, is at the same time specifically identified as an emerging nation, a nation in the throes of being born, of coming into being as such.

The novel's deceptively simple opening sentence highlights its concern with the founding myth of England: 'You would have searched for a long time for the sort of winding lane or tranquil meadow for which England later became celebrated' (*BG* 3). England is known, established, 'celebrated' even; and it is by implication the place from where the narrator narrates and from when the implied reader reads. But the sentence also points to a time *before* the existence of the geographical features that characterize 'England', for which it is known. The events are set in an England that has yet to be formed, both geographically and as the imaginary site of belonging that constitutes a nation. This is a novel that is about – even though it can't yet be what it is later to become – England. It specifically presents the 'origins' of England in a place that is not, or not yet, England.[9]

The opening sentence also picks up on the vaguely unsettling familiarity of second-person address that seems to imply a specific identity for the speaker's interlocutor – an effect that is similarly at work in *The Remains of the Day* (where Stevens's implied interlocutor is a butler) and in *Never Let Me Go* (where Kathy H. seems to be speaking to another clone): the opening sentence of *The Buried Giant* defines the person addressed (the implied reader, in a sense) as living in a time that is contemporary with the late- (or later-)medieval frame-narrator. The sentence is grammatically complicated in its use of the conditional perfect tense ('would have searched') and its specification of a middle time in the past between the narrative present and the time of the events that are about to be related ('for which England later became celebrated').[10] But most remarkable and unnerving, perhaps, is the use of the word 'England', since it immediately marks an origin for a place that is yet to exist. Ishiguro marks 'England', in other words, as a place that, even in its physical topography ('tranquil meadow'), is created, imagined, or invented.[11] There is an immediate paradoxicality, then: the narrator needs to talk about a place, to name it, before it can be named. He calls it 'England', but it is not England – because England is not just a place but a set of assumptions, connotations, and myths that are ultimately founded on a set of practices and customs that have nevertheless literally etched themselves onto the landscape (and are now 'celebrated', but only *since* the events related). And in its sly nostalgia for a sense of an original England that never was England – for an origin of England in not-England, the sentence simultaneously indicates that the origin of the place that is imagined as being England, now, was not 'tranquil' but was rather characterized by murderous colonization, internecine warfare and atrocity, and deliberate tribal cruelty.

In this sense, the opening to *The Buried Giant* chimes with the poem that Ishiguro acknowledges as its original inspiration, *Gawain and the Green Knight* – both in terms of the way that the fourteenth-century Romance poem acts as a model for the novel's narrative framing and in the shared concern in the two works with a mythical or imagined origin for 'England'. It is notable that the frame-narrative in *Gawain* is specifically reworked in Ishiguro's novel with regard to the positioning of the narrator, who (at least in one interpretation) speaks to a 'modern', late-medieval audience and thereby produces a mythico-historical version of England as such. In interviews, Ishiguro has cited as the initial inspiration for the setting of *The Buried Giant* a short section from Part II of *Gawain* in which the eponymous Arthurian hero rides in search of the Green Knight from one castle to another on the wild and forbidding borderlands of what are now England and Wales (lines 670–762).[12] It is notable that the passage to which Ishiguro refers begins with a geolocational specification that employs the Celtic word for the place that is not yet, but will one day be, England: *Logres*. 'Now rides this knight through the realm of Logres', the narrator says.[13]

The opening lines of *Gawain and the Green Knight* detail the colonial expansion of Rome after the fall of Troy, before homing in on the mythical founding of Britain by Felix Brutus:

> And, joyfully, far over the French sea,
> Felix Brutus founds Britain [*settes Bretayn*] by ample down and bay;
> Where war, and joy, and terror
> Have all at times held sway;
> Where both delight and horror
> Have had their fitful day.
> And after Britain was founded [*bigged*] by this brave fighter
> Rough fellows were fathered here who relished a fray
> And made much mischief in troubled times.   (lines 13–22)

The early lines from *Gawain and the Green Knight* emphasize that the founding of Britain takes place between two unstable periods: a period of terror (*wrake*) and horror (*blunder*) before, and a period dominated by 'Rough fellows ... who relished a fray' (*baret þat lofden*) and cause mischief (*tene*) afterwards. And this is the founding framework for Ishiguro's narrative, too: the events of the novel take place in a relatively peaceful (but still unpredictably dangerous) interval between two times – a time of trouble, affray, slaughter, and war, before the events related; and a time of strife to come after the events related but before the narrator's present – which has itself emerged out of an intervening period of internecine strife that is set to follow the slaying of the dragon.

The word 'England' only appears once in *The Buried Giant*, and by the fourth paragraph it has been replaced with 'Britain' ('I have no wish to give the impression that this was all there was to the Britain of those days' (*BG* 4)).[14] But this slippage might help us further understand the slipperiness of nation-based nomenclature in the context of a nation's founding myths. The terminology is difficult and movable because there is no Britain, and no England, at the time in which the story is set, even while some of the characters in it are called 'Britons'. But this is part of Ishiguro's point, I think (and the point that the frame-narrator is emphasizing in his use of 'England' in the first sentence). Glossing over centuries of change and mutability, of competing fiefdoms and kingdoms, and of an emerging sense of 'England' that is related to but different from and only partly 'Britain',[15] Ishiguro positions his *narrator* in a time when there *is* such a thing as England, while the *events* recounted take place at a time before that place and that identity have emerged out of warring factions and out of multiple tribes, languages, allegiances, and cultural identities.

This, in a sense, is the significance of the theme of forgetting in *The Buried Giant*, its whole point and purpose: to allow for a stable, unified sense of a community to exist, without internecine savagery, warfare, and atrocity. With the exception of one individual (the Saxon knight Wistan), all of the people in this land have had their medium- to long-term memories wiped by a dragon's breath that envelops the population in a mist of forgetting. Set at a time that would otherwise be within living memory of the atrocity-laden war between the invading Saxons and the indigenous Britons, it is in this sense that *The Buried Giant* concerns the founding myth of England. It is in the amnesia-enabled peace between the two warring tribes or factions that a nation – England – can begin to be born. England is founded in the violent merging of (more than) two tribes, out of conflict, out of violence.[16] And it also therefore emerges out of forgetting, out of a necessary amnesia.[17]

The place that Ishiguro invents or imagines in *The Buried Giant* is one in which an unstable peace between the Saxons and the Britons pertains. Each tribe has its own habits and customs, architectural practices, and languages, and there is a certain distrust between the separate communities, with a sense that the peace between them is tentative and fragile. And yet the novel also emphasizes the possibility of ethnic mixing and intermarriage. The mingling of the different tribes is highlighted in the inter-tribal identities and experiences of at least four characters: unlike Axl, Beatrice is familiar with the Saxon village that they visit early in the novel, and seems to speak fluent Saxon, having often traded there (*BG* 53–62); Ivor, the chieftain of the Saxon village that Axl and Beatrice pass through on the first night of their travels, is 'A Briton living here among Saxons' (65); Wistan, the Saxon warrior who has been tasked with slaying the dragon (and thus with bringing back the memory of internecine warfare), tells Axl that while his blood is 'Saxon through and through', he was brought up 'in a country not far from here and was often among the Britons' (78);[18] and Edwin, the Saxon boy who is destined to become a warrior is taken in hand by the Britons Axl and Beatrice so that he can be delivered to a Christian Briton village, where he will be safe, despite his alien origin and the mark of a bite by a 'fiend', (81) for which, however, he would be superstitiously feared and probably killed within his own pagan Saxon community.

But these forms of multicultural intermixing, and the fragile peace and mutual acceptance between two communities that they entail, has emerged out of bloodshed, violence, and tribal vengeance. And with the dragon's death, the land is set to be plunged into murderous intercommunal violence once again. Ishiguro's novel, in other words, is concerned with the invention of an unstable place in a time before England, out of which England is to emerge. If 'England' is itself a myth of origins (and what else is a nation, what else can it be?), *The Buried Giant* performs the mythico-archaeologico function of imaginatively unearthing the unstable, heterogeneous, and violent basis on which such an entity is founded.

Gloucestershire

Part Seven of Ishiguro's fifth novel, *When We Were Orphans*, constitutes a kind of coda that will offer the opportunity for a kind of coda to this chapter. Set in 1958, the world-famous detective Christopher Banks recalls finally locating the woman he believes to be his long-lost mother. She is being cared for by nuns in Roseland Manor, an old people's home for 'Westerners' in Hong Kong (*WWWO* 300, 302). Now long lost to what seems to be dementia, Banks's mother fails to recognize Christopher and cannot understand why he asks her for forgiveness. Later, back in England, Banks tells his adoptive 'niece', Jennifer, that he realizes both that his mother 'never ceased to love me' and that his attempt to find her and to 'save the world from ruin ... wouldn't have made a difference either way' (306). The thirty-one-year-old Jennifer, who is recovering from the difficult ending of a relationship (and a suicide attempt) a year earlier, now lives a cramped, somewhat impoverished life in Gloucestershire lodgings (307). Banks lives in London, but Jennifer jokingly suggests that she will meet a 'decent' man and get married so that Banks can come to live with the couple (309). Banks seems to know that this will never happen – and if he doesn't, we do – and the novel ends with a meditation on his self-confessedly 'smug' sense of contentment with his quiet, settled bachelor life in London. Noting the oxymoronic thought that there are times when 'a sort of emptiness fills my hours', however, Banks tells himself that he will give Jennifer's invitation 'serious thought' (313).

The invitation itself is issued when Banks and Jennifer are standing in a church graveyard looking out over the Windrush Valley in Gloucestershire – an almost impossibly 'English' scene and also one that is nominally imbued with echoes of the HMT Empire Windrush. By the final decade of the twentieth century – when the novel was written – the name 'Windrush' had become a kind of cultural shorthand for West Indian (post)colonial migration, and for the beginnings of mass migration into and the transformation of the UK (and England within it), into a modern, ethnically diverse, multicultural state that in fact constitutes a return, in a sense, to the culturally and ethnically heterogeneous historical space that is often elided in the stories it tells itself. Both Jennifer and Banks are orphans; both are immigrants. And the final section of the novel offers a subtle meditation on the constitutive condition of colonial migration – on the rootless, homeless condition that Jennifer, Banks, Banks's mother, and Sarah Hemmings (all of whom feature in this ending) differently and separately experience. The England in which Banks finds himself – whether in its instantiation as cosmopolitan London or as rural Gloucestershire – is a 'home' that is layered and complexified by fiction and imagination, by history and stories, by colonialism and migration, and by the heterogeneous, the unstable, and the uncertain.

The ending to *When We Were Orphans*, then, points up Ishiguro's continuing fascination with the idea of England as generated out of a sense that cultural, national, ethnic, and even racial identities are unstable, diversely imagined forms of chimera, and that in fact the single or homogenous, stable or permanent condition that marks a human community is permanent only in its heterogeneity and instability, in its fragile and conflicted status, and in the varied and ever-changing terms in which it talks to itself about itself. Ishiguro's novels repeatedly return to and continually reinvent a kind of Englishness – including, in *The Buried Giant*, an England that will only later become the England to which the novel occasionally alludes – because they recognize that England is an invention, a phantasm that can therefore only be 'truly like' itself, not itself. And in this sense the novels – novels that often seem to be compelled in large part by this concern – are not, or not only, about England but also about any place, any nation, and about the fragile, precarious, untethered, and finally un-nationed condition of human communities.

Notes

1 See Ishiguro's comment that 'I don't have a deep link with England like, say, Jonathan Coe or Hanif Kureishi might demonstrate. For me it is like a mythical place' (Tim Adam, 'For Me, England Is a Mythical Place': interview with Kazuo Ishiguro, *The Guardian*, 20 February 2005). But even the novels not set in England tend to go out of their way to make mention of England. *The Unconsoled* frequently refers to Ryder's childhood in England, and he comes across two English childhood friends in his confusing odyssey around the unnamed central European city that Ishiguro's epic novel never really leaves; in *Klara and the Sun*, Ishiguro is careful, but for no apparent reason, to specify that Josie's friend Ricky has an English mother. The one exception is perhaps *The Artist of the Floating World*, which is entirely set in Japan and has no obvious concern with England. But even here it is notable that Ishiguro's manuscript notes for the early version of the novel set it in a post-industrial England and mention the decision to 'say things about Britain' (quoted in Jane Hu, 'Typical Japanese: Kazuo Ishiguro and the Asian Anglophone Historical Novel', *Modern Fiction Studies*, 67:1 (2021): 123–48 (132)). In addition to Ishiguro's published novels and stories, his unpublished short story from 1983 'England in October' is thematically as well as in title, concerned with the idea of England (see Vanessa Guignery's chapter, in this volume, p.103–4).

2 Ishiguro comments that *The Remains of the Day* 'revisits P.G Wodehouse with a serious political dimension' (*CKI* 46; see also 74). In another interview, he remarks that Guildford epitomizes a certain, somewhat dated, sense of 'Englishness': 'I grew up in Guildford, the town P.G. Wodehouse was born in. It's kind of a haven of comfortable, middle class, old-fashioned, conservative England. I think it has the lowest crime rate in England. If you grew up there, you kind of had an instinct for what England was like before WWII' (Interview, *AERA English*, 6 (June 2011), 28–9).

3 The focus is on England specifically because I take that to be Ishiguro's primary topic. As he comments in a 1999 interview of 'the Britain or the England of *Remains of the Day*', 'I make this distinction because I think Scotland and Wales are something else' (*CKI* 13). See Robert J. C. Young, *The Idea of English Ethnicity* (Oxford: Blackwell, 2008), for an account that chimes in many ways with the representation of England in Ishiguro's novels: Young brilliantly analyses the 'curious emptiness of Englishness', which is 'never really here' but always 'there, delocalized, somewhere else', its story one of 'progressive diffusion' rather than homogeneous racial or indeed ethnic identity (pp.236, xi).

4 Susannah Hunnewell, 'Kazuo Ishiguro, The Art of Fiction No. 196', *The Paris Review* 184 (2008): n.p. (accessed online at www.theparisreview.org/interviews/5829/the-art-of-fiction-no-196-kazuo-ishiguro).

5 Benedict Anderson, *Imagined Communities: Reflections on the Origin and Spread of Nationalism* (Verso: London, 1983).

6 See, for example *CKI* 215; and see Myra J. Seaman, 'Becoming More (Than) Human: Affective Posthumanism, Past and Future', *Journal of Narrative Technique* 37:2 (2007): 246–75 (266–8).

7 The first part of Ishiguro's novel explicitly riffs on the conventions of the English boarding-school novel from Thomas Hughes's *Tom Brown's School Days* (1857) to Anthony Buckeridge's Jennings books (1950–94) and even to J. K. Rowling's Harry Potter series (1997–2007).

8 See, for example, Alex Clark, 'Kazuo Ishiguro's Turn to Fantasy', *The Guardian*, 19 February 2015.

9 For Jane Hu, *The Buried Giant* 'narrates Pax Britannica's colonial narratives about imperial modernization and global expansion as radically underdetermined – as perhaps having happened any number of other ways' ('Typical Japanese', 145). And see Hu's comment that Ishiguro's 'novel about pre-England estranges what readers take to be typical of the British, and later Anglophone world, by drawing out the mythical, elusive, and indeed oneiric origins of its national formation' (ibid., 146).

10 The distance between the narrative now and the time of the events narrated in *The Buried Giant* is uncertain, sometimes seeming to be within living memory (the narrator refers to the inhabitants of Axl and Beatrice's village as 'our villagers' at one point' (*BG* 15)), and sometimes some centuries ago (a time long enough ago for whole landscapes to have fundamentally changed); see Matthew Vernon and Margaret A. Miller, 'Navigating Wonder: The Medieval Geographies of Kazuo Ishiguro's The Buried Giant', *Arthuriana* 28:4 (Winter 2018): 68–89, on the time difference being 'a few decades' (80); Catherine Charlwood discusses the unstable temporalities involved, in 'National Identities, Personal Crises: Amnesia in Kazuo Ishiguro's The Buried Giant', *Open Cultural Studies* 2 (2018): 25–38 (31–3).

11 As Vernon and Miller put it, *The Buried Giant* imagines a 'mythical medieval Britain ... as it existed before nations' ('Navigating Wonder', 69); they argue that the novel 'attempts to recover the strangeness of medieval English romance's use of migration and conquest narratives to imagine British sovereignty. The patterns of movement and interpenetration of spaces that Ishiguro recovers militate against current claims of an always-already British nation' (70).

12 See, for example, Clark, 'Kazuo Ishiguro's Turn to Fantasy'.

13 *Sir Gawain and the Green Knight*, trans. Keith Harrison, ed. Helen Cooper (Oxford: Oxford University Press, 1998), p.26 (l.691) (translation modified): further quotations are from this translation; the original medieval English text is cited from the Clarendon Press edition, ed. J. R. R. Tolkien and E. V. Gordon (1967), accessed online at http://name.umdl.umich.edu/Gawain (p.20). See *Sir Gawain*, pp.98–9, n.: Logres is 'a Celtic-derived term for England, "England" itself being anachronistic as a name in an Arthurian story set before the coming of the Angles'.

14 The only other mention of England is in the use of the adjective 'English' on p.87, where the word is used in a way that is not dissimilar to 'England' in the novel's first sentence: 'The view before them that morning may not have differed so greatly from one to be had from the high windows of an English country house

today.' One might wonder whether the reference to 'high windows' doesn't slyly, and distantly, echo the poem of that name by Philip Larkin – in a particular kind of way that most 'English' (and perhaps not so much British) of twentieth-century poets.

15 We are referring here both to a 'Britain' that is allied with 'Britannia' as conceived or invented by a Graeco-Roman culture prior to the retreat of the Romans in the fifth century, and to a Britain as the invention (in both senses) of a unified Kingdom under King James VI and I that is constitutionally inaugurated in 1604.

16 Vernon and Miller argue that this is conflict without origin: 'as *Gawain* shows, there is quite literally no getting to the bottom of the conflicts on the island. The lurking evidence of previous massacres points to a Britain beyond memory and beyond the scale of the disputes between the Britons and Saxons' ('Navigating Wonder', 84). Hu links the unstable cultural/political/national condition represented in the novel with the multiple and unstable narrative perspectives (predominantly variously focalized third-person omniscient perspectives but with passages of first-person storytelling) ('Typical Japanese', 144–5).

17 As Matthew Eatough reminds us, collective amnesia is, for Ernst Renan, 'essential to the formation of the modern notion of the state' ('"Are They Going to Say This Is Fantasy?": Kazuo Ishiguro, Untimely Genres, and the Making of Literary Prestige', *Modern Fiction Studies* 67:1 (2021): 40–66 (51)); see Renan, 'What Is a Nation' (1882), in *What Is a Nation and Other Political Writings*, ed. M. F. N. Gigliolo (New York: Columbia University Press, 2018), ch.9 (p.251).

18 Wistan wears his sword like a Briton and was taught his swordsmanship by Britons; later we learn he was 'taken' as a boy from his own village (*BG* 156).

2

YOSHIKI TAJIRI

Ishiguro and Japan

History in *An Artist of the Floating World*

It is well known that for Kazuo Ishiguro it is not a primary purpose to depict history accurately in his novels. As regards his second novel set in Japan, *An Artist of the Floating World*, he explicitly says, 'I very much wanted to put down onto paper this particular idea of Japan that I had in my own mind, and in a way I didn't really care if my fictional world didn't correspond to a historical reality' (*CKI* 53). For him, history is little more than a background against which characters' psychological dramas are staged. He likens it to a location that a film director can freely choose and use for his purpose:

> What I started to do was to use history. I would search through history books in the way a film director might search for locations for a script he has already written. I would look for moments in history that would best serve my purposes, or what I wanted to write about. I was conscious that I wasn't so interested in the history per se, that I was using British history or Japanese history to illustrate something that was preoccupying me. I think this made me a kind of writer that didn't actually belong. (*CKI* 58)

This sense of aloofness from particular history (British or Japanese) makes him concerned that '[his] books were being used as a sort of historical text' (130). He also contends that 'as a writer of fiction you should have quite a lot of license to go and change things and muck around a little bit' up to a certain point (131).

Ishiguro's attitude towards history is thus very clear. It is undeniable, however, that regardless of the author's intentions, history portrayed in fiction can have its own signifying function. Even if it is marginalized to the background, it might appeal to our particular historical sense as long as

This chapter evolved (but departs substantially) from my Japanese essay '*Ukiyo no Gaka* wo Rekishi totomoni Yomu [Reading *An Artist of the Floating World* with History]', in Yoshiki Tajiri and Kunio Shin, eds., *Kazuo Ishiguro to Nihon: Yurei kara Senso Sekinin made* [*Kazuo Ishiguro and Japan: From Ghosts to War Responsibility*] (Tokyo: Suiseisha, 2020). My research weas supported by JSPS KAKENHI Grant No. 20H01244.

it is concretely presented. This is especially true of *An Artist of the Floating World*, which, giving specific dates (October 1948, April 1949, November 1949, June 1950), describes Japan in the crucial historical period immediately after the end of the Pacific War, when the foundations of contemporary Japan were formed, and also deals with the subject of war responsibility that has been highly controversial and sensitive in post-war Japan.

The narrator of the novel Masuji Ono is a retired painter who thrived as a propaganda artist contributing to war efforts. While Japan is forced to change fundamentally under the US occupation after the war, he is psychologically threatened by the younger generation with new values that reproaches people like him for taking no responsibility for their participation in the disastrous war. He is worried that his own tarnished past may cast a shadow over his second daughter Noriko's marriage arrangement. Though he admits his mistakes, he also justifies himself by thinking that he did his best for the nation before the end of the war. The novel thus focuses on Ono's psychological struggles with his own past against the backdrop of the Occupation period in which Japan was rapidly changing.

Since the atmosphere of the period is vividly represented, readers (particularly, Japanese readers) familiar with its history or interested in the subject of war responsibility will naturally be attentive to the details of history evoked in the novel or curious to know the actual historical facts about the period. Therefore it is meaningful to refer to some of those facts to enrich readers' understanding of the historical background. In addition, such references will be helpful in highlighting what kind of changes Ishiguro made to history and what points in history he wanted to emphasize. Needless to say, this is not to criticize him for misrepresenting history. Such an attempt would be pointless for an author who openly declares that he is not interested in accurately representing history. Ishiguro is indeed quite nonchalant about historical facts in *An Artist of the Floating World*, freely moving the release date of the monster film *Godzilla* from 1954 to 1948, for instance.[1] But when it comes to more momentous matters in history, to have information about actual historical facts can have significant effects on our reading.

In his essay on *An Artist of the Floating World*, Timothy Wright stresses the fact that the last of the four dates given in the novel, June 1950, indicates the month when the Korean War started. This war between North Korea and South Korea was a manifestation of the Cold War as the former was supported by the Soviet Union and the new communist China and the latter by the United Nations, mainly the USA. Thanks to this war (1950–3), Japan could get out of the economic crisis and lay foundations for the rapid economic growth that started in the mid-1950s. In other words, Japan could start to recover from the devastations of the Pacific War by taking advantage of the new war in Korea, its former colony. Although the novel never mentions this war, Wright argues that it is behind Ono's serene acceptance of the new post-war regime at the end of the novel.

> With this elided historical background in place, Ono's final acceptance of his new position seems less the result of grace or repentance than a convenient complicity, secretly informed by the sense that, with the economic upturn triggered by the Korean War, the new regime is cemented in place, and the possibility of an alternate history, of which he had still been able to entertain fantasies prior to the Korean War, is finally banished.[2]

The new regime is tied up with 'Japan's assumption of a crucial role within the new, violent battle for a total global *imperium* that we call the Cold War'.[3] In other words, it is just as problematic as the old regime, and therefore not in a position to judge the old one. In consequence, Wright is cautious in judging Ono guilty:

> The critical tendency to find Ono guilty, while not misplaced, has the unintentional effect of recapitulating in a different form the very act of judgment by which the new order of postwar Japan finds Ono guilty (and itself, by implication, innocent). Rather than refute the previous critical readings of the novel, then, I wish to extend them, showing how Ono's personal self-deceptions and concealments point to much larger forms of self-deception and concealment at the level of the nation.[4]

This is a valuable insight not least because how the old generation is judged by the new generation is a major theme of the novel and preoccupies Ono's mind throughout. But it is also to be noted that in fact what Wright calls 'self-deception and concealment at the level of the nation' was occurring in an even more significant way. In historical reality, some of the old generation tended to resent the way the new generation criticized them because in their view the new democratic values with which the latter judged the former were simply provided 'from above' by the US Occupation forces (General Headquarters/the Supreme Commander of the Allied Powers, or for short, GHQ/SCAP) led by Douglas MacArthur, which forcefully launched a series of fundamental democratic reforms while they occupied Japan between September 1945 and April 1952. In this sense as well, the new regime could not really be triumphant over the old one or boastful of itself. In a sense, the new generation deceived itself into thinking that it created new democratic values by itself when in fact it did not. The same was true of those many older people who quickly changed from fanatic nationalists to liberalists without any internal conflict and got satirized for their lack of consistency. This is another aspect of the 'self-deception and concealment at the level of the nation', which has been continuously debated ever since in Japan.[5]

The introduction of a historical fact omitted from the text can thus significantly alter our reading or invite us to think more deeply about the historical
background. In a similar way, I want to provide some important information
about history in reading *An Artist of the Floating World*. But before doing
that, it may be meaningful to have a brief look at how much Ishiguro
researched Japanese history while writing the novel. Although he says that
he 'wasn't terribly interested in researching history books' in an interview
(*CKI* 53), the archives show that he did read and study several books on the
history of Japan. The section entitled 'Research Notes' in the papers for *An
Artist of the Floating World* (Container 1.4) contains Ishiguro's notes from
them.[6] He spends most space (about nine pages) on the famous American
Japanologist Edward Seidensticker's book *Low City, High City* (1983),
which with great erudition in history and literature portrays the vicissitudes
of Tokyo from 1867 to 1923, that is, from the beginning of the Meiji period,
when Japan started modernization, to the late Taisho period, when the Great
Kanto Earthquake ruined a large part of the capital. Ishiguro pays particular
attention to such details as rickshaws, *ukiyo-e*, bricks, and fires, but he seems
most impressed with a sense of 'evanescence' that permeated the capital when
the culture of the Edo period (1603–1867) had its heyday, and considers using
this word as the title of the novel. Although this book does not cover the
immediate post-war period in which *An Artist of the Floating World* is set, it
may have been helpful in imagining and creating Ono's formative years,
particularly the time when he was apprenticed to Seiji Moriyama, who
emphasized the aesthetics of evanescence.

Ishiguro takes four pages of notes from Edward S. Morse's *Japanese
Homes and Their Surroundings* (1886), and another four pages from
Richard Storry's *A History of Modern Japan* (1960). Morse was an
American zoologist who lived in Japan in the Meiji period and contributed
to the development of science in Japan. Ishiguro takes meticulous notes
about the details of Japanese houses and their interiors but it is uncertain
how this kind of information helped him in the creation of the inner spaces in
An Artist of the Floating World. Storry was an English historian who lived
and researched in Japan before and after the Pacific War. Although his book
covers Japan up to the 1950s, Ishiguro's notes are limited to the period
between 1921 and 1937, when Japan was gradually drawn towards the fatal
war. Again, these notes might have been helpful for Ono's formative years if
not his present. The longer notes about the idea of 'Showa Restoration' at
the end of the 1920s are particularly remarkable because in *An Artist of the
Floating World* Chishu Matsuda, who influenced the young Ono, shares this
idea that Japan should reform itself by restoring the political power back to
the Emperor and eliminating corrupt politicians and capitalists.

Ishiguro spends less space on Akira Kurosawa's autobiography *Something Like an Autobiography* (1983), Saburo Shiroyama's biography of Koki Hirota, *War Criminal: The Life and Death of Hirota Koki* (1977), and a book entitled *World at War* about the Pacific War.[7] Ishiguro has expressed his admiration for the work of the Japanese film director Akira Kurosawa, but his notes from the autobiography are principally about the details of social mores and history from the 1910s to 1940s. In other words, he read this interesting autobiography as a history book. Koki Hirota was once the prime minister (1936–7) and was the only civilian to be executed after being sentenced to death at the Tokyo Trial (the International Military Tribunal for the Far East). The topic of war responsibility is important for *An Artist of the Floating World*, but Ishiguro's half-page of notes follows Hirota's career only roughly and incompletely. The notes from *World at War* mark some important military events during the Pacific War but these are not relevant to the novel.

These archival records show that Ishiguro did not take notes about the immediate post-war period in which he was to set *An Artist of the Floating World*. But this does not mean that he did not do substantial research about that period. In fact, it seems that the opposite is true, given the relative accuracy of his descriptions of Japan between 1948 and 1950. One instance is his impressive knowledge of the educational reforms. As regards Ono's former colleague, nicknamed 'the Tortoise', we read, 'The most he did was eventually to gain a post as art teacher at a high school in the Yuyama district a few years before the war – a post, I am told, he still holds today [October 1948], the authorities seeing no reason to replace him as they did so many of his fellow teachers' (*AFW* 67). The replacement of many school-teachers here probably points to the wholesale reorganization of the Japanese educational system carried out between 1947 and 1950 with the initiative of GHQ/SCAP. 'The Tortoise' was so mediocre and invisible that he was probably left alone in the massive personnel rearrangement.[8] Also, Ono's disciple Shintaro is ambitious to 'gain a teaching post at one of the new high schools' at the end of 1948 (*AFW* 100). The 'new high schools' here of course means those under the new educational system, which were officially inaugurated in April 1948.

In this novel, Ishiguro also evokes more or less accurately other aspects of the Japanese society that was forcefully changed by GHQ/SCAP. One of the most significant of them is the purge of public service personnel by GHQ/SCAP, which started in January 1946. This measure was intended to exclude war criminals, war collaborators, militarists, and ultra-nationalists from public service and private enterprises. In the 'October 1948' section, Ono remembers meeting Jiro Miyake (Noriko's prospective bridegroom then) by chance. Since it was 'just over a year ago' (*AFW* 53), the meeting must have taken place before October 1947. While Miyake tells Ono that the president of his company committed suicide, he mentions that '[t]wo senior men were already dismissed by the Americans, but our President obviously felt it was not enough' (*AFW* 55). The dismissal was evidently part of GHQ/SCAP's purge. Towards the end of the 'November 1949' section, Ono remembers saying to Taro (the newly married husband of his second daughter Noriko), 'is it in your opinion entirely for the good that so many sweeping changes were made at your firm after the war? I hear there is hardly any of the old management left' (*AFW* 185). This suggests that GHQ/SCAP purged Taro's company of 'the old management' suspected of contributing to the war.

The purge inevitably had its limits: not all dubious people were eliminated. Suichi (the husband of Ono's first daughter Setsuko) says to Ono at the funeral of Kenji (Ono's son who was killed in the war) in September 1946, '[t]hose who sent the likes of Kenji out there to die these brave deaths, where are they today? They are carrying on with their lives, much the same as ever. Many are more successful than before, behaving so well in front of the Americans, the very ones who led us to disaster' (*AFW* 58). Those leaders directly responsible for the war had been arrested or purged by 1946. Suichi here means more broadly those people who cooperated with the war, including artists like Ono, and his resentment cannot have been exceptional in those days.

The purge drastically changed its meaning as well. After around 1948, GHQ/SCAP began to change its policy and repress communists whom it had legalized immediately after the war in the effort to promote democracy. It started to regard Japan as a bulwark against China and the Soviet Union in the mounting tension of the Cold War. In this 'reverse course', the target of its purge openly switched to communists and their sympathizers in 1950 (the 'Red Purge'). Meanwhile, those formerly purged people began to be de-purged mainly between 1950 and 1952. Miyake says to Ono, '[t]here are plenty of men already back in positions they held during the war' (*AFW* 56). This remark sounds a little anachronistic since in 1947 the number of de-purged people was quite limited.

On the other hand, Chishu Matsuda tells Ono in October 1948 that although old nationalists like them are now condemned, the tide will soon change: 'Never mind what people today are all saying. Before long, a few more years, and the likes of us will be able to hold our heads high about what we tried to do' (*AFW* 94). This suggests that Matsuda correctly read GHQ/SCAP's tendency to reverse its course. Already in 1948 there were many events that indicated the reverse course, such as repressions of labour disputes. It is possible to argue that the novel starts (in October 1948) exactly when people like Ono and Matsuda could begin to feel less uncomfortable due to the policy reversal. Wai-chew Sim is certainly correct in suggesting that this is behind Ono's ambiguous position of being 'blame-worthy (but less so)' at the same time.[9]

There are other references to the power of GHQ/SCAP, which tried to democratize and demilitarize Japan before it took the reverse course. Ono says rather bitterly of the disbanding of the Okada-Shingen Society, the right-wing society of artists to which Matsuda belonged: 'The Okada-Shingen Society no longer exists today – one of many such victims of the occupying forces' (*AFW* 88). The word 'victims' here eloquently suggests Ono's anti-American stance. When Shintaro applies for a high school post at the end of 1948, he wants to impress on the committee that he was initially worried about following his master Ono and producing propagandistic posters about the China crisis in 1937. This is because '[a]fter all, there are the American authorities to satisfy' (*AFW* 102). It is plausible that someone like Shintaro at this time really needed to dissociate himself from any past involvement with war efforts.[10] On the other hand, Kuroda, Ono's most talented disciple, was treated well in society after the war, finding little difficulty in getting a teaching post at a college. He was imprisoned and tortured during the war because by betraying Ono he had become a left-winger. In April 1949, Ono comments: 'Kuroda, it seems, had not fared at all badly since his release at the end of the war. Such are the ways of this world that his years in prison gave him strong credentials, and certain groups had made a point of welcoming him and seeing to his needs' (*AFW* 108). This reflects the historical fact that GHQ/SCAP was generous towards left-wingers before the reverse course and the Red Purge while the imprisoned communists were hailed in some quarters as heroes who bravely fought against the state. The phrase '[s]uch are the ways of this world' faintly implies Ono's antipathy towards the trend.

Ishiguro's evocation of the Occupation period is thus largely accurate. However, there is one point in which Ishiguro significantly changed history. During Ono's chance meeting with Jiro Miyake sometime before October 1947, Miyake tells him about the suicide of the president of his company. The president took his own life because he felt guilty of his company's involvement with the war: 'His act was an apology on behalf of us all to the families of those killed in the war' (*AFW* 55). Ono's response is characteristic:

> The world seems to have gone mad. Every day there seems to be a report of someone else killing himself in apology. Tell me, Mr Miyake, don't you find it all a great waste? After all, if your country is at war, you do all you can in support, there's no shame in that. What need is there to apologize by death? (*AFW* 55)

In historical reality, there were many high-ranking militaries and politicians who killed themselves between August 1945 and March 1947. But they did so in order to apologize to the Emperor or to escape from being tried as war criminals in the Tokyo Trial.[11] They usually did not intend to apologize to 'the families of those killed in the war'. In addition, we cannot find any reports in the newspapers at that time about civilians such as company presidents committing suicide to take responsibility for war victims. Such a case was at least not a social phenomenon.[12] Here Ishiguro recreates history by making inflated use of the stereotype about Japanese people's penchant for suicide. This promotion of the stereotype makes an interesting contrast to the critical distance he keeps from it in *A Pale View of Hills* and 'A Family Supper'.[13]

The same applies to the suicide of the fictional composer Yukio Naguchi that Ono and his grandson Ichiro discuss in the 'November 1949' section. Since Naguchi composed many war songs that were popular 'all over Japan' (*AFW* 155), he took his own life, feeling responsible for people who lost their family members in the war. In reality, there were several influential composers like Naguchi, but none of them committed suicide after the war. Here again, Ishiguro goes against history and emphasizes the element of Japanese moralistic suicide. This emphasis has the effect of accentuating Ono's refusal to follow the likes of Naguchi and thus his self-justification. Ono approves of Naguchi, saying, '[h]e was brave to admit the mistakes he'd made' (*AFW* 155), and he himself also admits his own mistakes in Noriko's *miai* (her family matchmaking meeting). But he seems to have no intention to consider suicide because he justifies himself by believing that he did his best during the war and that 'there is no shame in that'.

How did the composers like Naguchi cope with their war responsibility in historical reality? The most important composer in modern Japan, Kosaku Yamada, was very active in organizing and centralizing the musical world in line with the militarized state during the war. He was the vice-president (later the president) of the Society of Musical Culture, the authoritarian organization that kept all musicians strictly under control. He also composed many war songs that were popular 'all over Japan' just like those of Naguchi. Therefore it was natural that immediately after the war, Yamada was accused as a war criminal. In the *Tokyo Shimbun* newspaper in December 1945, the music critic Ginji Yamane openly called Yamada 'a typical war criminal' and criticized him for now cooperating with GHQ/SCAP's attempts to know Japanese musical culture, although until recently he had been denouncing the Americans and their music as 'beastly'. In a counter-argument Yamada defended himself by saying that he did indeed make modest efforts to raise the nation's fighting spirit as the vice-president of the Society of Musical Culture, but it was a perfectly natural action for a citizen who hoped for the victory of the nation. He went on: 'If such a patriotic action demanded by the state during the war is a war crime as you say, then all Japanese people must be imprisoned as war criminals'.[14]

Here is a typical rhetoric that enabled suspicious people to evade responsibility: everyone did that, so why do you accuse only me? This dilution of responsibility was actually the official idea of the Japanese government. Prince Higashikuni, who was the prime minister immediately after the war, declared that 'the military, civilian officials, and the people as a whole must thoroughly self-reflect and repent'.[15] On the other hand, in 1945 and 1946, there were vigorous attempts among citizens to nominate war criminals, apart from GHQ/SCAP's punitive measures.[16] Yamane's denunciation of Yamada was a manifestation of this trend. Ono in the novel constantly feels threatened by the lingering atmosphere created by the same trend. In reality, people's feelings wavered between the two poles: everyone was wrong or some were more wrong than others.[17] The following dialogue between Ono and Miyake reflects this divide:

> 'But those who fought and worked loyally for our country during the war cannot be called war criminals. I fear that's an expression used too freely these days.'
> 'But these are the men who led the country astray, sir. Surely, it's only right that they should acknowledge their responsibility. It's a cowardice that these men refuse to admit to their mistakes ....'　　　　　　　(AFW 56)

Ono's self-defensive position here would excuse leaders from taking responsibility because they can say they also did their best for the country just like all the rest of the nation, whereas Miyake insists that they have more responsibility than others who just followed them. Miyake's opinion here might have led Ono to admit to his mistakes in Noriko's *miai* later in the novel.

In the world of painters, there was also a debate similar to that between Yamada and Yamane. During the war, under the demand of the military authorities, many painters went to the front and produced 'war (record) paintings'.[18] Those paintings were exhibited all over the country to boost the fighting spirit. The leader of this move was Tsuguharu Fujita, who was a member of the École de Paris and the only internationally acclaimed Japanese painter. Just like Kosaku Yamada, he was inevitably denounced after the war. In the *Asahi Shimbun* newspaper in October 1945, a painter, Shigeo Miyata, criticized Fujita and others for now cooperating with GHQ/SCAP, although until recently they had been 'riding on fascism'. Denying the alleged contribution to the Americans, Fujita defended himself in the same way as Yamada did: as soon as the war started, all the nation supported the war, and many painters simply accomplished their national duties.

Goro Tsuruta, another painter blamed by Miyata, repeated this familiar excuse but added, 'it is wrong to criticise painters who produced war paintings for being inconsistent in painting other things in peace time. We are painters. We paint whatever we like. We are not ideologists.'[19] The implication here is that painters transcend world affairs. This in fact was another way painters tried to escape from their responsibility.[20] Kazumasa Nakagawa, the famous painter, is reported to have said after the war that painters should not boast of being criminal because they cannot be war criminals unless they are extremely talented.[21] In other words, paintings (including war paintings) are in essence powerless in society.

In *An Artist of the Floating World*, Chishu Matsuda often expresses the same opinion. When young he converted Ono to nationalism by advocating the need for Japan to restore the power to the Emperor, expand its empire, and save itself from poverty – the typical right-wing ideology in the 1920s. But even in his heated assertion he says in the end, 'But this is largely for others to worry over. ... The likes of us, Ono, we must concern ourselves with art' (*AFW* 174). This sounds like a contradiction because he is clearly urging artists to contribute, even if indirectly, to the national reform. In their final meeting in 1950, Matsuda says in a similar vein: 'Army officers, politicians, businessmen ... [have] all been blamed for what happened to this country. But as for the likes of us, Ono, our contribution was always marginal. No one cares now what the likes of you and me once did' (*AFW* 201).[22] Both Matsuda and Ono believe that they did their best during the war and that they can justify themselves. But Ono does not share Matsuda's view that the artist's role is marginal in society. This is because he is so proud that he wants to believe that he was an influential artist during the war. There were two ways in which artists excused themselves from war responsibility: one is to say that the whole nation was united to support the war, and the other is to say that after all art was irrelevant to politics and the war. Ono took only the former option because his pride did not allow him to accept the latter.

No musician or painter was purged by GHQ/SCAP.[23] To borrow Suichi's words in September 1946, it appeared that '[t]hey [were] carrying on with their lives, much the same as ever' (*AFW* 58). And the debates over war responsibility among them were quickly forgotten and led to no further discussion, to the regret of some later critics. It was inevitable that they petered out mainly because the attackers were also guilty after all: Yamane occupied an important position in the Society of Musical Culture as Yamada himself points out in his counter-argument; Miyata who denounced Fujita had also produced war paintings. In literature, the situation was more or less the same, although several famous authors were purged by GHQ/SCAP and the debates over war responsibility, prolonged until the mid-1950s. Here again, very few authors were completely innocent after all, and as Japan began to grow economically, the issue of war responsibility of the literati was forgotten. Post-war Japanese literature practically did not address this issue either, despite its extraordinary richness and diversity.[24]

In this manner, war responsibility in music, art, and literature became an embarrassing problem that few people wanted to explore. That is why in 1988 the literary critic Masashi Miura could write in his review of the Japanese translation of *An Artist of the Floating World* that 'the artist's war responsibility is a long past subject, but it may look different from abroad'.[25] He takes it for granted that the issue is dead. Indeed, when the Japanese translation appeared in 1988, critics and reviewers did not dig up the old embarrassing theme, focusing instead on the quality of translation. This remains the same to the present. In a sense, an English novelist, who hardly shares the post-war Japanese historical context, explored the old subject that Japanese people and Japanese literature avoided and forgot as a kind of taboo.

It is unlikely that Ishiguro was interested in or even conscious of the actual historical debates on war responsibility in music, art, and literature. But as long as his novel touches directly on such an issue, Japanese readers are better advised to at least remember the historical facts when reading this novel. Even if this is an imaginary Japan, the specific history depicted in the novel invites them to reconsider the related historical problems, because, after all, the Japanese at present are still haunted by problems that originated in the immediate post-war period, including not least war responsibility.[26] Discussing how the Japanese translation of the novel tones down the sensitive issue of war responsibility, Motoko Sugano rightly says:

> Allusions to history in *An Artist of the Floating World* are fictionalized and displaced for the reader in English; however, when they are translated back to Japanese, there appears to be only a fine line of difference between a historical parable that aims to achieve universality and the 'real' history, which must be considered in this particular situation.[27]

Despite Ishiguro's and the Japanese translator's intention to stress the universality of the novel, the history in it demands to be interpreted in the local context when it is concerned with vital national problems.

This claim may sound rather parochial as it goes totally against the tenor of Ishiguro's work, which seems to transcend national particularities. But many of Ishiguro's characters are inextricably embedded in particular historical contexts: it is difficult to imagine Ono in other countries than Japan or Stevens in *The Remains of the Day* in other countries than England, even if Ishiguro says that for him history is secondary like a location for a film director. It is more rewarding than distracting therefore to know and understand the historical background, including sensitive issues in it. And this is true for non-Japanese readers of *An Artist of the Floating World*. Even though they are not directly involved in the historical problems of Japan, they may be induced to imagine what those problems mean for the Japanese if they pay attention to history. Similarly, non-British readers (like myself) of *The Remains of the Day* may not be as familiar with the British historical context as the British are, but they can imagine how British people respond to the portrayal of British history in the novel.[28] I believe that in such an imaginative endeavour can be envisioned a higher level of universality where characters are understood in terms of (the interpretation of) the particular historical and cultural context, instead of the simple, facile kind of universality in light of which characters appear to be so abstracted and unmoored from history that they could have been placed anywhere, as if in a parable.

Notes

1 There are other similar instances: *The Lone Ranger* and *Popeye the Sailorman*, about which Ono's grandson Ichiro is enthusiastic in 1948 and 1949, began to be truly popular in Japan when they were shown on TV in 1958 and 1959 respectively.

2 Timothy Wright, 'No Homelike Place: The Lesson of History in Kazuo Ishiguro's *An Artist of the Floating World*', *Contemporary Literature* 55.1 (2014): 58–88 (73).

3 Ibid., 72.

4 Ibid., 63.

5 The fact that the Japanese did not create the new post-war order by themselves has put the authenticity of post-war values in doubt. The most controversial issue in this context is the Japanese Constitution, including Article 9 about the renunciation of war and no maintenance of armed forces. While liberals embrace and value it as their own, conservatives insist that it should be revised, since it was 'imposed' by GHQ/SCAP.

6 For more details about these books, see Kunio Shin, 'Ishiguro to Kindai Nihon no Rekishi [Ishiguro and the History of Modern Japan]' and 'Ishiguro to Edward Seidensticker [Ishiguro and Edward Seidensticker]' in Yoshiki Tajiri and Kunio Shin, eds., *Kazuo Ishiguro to Nihon: Yurei kara Senso Sekinin made* [*Kazuo Ishiguro and Japan: From Ghosts to War Responsibility*] (Tokyo: Suiseisha, 2020), pp.217–20.

7 Kunio Shin surmises that it is a book by an English journalist Mark Arnold Forster, published when ITV showed a documentary programme *The World at War* in 1973–4. See his 'Ishiguro to Kindai Nihon no Rekishi [Ishiguro and the History of Modern Japan]', p.192.

8 Alternatively, the passage may refer to the replacement of ultra-nationalist teachers by the prefectural authorities before the formal screening process started in June 1946 (see note 10). At least in Nagano prefecture such a precautionary personnel rearrangement is known to have occurred on a large scale (Yasohachi Morimoto, *Sengo Kyouiku no Shuppatsu: Naganoken Kyouin Tekikaku Shinsakai no Kiroku* [*The Start of the Postwar Education: The Records of Nagano Prefectural Teachers' Screening Committee*] (Ginga Shobo, 1977), p.47). In this case, 'the Tortoise' had been so aloof from the general militarism of society that the authorities judged he was 'safe' and not worth replacing. It is also to be noted that high schools in the old system were actually quite prestigious and most of them were promoted to universities in the new system. It is rather implausible that such an obscure man as 'the Tortoise' could get a post at a high school before the war. That is why the Japanese translator translates 'high school' here as 'junior high school'.

9 Wai-chew Sim, *Kazuo Ishiguro* (London: Routledge, 2010), p.43. During Noriko's *miai* in December 1948, Dr Saito mentions 'more demonstrations in the city centre today', in which some people seem to be injured (*AFW* 119). But in 1948, under GHQ/SCAP's pressure, demonstrations began to be controlled by public security regulations. As Kunio Shin says, Ishiguro here may have had in mind the 'Bloody May Day' in 1952 in which many demonstrators were injured in their clash with the police in Tokyo ('Ishiguro to Kindai Nihon no Rekishi [Ishiguro and the History of Modern Japan]', p.192). Ishiguro uses such an incident as a symbol of the difficult birth of the new, democratic Japan.

10 From June 1946 to the end of the Occupation, following GHQ/SCAP's purging efforts, each prefecture had a teachers' screening committee which eliminated those with dubious past records. But only a small number (fewer than 1 per cent) of teachers were ousted by this committee. Ogata in *A Pale View of Hills* might have been judged inadequate and dismissed by the committee.

11 The Tokyo Trial culminated in November 1948, one month after the starting date of the novel, when major war criminals were sentenced. Seven of them sentenced to death by hanging were executed the next month.

12 The president of Miyake's company 'tried harakiri first' (*AFW* 55). This would also have been unusual because even high-ranking militaries often used a pistol, though some fanatic civilian nationalists committed mass harakiri immediately after the war.

13 Towards the beginning of *A Pale View of Hills*, the narrator Etsuko soberly writes, '[t]he English are fond of their idea that our race has an instinct for suicide' (*PVH* 10). Regarding 'A Family Supper', in which readers are led to suspect that the family are committing mass suicide at the end, Ishiguro says, '[t]he story was basically just a big trick, playing on Western readers' expectations about Japanese people who kill themselves' (*CKI* 10–11).

14 These exchanges appeared in *Tokyo Shimbun* on 23 December 1945. Translations are mine.

15 Quoted in John W. Dower, *Embracing Defeat: Japan in the Wake of World War II* (New York: W. W. Norton, 1999), p.496.

16 Ibid., pp.475–6.

17 Ibid., pp.504–5.

18 For more details, see Motoko Sugano, '"Putting One's Convictions to the Test": Kazuo Ishiguro's An Artist of the Floating World in Japan', in Sebastian Groes and Barry Lewis, eds., *Kazuo Ishiguro: New Critical Visions of the Novels* (Basingstoke: Palgrave Macmillan, 2011), pp.75–8.

19 Miyata's first attack appeared in the *Asahi Shimbun* newspaper on 14 October 1945, and Fujita's and Tsuruta's responses on 25 October 1945. Translations are mine.

20 Compared with composers who wrote war songs, it was easy for painters to assert that the meaning or message of their war paintings was ambiguous. It was always possible for them to claim that those paintings in fact were intended to oppose the war. Ono seems more culpable because his paintings were explicitly propagandistic.

21 Quoted in Giichi Nakamura, *Zoku Nihon Kindai Bijutu Ronso Shi* [*More History of the Debates in Art in Modern Japan*] (Tokyo: Kyuryudo, 1982), p.257.

22 Ono's first daughter Setsuko is of the same opinion: 'Father was simply a painter. He must stop believing he has done some great wrong' (*AFW* 193). As Wai-chew Sim says, this must be because Setsuko is worried that her father Ono might blame himself too much, as the song-writer Naguchi does (*Kazuo Ishiguro*, p.42).

23 The music critic Seiji Choki argues that compared with the de-Nazification of German musicians, GHQ/SCAP's attitude towards Japanese musicians was very soft maybe because they did not take them seriously. See his 'Undo Toshiteno Sengo Ongakushi [The Post-War History of Music as a Movement] (2)', *Record Geijutsu* [*Record Art*] 51:2 (2002): 86–90 (90).

24 For left-wing writers, the experience of conversion (from left to right) before the war was more important than that of cooperation with the war itself. There are many novels about this conversion.

25 Masashi Miura, 'Senzen no "Shinnen" wo tou [Questioning the 'Belief' of the Prewar Period]', *Asahi Shimbun*, 4 April 1988, the morning edition (my translation).

26 Those problems include the problematic status of the Japanese Constitution, the ambivalent attitude towards the USA (dependence and resistance), and the awkward diplomatic relations with neighbouring Asian countries, to name a few.

27 Sugano, 'Putting One's Convictions to the Test', p.79.

28 In the process, the following questions come to mind, for example: How do British people think of the Suez crisis, which occurred in 1956, the year in which the novel is set even though it is never mentioned in the text?; How are those appeasers in the 1930s (represented in the novel by Lord Darlington) placed in British people's minds now?; Is there a controversy over their responsibility?; Are their memories suppressed in the United Kingdom just as the memories of cooperation with war efforts tend to be suppressed in Japan?

3

LIANI LOCHNER

Ishiguro and Colonialism

Kazuo Ishiguro is 'very suspicious of postcolonial writing as a category' when it is defined by writers' biographies, including their race or country of origin, 'rather than by their writing'.[1] It is an unsurprising stance for the Nagasaki-born British author who, because of his name and the subject matter of his early novels, was either bracketed in the same multicultural category of British literature as Salman Rushdie and other writers of Commonwealth origins or considered an 'exotic writer' and asked repeatedly to account for the supposed Japanese qualities of his writing.[2] Yet, the inclusion of Ishiguro and Rushdie in 1983 on the *Granta 7: Best of Young British Novelists* list of upcoming writers under the age of forty also signalled a transformation of the literary scene and the redefinition of the English novel at a time when Thatcherism worked hard to exclude immigrant communities from definitions of British identity.[3]

Ishiguro is not a colonial subject, and his novels cannot be considered postcolonial when held up against a definition of these and world literatures as '"closed" in the sense that they clearly delineate forms that derive their meaning from opposition to and correction of a colonial context and experience'.[4] Maintaining this distinction, critics tend to recognize in *The Remains of the Day* an 'anti-imperial stance' also present in Rushdie's early work. Rebecca L. Walkowitz identifies allegorical readings of the novel as exposing 'the hypocrisy of English liberalism in the face of colonial exploitation abroad and anti-Semitism at home'.[5] And John McLeod points out that the novel's subtle examination of pro-Nazi leanings in the British aristocracy in the lead-up to the Second World War makes it part of 'the wider literary critique of the nation's chequered history at the heart of postcolonial representations of Britain'.[6] It is in this frame, then, that *The Remains of the Day* is considered a response to the Thatcher government's nativism and nostalgia for Empire, as representing a time when Britain still had a significant presence on the world stage.[7] Distinguishing between colonialism and imperialism becomes less important when considered against postcolonial studies' insight that 'both the "metropolis" and the "colony" were deeply altered by the colonial process'.[8]

Colonialism is only alluded to in *The Remains of the Day*: although he seems blithely unaware of it, Stevens's road trip occurs in July 1956, the month in which the Suez Crisis, seen as 'the last feeble fling of an older imperial tradition' and symbolizing the decline of British international influence, was initiated.[9] American neo-imperialism and post-war occupation of Japan from 1945 to 1952 is the largely unstated context of *A Pale View of Hills*, but *An Artist of the Floating World*, *When We Were Orphans*, and the Ishiguro-scripted film *The White Countess* represent Ishiguro's most direct encounter with the question of British and Japanese imperialism and colonialism in China. These works are set against the backdrop of what the historian Richard Overy calls the 'long Second World War' that starts with the Japanese invasion of Manchuria in 1931 and comes to a conclusion only in the insurgencies and civil conflicts that marked the beginning of the end of many centuries of colonialism and territorial empire after the armistice in 1945. Considering the imperial ambitions of Japan, Italy, and Germany – the so-called Axis states – as leading causes, Overy recasts the Second World War as 'the Great Imperial War': the existence of 'a global imperial order' dominated by Britain and France 'shaped and stimulated the fantastic ambitions in Japan, Italy and Germany, the so-called have not nations, to secure their national survival and express their national identity by conquering additional imperial zones of their own'. Being an empire 'came to be seen as a way of defining the identity of the late-century nation state as a progressive "civilizing" agent for the rest of the world, and partly as a symbol of national prestige'.[10] Britain and Japan's imperial fantasies thus may have played out on colonial soil, but were also crucial to forming the self-image of the nation. Ishiguro's engagement with colonialism takes place against this broader understanding of the notion of the postcolonial, as Ato Quayson formulates it: 'as much a reflection on conditions under imperialism and colonialism proper as about conditions coming after the historical age of empires'.[11]

Considering the settings of his early novels, Sebastian Groes and Barry Lewis call Ishiguro a *Nachkriegskind*: 'a child born into a generation that lives, and writes, in the shadow of the Second World War'.[12] Significantly, though, Ishiguro repeatedly asserts that setting is only a secondary consideration in his writing; his works offer a literary rather than documentary engagement with the nation-empire. *An Artist of the Floating World*, for example, is set in an imaginary Japanese city, as Ishiguro did not want it to be read as 'some kind of realist text telling you what Tokyo was like after the war' (*CKI* 8), and it is impossible to read Christopher Banks's nightmarish descent into the district of Chapei in *When We Were Orphans* as a historical account of the 1937 Battle of Shanghai. Moreover, his interest in these periods of political transformation is in the nation's narratives of itself, its motivations and elisions, as focalized through the concomitant demands on individuals to align themselves with the dogmas of the day. 'What's important', Ishiguro asserts, 'is the emotional aspect, the actual positions the characters take up at different points in the story, and why they need to take up these positions' (*CKI* 10).

Unlike Rushdie, Ishiguro does not write from the perspective of the colonized subject, and when he explores notions of subaltern identity in novels like *Never Let Me Go* and *Klara and the Sun*, his ahistorical settings – respectively, a late-1990s Britain where cloning is a reality and a futurist dystopian America – invite allegorical readings rather than voicing the experiences of a specific context. The postcolonial tenor of Ishiguro's work is thus perhaps more evident when compared to that of J. M. Coetzee, the South African author and fellow Nobel laureate, to whose prose his pared-down style is frequently likened. Coetzee, too, as David Attwell points out, has resisted being assigned a writerly identity, 'of having South Africanness in various forms (as a legal structure of citizenship, an historical identity, and the cultural edifice of being a South African writer) forced upon him by an accident of birth'.[13] But possibly the most significant comparison for the purposes of this chapter is that, like Coetzee, Ishiguro examines colonialism from the 'inside', so to speak – from the perspective of individuals who are on the side of empire and, therefore, of colonial rule, and who are unwittingly complicit in its structures of oppression. They, too, are subjects produced by colonial and imperial discourses. Interested in the 'emotional and historical reverberations' of his settings,[14] Ishiguro concentrates on 'the small and the private' (*TCE* 30) of his characters' lives and offers intricate, complex, and unsettlingly sympathetic depictions of the psychological denials and displacements that allow them to operate within these regimes. Focusing on *An Artist of the Floating World*, *When We Were Orphans*, and *The White Countess*, this chapter responds to the ways in which Ishiguro's fiction attends to the relationship between individual and collective responsibility and historico-political forces.

Responsibility and Identity

A consistent premise of Ishiguro's writing is the inability of individuals to take on an extra-discursive or extra-ideological stance from which to assess the values of their community and the historico-political forces that shape them. Indeed, he considers it to be a universal truth that we are all insiders: like Stevens in *The Remains of the Day*, we typically are far from 'where the big decisions are made';[15] we 'take our orders, we do our jobs, we accept our place in the hierarchy, and hope that our loyalty is used well'.[16] Ishiguro's unreliable narrators, and the use of the presumptive 'you', creates an unsettling effect in that the reader is unable to critique these flawed characters, even as they face plenty of judgement within the texts. The lingering fear, haunting the reading of Ishiguro's work, is that we could end up like the butler who realizes, 'too late in his life, that he has lived his life by the wrong values' (*TCE* 19). This is usually where readers encounter Ishiguro's narrators – at points when, either through public opprobrium or the realization of irrevocable losses, they come to recognize, though perhaps not to accept, that they have dedicated their lives to a wrong or shameful cause; in an attempt to make sense of their present predicaments, they are looking to their pasts to reassess their orienting values and commitments. The retreat of Ishiguro's characters in nostalgia might be, as Patricia Waugh argues, the only way to 'survive psychically' the various 'personal, national, international' traumas they have suffered:[17] the deaths of Masuji Ono's wife and son during the Second World War in *An Artist of the Floating World*; the disappearance of Christopher Banks's parents in colonial Shanghai in *When We Were Orphans*; and, in the same city in *The White Countess*, Todd Jackson's loss of his wife and daughter in anti-foreigner riots. Traumatic histories, Waugh claims, produce 'kinds of mental dislocation' that result in 'a sense of blockage, suspension, the inability to move on'.[18] Focusing on the war propaganda artist Masuji Ono, a character born out of a subplot of *A Pale View of Hills* in which Ogata, an influential former teacher is publicly excoriated by an erstwhile student for his pro-imperialist teachings,[19] I will argue that Ono's emotional stasis is, rather, the result of his attachment to the 'wrong values', which can be ascribed to the constitutive desire for identity.

In *The Psychic Life of Power*, Judith Butler builds on what she describes as the little-explored role of conscience in Althusser's theory of subjection. She reads the scene in which Althusser himself runs after the authorities to confess to the murder of his wife as an account of reverse interpellation: it is the guilty subject who, in a bid for social recognition and status, calls out to the law. The subject turns towards the law out of 'a prior desire for the law, a passionate complicity with law, without which no subject can exist'.[20] The process of subjectivation is, therefore, based on a founding subordination. By repeating and rehearsing the norms and values by which subjection is secured, the subject achieves social identity. Masuji Ono's reminiscences of Japan in the lead-up to the Second World War in *An Artist of the Floating World* are of a time that saw an intensification of the mobilization of public life in preparation for the country's entry as a nation-empire onto the world stage, a process that had already begun during the Meiji era. From 1931 onwards, the military leadership ran a concerted campaign 'to raise national awareness and enthusiasm for territorial expansion' playing on 'the themes of national honour and sacrifice for the nation', in Japan's desire to become the 'Great Britain of the East'.[21] The role of educators was to create 'subjects to serve the nation' who would advance government policy.[22] Ishiguro creates an atmosphere of radical certainties and fierce loyalties that was inspired, he reveals, by the period of 'often fractious and bitter transition in [1980s] Britain' in which he wrote the novel.[23] At the height of his influence, Ono tells his students that 'a finer, more manly spirit is emerging in Japan' of which they are 'the spearhead' (*AFW* 73–4). Japanese identity becomes equated with the imperial cause. When Hirayama, a developmentally delayed local from Ono's village, parrots pro-imperial slogans like 'The village must provide its share of sacrifices for the Emperor! Some of you will lay down your lives! Some of you will return triumphant to a new dawn!' (60), he is praised by the villagers for having the 'right attitude. He's Japanese' (61). After the war, Hirayama will get physically attacked for still singing the war songs and shouting the same mottos now deemed regressive.

Arguably, Hirayama and Ono are not what Hannah Arendt calls 'convinced adherents' of pro-imperialism, unlike Ogata, the narrator Etsuko's father-in-law in *A Pale View of Hills*. True supporters of the war effort 'could not feel guilty but only defeated'.[24] Ogata refuses to consider the question of personal responsibility for the horrors inflicted on the younger generation by Japanese imperialist expansion. Rather, he is proud of his hard work to ensure the 'correct values' (*PVH* 147) and the 'proper qualities' (66) were handed down and wants an apology from Shigeo Matsuda, the former pupil and friend of his son who published an article critical of his teachings. So deeply ingrained is his belief in self-effacement, the sublimation of the individual to the nation's goals, that he sees no volition in the younger generation's critique: he thinks Matsuda is swayed by Communism or that his own son, Jiro, is simply aping the way of the enemy, namely American individualism. He fears for the impact of the occupier's values on Japanese society: 'Discipline, loyalty, such things held Japan together once ... People were bound by a sense of duty. Towards one's family, towards superiors, towards the country' (65). Individualism and the universal suffrage granted in a democracy are equated with selfishness and people forgetting their obligations.

Ono's recollections of his formation as an artist in the 1930s, on the other hand, are prompted by the marriage negotiations – the second after a failed first attempt – of his younger daughter, Noriko, that will include an investigation into the family history by her fiancé's family. His diary entries, dated between 1948 and 1950, seem to be driven by the realization, as Ishiguro claims, that his career as an artist, which included creating propaganda posters for the imperial war effort, has 'becomes contaminated because he happens to live at a certain time'.[25] Ono is flummoxed when he learns that the president of a company involved in the war effort committed suicide as an apology to the families of those killed: 'After all, if your country is at war, you do all you can in support, there's no shame in that' (AFW 55). The notion of duty that Ono – like Ogata – subtly evokes here suggests the subjection of the individual to the values of the time and thus the displacement of responsibility onto politico-historical forces. Swept up in a wave of fervent nationalism, people hesitate to judge collaborators, because of the suspicion, as Arendt argues, that in such a climate 'no one is a free agent, and hence the doubt that anyone is responsible or could be expected to answer for what he has done'.[26] This suggests collective guilt, which in turn means that no one is responsible. Arendt, however, is careful to distinguish between the 'political responsibility' assumed by 'every nation for the deeds and misdeeds of the past' and the 'personal responsibility' of individuals who implicitly supported the constitution of the 'common enterprise', unlike revolutionaries such as like Kuroda, whom Ono denounces for unpatriotic activities in *An Artist of the Floating World*, and the five teachers who get imprisoned in *A Pale View of Hills* who have withdrawn 'this tacit consent'.[27] The question that Ono's unreliable narration circles but does not face head on, as evident in his need to deflect and displace his feelings of guilt onto his social milieu, is the same one Arendt asks in *Responsibility and Judgment*: 'Why did you *support*?'[28]

Ono's feeling of culpability can be traced to the paternal relationships, including between master and teacher, that form the core interpersonal connections in the novel. Ono's need for recognition is evident from the first diary entry in which he mentions that he was especially chosen for his 'good character and achievement' to buy Akira Sugimura's house, the 'exaggerated respect' his pupils had for him (AFW 8), and demurs that he was surprised at the high esteem in which he was held, as he himself has never been aware of his 'own social standing' (19). Arguably, his longing for status and influence is born out of his businessman father's rejection of his childhood dreams of becoming an artist. However, his narrative reveals the creeping realization that perhaps his teacher Mori-San was right, that he did betray his artistic integrity by following Chishu Matsuda to create propaganda posters for the Okada-Shingen Society's China Crisis – presumably a reference to the invasion of Manchuria – and New Japan campaigns. When he wins the Shigeta Foundation Award in 1938, it does not bring him the 'deep triumph and fulfilment' (202) that he expected. He feels 'triumph and satisfaction' only looking down at Mori-San's villa, having overcome his doubts that he would achieve 'something of real value and distinction' (204). However, it is catching the train of history that enables Ono to succeed in his 'endeavour to rise above the mediocre' (204).

Ono's subjection to the patriotic values of the pro-imperialism period initiates and sustains his agency: he becomes a Sensei with students of his own, an advisor to the Committee of Unpatriotic Activities, and plays a significant role in the advent of the Migi-Hidari, which becomes the hangout of artists, playwrights, and journalists 'unflinchingly loyal to his Imperial Majesty the Emperor' (AFW 64) and refuses patrons who are 'incompatible' with 'the new patriotic spirit' (63). Ono's insistence that for this, too, he derived 'so much personal satisfaction' (64) is in marked contrast to his lack of stated emotion over the deaths of his son Kenji in Manchuria and his wife Michiko in a freak shelling towards the end of the war. According to his diary entries, only others feel the expected feelings of anger or sadness at these losses. It thus seems significant that, when Kuroda's student calls him a traitor for his denunciation of Kuroda, he mentions that he was not 'unduly' (114) upset about this but only concerned about how it would affect Noriko's marriage negotiations. The Kuroda incident, too, represents an event in his life that he is unable to confront directly: the reader never learns what Kuroda is accused of, thus raising the suspicion that Ono betrayed him because he thought him disloyal to his teachings rather than a traitor to the nation; this seems to be affirmed by Ono's anticipatory passages in which he excuses teachers who act rashly because they feel betrayed by students developing their own techniques as artists. He tries to reassure himself that Kuroda landed on his feet, because his time in prison means that he is on the right side of history after the war, but unlike Kuroda and his family, Ono never faced any financial loss. Not significant enough in the hierarchy to be prosecuted, he and Matsuda manage to hold on to their assets after the war.

Masuji Ono's assertions, towards the end of the narrative, that his actions were 'at the time in the best of faith' (AFW 202), indicate his inability to turn away from the 'wrong values' that have been so constitutive of his identity. 'For the "I" to launch its critique,' Butler writes in The Psychic Life of Power, 'it must first understand that the "I" itself is dependent upon its complicitous desire for the law to make possible its own existence.' 'One cannot criticize too far the terms by which one's existence is secured.'[29] An Artist of the Floating World depicts Ono as a man in search of lost authority: his daughters no longer live in fear of him, but rather treat him like an old man, and his grandson, enamoured with American popular culture figures like Popeye and the Lone Ranger, ignores his cultural guidance. When a former student comes, like before, to ask him for a favour, Ono initially feels 'something akin to relief, as though things were returning to a more familiar footing' (*AFW* 100). Until the end, he denies that he compromised his artistic integrity in pursuit of the reflected glow of the pro-imperialist movement of the 1930s, insisting that Dr Saito, an eminent art critic and his daughter's new father-in-law, has always been aware of his stature as a painter. But perhaps the harshest truth the text reveals through the dramatic irony of Ono's narration, the one that he simply cannot face, is that his wife and son died as the result of a cause that he helped to promote, not because he believed in it but for the status and influence it conferred. He was not a convinced adherent. As Matsuda reminds him, 'you wanted so badly to make a grand contribution' (199). *An Artist of the Floating World* ends with what can be interpreted as a cautionary note, warning against the possibility of simply replacing one code with another, to be followed by a new generation of patriots: 'Our nation, it seems, whatever mistakes it may have made in the past, has now another chance to make a better go of things. One can only wish these young people well' (206).

Fantasy and Sacrifice

They do not need to blame themselves unduly, Chishu Matsuda tells Masuji Ono, because in the end, their misfortune was simply that they were '[o]rdinary men with no special gifts of insight' (*AFW* 200). In Hannah Arendt's terms, for whom the faculty of thinking is world-questioning, their failure is their inability to think and judge for themselves: thinking requires, or even means, a singular responsiveness to each context 'instead of applying categories and formulas which are deeply ingrained in our mind, but whose basis of experience has long been forgotten and whose plausibility resides in their intellectual consistency rather than in their adequacy to actual events'.[30] How children acquire a world-view and internalize its hierarchies, articulated both discursively and spatially, is a repeated concern staged in Ishiguro's *oeuvre*; his first novel, *A Pale View of Hills*, already foregrounds the role of educators to align the values of children with the goals of the nation-empire. Shigeo Matsuda remarks to his former teacher Ogata: 'In your day, children in Japan were taught terrible things. They were taught lies of the most damaging kind. Worst of all, they were taught not to see, not to question. And that's why the country was plunged into the most evil disaster in her entire history' (*PVH* 147). Ogata's son, Jiro, remembers having to memorize lessons 'all about how Japan was created by the gods ... How we as a nation were divine and supreme' (66), echoing the nationalist teachings telling Japanese children that they were 'a chosen people, a divinely favored race'.[31] This imperial fantasy of 'the fulfilment of a manifest destiny', like

48

other powerful colonial myths about the 'settlement of wild frontiers, or the prospect of an Eldorado of riches',[32] was the redeeming ideal that would justify to the nation the violence and sacrifice imperialism demanded and that would turn the people into unthinking subjects.

In Britain, presenting imperialism as a civilizing mission by claiming the inferiority and childlike nature of colonized peoples ensured the nation's commitment to the colonial mission, while masking the importance of capitalist acquisition and exploitation for smoothing over domestic inequalities and maintaining international prestige.[33] In *When We Were Orphans*, the Banks's family friend, Uncle Philip, recognizes how the idea of a Western civilization trades on people's need to belong: 'To a nation, to a race' (*WWWO* 77); simultaneously, populations were kept ignorant of the nature of colonial acquisition, of how territories were acquired and indigenous resistance was overcome. The 'greatest leaders' from the 'greatest countries' in the world are revered for their accords, like the Treaty of Versailles after the end of the First World War, establishing the 'foundations of our future civilisation', as the Japanese imperialist Matsuda remarks in *The White Countess*.[34] In *When We Were Orphans*, it is Sir Cecil Medhurst, an architect of the League of Nations – seemingly named after Lord Cecil, an establishment figure and member of the British League of Nations Union[35] – who claims that 'the forces of civilisation had prevailed and legislated' to limit the horrors that can be inflicted with the use of modern weaponry (*WWWO* 42). This soaring rhetoric, which Ishiguro's characters deploy, obscures Britain's use of its technological advances to gain control of the colonies or the attempts by Britain and France in the League of Nations to secure their own interests in China by limiting Japanese colonialism. Japan withdrew from the organization in 1933 to further pursue its imperial ambitions after the League recognized China's right to sovereignty in condemnation of the invasion of Manchuria.

According to Alexander Bain, Ishiguro's Shanghai narratives, including the film *The White Countess*, are about the revelations – to the novel's English detective, Christopher Banks, and the film's former American diplomat, Todd Jackson – of 'a broader convergence of global interests, war, and state power which has, with or without their comprehension, shaped their lives'.[36] Christopher travels to Shanghai in 1937 with the improbable mission of finding his parents who disappeared from the International Settlement over two decades ago; he learns that, in return for his safety and financial security, his mother was enslaved by the Chinese warlord, Wang Ku, active in the very opium trade she campaigned against and which was also the source of wealth of his father's British employer, Morganbrook and Byatt. While Christopher rails against the 'denial of responsibility' and

the lack of shame of the British settlers who are 'at the heart of the mael-
strom threatening to suck in the whole of the civilised world' (*WWWO* 162),
he comes to realize his own complicity as a benefactor of a system of
economic exploitation created to secure the interests of people like him.
Thus, *When We Were Orphans* stages the question of collective responsibility, which, unlike the individual responsibility betrayed by Masuji Ono's
feelings of guilt in *An Artist of the Floating World*, does not result from
Christopher's own actions, but rather from that which has been done in his
name. In Arendt's understanding of the term collective responsibility, the
individual is considered responsible because of their involuntary 'member-
ship in a group (a collective)', in this case, the British nation and body
politic.[37]

Raised in the International Settlement in Shanghai before moving to
England, Christopher Banks is 'a bit of a mongrel' (*WWWO* 76), and
although he vehemently denies being ostracized and insists on his successes
mimicking English culture, he fails to circulate inconspicuously in upper-
class British society. As a colonial, 'tainted' by his time in the colony, he is
marked by and bullied for his differences by his peers at his boarding school,
at university, and later at a society wedding he attends as an adult.
Moreover, his narrative is marked by the 'mad logic' (*CKI* 158) that associ-
ates solving the mystery of his parents' disappearance twenty-two years
earlier with stopping the Second World War. This emotional need for his
childhood home, from which he was ripped too soon, drives a peculiar
narcissism that makes the Chinese and Japanese officers and soldiers
engaged in the 1937–45 Sino-Japanese War bit players in his drama. This
myopic focus defamiliarizes the depiction of colonial Shanghai, bringing into
sharp relief the occlusions of the imperial fantasy; in other words, while his
focus is elsewhere, what emerges from Christopher's nightmarish account is
an image of a people and their environment that were fundamentally altered
by British colonialism, including its trade in opium imported from India.
When We Were Orphans thus reveals the transformation of colonial spaces
in the image of an imperial fantasy and, consequently, the blindness to the
collateral damage.

Similarly, the fervent wish of Japanese imperialists in *An Artist of the
Floating World*, *When We Were Orphans*, and *The White Countess* is for
Japan 'to take her rightful place amongst the world powers', by 'forg[ing] an
empire as powerful and wealthy as those of the British and the French' (*AFW*
174). Another Matsuda, in *The White Countess*, tells Todd Jackson that his
'cherished dream' is 'to see Japan become a truly great nation. As great as
Britain or France' or America. When Jackson remarks that Matsuda's vision,
the Japanese empire that he is orchestrating by sketching on the world

canvas through Japanese aggression in China, will 'come and crush my little world in here. Just like it's crushing all those other little worlds right now', Matsuda's answer is dismissive: 'Most regrettable, but that is in the nature of things'.[38] His words echo those of the Japanese colonel Hasegawa, who, when Christopher Banks asks if he, as a 'cultured man', has misgivings about 'all this carnage caused by your country's invasion of China', smiles calmly and answers, '[i]t is regrettable, I agree. But if Japan is to become a great nation, like yours, Mr Banks, it is necessary. Just as it once was for England' (*WWWO* 278).

This 'necessary' feature of the imperial fantasy and the blindness it engenders is evident when, shortly after arriving in Shanghai, Christopher Banks attends an evening in the ballroom of the Palace Hotel, where, in one of the novel's most surreal scenes, he is handed a pair of opera glasses to view the fighting between the Japanese and Chinese nationalist forces (the Kuomintang). When a troupe of dancing girls appear, the room loses all interest in the battle across the water, as though 'one entertainment had finished and another had begun'. Christopher is outraged that the so-called elite of Shanghai could treat 'with such contempt the suffering of their Chinese neighbours across the canal' (*WWWO* 162). But, evidence of ingrained British colonial attitudes towards the Chinese, and the effects of colonial space-making in Shanghai, is littered throughout the novel: Christopher remembers Uncle Philip resigning from Morganbrook and Byatt over a 'profound disagreement with his employers over how China should *mature*' (*WWWO* 74, emphasis added); social ills like alcoholism and opium addiction are simply '[u]sual Chinaman stuff' (198); and the deplorable housing conditions of the Chinese factory workers in the warren make Lieutenant Chow exclaim, '[y]ou would not believe human beings could live like that' (235). Perhaps suggesting his own impending myopia if he were to stay in this environment for too long, Christopher, when driving through the city with a former school acquaintance, Morgan, comments that he has grown used to seeing the suffering but, while he is still dismayed at the sight of these 'huddled figures' (182), the refugees fleeing the conflict, his friend shows none, not even registering concern that the 'bundle' they have run over might have been a 'sleeping form' (183). The blindness of the British to those, like the factory workers in Chapei, whose suffering they never see because foreigners rarely enter the warren, can be explained by the colonial-era compartmentalizing of the city into separate nationalities and classes; similarly, the '[p]lenty of death over there in Chapei' (161) simply affects an unindividuated mass. However, this same logic when applied to Christopher's personal losses makes the reader realize the horror denied by those for whom colonial inequalities and attitudes have become systemic and ingrained. Christopher remembers contemplating the notion, after his father's disappearance, 'that I need not mind so much since Uncle Philip could always take my father's place' (118); and of his journey to England, '[o]f course, I did miss my parents at times, but I can remember telling myself there would always be other adults I would come to love and trust' (27).

In the Chapei 'warren', realizing that among the debris 'lay cherished heirlooms, children's toys, simple but much-loved items of family life', Christopher's anger again erupts, supposedly at 'those pompous men of the International Settlement' (*WWWO* 241), but perhaps more broadly at the sacrifices of personal connection, the creation of so many orphans, in the name of the nation-empire. He comes across some children 'poking with sticks' at something on the ground, as if it was 'some dark ritual' (248); it is an injured Japanese soldier whom Christopher professes to recognize as his childhood friend, Akira. The novel maintains the reader's doubt about whether this really is the same Akira, but it seems no coincidence that the boy who once bragged of Japanese superiority and believed that if he was Japanese enough, he would be like the twine holding the metaphorical blinds of his family together, returns as a Japanese soldier, bound in twine by his captors (73, 252). The scene evokes Masuji Ono's painting entitled 'Complacency' in *An Artist of the Floating World*, created in response to a similar encounter with three small boys torturing an animal Ono comes across with Matsuda in the deprived shanty district of Nishizuru. Ono's painting indicts the neglect of the 'three fat, well-dressed men', presumably representing the business class (*AFW* 168). A few years later, he transforms this painting into 'Eyes to the Horizon' in which the three men, now resembling three prominent politicians, wear nervous expressions, and the three poverty-stricken boys had become stern-faced soldiers, pointing the way forward, 'west towards Asia' (169).

Christopher's realization that his mother loved him enough to sacrifice herself for his safety, without him having to earn it by performing an idea of Englishness, releases him from the delusion that he is individually responsible for the war. In *The White Countess*, too, the personal connection offered by the countess, Sofia Belinsky, offers redemption to Todd Jackson. A White Russian refugee living in Shanghai, she works as a taxi-hall dancer, and, it is suggested, sometimes engages in prostitution to support her daughter and her deceased husband's family. She faces no end of condemnation and judgement from her sister- and mother-in-law who, while excoriating her as bringing shame on their aristocratic Russian family name, are happy to be supported by her work. Clear-eyed about what she is doing, Sofia refuses to join her friend Maria in judging other women who offer their customers more than dancing. 'Isn't it the same? For all of us? You and me too?' she asks. She denies Maria's useful fiction of grand passion to mask the true nature of the exchange: 'We all have to fall in love from time to time. To feed our children, feed our mothers, our sisters.'[39] Sofia demonstrates a willingness to sacrifice herself, to efface her identity and status as a former aristocrat, for her child. Unlike characters like Ogata, Masuji Ono, and even Christopher who have sacrificed the personal in pursuit of a career (in the latter's case, a relationship with his orphaned ward, Jennifer), Sofia feels no regret. The pathos of these males' narratives is in the sense that, without the identity that a life dedicated to the wrong values has given them, they have nothing. The white countess thus offers redemption to Todd Jackson in a way that his bar, The White Countess, could not – a meaningful connection that offers a reprieve from the transactional nature of relations in Shanghai.

Conclusion

'If you want to draw a parallel between how individuals come to terms with their past and decide what to do next, and how a nation or community approaches such things,' Ishiguro claims, 'then the issue of storytelling is an important one.'[40] The motivations for these stories, the desire to comfort or to deceive, are revealed in their omissions and misdirection. Set against the backdrop of Japanese and British imperialism and colonialism, *An Artist of the Floating World*, *When We Were Orphans*, and *The White Countess* reveal the disastrous successes of imperial discourse to form the world-view also of colonizing subjects, which is enacted and reinforced through their everyday negotiation of the identities and spaces transformed by imperialism.

Haruki Murakami likens Ishiguro to 'a painter working on an immense painting' to which the reader gains access, with each publication, only in sections: 'we have yet to gain a bird's-eye view of the total work.'[41] Murakami's metaphor of course evokes Todd Jackson's realization, in *The White Countess*, that his cosmopolitan bar bringing together all the forces in Shanghai that would soon erupt into one of the first conflicts of the Second World War, was only a small picture unwittingly contributing to the canvas of Matsuda's larger imperialist ambitions. Similarly, as this chapter has shown, ordinary people, with no special vision, trying to make sense of their small portion of the world, finding social identity in a sense of duty or career, perhaps unwittingly support bigger notions of belonging such as culture, race, or nation. These can become corrupted, sending individuals adrift and into questioning their identity from the wrong side of history: 'Sometimes people base their whole lives on a sincerely held belief that could be wrong.'[42] Ishiguro's strategies of defamiliarization, confining the reader to the minds of his narrators whom we are simultaneously invited to and unable to judge, awaken our own faculties of thinking, questioning the historico-political forces, the relations they condition, and the spaces they transform. In the end, for Ishiguro, the need for external recognition, to have social identity conferred from the outside, is treacherous; redemption from the consequences of our inability to fully see our historical situatedness lies in the kinds of personal connection that would make the sacrifice of children and parental relations to these forces unthinkable.

Notes

1 Kazuo Ishiguro, 'The New Seriousness: Kazuo Ishiguro in Conversation with Sebastian Groes', in Sebastian Groes and Barry Lewis, eds., *Kazuo Ishiguro: New Critical Visions of the Novels* (Basingstoke: Palgrave Macmillan, 2011), p.263.
2 Rebecca L. Walkowitz, 'The Post-Consensus Novel: Minority Culture, Multiculturalism, and Transnational Comparison', in Robert L. Caserio, ed., *The Cambridge Companion to the Twentieth-Century English Novel* (Cambridge: Cambridge University Press, 2009), p.225; Cynthia F. Wong, *Kazuo Ishiguro* (Horndon: Northcote House, 2000), p.8. See also Susie O'Brien, 'Serving a New World Order: Postcolonial Politics in Kazuo Ishiguro's The Remains of the Day', *Modern Fiction Studies* 42:4 (1996): 787–806 (especially p.798, for a summary of typical reviews of Ishiguro's early works).
3 Bridget Chalk, 'The 1980s', in Peter Boxall, ed., *The Cambridge Companion to British Fiction: 1980–2018* (Cambridge: Cambridge University Press, 2019), p.17. See also Walkowitz, 'The Post-Consensus Novel', pp.223–6.
4 Sean Matthews and Sebastian Groes, 'Introduction: "Your Words Open Windows for Me": The Art of Kazuo Ishiguro', in Sean Matthews and Sebastian Groes, eds., *Kazuo Ishiguro: Contemporary Critical Perspectives* (London: Bloomsbury, 2010), p.2. It should be noted that postcolonial literary theory has moved on from this definition. See, for example, Elleke Boehmer's *A Postcolonial Poetics: Twenty-First Century Critical Readings* (Basingstoke: Palgrave Macmillan, 2018).
5 Rebecca L. Walkowitz, 'Unimaginable Largeness: Kazuo Ishiguro, Translation, and the New World Literature', *Novel: A Forum on Fiction* 40:3 (2007): 216–39 (228).
6 John McLeod, 'Postcolonial Writing in Britain', in Ato Quayson, ed., *The Cambridge History of Postcolonial Literature*, Vol. 1 (Cambridge: Cambridge University Press, 2012), p.593.
7 See Christine Berberich, 'Kazuo Ishiguro's The Remains of the Day: Working Through England's Traumatic Past as Critique of Thatcherism', in Groes and Lewis, eds., *Kazuo Ishiguro*, pp.124–8.
8 Ania Loomba, *Colonialism/Postcolonialism*, 2nd ed. (London: Routledge, 2005), p.22.
9 Richard Overy, *Blood and Ruins: The Great Imperial War, 1931–1945* (Penguin Kindle Edition, 2021), p.858. See John P. McCombe, 'The End of (Anthony) Eden: Ishiguro's *The Remains of the Day* and Midcentury Anglo-American Tensions', *Twentieth Century Literature* 48:1 (2002): 77–99.

10 Overy, *Blood and Ruins*, pp.xi, 3.

11 Ato Quayson, 'Introduction: Postcolonial Literature in a Changing Historical Frame', in Quayson, ed., *The Cambridge History of Postcolonial Literature*, p.6.

12 Sebastian Groes and Barry Lewis, 'Introduction: "It's Good Manners, Really" – Kazuo Ishiguro and the Ethics of Empathy', in Groes and Lewis, eds., *Kazuo Ishiguro*, p.5.

13 David Attwell, 'Coetzee's Estrangements', *Novel: A Forum on Fiction* 41:2–3 (2008): 229–43 (232).

14 Susannah Hunnewell, 'Kazuo Ishiguro, The Art of Fiction No. 196', *The Paris Review* 184 (2008): n.p. (accessed online at www.theparisreview.org/interviews/5829/the-art-of-fiction-no-196-kazuo-ishiguro).

15 Ibid.

16 Sean Matthews, '"I'm Sorry I Can't Say More": An Interview with Kazuo Ishiguro', in Matthews and Groes, eds., *Kazuo Ishiguro*, p.115.

17 Patricia Waugh, 'Kazuo Ishiguro's Not-Too-Late Modernism', in Groes and Lewis, eds., *Kazuo Ishiguro*, p.16.

18 Ibid., p.16.

19 Hunnewell, 'Kazuo Ishiguro, The Art of Fiction No.196'.

20 Judith Butler, *The Psychic Life of Power: Theories in Subjection* (Stanford, CA: Stanford University Press, 1997), p.108.

21 Overy, *Blood and Ruins*, p.35; Hyman Kublin, quoted in Ching-chih Wang, *Japanese Imperialism in Contemporary English Fiction: From Dejima to Malaya* (Singapore: Palgrave Macmillan, 2019), p.36.

22 Alexis Dudden, 'Japanese Colonial Control in International Terms', *Japanese Studies* 25:1 (2005): 1–20 (14).

23 Kazuo Ishiguro, 'Introduction' to *An Artist of the Floating World* (London: Faber & Faber, 2016), p.xii.

24 Hannah Arendt, *Responsibility and Judgment*, ed. Jerome Kohn (New York: Schocken Books, 2003), p.35.

25 Hunnewell, 'Kazuo Ishiguro, The Art of Fiction No. 196'.

26 Arendt, *Responsibility and Judgment*, p.19.

27 Ibid., pp.27, 47.

28 Ibid., p.48.

29 Butler, *The Psychic Life of Power*, pp.108, 129.

30 Arendt, *Responsibility and Judgment*, p.37 (also see pp.159–89).

31 Wang, *Japanese Imperialism in Contemporary English Fiction*, p.36.

32 Overy, *Blood and Ruins*, p.4.

33 Bill Ashcroft, Gareth Griffiths, and Helen Tiffin, *Postcolonial Studies: The Key Concepts*, 3rd ed. (London: Routledge, 2013), pp.50–8.

34 Kazuo Ishiguro, *The White Countess: An Original Screenplay by Kazuo Ishiguro* (unpublished manuscript, 2005), New York Public Library of the Arts, Billy Rose Theatre Division, 147 pages, pp.92–3.

35 Overy, *Blood and Ruins*, p.70.

36 Alexander M. Bain, 'International Settlements: Ishiguro, Shanghai, Humanitarianism', *Novel: A Forum on Fiction* 40:3 (2007): 240–64 (243). See also Carey Mickalites, 'Kazuo Ishiguro and the Remains of Empire', *Critique: Studies in Contemporary Fiction* 60:1 (2019): 111–24.

37 Arendt, *Responsibility and Judgment*, p.149.

38 *The White Countess*, p.132.
39 Ibid., p.10.
40 Matthews, 'I'm Sorry I Can't Say More', p.117.
41 Haruki Murakami, 'Foreword: On Having a Contemporary Like Kazuo Ishiguro', in Matthews and Groes, eds., *Kazuo Ishiguro*, p.viii.
42 Hunnewell, 'Kazuo Ishiguro, The Art of Fiction No. 196'.

4

JERRINE TAN

Immigration and Emigration in Ishiguro

In an interview with Nobel winner Kenzaburō Ōe, Kazuo Ishiguro once admitted to feeling like 'a kind of homeless writer' (*CKI* 58). Indeed, Ishiguro's fiction is pervasively concerned with questions of home and homelessness – characters immigrate to other countries or are otherwise displaced; they are marked by a sense of unbelonging, of cultural otherness, or characterized in one way or another as 'the Other'. All this is characteristic of the immigrant condition, and indeed can be traced to Ishiguro's own experience of relocation. Born in Nagasaki, Japan on 8 November 1954, Ishiguro moved with his family to the United Kingdom at the early age of five in 1960, due to his father's job. Despite assuming that the move would be temporary, the family eventually stayed on in the UK.

Characters in Ishiguro's novels are endlessly on the move. There is an irony in this constant motion as it is juxtaposed against the internal stasis that the characters are often trapped within – metaphorically and sometimes also literally. Sachiko in *A Pale View of Hills* talks frequently of moving to America with her lover Frank; we learn that Etsuko, our narrator, has immigrated to England from Nagasaki under unknown circumstances. In *An Artist of the Floating World*, Masuji Ono meanders the streets of the 'floating world' of his town (a town very much like Nagasaki), finding himself continually entangled in the annals of Japan's war history. Stevens in *The Remains of the Day* ends his narrative in, and recounts his experiences from, an extended road trip. In *The Unconsoled*, Ryder circles an unspecified central European city, getting increasingly frustrated with the web of appointments and promises he seems unable to keep, walking endlessly but getting nowhere. We follow Christopher Banks in *When We Were Orphans* on his deceptively teleological quest to find his parents – themselves not only displaced but *disappeared* – and perhaps avert catastrophe. His journey takes him not only from Shanghai to London and back again, but also into, around, and through the different neighbourhoods and pockets of Shanghai that denote and symbolize different national and cultural enclaves.

Kathy H. in *Never Let Me Go* is constantly ferrying herself from place to place in her role as Carer, even though her efforts will tragically make no difference to her ultimate destination – to 'complete' like her friends before her. The characters and narrators in *Nocturnes* are variously displaced and exiled. Axl and Beatrice in *The Buried Giant* undertake a journey to reach a son they are already beginning to forget and, along the way, meet others on quests of their own. Finally, in Ishiguro's latest novel, *Klara and the Sun*, Klara similarly beseeches other characters for help, stumbling through fields and making her way through the city as she endeavours to 'save' Josie, before ending up in a trash heap where she waits out her last days.

Ironically, many of the journeys these characters take are characterized by a degree of futility or stasis. Frustratingly naive, or displaying an abundance of misplaced faith in broken systems, these characters go nowhere, arrive at no great revelation, and seem to face no moral reckoning. By the end of the Ishiguro novel, the fates of his characters usually remain unchanged and it is questionable whether they have achieved any true understanding of their lives. The pathos of this internal stagnation is made more poignant when it is set against the journey or quest that almost all of them undertake.

Together with several of his stories, two of Ishiguro's novels directly and explicitly address the question of migration from one country – and one continent – to another: *A Pale View of Hills* concerns the trauma of moving from Japan to England, while *When We Were Orphans* is also centred around an intercontinental move, from pre-communist Shanghai to pre-war Britain. This chapter will focus on these two novels in order to consider more widely the importance of immigration and the condition of being nationally and ethnically ungrounded in Ishiguro's work. In addition to these two novels, this chapter will also examine Ishiguro's latest novel, *Klara and the Sun*, to discuss immigration alongside attendant issues of race and labour.

It is difficult to categorize Ishiguro within any one genre. Firstly, no Ishiguro novel is stable in terms of genre; many of his novels appear to traffic in the tropes of certain genres only to bend, exceed, or fail to adhere to the norms of those genres (*When We Were Orphans* is not quite a detective novel; *Never Let Me Go* dabbles in science and dystopia but deviates from typical sci-fi). Secondly, it is almost impossible to define Ishiguro as a novelist in terms of the predominant genre of his *oeuvre* precisely because he writes across and does not appear to be bound to any single genre. The settings of his novels and his protagonists are myriad, hopping across continents, shifting across periods, and even reaching into the realm of fantasy and science fiction. Further, Ishiguro's Anglo-Japanese background seems to have led to a compulsion among critics either to sidestep his racial and national identity (glossing his hybridity and his sparseness in style as something post-racial and universal) or to reduce his name and face to biographical details (and thus read his work as if it were imbued with some 'Japanese quality').[1] Because of this, Ishiguro's body of work invites a serious reflection on how critics approach texts in World Literature by authors with complex hybrid identities. In fact, the Ishiguro novel should be cherished not for the ways that it blurs the boundaries of culture, nation, and politics as such in order to universalize human experience, but precisely because it invites us to meditate on these boundaries. Paying attention to immigration and emigration in Ishiguro's works is important because doing so compels us to contend with key moments in world history, grounded in specific contexts that have often been overlooked or forgotten. This approach is key to pushing against modes of reading Ishiguro that problematically universalize his work, as if it were unyoked from the particularities of nation, language, empire, race, and history.

Ishiguro's claim that he does not begin with a location for his novel in mind does not demonstrate a disregard for setting, but rather a deep investment in the ethical conundrums of the specifics of world history. Describing his process, he explains, 'I would search through history books in the way that a film director might search for locations for a script he has already written. I would look for moments in history that would best serve my purposes ... I was conscious that I wasn't so interested in the history per se, that I was using British history or Japanese history to illustrate something that was preoccupying me' (*CKI* 58). Rather than simply presenting stock images of an orientalized Nagasaki or Shanghai, Ishiguro's novels set in Asia in fact engage deeply not only with the same ethical conundrums addressed in his later novels, but also with the specific historical, sociopolitical issues of their localized contexts.

As widely circulating and widely translated and translatable texts, Ishiguro's novels are a bit like immigrants themselves. Rebecca Walkowitz points out that 'because a text's network will continue to grow and multiply, as that text is circulated and read in numerous regions and languages, its geography and culture will be dynamic and unpredictable. It is no longer simply a matter of determining ... the literary culture to which a work belongs.' Ishiguro's novels are part of what Walkowitz calls 'new world literature'.[2]

Following his 2017 Nobel Prize in Literature, both Japan and the UK have claimed the author as their own. Even though Ishiguro has not lived in Japan since he left Nagasaki at the age of five, and even though the early Japanese reception to his work was in fact lacklustre, Japan often cites Ishiguro as its third Nobel Prize-winning author.[3] Despite early success in Britain,[4]

Ishiguro's work did not enjoy the same reception from Japanese readers. Summarizing the argument of scholars such as Gayatri Spivak, Emily Apter, and Aamir Mufti, who criticize a brand of Western-centric, 'one-world' vision in world literature, Rebecca Suter explains in her book, *Two-World Literature: Kazuo Ishiguro's Early Novels*, that:

> While "world literature" has expanded to include an increasingly broad range of different languages and cultures, it still evaluates them from a single aesthetic and moral point of view that ultimately coincides with that of the dominant (Anglophone and/or Euro- American) culture …. Attributing Ishiguro's stylistic and thematic choices to some kind of 'specific attention to oriental ways and modes' was a recurrent feature of critical responses to this author in the late 1980s and early 1990s.[5]

Suter suggests that 'by creatively exploiting his double cultural positioning … Ishiguro has been able to produce texts that look at broad human concerns in a significantly different way from the kind of 'world literature' discussed by these scholars'.[6]

As an immigrant to the UK from a defeated Japan after the Second World War, Ishiguro has been a stumbling block to modes of categorization in postcolonial theory and world literature, and even in critical race theory, since such a figure produces fraught impasses to easy reductive ways of thinking about empire, imperialism (and less-discussed East Asian imperialism), and race. Commenting in 1995 on how some of Britain's strongest writing of the 1980s and early 1990s had emerged from its former colonies, his friend Pico Iyer mentioned Ishiguro together with Salman Rushdie and Timothy Mo.[7] But unlike India and Hong Kong, Japan was never a colony. In the nineteenth and early-twentieth centuries, Japan was in fact the perpetrator of an aggressive East Asian imperialism with an expansionist agenda, colonizing large swathes of Asia during and before the Second World War.

Ishiguro himself has often intentionally distanced himself from, or even disavowed, his own Japaneseness, reiterating the claim that he speaks Japanese like a five-year-old and frequently citing cherished canonical Western writers. In interviews and most recently in his Nobel Prize acceptance speech, he has been candid about the pressures he experienced as an Asian writer in the UK. 'It's very difficult for me to distinguish how much Japanese influence I've actually inherited naturally', he comments in a 2015 interview, 'and how much I've actually generated for myself because I felt I ought to': 'I think I certainly do have a tendency to create a Japaneseness about my writing when I do write books in a Japanese setting', he remarks.[8] Some critics, the harshest of whom is Sheng-mei Ma,[9] viewed Ishiguro's Japanese novels as a concession to the literary marketplace, serving up an exoticized Japan to the West; for various reasons, Japanese readers also had a muted response to Ishiguro's early novels and were seemingly unimpressed.[10] Yet, Ishiguro's assertion that his Japan is merely a 'fictional world' is suspect (*CKI* 53). Even though Ishiguro talks about the 'particular idea of Japan that [he] had in [his] own mind' (ibid.), he had formed these ideas and images based on Japanese films by Akira Kurosawa and Yasujiro Ozu, as well as on 'comics, magazines, and educational digests' sent to him by his grandfather in Japan (*TCE* 11). Ishiguro is acutely and immensely conscious of his racial difference, his immigrant status, and his liminal position as a Japanese-born British writer.[11] As Suter writes, 'the experience of growing up between two cultures lies at the core of the literary strategies deployed in Ishiguro's fiction. The author's career was built on playing with, and often defying, readers' and critics' expectations about his ethnic and cultural belonging.'[12]

In his conversation with Ōe, both writers speak to the perceived affectlessness of his style and consequent assumptions regarding his ethnicity, and national and cultural identity. Ishiguro claims that he does not in fact try to be 'a quiet writer' but acknowledges that 'there's a surface quietness to my books', even though they 'deal with things that disturb me the most and questions that worry me the most. They're anything but quiet to me' (*CKI* 58). Ōe observes that because Ishiguro is described as a 'very quiet and peaceful author', he is therefore *mistaken as* 'a very Japanese author' (*CKI* 157). Rather, Ōe feels that Ishiguro has a 'tough intelligence', and that 'this kind of strength [is] not very Japanese', but in fact very English.

Something of the immigrant position can also be observed in what might be interpreted as Ishiguro's excessive gratitude towards the British public. In his Nobel acceptance speech, he recalls that when he first moved to England it 'was less than twenty years from the end of a world war in which the Japanese had been [the country's] bitter enemies', and that he was 'amazed by the openness and instinctive generosity with which [his] family was accepted by this ordinary English community' (*TCE* 10). His comment poignantly illuminates the alienation that (mostly non-white) immigrants feel in the West, their pre-emptive assumption that they will be viewed suspiciously, as perennial foreigners who do not belong, revealed in their surprised gratitude even for basic decency. Across the Atlantic, in America, after Pearl Harbour and after disseminating narratives about robotic kamikaze pilots in order to justify their dropping of the atomic bombs,[13] there was an indifference towards the Japanese that masqueraded as benevolence and perhaps soothed any sense of guilt on the part of the victorious West to be magnanimous to those they had triumphed over, through terrible, violent forces.

Ishiguro is acutely aware of stereotypes surrounding Japanese people – that they have 'an instinct for suicide' (*PVH* 10) – and has even manipulated this for both commercial and subversive purposes. Ishiguro plays with the theme of suicide in one of his earliest works, the short story 'A Family Supper' in order to parody and satirize Western readers' fixation on such stereotypical qualities of the Japanese.[14] He does this to an even greater degree in his first novel, using suicide as the foil to his complex engagement with culture and violence.

A Pale View of Hills

Ishiguro's debut novel opens with Etsuko, a Japanese woman who had earlier moved to England and married an Englishman named Sheringham, ruminating on her daughter Keiko's suicide. Keiko is her 'pure Japanese' daughter from an earlier marriage to a Japanese man named Jiro (*PVH* 10). Niki, her half-English daughter, is visiting from London for the weekend. Etsuko reflects on her time in Nagasaki just after the war, and recalls an acquaintance, Sachiko, whose story is uncannily similar to Etsuko's.

Largely engaging in a form of orientalism, early reviews and criticism of Ishiguro often insistently referred to '[his] Japanese face and [his] Japanese name', the fact that he was born in Nagasaki, Japan, and observations on the 'Japaneseness' of his work (*CKI* 70). Many such critics offered superficial analyses of his novels as literary reflections on Japanese philosophical notions such as *mono no aware*, loosely translated as 'the pathos of things', which is often misinterpreted by non-Japanese readers.[15] But paying attention to descriptions of Nagasaki in Ishiguro's first novel forces us to confront the histories of the land, challenging the dominant view of Japan and its people as pure surface with no 'innerness'.[16] Critics such as Lewis argue that the novel obstructs realist readings by persistently echoing Giacomo Puccini's *Madam Butterfly*, also set in Nagasaki and which only 'satisfied a Western demand for stock images of an alien and aestheticised Far East'.[17] It is true that these references serve not to authenticate, but rather to satirize. Nonetheless, the novel *does* engage a mode of realism that allows for and invites serious contemplation of historical violence.

Even though Keiko (or Keiko's death) is at the centre of the novel, she remains an absent centre and only a liminal presence in the text. Compelling the reader to confront the lack of curiosity and sympathy surrounding Keiko's death, tellingly, and tragically, Etsuko explains that her death was revealed in a trenchant newspaper report: 'The English are fond of their idea that our race has an instinct for suicide as if further explanations are unnecessary; for that was all they reported, that she was Japanese and that she had hung herself in her room' (*PVH* 10). No further explanations were necessary because *that was the explanation*. This callousness bespeaks the attitude of many in the West towards the Japanese as an ethnic monolith, not only with regard to those they defeated far away, but even towards those immigrants at home, whom they should view as their own brethren. This demonstrates the entrenched ways in which racial difference continues to be understood as a manifestation of (usually negative) innate traits, that preclude sympathy and empathy in those who view immigrants as Others. Empathy and sympathy for Keiko are impossible because her being 'pure Japanese' marks her as foreign. *A Pale View of Hills* is the kind of fiction that exhibits 'the blindness of a certain kind of person to the pain of another kind of person', thereby demonstrating to the reader that they may have been similarly blind.[18] As Richard Rorty writes, the ability to avoid being cruel is 'achieved not by inquiry but by imagination, the imaginative ability to see strange people as fellow sufferers'.[19]

Ishiguro echoes Partha Chatterjee's critique of the myopia and exclusions of *imagined communities* in his essay 'Whose Imagined Community?' Indeed, *A Pale View of Hills* reveals the imagined community to be the British newspaper-reading public, the stereotypes they widely believed in, and their imagined Other. Etsuko's late husband, Sheringham, as a British journalist, was also part of this system. As Etsuko reveals, her husband held clear prejudices against the Japanese race because 'although he never claimed it outright, he would imply that Keiko had inherited her personality from her father' (*PVH* 194). Niki also discusses how Sheringham was never really kind to Keiko: 'I suppose Dad should have looked after her a bit more, shouldn't he? He ignored her most of the time. It wasn't fair really' (175). *A Pale View of Hills* suggests that, as the dominant medium for the dissemination of information, newspapers not only compound, enforce, and circulate racist stereotypes (often about immigrants) held by the hegemonic demographic but also create them.

Keiko's solitude and isolation – her trauma of relocation, immigration, and of living in post-war Japan notwithstanding – is set against her 'half-English' sister Niki's easy assimilation into contemporary British society. For Niki, her 'residual' Japaneseness is an exotic quality that even affords her greater cultural currency and can be commoditized, as we learn that she peddles Etsuko's narrative to curious British poet friends – a narrative that Etsuko does not even agree with, and that we know Niki learned almost purely from her English father. This uneasy and unequal dynamic within the family sheds light on the difficulties that each of them faces in their various racial and immigrant categories.

The novel also interrogates the specific position of the immigrant mother. Sachiko and Etsuko have often been read as doubles: Sachiko is either read psychoanalytically, as Etsuko's projection of herself, or she is read as a narrative tool for Etsuko to explore her own story. Either way, for the twinned mothers, integration and assimilation are their key worries – more with regard to their children than to themselves. Addressing her plan to move to the USA with Frank, Sachiko, who up till that moment had insisted that she had Mariko's best interests at heart, finally admits: 'Do you think I imagine for one moment that I'm a good mother to her?' (*PVH* 171). At a later moment, Etsuko also confesses to Niki that she 'knew all along [Keiko] wouldn't be happy over here. But … decided to bring her just the same' (176).

Beyond the mirrored immigrant positions of these mother–daughter pairs, the novel is an immigrant narrative twice over in other ways as well: our narrator, Etsuko, is a Japanese immigrant to the UK, and so is the novel's author, Ishiguro. As immigrant narratives go, however, it is an unusual one because there is no *narrative of immigration*: the process and experience of immigration is omitted, even though the attendant pain and loss is alluded to. Similarly, Etsuko's interiority is fiercely guarded: she barely betrays any emotion, despite her repeated paraliptical desires. That she remembers Keiko even as she insists that she has 'no great wish to dwell on Keiko, it brings [her] little comfort' (*PVH* 11) – memorializing even as she disavows her compulsion to remember – suggests the depth of her well of pain.

But the story of Etsuko's emigration to England is ultimately not Niki's friend's to tell. 'A friend of mine's writing a poem about you', Niki declares to her mother during her visit. Etsuko reacts with astonishment: 'Why on earth is she doing that? … A poem about me? How absurd. What is there to write about? She doesn't even know me', she says. And it's true – Niki's friend has never met Etsuko and knows only what she has been told. Niki continues, 'I was telling her about you and she *decided* she'd write a poem', as if the story, and the right to tell it, belonged to the poet friend (*PVH* 89; emphasis added). In the end, Etsuko gives Niki a photograph for her poet friend, one that depicts the pale view of hills over Nagasaki, a precious scene to Etsuko because she recalls sharing the view with Keiko on a rare happy occasion. One can assume that Niki's 'brilliant poet' friend will produce an ekphrastic poem based on Niki's stories, but it would be an artefact completely divorced from Etsuko's experiences of war and immigration. The novel thus embeds a criticism of the appropriation and commoditization of immigrant narratives, often by white writers, and simultaneously performs a refusal to engage in the same fetishization of immigrant pain.[20]

The reader must contend with the fact that Etsuko's narrative will be transformed, manipulated, adapted, and circulated through and by different forms and media, and sometimes without her consent. This speaks to the complexity and compounded nature of the immigrant narrative and also alludes to the impossibility of conveying the immigrant narrative, which will always be fragmented, layered, and challenging.

As much as Ishiguro has at times disavowed the influence that his Japanese background has on his work, his archives, now owned by the Harry Ransom Center at the University of Texas, Austin, suggest otherwise. Many of his descriptions of the waste ground in A Pale View of Hills mirror scenes in Akira Kurosawa's 1952 Ikiru (生きる), a film Ishiguro closely reflected on while writing Never Let Me Go, as detailed in his notebooks, 'Ideas As They Come'.[21] Ishiguro was surely influenced by sociopolitical issues that defined Japan at the time and had been well acquainted with these films for years: the opening scene in Ikiru shows women gathering at the reception area of a bureaucratic office, demanding that the waste grounds in front of their houses be cleared. Oliver Hermanus's 2022 film, Living, an adaptation of Kurosawa's Ikiru, with a screenplay written by Ishiguro himself, retains this scene and plot point: a group of women come to County Hall to petition for a waste ground to be turned into a children's playground.

Ishiguro's immigrant identity and personal history has left an indelible mark on his writing, and is inscribed even into the very existence of his career. When he initially conceived of the story for A Pale View of Hills, he planned to set it in Cornwall, but later realized that if he 'told this story in terms of Japan, everything that looked parochial and small would reverberate'.[22] In the same interview, Ishiguro mentions discovering that his 'imagination came alive when I moved away from the immediate world around me'. In his Nobel Prize speech, he elaborates on how during his Creative Writing MA at the University of East Anglia he would 'tinker' with 'some ideas for short stories not set in Japan, only to find my interest waning' (TCE 6–7).

It is striking, then, to consider Sheng-mei Ma's criticism of Ishiguro in this light. Ma has accused Ishiguro of writing in 'whiteface', and chides Ishiguro for the fact that none of Ishiguro's protagonists, except Etsuko, share his Anglo-Japanese identity.[23] Putting aside how this demand for autofiction from a writer of colour is problematic on several levels, Ishiguro is in fact there in A Pale View of Hills. He makes an auteur-like cameo in his very first novel, inscribing himself into the novel he wrote in order to preserve his own private Japan, and also himself: Mrs Fujiwara's only surviving family member is named Kazuo. He may even have more similarities with Keiko, who, like himself, is transplanted from Japan to England. Like Etsuko, Ishiguro's mother is a Nagasaki atomic bomb survivor.

When We Were Orphans

Describing himself as 'a kind of homeless writer' in an interview from 1989, Ishiguro goes on to explain that this sense stemmed from his feeling that he 'wasn't a very English Englishman', nor 'a very Japanese Japanese', and therefore 'had no clear role, no society or country to speak for or write about. Nobody's history seemed to be [his] history' (*CKI* 58). These same concerns with not being English enough, nor Japanese enough, are expressed almost verbatim by the two children, Akira and Christopher Banks, in *When We Were Orphans*. Even though Ishiguro demurs that he thoroughly researches his books or the locations in which they are set, professing that he was not 'terribly interested in researching history books' (*CKI* 53) in the case of *The Artist of the Floating World*, Ishiguro's descriptions of his settings, particularly Nagasaki and Shanghai, are uncannily accurate and reveal an intimate knowledge of the ins and outs of these cities. In fact, *When We Were Orphans* is infused with yet another branch of Ishiguro's family history. In an interview from 2008, Ishiguro revealed that '[his] father wasn't typically Japanese at all because he grew up in Shanghai'.[24] His Japan novels are set in Nagasaki (whether explicitly or implicitly), where his mother survived the bombs. *When We Were Orphans*, Ishiguro's first return to an Asian setting, ventures to Shanghai, where his father grew up with 'a Chinese characteristic'.[25] This novel enables him to explore his complex relationship not just with Japan, but also with East Asian and Western imperialism in China, and with internationalism more broadly. Through the novel, Ishiguro posits that the international writer is not unlike an orphan – a notion that seems embedded in his remark about being a 'homeless writer'.

When We Were Orphans follows Christopher Banks, a highly respectable detective in London, who returns to Shanghai to solve the mystery of his parents' disappearance. In Shanghai, he reminisces about his childhood and about a childhood friend, Akira – a Japanese boy with whom he used to play in the International Settlement, where both their families lived. On the cusp of the Second Sino-Japanese war, and after the Anglo-Chinese Opium Wars, Banks finds himself mired not only in the throes of his family tragedy, but in the vicissitudes of world history as well.

In fact, Christopher Banks's conflicts about home and belonging might be based on Ishiguro's own feelings as an immigrant. Ishiguro has described in the past how he felt that his Japanese name and face act as a straitjacket, as if he were only Asian on the outside, and British on the inside. If this is so, he may find a kindred spirit in a combination of his two characters in the novel: Christopher Banks, who is white, but feels that the International Settlement in Shanghai is home, and Akira, Banks's childhood friend, an immigrant Japanese boy in Shanghai who does not want to return to Japan.

This idea of mixing is offered by Uncle Philip, who posits the fantasy of a 'mixed' universe in which peace is achieved not by segregation, nor standardization and conformity, but through a universal *mixing*:

> [I]t's true, out here, you're growing up with a lot of different sorts around you. Chinese, French, Germans, Americans, what have you. It'd be no wonder if you grew up a bit of a mongrel. ... You know what I think, Puffin? I think it would be no bad thing if boys like you all grew up with a bit of everything. We might all treat each other a good deal better then. Be less of these wars for one thing. Oh yes. Perhaps one day, all these conflicts will end, and it won't be because of great statesmen or churches or organisations like this one. It'll be because people have changed. They'll be like you, Puffin. More a mixture. So why not become a mongrel? It's healthy. (*WWWO* 79)

Here, Uncle Philip subverts the use of the word 'mongrel', typically used pejoratively to describe mixed-breed animals and as a slur for mixed-race children, recasting it positively as the hope for the future. The irony of course is that Christopher is British and white, so if he is a mongrel, he would only be a mongrel 'on the inside', continuing to circulate as he always has based on his 'outside'. However much Christopher may profess to love the multiplicity of the International Settlement or Shanghai, he is still, by blood and by appearance, a pedigree.

But the space of the International Settlement nonetheless offers hope to the dream of mutual understanding and cooperation, because for Banks personally it was a space where he and Akira, two little boys from different cultural backgrounds, played with a shared understanding. Recalling their childhood, Banks gets their stories confused, 'I had a feeling we acted out scenes from *Ivanhoe*, which I was reading at that time – or perhaps it was one of Akira's Japanese samurai adventures' (*WWWO* 113). This suggests the interchangeability and relatability of these stories across cultures, offering the possibility that shared understanding can nonetheless be achieved across difference. Yet, this idyllic harmony only occurs during their childhood in the safe space of the home, and is soon demystified.

The space of the home is also an interesting architectural monument to the immigrant's 'double consciousness'. Christopher's and Akira's houses had been built by the same British firm, but Akira's parents had created a pair of 'replica' Japanese rooms at the top of the house. 'Once inside ... one could not tell one was not in an authentic Japanese house made of wood and paper ... the doors to these rooms [were] especially curious; on the outer, 'Western' side, they were oak-panelled with shining brass knobs; on the inner, 'Japanese' side, delicate paper with lacquer inlays' (*WWWO* 75). Akira's house, doubly surfaced, destabilizes the notion of authenticity and of what is within and without, and recalls Ishiguro's comments about his feelings of his own duality with regard to his immigrant identity. The doors to the room at once seal *in* and seal *out* 'Englishness' and 'Japaneseness', simultaneously concealing and revealing, and are the sites where 'Japaneseness' is enclosed and disclosed, thereby serving as an architectural metaphor to Ishiguro's double consciousness.[26]

Ishiguro's childhood home in Nagasaki in fact had a similar design. Ishiguro has reminisced about the house, saying, '[t]here was a room on the top floor with Portuguese furniture'.[27] Contrary to Sheng-mei Ma's claims that Ishiguro's novels do not offer any autobiographical detail, *When We Were Orphans* might be Ishiguro's extended meditation on national identity, immigration, ethnicity, and belonging, and his own in particular.[28] Like Christopher, Ishiguro's identity encapsulates a dichotomous outside-inside. Japanese-British Ishiguro is embodied by Christopher and Akira – inspired by both canonical Western and Eastern stories. Yet he shares Akira's and Christopher's compulsive fear of not being either 'Japanese' or 'English' enough, as if his inability to perform both sufficiently would lead to the breakdown of the world – indeed, to an epistemological collapse. It was by practising 'Japaneseness' or 'Englishness' that Akira believed they did their part to keep the world in harmony: 'we children ... were like the twine that kept the slats held together ... We often failed to realize it, but it was we children who bound not only a family, but the whole world together. If we did not do our part, the slats would fall and scatter over the floor' (*WWWO* 73).

This particular scene in *When We Were Orphans* directly echoes statements Ishiguro has made about himself and his sense of identity. He has, in the past, expressed a profound desire to be an 'international writer': 'If the novel survives as an important form into the next century, it will be because writers have succeeded in creating a body of literature that is convincingly international. It is my ambition to contribute to it', he comments.[29] Banks feels unmoored between Shanghai and London; likewise, Ishiguro's sense of homelessness stems from not feeling Japanese or English enough. Banks's cathexis to the International Settlement as his comforting 'home village' (a symbolic space of internationalism) where peace can be attained through mixing maps onto Ishiguro's wish to be part of a surviving literary world that thrives on being convincingly international. But just as Banks's childhood and the International Settlement are eventually revealed to be more complex than they seemed on the surface, internationalism, too, is not simply a perfect solution. It is ultimately 'fragile', as Akira insists, at risk of falling apart at the wave of a hand.

Klara and the Sun

In *Klara and the Sun*, Ishiguro broaches race alongside immigration and labour, but in the subtle, oblique fashion that is characteristic of the Ishiguro novel. In the novel, Klara only addresses one character with a 'last name': Melania Housekeeper. But we understand, of course, that this naming denotes Klara's misunderstanding. It's likely that she does not think Melania's last name is actually 'Housekeeper', since she also seems to understand the role of a housekeeper and that Melania *is* one. Melania Housekeeper then, is named *as* her menial job, interpellated as her vocation – her identity, in other words, is tied to and defined by it.

The reader is invited to note the differences, broadly, among characters – lifted and unlifted; B3s and other models; substituted and not substituted. Another difference that is often remarked upon in the novel is a character's accent or linguistic ability – a giveaway of class, place of origin, or mother tongue. Rick's English accent is remarked upon as foreign (*KS* 63). In the novel, there is an alignment of accent not only with class, but also with the suggestion of racial, immigrant, and vocational status. Rick and Melania Housekeeper are both marked by accents, but in different ways to connote different things. While Rick speaks with an English accent Melania speaks in broken English and in vernacular. Melania often makes ungrammatical statements such as, 'All right, but only short', or 'Okay hurry up!' or 'Wind too strong! You want die up there or what?' eliminating articles in the way non-native speakers do (63, 30). It is possible to detect a version of this in Klara's programmatic language – which is generally grammatically correct but awkward or somehow *off* in subtle ways. The way she says 'give privacy', for example, is an awkwardness that Rick notes at one point in the novel. It is suggested that Melania is an immigrant and the AFs, Artificial Friends like Klara, embodying a not dissimilar role and space in the household, in many ways, serve as clear allegories for immigrants and their labour.

Melania and Klara have more in common than they think or are aware of and should, from the start, be in community rather than in competition. This can be observed in one of the many ways in which Klara misunderstands a situation: once, when they are outside, Klara describes how

> Melania Housekeeper came between us, and before I was fully aware, had taken
> Josie's arm, tucking it under her own. Josie too was surprised by this, but didn't

protest, and I appreciated that Melania Housekeeper had concluded I might not be able to protect Josie reliably while outdoors due to my unfamiliarity. (*KS* 59)

Klara makes excuses for or misunderstands what seems to be Melania's insecurity about her position in the household – one defined by her utilitarian value.

The many Others in the novel are marked throughout in subtle ways – through their accents, their positions, their jobs, the way they interact with others, etc. But not all Others are cast the same. We understand that Josie's father is one of the 'substituted'. And yet he manages to have a decent and comfortable life, even taking a superior and defensive position towards others – a position that Rick's mum, Miss Helen, notes as 'fascist'. Josie's father can be read analogously to a growing far-right, predominantly white movement whose members view themselves as victims of a growing (usually non-white) immigrant class, who fear and resent the fact that they may be "replaced" by a non-white, immigrant workforce.[30]

Perhaps it is that, in 2021, nothing is innocent. *Klara and the Sun* is Ishiguro's first novel since his Nobel Prize, published in a post-Brexit, post-Trump, pandemic-roiled world. So when Josie's father insists that he is sharing his life with some 'very fine people' – white people who arm themselves and live in a gated community – one cannot but hear Donald Trump's defence of the 'very fine people' of Charlottesville, where the white suprema-cist Unite the Right rally took place in 2017.[31] It's not just any difference that renders one menial and abject. Some differences, it seems, are better than others. We know, after all, that the book is *not* set in England, and set in a place that very much resembles America. It's worth noting the irony, then, that Melania Housekeeper shares the same first name as Trump's immigrant wife – who visited an immigrant children's shelter at the US–Mexico border in 2018 wearing a jacket that read 'I really don't care. Do you?'. Suffice to say, Ishiguro's latest book offers a timely and piercing critique of some of the most pressing issues of our contemporary moment – that of an increasingly indignant and violent right, a continuing immigrant and labour crisis, discrimination towards immigrants and people of colour, as well as how these issues intersect.

In her book, *Anatomy of a Robot: Literature, Cinema, and the Cultural Work of Artificial People*, Despina Kakoudaki describes how '[t]he fantasy of the robotic servant, worker, or slave promises that if the enslavement of real people can no longer be tolerated in the modern world then mechanical people may be designed to take their place, and their labor will deliver the comforts of a laborless world for the rest of us'.[32] The word 'robot' was coined in 1920 by Karel Čapek to describe artificial workers and it was derived from the Czech word *robota*, which refers to serf labour, to drudgery and hard work.[33] The concept thus 'unites old and new types of oppression and obliquely connects serfs and chattel slaves to the modern and newly awakened proletariat classes of the twentieth century',[34] which artificial people seem to embody.

This dovetails with the concept of racial capitalism, a term coined by Cedric J. Robinson that is broadly defined as the process of deriving social and economic value from the racial identity of another person. Jenkins and Leroy explain how '[r]ace serves as a tool for naturalizing the inequalities produced by capitalism, and this racialized process of naturalization serves to rationalize the unequal distribution of resources, social power, rights, and privileges'.[35] As a tool, then, race, as an attendant factor to immigration, serves as an illuminating scalpel for understanding the subtle yet extant structures of power and oppression in the world of *Klara and the Sun*. Referring to 'the unnatural cyborg women making chips in Asia' as enabling the 'night dream of post-industrial society', Donna Haraway suggests that '"women of colour" might [already] be understood as a cyborg identity'.[36]

Notes

1 Gregory Mason, 'An Interview with Kazuo Ishiguro', *Contemporary Literature* 30:3 (1989): 335–47 (336).
2 Rebecca L. Walkowitz, 'Unimaginable Largeness: Kazuo Ishiguro, Translation, and the New World Literature', *Novel* 40:3 (2007): 216–39 (216).
3 Motoyuki Shibata describes the lukewarm reception of Ishiguro's Japanese novels in Japan in examining the Japanese translations of Ishiguro's early novels against their English originals ('Lost and Found: On Japanese Translations of Kazuo Ishiguro', in Sebastian Groes and Barry Lewis, eds., *Kazuo Ishiguro: New Critical Visions of the Novels* (Basingstoke: Palgrave Macmillan, 2011).
4 Ishiguro was included in *Granta* magazine's 'Best of Young British Novelists' list twice (1983 and 1993).
5 Rebecca Suter, *Two-World Literature: Kazuo Ishiguro's Early Novels* (Honolulu: University of Hawai'i Press, 2020), pp.2, 5.
6 Ibid., p.14.
7 Pico Iyer. "The Empire Strikes Back". *The New York Review*. 22 June 1995.
8 Alex Clark, 'Kazuo Ishiguro's Turn to Fantasy', *The Guardian*, 19 February 2015 (accessed online at www.theguardian.com/books/2015/feb/19/kazuo-ishiguro-the-buried-giant-novel-interview).
9 Sheng-mei Ma, 'Kazuo Ishiguro's Persistent Dream for Postethnicity: Performance in Whiteface', *Post Identity* 2:1 (Winter 1999): n.p. (accessed online at http://hdl.handle.net/2027/spo.pid9999.0002.103).
10 Issues around accuracy and omissions in translations also contributed to this reception by Japanese readers as Motoko Sugano explores in '"Putting One's Convictions to the Test": Kazuo Ishiguro's *An Artist of the Floating World* in

Japan', in Groes and Lewis, eds., *Kazuo Ishiguro*; Motoyuki Shibata and Motoko Sugano, 'Strange Reads: Kazuo Ishiguro's *A Pale View of Hills* and *An Artist of the Floating World* in Japan', in Sean Matthews and Sebastian Groes, eds., *Kazuo Ishiguro: Contemporary Critical Perspectives* (London: Bloomsbury, 2009).

11 In the opening sentence of his Nobel Prize speech he notes his complex unplace-ability: 'If you'd come across me in the autumn of 1979, you might have had some difficulty placing me, socially or even racially', explaining that his 'features would have looked Japanese' but that his hairstyle and dressing reflected the trends in Britain at the time, and further – hyper self-consciously – that if there were a traceable shibboleth to his speech, it reflected his upbringing in the southern counties of *England*, and not Japan (*TCE* 1).

12 Suter, *Two-World Literature*, p.10.

13 See, for example, Ruth Benedict, *The Chrysanthemum and the Sword* (Boston, MA: Houghton Mifflin, 1946).

14 Kazuo Ishiguro, 'A Family Supper', in Malcolm Bradbury, ed., *The Penguin Book of Modern British Short Stories* (London: Viking, 1987).

15 Barry Lewis offers an overview of this approach in *Kazuo Ishiguro* (Manchester: Manchester University Press, 2000). Further, such aestheticist approaches in Japanese philosophy are often misunderstood by Western audiences, as eluci-dated in Ria Taketomi's '*Mono No Aware* in Ishiguro's *A Pale View of Hills*', *Comparatio* 18 (2014): v–xvii (accessed online at https://catalog.lib.kyushu-u.ac.jp/opac_download_md/1518296/p(v).pdf).

16 See Roland Barthes, *Empires of Signs*, trans. Richard Howard (London: Cape, 1983).

17 Lewis, *Kazuo Ishiguro*, p.23.

18 Richard Rorty, *Contingency, Irony, and Solidarity* (Cambridge: Cambridge University Press, 1989), p.141.

19 Ibid., p.xvi.

20 See Jerrine Tan, 'Kazuo Ishiguro's Early Japan Novels and the Way We Read World Literature', *Modern Fiction Studies* 67:1 (Spring 2021): 89–122 (105).

21 In his early conception of *Never Let Me Go*, Ishiguro was thinking of Tommy in relation to the main character of Akira Kurosawa's *Ikiru* (1952), but he aban-doned this idea. I learned about this in an illuminating talk given by Yoshiki Tajiri, titled 'Art or Utilitarian Activities? – Ishiguro's Decision in an Early Plan for *Never Let Me Go*', at the conference 'Twenty-First Century Perspectives on Kazuo Ishiguro: An International Celebration' held at the University of Wolverhampton, UK, in February 2020.

22 Susannah Hunnewell, 'Kazuo Ishiguro, The Art of Fiction No. 196', *The Paris Review* 184 (2008): n.p. (accessed online at www.theparisreview.org/interviews/5829/the-art-of-fiction-no-196-kazuo-ishiguro).

23 Ma, 'Kazuo Ishiguro's Persistent Dream for Postethnicity'.

24 Hunnewell, 'Kazuo Ishiguro, The Art of Fiction No. 196'.

25 Ibid.

26 See Jerrine Tan, 'The International Settlement: The Fantasy of International Writing in Kazuo Ishiguro's *When We Were Orphans*', *American, British, and Canadian Studies Journal* 31 (2018): 47–64 (53).

27 Quoted in Ria Taketomi, 'Kazuo Ishiguro and Japanese Films: Concerning the Visual and Auditory Effects and Images of Danchi', *Comparatio* 17 (2013):

xvi (accessed online at https://catalog.lib.kyushu-u.ac.jp/opac_download_md/1456054/p(vii).pdf).

28 Jerrine Tan, 'The International Settlement', 54.

29 Wai-chew Sim, *Kazuo Ishiguro* (Abingdon: Routledge, 2010), p.20.

30 This far-right, white nationalist ideology has gained popularity in recent years, and has inspired violent crime in the USA. The Buffalo shooter in 2022 was said to have been inspired by the racist conspiracy. See *The Guardian* article by Steve Rose, 'A Deadly Ideology: How the Replacement Theory Went Mainstream', 8 June 2022 (accessed online at www.theguardian.com/world/2022/jun/08/a-deadly-ideology-how-the-great-replacement-theory-went-mainstream).

31 Katie Fitzpatrick, 'More Than Love: Kazuo Ishiguro's Futuristic Inquiries into the Present', *The Nation*, 5/12 April 2021 (accessed online at www.thenation.com/article/society/kazuo-ishiguro-klara-and-the-sun/).

32 Despina Kakoudaki, *Anatomy of a Robot: Literature, Cinema, and the Cultural Work of Artificial People* (New Brunswick, NJ: Rutgers University Press, 2014), p.116.

33 Ibid.

34 Ibid.

35 Destin Jenkins and Justin Leroy, 'Introduction: The Old History of Capitalism', in *Histories of Racial Capitalism* (New York: Columbia University Press, 2021), p.3.

36 Donna Haraway, 'A Cyborg Manifesto: Science, Technology, and Socialist-Feminism in the Late Twentieth Century', in *Simians, Cyborgs, and Women: The Reinvention of Nature* (Routledge: New York, 1991), pp.154, 174.

5

REBECCA KARNI

Ishiguro and Translation

Translation, and more specifically the work of the translator and reading in translation, have received increased attention in literary studies since the turn of the twenty-first century, a development that has gone hand in hand with shifts in critical perspectives towards a heightened awareness of the circumstances of production, circulation, and reception of the literary work. And as this chapter will highlight, considering Kazuo Ishiguro's *oeuvre* from the perspective of translation points to translation as both formally and thematically at the very core of his writing – as its origin, strategy, and target.[1] Already translated into over forty languages, Ishiguro is in fact among a growing group of writers – including, among others, contemporary world authors such as Haruki Murakami, David Mitchell, Yoko Tawada, Jhumpa Lahiri, Roberto Bolaño, and Orhan Pamuk – whose novels Rebecca Walkowitz has referred to as 'born-translated' because '[t]hey have been written for translation from the start' so that translation 'is a condition of their production'.[2] Based on the ways in which their language and style have been shaped by their affiliations and artistic engagements with two or more languages and cultures, these writers' prose can be seen as inherently translated.

Ishiguro stands out among these authors in terms of his self-consciousness with regard to aspects of translation – in terms of a reflexivity that is in turn mirrored in his fiction on the level of both form and content. He has, for example, stated that he would like his prose to make sense to readers across the globe and for it to 'survive translation'.[3] Ishiguro has also commented that in order to create characters that are ostensibly narrating and speaking in Japanese he was obliged in his first two novels to use language that functions 'almost like subtitles, to suggest that behind the English language there's a foreign language going on' (*CKI* 13). Thus in *A Pale View of Hills* and *An Artist of the Floating World*, a formal, slightly stylized English reflects narration and dialogues supposedly conducted in Japanese. I would argue, however, that the 'originary translation' required of the particular narrative situation of Japanese speech imagined in English helped the author develop and sharpen his awareness of the 'translationese' that has become a key stylistic element of his prose ever since.[4]

Hence, besides Ishiguro's own fundamentally translated experience tied to his double (non-)affiliation with both Japan and England, his artistic attraction to and engagement with the relationships between these two cultures and respective languages reflected particularly in his first three novels as well as in *When We Were Orphans* are crucial to considerations of his inherently translated style and fictions and will be the focus of the first part of this chapter. More specifically, this section will consider the construction of a subtly self-consciously translated, mediated yet culturally rooted Japaneseness and, in turn, Englishness in Ishiguro's early novels. This part of the chapter ultimately foregrounds the ways in which Ishiguro's texts, through what I refer to as a 'translational realism' at the core of a poetics of 'originary translatedness', implicitly perform and gesture towards their own constructions of 'Japaneseness' and 'Englishness' precisely *as* such, thus involving us in a critique of both cultural essentialism and universalism while making visible the translation processes, assumptions, and expectations underlying these constructions and their readers' assessments.

While this inherently translated dimension of Ishiguro's novels is tied intimately to the text's manufactured Englishness and Japaneseness in the texts mentioned above, it is not limited to these works. The early novels' intrinsically translated voice is a crucial element in all his texts and is in many ways even more conspicuous in the author's subsequent work, where it is strangely and markedly disconnected from any specific language and culture, and where it becomes associated with just that disconnect and displacement. The chapter will therefore also examine this translated narrative voice – a voice appearing on one level, and often (explicitly or implicitly) read as, that of someone whose values and understanding differ significantly from our own – in *Never Let Me Go*. In drawing our attention to its own 'translated' nature and liminality, this voice itself embroils us in questions of the limits of knowing, and by extension in the ethics of story, narrative, and interpretation.

Ultimately, I will argue that Ishiguro's poetics of translation – or more precisely the liminalities of its subtly self-reflexive translational realism and voice – draws attention to itself *as* such, thereby both demanding reflection and training us in novel ways of reading. In this way, Ishiguro's novels embroil us in the characters' affective and ethical quandaries as well as those involved in their reading, interpretation, and critique. The novels thus extend their concerns to an ethics of reading – one that is immanent to Ishiguro's fiction and that models an ethics for reading world literature.

Originary Translatedness

Ishiguro's critical reception is notable not least for the extent to which it has attributed signs of 'Japaneseness' and 'Englishness' mimetically to both the form and the content levels of his narratives. Instead of reading aspects of Ishiguro's texts as signifiers of a purportedly authentic Japaneseness or Englishness, in this part of the chapter I want to highlight instead the inherently translated nature of this putative Britishness and Japaneseness – which, notably in *The Remains of the Day*, in various intriguing ways overlap – as central to the originary translatedness of his prose. This translatedness may be seen as emerging, in part, from a 'mythical' dimension that is at the heart of Ishiguro's writing – understood in terms of Roland Barthes's conception of 'myth' outlined in *Mythologies*, according to which a level sensitive to secondary meanings, or connotations, is attached to specific cultural signs and representations.[5] Ultimately, my discussion of *A Pale View of Hills, An Artist of the Floating World*, and *The Remains of the Day* will foreground the ways in which this mythical dimension helps create what I will call a 'translational realism' in Ishiguro's novels that involves both drawing attention to and critiquing the culturally essentialist and/or universalist, stereotypical responses that it simultaneously evokes. In so doing, I will also highlight the central roles of genre, mood, narrative voice, and style for Ishiguro's poetics of originary translatedness.

Especially in early criticism of the author's work, Ishiguro's prose style and his characters are both commonly described in terms of attributes associated with Japanese painting and poetry. Many reviewers and critics have read not only the two novels set in Japan, *A Pale View of Hills* and *An Artist of the Floating World*, but also *The Remains of the Day*, set in England, as essentially 'explanations, even indictments, of Japaneseness'.[6] Western critics have thus highlighted either the idealized or the more 'inscrutable' aspects of this perceived Japaneseness in the novels' first-person narrators, or both, thereby reading them in terms of two well-known orientalist tropes. The majority of assessments of Ishiguro's work are somewhat vague in this respect and speak both of the author's prose style and his themes as exuding a certain Japanese sensibility and mood.[7] Even to Haruki Murakami – a novelist whose work has itself been read, both in Japan and elsewhere, in terms of its ostensible 'Japaneseness', 'un-Japaneseness', or 'Americanness' – *The Remains of the Day* 'looks like a Japanese novel' in its 'mentality, its taste, its colour'.[8] The Japanese novelist and Nobel Prize winner Kenzaburō Ōe, on the other hand, regards Ishiguro's style as distinctly un-Japanese (*CKI* 57–8). And when Malcolm Bradbury remarked that translating *A Pale View of Hills* must be an easy task, the Japanese translator is said to have replied: 'On the contrary, it is very hard because it is such an English book.'[9] Particularly these early assessments of Ishiguro's novels thus reflect more disagreement about these matters among Japanese readers and translators than there is in their Western counterparts. Additionally, while Ishiguro's first three novels are read by many as revealing his 'deeper interests' to be 'firmly Japanese', *The Remains of the Day* is often considered a kind of Japanese novel in disguise.[10]

Since *The Remains of the Day*, Ishiguro's writing has also been seen, both from within and from outside the UK, to be quintessentially 'British'. According to *The Times Literary Supplement*, for example, Ishiguro is 'purer than most English novelists'.[11] While Ishiguro did not significantly change his prose style in writing his first three novels, one of the favoured Western press clichés about *A Pale View of Hills* and *An Artist of the Floating World* involved a British writer producing 'authentic' Japanese fiction, while the cliché about *The Remains of the Day* entailed a Japanese writer fashioning a 'super-English' novel – one that, as Ishiguro has commented, seems to be 'more English than English' (*CKI* 73). And while such culturally essentialist lenses were central especially to the early reception of Ishiguro's work, his shift to a more overtly experimental style and to the less specific setting of *The Unconsoled* and the more global setting of *When We Were Orphans* did not significantly alter these assumptions.

This critical concern with the alleged 'British' and 'Japanese' characteristics of Ishiguro's works is both cause and effect of the author's own preoccupation with such matters, which can in turn be seen as at the heart of the translational nature of Ishiguro's prose. With regard to the Japanese setting of his first three short stories and two novels, Ishiguro has emphasized in interviews that this 'Japan' is a 'mixture of memory, speculation, and imagination' that provides him with the backdrop, with a certain political climate, atmosphere, and mood for his themes (*CKI* 129). As I will argue, this context in turn allowed Ishiguro to fashion stories and a prose style that, while functioning (at any rate in his first three novels) as a kind of personal, self-conscious Japonaiserie – an evocation of, and play on, a certain Japaneseness through content, form, style, and mood – simultaneously compels and trains us to read closely and sharpens our awareness of the translated aspects of the author's work.

It was, in part, the culturally essentialist reception of Ishiguro's early work and the classification of his novels as 'Japanese' that prompted a change of setting for *The Remains of the Day*: 'Before I knew anything about the book', he told Bill Bryson in an interview, 'I knew that it wasn't going to have anything to do with Japan or Japanese people.'[12] Yet, interestingly, the novel is in various ways a translation of *An Artist of the Floating World* into a British context.[13] In this way, the classification of Ishiguro's writing on the levels of both form and content in terms of its purportedly 'British' or 'Japanese' characteristics, and its critical reception in general, have become integral to the *oeuvre* itself. In this sense, Ishiguro has been, from the very start of his career, extraordinarily self-conscious with regard to the global reception of his work and its national and international resonances. And central to this awareness is Ishiguro's sensitivity to the ways in which his prose is read in translation.[14] This consciousness helped shape the subtly demythologizing and deorientalizing functions at the heart of his translational realism.

Contributing further to the self-consciously translational and demythologizing nature of Ishiguro's writing is his preoccupation with national and cultural myths as they are reflected on the level of both form and content in his fiction since the early short story 'A Family Supper'.[15] It makes sense that the author, who considers himself neither 'a very English Englishman' nor 'a very Japanese Japanese' (*CKI* 58), would be particularly sensitive to the myths and stereotypes associated with the two cultures that constitute his double cultural affiliation and on which his outsider-insider position offers him a unique perspective. In the end, myth-making and a certain mythical mode of writing, going hand in hand with the cultivation of a peculiar, productive, culturally rooted distance that implicates readers formally, thematically, and critically has turned into a conscious aesthetic, poetic, and ethical endeavour for Ishiguro – such that it is central to the subtly performative and inherently translated qualities of his fictions.

Translational Realism

Ishiguro's interest in a particular Japanese film aesthetic itself inspired and helped shape the intriguing translational realism of his writing. While he has carefully avoided easy associations with Japanese literature, Ishiguro has readily affirmed the influence of Japanese cinema on his work: 'Cinema is the one area of Japanese "culture" which I believe has had a direct effect on my writing', he commented in an interview in 1982.[16] It is especially the *shōmin-geki*, or domestic drama, associated notably with Yasujirō Ozu's mature films, that helped Ishiguro create his own partly remembered, partly imagined 'Japan' by providing him with a generic model through which both to access his country of origin's past and his childhood memories, and to subvert reductive notions of Japanese culture centring on samurais and suicide.[17] Ishiguro considers the *shōmin-geki* 'a profound, respectable genre, and distinctively Japanese. It's concerned with ordinary people in everyday life, and it has that sort of pace: a pace which reflects the monotony and melancholy of everyday life.'[18]

The *shōmin-geki* genre – or Ishiguro's perception of it – is reflected in the author's 'Japanese' fictions not only in their focus on the domestic, in particular the family, but also in their wistful mood. Hence their dominant themes and tones of nostalgia and remorse. The genre entails another topos central to Ishiguro's narratives: the expression of life's impermanence and flux. The fictional territory he has chosen to explore is one of hesitation and transition: there is an 'unmistakable air of transience' about the Nagasaki apartment complex that Etsuko remembers in *A Pale View of Hills* (*PVH* 12), for example, as there is in Ono's recollections and narrations in *An Artist of the Floating World*. But an air of transience in fact characterizes all of Ishiguro's novels to date. The early novels also juxtapose pre- and post-Second World War values: both Ogata, Etsuko's father-in-law, and Ono, for instance, lament the loss of discipline and loyalty supposedly brought about by the imposition, post-surrender, of American-style democratic institutions and values. And implicitly or explicitly, both characters are judged by the younger generation for their support for Japan's wartime efforts.

But much as the *shōmin-geki* inspired and helped shape Ishiguro's themes and fictional mood, as well as an intrinsically mediated Japaneseness on the levels of both narrative content and form, unlike critics who have established direct links between Ishiguro's *oeuvre* and Japanese literature, film, and/or culture, the main point I would like to make about the ways in which the genre relates to the author's narratives is that it does so precisely *as genre*, and a very stylized one at that. Characterized by a marked stylization and thus by a certain distancing as well as by their images of everyday life, Ishiguro's 'Japanese' fictions reflect on their ostensible 'Japaneseness' as a manufactured and translated yet culturally specific one, thus sustaining the author's demythologizing and deorientalizing endeavours. In foregrounding their own intrinsically translated qualities, these narratives reflect on their constructed nature as well as on readers' expectations precisely *as* such, thwarting assumptions about their cultural authenticity, while questioning notions of 'originality' and 'authenticity' in general.

In this way, techniques adapted from Japanese film aesthetics helped shape the tempered realism at the core of Ishiguro's fictional worlds, a mode of writing that balances realism with a distinctive focus on form and a consciousness of its own construction. Only slightly removed from conventional realism, it is precisely through this proximity and through a nuanced self-reflexivity that Ishiguro's fiction *thematizes* its own degree of realism and representations of the world.[19]

Further contributing to the demythologizing and inherently translated nature of Ishiguro's prose are the ways in which – most markedly so in his early work – the formulation of an enigma both on the level of form and on the level of content appears to be linked inextricably to cultural meanings. Readers' cultural preconceptions are an integral aspect of this originary translatedness in that signs ostensibly signifying a certain 'culture' become inextricably entangled, and indeed interchangeable, with clues pointing to an 'enigma' seemingly central to the narratives. Thus, for example, Ishiguro's early short story 'A Family Supper' and his first two novels play on expectations related to suicide – itself a strategy associated with 'Japaneseness' – as key to the texts' seemingly central mysteries.[20] But these are expectations that are ultimately resisted and even negated by the narratives. Ishiguro's fictional worlds thus appear simultaneously disquieting, disorienting, strange, and foreign; narrative estrangement seems to suggest at once emotional-psychological and cultural difference. Creating a particular form of cross-cultural poetics and ethics, the author gestures in this way towards the hazards of mistaking narrative estrangement in his fictions for Japanese otherness.

Instrumental to the creation of fictional worlds that are culturally both distanced and rooted is a kind of originary translatedness in Ishiguro's prose and in his characters' language – their air of being *written* in translation. The author has stated that, in order to achieve this effect, he 'can't be too fluent' and 'can't use too many Western colloquialisms', and he comments that in order to indicate that his first two novels are narrated by Japanese speakers, he was obliged to use a type of what he calls 'subtitled language' (*CKI* 136). But, as I have argued, this effect is also a central characteristic of Ishiguro's subsequent texts. The seemingly foreign obliqueness and formality of the prose together with its oral or spoken qualities reflect a combination of artifice and naturalness that results in an intrinsic distance and stylization. Often read as culturally conditioned or as a sign of otherness, the stylized linguistic and rhetorical tenor that results is at the heart of the self-consciously translational realism and originary translatedness of Ishiguro's fictional worlds.

A Mediated Englishness and Japaneseness and an Ethics of Reading

But with *The Remains of the Day*, Ishiguro takes the 'translated' quality of his prose to a new level. Since the novel constitutes a conscious attempt to avoid being compared to modern Japanese authors or categorized simply as a 'Japanese' novelist and is in many respects, as I have said, a rewriting of *An Artist of the Floating World* in an English setting, it can be seen as even more self-consciously 'translational' than his earlier 'Japanese' work. The novel produces a kind of translated Englishness and Japaneseness – aspects of which in intriguing ways overlap – that are manifested in both thematic and formal ways. At its core, this Englishness and, respectively, Japaneseness, like the Japaneseness of Ishiguro's earlier works, involves what Roland Barthes refers to as the culturally 'already-written'.[21] Like the later novel, *When We Were Orphans*, *The Remains of the Day* rewrites traditional motifs of the English literary tradition, thereby invoking and building on, but also thwarting reader expectations both on the level of cultural stereotypes in general and with regard to the literary tradition itself. Thus, for example, the idyll of the country-house novel is sustained only on the surface and is undermined by the reality of Lord Darlington's dark political manoeuvrings. And the peaceful English countryside offers a nostalgic picture of a country that never was.[22] This deceptive Englishness is central to the novel's mythical and translational realism: it compels us to read beyond the stereotypes (and our own interpretative assumptions) and with an increased sensitivity to our own positions, perspectives, and presuppositions.

Much more could be said about the ways in which *The Remains of the Day* works to expose the fictional nature of its own Englishness (and, to some extent, of Englishness in general) both on a literary level and in terms of national-cultural myths and stereotypes. But what is particularly remarkable about *The Remains of the Day* is the way in which, alongside its Englishness, the novel simultaneously rewrites some of the mediated Japaneseness of the previous two texts. This is registered emblematically in the intrusion of a putative signifier of Asian otherness into the ostensibly ordered Englishness of Darlington Hall in the scene in which Stevens the butler – unwilling and unable to admit to himself or to Miss Kenton the obvious errors of his ageing father, now the under-butler at Darlington Hall – repeatedly refuses even to look at a 'Chinaman' (a colonialist decorative figure that has been placed incorrectly after cleaning by Mr Stevens Sr). As an increasingly angry Miss Kenton insists: 'The fact is, Mr. Stevens, all the Chinamen in this house have been dirty for some time! And now, they are in incorrect positions!' (*RD* 59). While on one level the Chinamen figures gesture at Britain's colonial past and communicate a certain orientalism, this particular scene, partly by means of the seven repetitions of 'Chinaman' or 'Chinamen' over half a page, draws attention to them primarily or only as misplaced objects. In this way, the text presents the porcelain figurines as disconnected from their usual signifying contexts. In thus (literally) figuring, on one level, a certain orientalism or Asian otherness that, on another level, the figurines simultaneously defy, the text dramatizes self-reflexively its own resistance to easy associations with a perceived Asian difference as well as to the misplaced orientalist readings to which Ishiguro's *oeuvre* has itself been subjected and that it has made an important aspect of its thematic and formal focus.

The Remains of the Day may be said to 'rewrite' a certain kind of Japaneseness with respect to the novel's remediations of characteristics associated with Japanese literature and culture – including some that are stereotypically 'Japanese'. Ishiguro's rendering of the effects of light and darkness, in particular his preference for a 'pale view' of things, for example, also bears a striking resemblance with Jun'ichirō Tanizaki's 'praise of shadows' in his famous eponymous essay on 'Japanese' aesthetics – 'Japanese' since, in many ways, *In'ei raisan* (1933) is written in the same subtly distanced and partly self-conscious mode as Ishiguro's texts.[23] The conventional reading of Tanizaki's essay has been as an ahistorical treatise on 'Eastern aesthetics', wherein the author's praise for the ways in which 'the East', and particularly Japan, has traditionally preferred darkness to the stark light of 'the West' is taken at face value. Later readings have been more sensitive to the relationships between Tanizaki's self-orientalizing East–West discourse and the different East–West discourses and counter-discourses prevalent in Japan during his time and have emphasized the distance between author and narrator as well as the text's partly ironic and satiric tone. Drawing attention to the intertextual echoes between Tanizaki's essay and Ishiguro's novel will allow us to foreground how Ishiguro's project goes beyond the stereotyping in which, on one level, it engages.[24]

We might say, for instance, that the 'pale view' that dominates the mood of Ishiguro's fiction echoes Tanizaki's praise of 'dim shadows', a 'pale glow', or 'the delicate glow of fading rays clinging to the surface of a dusky wall'.[25] In doing so, however, we should not be seen as suggesting that there are any inherently 'Japanese' qualities to Ishiguro's prose, but rather as indicating that his prose shares with Tanizaki's a quietly self-conscious mode and mood, and thus a certain distance with respect to putative aspects of 'Japaneseness' that provide the basis for Ishiguro's translational realism. Faint light is emphasized in *The Remains of the Day* in ways that it was not in the previous novels. Related to his discussion with Miss Kenton in the summerhouse following the dismissal of two Jewish maids ordered by Lord Darlington, for instance, Stevens recalls 'a mist starting to set', 'the encroaching mist', 'the fading daylight', 'the thickening mist', and 'the great expanse of fog' (RD 151–2). An atmosphere of near-darkness, in fact, hovers over all the meetings between the butler and the housekeeper. In this way, light, mood, and setting all point indirectly to the butler's vulnerability in areas that his formal discourse is trying to hold at bay, while at the same time sustaining a type of self-conscious Japonaiserie and with it an intrinsically translational aesthetics, poetics, and ethics.

The Remains of the Day can also be seen to rewrite a certain mediated Japaneseness in terms of the *shōmin-geki*-inspired pathos mentioned above.

Indeed, in many ways, Stevens's voice reflects 'the monotony and melancholy of everyday life' that Ishiguro has associated with the *shōmin-geki* as well as articulating nostalgic yearning and remorse more poignantly than do Etsuko's and Ono's.[26] Stevens's reminiscences suggest a 'nostalgic longing' for 'Lord Darlington's days', when the house 'was filled with distinguished visitors' (*RD* 17, 180, 235). 'Nostalgic longing' is also what Stevens finds reflected in Miss Kenton's letter (180). And he loses himself in 'endless speculations' about the 'changing times' and about the 'turning points' in his life, which 'render[ed] whole dreams forever irredeemable' (16, 179, 180). To Stevens, the chasm between past and present seems unbridgeable, and the text's nostalgic mood is also linked closely to its expression of transience and transition.

Ishiguro also has *The Remains of the Day* gesture towards a certain mediated Japaneseness through the butler's character. Most notable in this respect are Stevens's rigid code of honour (what he calls 'dignity'), archaic formality, politeness, reticence, and indirectness – qualities that, tellingly for Ishiguro's project, are also putatively English. Especially in his boundless loyalty to Lord Darlington, his stoic professionalism, and his efforts more recently to come to terms with his new American employer, Stevens does indeed display the qualities associated with a samurai and, in the narrative present, that classic Japanese figure of the *rōnin*, the samurai who has lost his master. But while critics who have made such connections have either not elaborated on them or have seen them as a reflection of Ishiguro's Japanese background and an intrinsic connection to Japanese literature, it is important to highlight the self-conscious component of Ishiguro's stylized, yet culturally rooted, originary translatedness – its constructedness and the critical, and sometimes ironic, distance inherent in the mythic realism that underlies it, as well as the fact that the novel's qualities often associated with its 'Japaneseness' are also those commonly viewed as testaments to its 'Englishness'.

Aligned as it is with the previous novels, Stevens's 'translationese' – his formal, restrained language and communication strategies, marked by indirection and circumlocution – is at the heart of Ishiguro's translational realism and poetics. Ishiguro records that it was the praise received in reviews of his first two novels for his understated and indirect prose style that led him to hone qualities that he realized were anyway part of his 'natural voice' (*CKI* 26–7). More self-consciously than the previous texts, *The Remains of the Day* can be seen to explore the implications of this voice's characteristics on the levels of character, culture, and nation. Stevens is defined entirely by his language and speech behaviour, which mirror his experience and are cunningly made to reflect (on) the speech and behaviour associated – not only stereotypically – with both England *and* Japan.

In *The Remains of the Day*, then, an aesthetics and poetics of nostalgia and transience is linked in remarkable ways to an ethics of intercultural representation and its reading. By way of this mythical mode and the inherently translated, mediated aesthetics and poetics that it supports, Ishiguro's novels – and especially *The Remains of the Day* – embroil its readers simultaneously in the narrator-protagonists' affective and ethical conundrums, on the one hand, and in a critique of the layered textual and cultural translation processes that constitute them and that they subtly expose on the other. The novel in this way both demands and fosters a mode of reading sensitive to its mediations and distances, as well as to forms and the degree of myth in order to involve and train us in the work's own ethics of reading.

A Translated Voice

If the intrinsically translated voice of Ishiguro's first three novels draws attention to itself precisely *as* such, it is not limited to these novels and is in many ways even more conspicuous in his subsequent work, where it is markedly disconnected from any specific language and culture and is itself associated with just that sense of linguistic and cultural disconnect and displacement. Thus the narrators' curiously distanced voices, with their corseted, formal, flat idiom, appear on one level, and are often (explicitly or implicitly) read, as those of characters whose values differ greatly from ours, who do not fully grasp the true nature of their situations, and/or who are fundamental Others. This is particularly true of Kathy H. in *Never Let Me Go*, in relation to whom readers and critics have noted the discrepancy between an emotionally withheld language and the plight of the clones, whose truncated lives have been programmed for organ donations. This discrepancy is registered, for instance, in the 'euphemistic' expression sometimes ascribed to Kathy when she refers to dying as 'completing'.

But a careful consideration of the 'translated' dimension of Kathy's voice and its ways of involving readers in the narrative and its critique may complicate such a reading and suggest more nuanced ways of understanding Ishiguro's narrative voices. This is in part because such readings imply a distance between 'story' and 'discourse', between implied author and narrator, and between narrator and reader, and because they make assumptions as to what the narrator and the reader know and can know at a given point in the narrative – an effect that is intimately tied to a tacit perception of the text's narrative unreliability. It is my suggestion that Ishiguro's voices serve in fact to problematize these distances and assumptions underlying such readings, thus *in* their translatedness and liminality calling attention to, entangling us in, and asking us to reflect on the limits of knowing on the levels of character, reading, interpretation, critique, and beyond.

This aspect of the novel is also what classifications of Kathy's seemingly translated idiom in terms of a non-human quality in arguments that consider the clones as, in some form, Other overlook.[27] While on one level Ishiguro's narrators may appear as Others, the novels resist and offer a critique of such 'Othering' in other subtly self-conscious ways as well. Thus, for example, in *Never Let Me Go* Tommy's animal drawings, in their contradictory nature – 'metallic', mechanistic, but at the same time reflecting fragility, vulnerability, and an attitude of caring – come to emblematize the impossibility of separating the human from the non-human and to figure the intrinsic tension between the two (*NLMG* 188).

It is, among other things, this fundamental friction to which Kathy's inherently translated voice, in its subtle self-consciousness and liminality, draws attention. And just as with Ishiguro's translational realism, the voice's slightly 'off', curiously distanced quality both involves and trains readers in navigating its liminalities, prompting reflection on the novel's complex limit situations on both levels of form and content precisely *as* such. This includes questions related to the human–clone relationship – the text's story level – as well as to knowing and not knowing (what, for example, both the characters and we, as readers, can or should know at a given point in the narrative) and thus to ethical questions pertaining not only to the story, but also to its reading and interpretation. Additionally, in its subtly enacted liminality, Kathy's apparently translated and contained idiom gives expression to a pathos of restraint that is characteristic of Ishiguro's narrator-protagonists, but that can at the same time be seen as a reflection of a semi-conscious awareness of the limits and limitations of her situation and life – an awareness that ultimately aims to include the reader.[28] In its self-consciously translated narrative voice, the novel thus communicates, and implicates us in, an awareness of ontological and epistemological limits and limitations on the levels of character, interpretation, and critique.

Conclusion

The formal, indirect, withheld language of Ishiguro's prose – a register largely stripped of colloquialisms and regionalisms – demonstrates an acute awareness of language as fundamentally translated, as well as of translation and translatability as origin, strategy, and target of his fictions. In the author's intrinsically translated writing, nothing can be lost in translation, since translation, or a poetics of originary translatedness, *is* its mode and is the key to its mood. As this chapter has aimed to highlight, Ishiguro's skilled manipulations of genre, realism, mood, narrative voice, and style create a performative and self-reflexive translational realism that comments implicitly on its own constructedness as well as on our narrative and critical assumptions and expectations, thus fostering a mode of reading sensitive to the texts' layered textual and cultural translation processes. Similarly, Ishiguro's self-consciously translated narrative voices train us in navigating their liminalities, prompting reflection on the limits of knowing on the levels of story, narrative, interpretation, critique, and beyond.

In its quietly experimental involvement of readers in the story and its interpretation by manipulating the literary and cultural particularities that are essential to its narrative fabric, Ishiguro's translational poetics eschews relativism and entangles us in a critique of both cultural essentialism and universalism. It is in its subtly performative liminalities that the texts' translational realism and translated voices demand attention, reflection, and a certain self-reflexivity while embroiling us in the narrator-protagonists' affective and ethical quandaries. Ishiguro's poetics of originary translatedness ultimately, among other things in its reflexivity as to its own and readers' perspectives as well as in the modesty of its awareness of its own limits and limitations, involves us in an ethics of reading immanent to his fiction that also models an ethics for reading world literature.

Notes

1 See also my essay, 'Made in Translation: Language, "Japaneseness", "Englishness", and "Global Culture" in Ishiguro', *Comparative Literature Studies* 52:2 (2015): 318–48.
2 Rebecca Walkowitz, *Born Translated: The Contemporary Novel in an Age of World Literature* (New York: Columbia University Press, 2015), pp.3, 4.
3 Tim Adams, 'For Me, England is a Mythical Place', *Observer*, 19 February 2005: 17 (accessed online at www.theguardian.com/books/2005/feb/20/fiction.kazuoishiguro).
4 Ishiguro himself has characterized his language used in this context as 'translationese' (*CKI* 13).
5 Roland Barthes, *Mythologies* (Paris: Seuil, 1957).
6 Gabriele Annan, 'On the High Wire', *New York Review of Books*, 7 December 1989: 3.
7 '[T]here are distinct Japanese characteristics (such as indirectness) in Ishiguro's work, however much he may disclaim them', writes one reviewer (Anthony Thwaite, 'In Service', *London Review of Books*, 18 May 1989: 17). Novelist Angela Carter is reported as holding that Ishiguro's novels 'have the sort of mood in the writing – what she refers to as "elegiac reticence" and a "sense of the sadness of things"– that Japanese fiction has' (Jocelyne Targett, 'A Writer of the Floating World', *Weekend Guardian*, 13 May 1989: 6). And in the words of a French reviewer, the author's writing is of 'une lenteur que l'on prête à l'Asie' [a

slowness that we associate with Asia] (Jean-François Fogel, 'Ishiguro: Very British', *Le Point*, 19 February 1990: 17).

8 Quoted in Pico Iyer, 'Connoisseur of Memory', *Time*, 14 February 1994: 46.

9 Clive Sinclair, 'The Land of the Rising Son', *Sunday Times Magazine*, 11 January 1987: 37.

10 Valerie Purton, 'The Reader in a Floating World: The Novels of Kazuo Ishiguro', in Norman Page and Peter Preston, eds., *The Literature of Place* (London: Macmillan, 1993), p.174. According to Pico Iyer, for example, *The Remains of the Day* may seem like an English novel, but '[t]o anyone familiar with Japan ... the author's real intention' of highlighting the 'Japanese' characteristics of Stevens the butler 'slips out as surely as a business card from a Savile Row suit' ('Waiting upon History', in *Tropical Classical: Essays from Several Directions* (New York: Knopf, 1997), p.178).

11 Quoted in Iyer, 'Connoisseur of Memory', p.46. Similarly, 'Ishiguro: Very British' is the title of a French review (Fogel, 'Ishiguro: Very British', 17). 'Plus "british", tu meurs!' [More 'British', you'll die!] writes one critic (Nicole Zand, 'La confession d'un majordome fidèle', *Le Monde*, 23 February 1990: 28), and another speaks of *The Remains of the Day* as a novel 'durch und durch "britisch"' ['British' to the core] (Peter Münder, 'Immer im Dienst', *Neue Zürcher Zeitung*, 6 November 1990: 65).

12 Bill Bryson, 'Between Two Worlds', *The New York Times* Magazine, 29 April 1990: 44.

13 In a 1999 interview Ishiguro also conceded that his first three novels 'were really attempts to write the same novel' (*CKI* 153).

14 'I've always been aware that my prose must make sense in translation', Ishiguro remarks (Bryan Appleyard, 'Kazuo Ishiguro's Work Reflects the World', *Sunday Times*, 3 May 2009).

15 As Ishiguro has stated in an interview from 1990: '[A] nation's myth is the way a country dreams. It is part of the country's fabulized memory and it seems to me to be a very valid task for the artist to try to figure out what that myth is and if they should actually rework or undermine that myth' (*CKI* 74–5).

16 Nicholas De Jongh, 'Life after the Bomb', *The Guardian*, 22 February 1982: 11. See also his comment in a 1986 interview that '[t]he visual images of Japan have a great poignancy for me, particularly in domestic films like those of Ozu and Naruse, set in the postwar era, the Japan I actually remember' (*CKI* 4).

17 In this way, Ishiguro's fiction ultimately subverts, exposes, and critiques stereotyped notions of his work, Japanese culture, and the Japanese held not only by Western readers and critics but reflected also in the *Nihonjinron* (literally, discussions or theories about the Japanese), an essentialist discourse on 'Japanese uniqueness', or exceptionalism, that has been a long-standing tradition in Japan (Peter N. Dale, *The Myth of Japanese Uniqueness* (New York: St. Martin's Press, 1986)).

18 Christopher Tookey, 'Sydenham, Mon Amour', *Books and Bookmen*, March 1986: 34.

19 I discuss the gestural and more specifically subtly presentational qualities of Ishiguro's realism in Rebecca Karni, 'Ishiguro's Tempered Presentational Realism and Practice', in Peter Sloane and Kristian Shaw, eds., *Kazuo Ishiguro: Twenty-First Century Perspectives* (Manchester: Manchester University Press, 2023).

20 Suicide clearly does have its place within Japanese literature and culture and is a serious problem in contemporary Japan but is also a prominent stereotype often associated with essentialist notions of 'Japaneseness'.

21 Roland Barthes, *S/Z*, trans. Richard Miller (Oxford: Blackwell, 1990), p.26.

22 See also Ishiguro's comment in a 1996 interview that the country he invents in *The Remains of the Day* is 'not an England that I believe ever existed' (*CKI* 74).

23 See Jun'ichirō Tanizaki, *In'ei raisan* (Tokyo: Chūōkōronsha, 1975); translated as *In Praise of Shadows*, trans. Thomas Harper and Edward Seidensticker (New Haven, CT: Leete's Island Books, 1977).

24 This is despite the fact that Ishiguro's text is notably more self-conscious in this respect, as well as more affectively, ethically, and critically minded than Tanizaki's.

25 Tanizaki, *In Praise of Shadows*, p.18.

26 Tookey, 'Sydenham, Mon Amour', 34.

27 Shameem Black, for example, characterizes the style of narration attributed to Kathy and the aesthetics it creates as 'inhuman' (Shameem Black, 'Ishiguro's Inhuman Aesthetics', *Modern Fiction Studies* 55:4 (2009): 785–807 (786, 798)). Louis Menand, too, argues that it is not just the clones but Ishiguro's characters in general that are 'simulators of humanness, figures engineered to pass as "real"' and that '[t]here is something animatronic about them' (Louis Menand, 'Something about Kathy', *New Yorker*, 28 March 2005: 78 (accessed online at www.newyorker.com/magazine/2005/03/28/something-about-kathy)).

28 The latter is supported also by the limits of knowing foregrounded by Ishiguro's choice of central metaphors for his novels, reflected most notably in the limited diegetic perspectives and voices of the butler, the orphan, the clone, and the Artificial Friend.

PART II
Literature, Music, and Film

6

VANESSA GUIGNERY

The Ishiguro Archive

Vijay Mishra, who has studied the papers of Salman Rushdie, notes that an archive, defined as 'a body of material which a person has collected', 'begins as an autobiography'.[1] This is certainly the case with Kazuo Ishiguro's archive, which includes documents the writer carefully and purposefully selected, organized, and prepared before their transfer to the Harry Ransom Humanities Center of the University of Texas at Austin in 2015. The collection includes juvenilia, the typescripts of his first novel *A Pale View of Hills*, the drafts, notes, manuscripts, and typescripts of later novels and short stories up to *Nocturnes*, in paper and digital format, as well as working notes and unpublished material, notebooks, correspondence, drafts of song lyrics, and screenplays, photographs, and family papers. Such a collection offers a unique perspective on Ishiguro's art and craft by giving access to his writing practices and processes, enabling scholars to trace the trajectories of his published novels and short stories through an examination of the various stages of composition, the false starts and near-misses, and the ultimate choices as to what to retain.

Genetic criticism has established that the published work stands out 'against a background, and a series, of potentialities' and that 'we should consider the text as a *necessary possibility*, as one manifestation of a process which is always virtually present in the background'.[2] An exploration of the multiple options and discarded possibilities in Ishiguro's archive as well as the extensive notes he takes while planning and writing his texts can definitely enhance our understanding of the published works. This chapter will offer a brief description of the scope and contents of Ishiguro's papers before discussing his writing methods as revealed by the archives. It will conclude with a focus on the 'precursors' to *The Remains of the Day* in order to show how access to the archives and preliminary steps to a published text may illuminate the complex process of creation.

A Brief Description of the Archive

Ishiguro's archives at the Ransom Center were meticulously prepared by the author himself and then catalogued by Amy E. Armstrong, who provides a thorough description of their scope and contents on the library's website.[3] The total of eighty document boxes (33.60 linear feet), two oversize boxes, one oversize folder, four serials boxes, and fifty-one computer disks can seem considerable if one bears in mind that, at the time of acquisition of the archives in 2015, Ishiguro had published seven novels and one short-story collection, to which should be added four screenplays, seven uncollected short stories, and many song lyrics. The archives do not include any drafts or notes relating to *The Buried Giant* or *Klara and the Sun*, which were published after Ishiguro's papers arrived at the Ransom Center, while the genetic dossier of Ishiguro's first novel *A Pale View of Hills* is limited to two typescripts and the proofs (as well as the screenplays of later film adaptations), since all former documentation on this book was thrown away by the author. It is only in the late 1990s that Ishiguro began keeping all the material related to his published work and especially what he calls his 'rough' papers, that is, his first ideas, notes, outlines, plot sketches, working drafts, and rejected pages. In a piece entitled 'How I Write', written in 2014 'for the purpose of clarifying [the] papers' he entrusted to the Ransom Center, Ishiguro explains:

> For many years, I've been in the habit of keeping a large cardboard box under my desk into which I throw, more or less indiscriminately, all papers produced during my writing that I don't wish to file neatly and take into the next stage of composition: earlier drafts of chapters, rejected pages, scraps of paper with scribbled thoughts, repeated attempts at the same paragraph, etc.
>
> I'd originally started this box-under-the-desk system not because I'd anticipated one day preparing an archive, but because I was nervous I'd throw out work I'd need later to refer back to, or that an unrepeatable burst of inspiration would get taken away in error with that week's garbage. By the same token, I saw no reason to keep these papers once a novel was safely finished and had gone to the printers. So I'd have a diligent clear-out around the proof stage, and get the bin man to take it all away.
>
> Then, at some point in the late 1990s, a friend alerted me to the possibility that I would one day wish to prepare an archive, and advised me not to throw away anything at all produced at my desk. This struck me as extreme, but from then on, instead of giving the contents of the cardboard box to the refuse collectors, I began emptying them into plastic crates and storing them in the attic. (1.0)

Thus, the 'rough' papers relating to *When We Were Orphans*, *Never Let Me Go*, and *Nocturnes* have all been kept, sorted out by Ishiguro himself and placed into their respective folders ('bundled into freezer bags and ...

labelled as "Papers"' (1.0)) while the archives for *An Artist of the Floating World, The Remains of the Day*, and *The Unconsoled* are more partial: 'although I carefully preserved earlier drafts, plans, notes, etc, the "rough" papers from this period mostly no longer exist' (1.0). Therefore, the volume of archives varies considerably from one book to the next,[4] with consequences for the reconstruction of what theoreticians of genetic criticism have named the 'avant-texte' – that is, the sum of documents and writing operations that come before the published text and which the critic-geneticist has identified as such.[5] Until the early 1990s, Ishiguro typed the neat versions of his texts on a typewriter, but he then started using a word processor (in addition to handwriting); therefore, the archives from the time of *The Unconsoled* also comprise floppy disks containing early and revised drafts.

In addition to the sometimes voluminous genetic dossiers of published books and short stories, the archives include the notes, plans, and drafts of Ishiguro's screenplays (realized and unrealized); his notebooks from 1973 to 2013 (which comprise notes, reflections, plans, and personal diaries); juvenilia (including eight comic books made in 1960–2 and his very first story written at the age of ten, 'Run Melody Run'); along with song lyrics, non-fictional texts, correspondence, press clippings, photographs, and personal and professional papers. The archives also contain a large volume of unpublished material mainly dating from the 1970s, including two travel pieces,[6] a Western novella,[7] an untitled film script,[8] comedy sketches, a short play,[9] short stories,[10] two completed[11] and two uncompleted novels,[12] as well as a radio play.[13] The correspondence included in the archives is mainly professional, but one section labelled by Ishiguro '(slightly) more interesting correspondence' includes a few letters or cards by such writers as Julian Barnes, Angela Carter, Ian McEwan, David Mitchell, and Graham Swift (60.3–61.1). In a fascinating folder containing his 'random, impromptu thoughts on books read (sometimes films seen), with particular emphasis on useful lessons, etc, for [his] own writing' (49.5), Ishiguro unfortunately removed the pages with his comments on books by living authors, which formed the larger bulk of the file.

The utmost care with which Ishiguro selected, organized, and labelled his collection is remarkable and brings to mind the two principles at the heart of the archive or *arkhe* according to Jacques Derrida: 'the *commencement* and the *commandment*'. The archive is '*there* where things *commence*' but also '*there* where' the writer commands and exercises his authority.[14] This is manifested by the way in which Ishiguro sometimes provides a useful label for a grouping of material that does not appear on the original papers themselves ('Rough pages', 'Notes and plans', 'Ideas as they come', 'Rough drafts', 'First neat draft', 'Neat top copy', 'Rejected pages'). He also includes handwritten annotations on yellow sticky notes or longer typed notes offering detailed information about

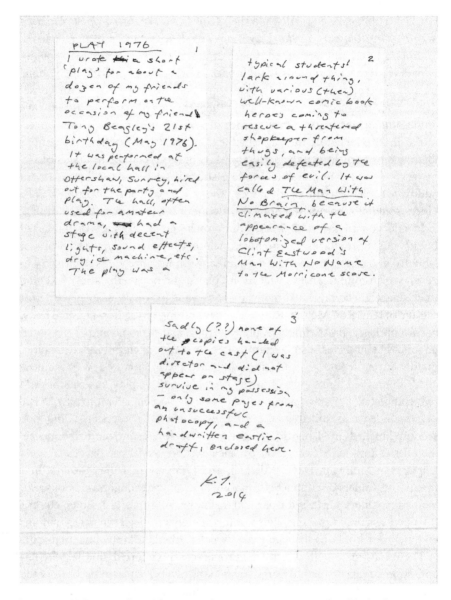

Figure 6.1 Sticky notes about 'The Man with No Brain' (51.4) (Reproduced by kind permission of Kazuo Ishiguro and the Harry Ransom Center, The University of Texas at Austin)

the date of composition of a text, the context of writing, or the identity of some key people, sometimes providing his own assessment of these pieces several years or decades later, as shown in the example (Figure 6.1) about a 1976 short play entitled 'The Man with No Brain' (51.4).

Ishiguro provides such indications for every single folder (even those containing just a single page) and, in the case of the unpublished novels and some sections of his notebooks, offers thorough explanations covering several pages. He also sometimes identifies texts or plans as sources for later books. For example, one note refers to various attempts which 'evolved into the short story called "Summer after the War" published in *Granta* 7 in 1983, and then into the novel *An Artist of the Floating World*' (1.1). These interventions demonstrate a high degree of thoughtfulness towards the scholar and prove very useful. They should, however, be used with caution as they may guide the reader in a specific hermeneutic direction, highlighting a trajectory while obscuring others. Such a posteriori metatextual commentaries as well as information about the creative process given in interviews are therefore illuminating but should not distract scholars from conducting their own exploratory research on the basis of all available genetic documents.

Ishiguro's Methods of Composition

A close examination of the Ishiguro archive helps to explain his conscientious methods of composition. First of all, the writer plans his work for a very long time (often over two or more years), making notes and writing down ideas for alternative plots before he actually starts penning formal drafts which are extensively revised or sometimes discarded altogether.[15] Although Ishiguro threw away all the preliminary papers relating to his first novel, *A Pale View of Hills*, when he started working on *An Artist of the Floating World*, he reminded himself of the amount of planning and discarding this earlier project had entailed: 'remember the last novel, how much planning went in at this same stage and how most of it got scrapped after several things had actually got written' (1.2). He feared a similar excess of preparatory work for his second novel: 'perhaps we've gone quite far in planning and we may be in danger of over-planning', he writes (1.2). The method developed by Ishiguro corresponds to what Louis Hay has called 'programme writing', which relies on a rigorous pre-established plan of writing, as opposed to 'process writing', when a writer proceeds without an entirely preconceived destination and when some form of instinctive freedom can lead to unexpected deviations.[16]

In his explanatory piece entitled 'How I Write', Ishiguro details the various stages of his drafting process, which starts after months or years of planning, and has remained consistent throughout his career:

> I would write an initial, improvised, very messy draft (usually marked 'Rough Draft') by hand for a segment roughly corresponding to a chapter, with

minimum pauses for thought and no revision. I would then read back through this draft, dividing the writing into numbered sections, marked out in ink or pencil in the left margin. (1.0)

Such a rough draft would typically cover ten to fifteen pages and include only a few marks of correction, as seen in the example from *When We Were Orphans* (Figure 6.2).

The next stage consists in making a brief summary of the rough draft (Figure 6.3):

I would then produce a handwritten sheet, usually headed 'As Is', with circled numbers going down the left of the page. The circled numbers would corres- pond to the divided sections of the rough draft, and I would write a one or two line summary beside each circled number of what the corresponding section 'did' or contained. (1.0)

In the example from *When We Were Orphans*, the first segment made up of one sentence in the rough draft ('I am sure though that over these past few months, despite the intimacy that had certainly grown between Sarah Hemmings and me, I revealed only a small part of these recollections', Figure 6.2) was summed up as 'But didn't reveal to Sarah' in the 'As Is' sheet (Figure 6.3), while the second segment of ten lines in the rough draft was summarized as '[u]nwise to have divulged what I did? Surely quarrel is trivial' (Figure 6.3). As a breakdown of the rough draft, the 'As Is' sheet gives Ishiguro 'a view of the overall shape and content of what [he]'d written'. He then carefully considers this sheet for a while, 'often writing thoughts on paper', before 'producing a Plan, in the form of a flow chart' with numbers in the left margin, which 'would sometimes follow roughly the structure of the As Is sheet' though 'sometimes it would differ significantly' (1.0).

In the example from *When We Were Orphans* (Figure 6.4), the first circled segment in the plan reads as follows: 'But didn't reveal much of this to Sarah. And in light of quarrel, thankful I didn't', which corresponds to the first two sections of the rough draft (Figure 6.2) and the 'As Is' sheet (Figure 6.3), thus confirming that the Plan sometimes differs from the 'As Is' summary. It is from this type of Plan that Ishiguro then produces what he calls a 'First Draft', working very carefully by hand through each numbered section, producing several versions of the same passage until he is satisfied with one which he marks with a tick in the left margin and types on his typewriter or computer before moving on to the next numbered section of the Plan. As noted by Ishiguro, 'it was sometimes necessary to go through the whole process again (and again!)' (1.0), and the polished typed pages also went through a process of rewriting and revisions. Referring to *The Remains of*

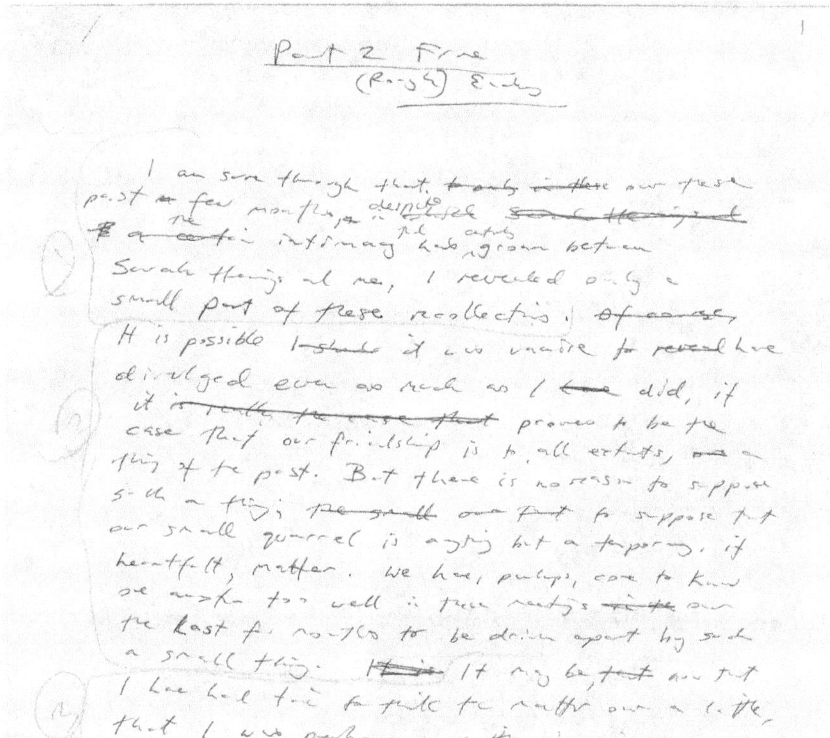

Part 2 Frame
(Rough) Ending

I am sure though that, over these past few months, despite the intimacy that has actually grown between Sarah Hemmings and me, I revealed only a small part of these recollections. It is possible it was unwise to have divulged even as much as I did, if it proves to be the case that our friendship is to all extents, a thing of the past. But there is no reason to suppose such a thing; to suppose that our small quarrel is anything but a temporary, if heartfelt, matter. We have, perhaps, come to know one another too well in these meetings over the last few months to be driven apart by such a small thing. It may be, now that I have had time to think the matter over a little, that I was perhaps a little insensitive towards her that night at Margaret Thompson's house; the onus might, in other words, be upon me to offer – if not exactly an apology, at least to take the first steps in a reconciliation. I am, so I must say, surprised by her sensitivity, given her outspoken manner in most matters. It is perhaps sufficient that I let the matter be, and it will heal itself of its own accord. She is perfectly capable

Figure 6.2 Rough draft of *When We Were Orphans* (1.0) (Reproduced by kind permission of Kazuo Ishiguro and the Harry Ransom Center, The University of Texas at Austin)

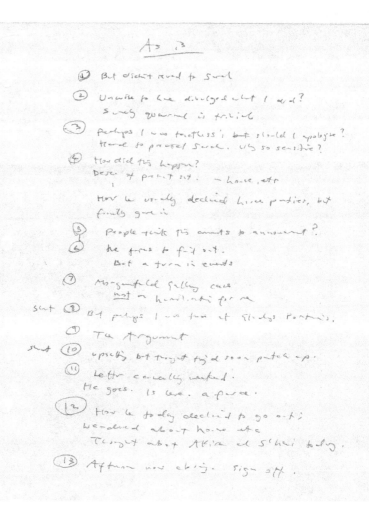

Figure 6.3 'As Is' sheet for *When We Were Orphans* (1.0) (Reproduced by kind permission of Kazuo Ishiguro and the Harry Ransom Center, The University of Texas at Austin)

the Day, Ishiguro commented: '<u>Remains</u> was written in sections of 40/50 pages, each section going from very rough to polished typed copy before I began to tackle the next section of the story (this was how I'd gone about the previous two novels too)' (18.1). On the other hand, he modified his routine for *Never Let Me Go*, as instead of meticulously drafting and revising each section before moving on to the next, he wrote a first rough draft of the whole novel before starting his revisions.

Ishiguro recalls that the composition of *The Remains of the Day* was particularly demanding because he adopted an intense working rhythm:

98

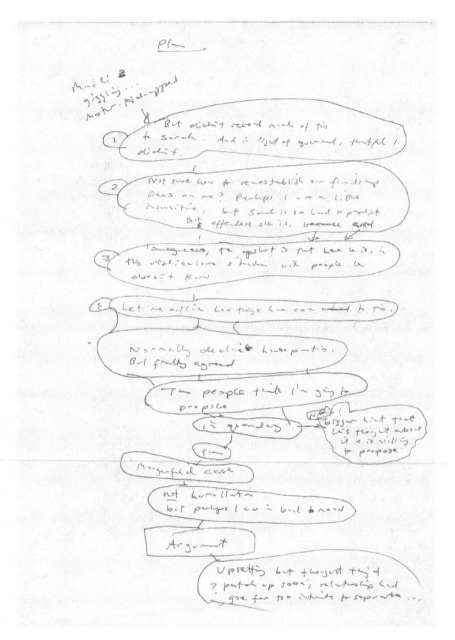

Figure 6.4 Plan for *When We Were Orphans* (1.0) (Reproduced by kind permission of Kazuo Ishiguro and the Harry Ransom Center, The University of Texas at Austin)

'the bulk of the writing was done during 1987 in concentrated "lock-in" sessions when, literally, I hardly left my study morning to night for 4 week blocks' (18.1). He explained further:

> Most memorably in July 1987, and occasionally thereafter, I undertook what Lorna and I called 'crash' periods. This entailed ruthlessly clearing the diary of all engagements for, say, a four week period, then working from morning till bedtime, with just an hour for lunch and two hours for dinner, six days per week. The idea was not simply to pack in more hours. It was a method we thought might drive me deeper into the world of my fiction (that world becoming more real than the real world!), producing valuable breakthroughs. The method proved immensely valuable in the writing of The Remains of the Day, when major revelations came during the 200 plus working hours of that 'crash'.   (62.6)

While planning and drafting his texts, Ishiguro also systematically writes down his impressions, analyses, reflections, and interrogations on what he has devised, is trying out, or has written so far, using the first-person plural pronoun (for example, starting with 'So what do we think after all this?' (48.5)). In these instances of extreme self-reflexivity, Ishiguro meditates on what he has tried to achieve, what works, what does not, and what he should experiment with next. For example, when writing *The War Artist* (which became *An Artist of the Floating World*), he noted: 'we need the momentum (suspense?) of the story in the past to be stronger' (2.3). Comments may concern the narrative voice or the plot as, for instance, in the early stages of *Never Let Me Go*: 'We have to decide on narrative position ... Does Katy narrate from a fixed pt. in time?'; 'Perhaps we need to immerse ourselves more ... Time to get on with voice ... for now, a bit of a blank on the plot side...' (3.1). These often handwritten and sometimes typed notes provide invaluable information on the writer's assessment on what seems 'right' to him, what is 'coming together', and what 'doesn't quite work' (16.8). These remarks that highlight Ishiguro's difficulties, doubts, and achievements may be compared to interior monologues, with the important difference that Ishiguro puts them down on paper, thereby allowing scholars to follow his thought processes.

The 'Precursors' to *The Remains of the Day*

Although the 'rough' papers and boxes of early drafts of *The Remains of the Day* were thrown away, the novel presents an interesting case study for genetic analysis since, when assembling his archives, Ishiguro gathered together four 'precursors' (the term featuring in the catalogue) to the book and included a great quantity of 'notes and ideas as they come', which bear some close or distant relation to the future novel. The final section of this chapter will focus on these preliminary texts and notes in the archives to show how they may have paved the way for *The Remains of the Day*. The four identified 'precursors' include an unpublished short story ('England in October', 1983), a screenplay that was made into a film (*A Profile of Arthur J. Mason*, 1984), and outlines for films that were never shot ('The Patron', 1982–5, and 'Service in Japan', 1987). The notions of 'precursors' and 'run-up' (the word used by Ishiguro)[17] are significant as they seemingly rely on the 'teleological illusion', which, in genetic criticism, consists of 'reading "avant-textes" as if they were sucked up by their future, the final text (or the last one chronologically), because of some necessity or internal causality'.[18] A retrospective glance may lead the writer and the reader to spot similarities between earlier projects and a published text, but one should be wary of perceiving the latter as the inevitable *telos* of a series of previous experimentations and mere stepping stones to a future (and supposedly better) text. And yet, Ishiguro himself seems to embrace the teleological illusion as suggested by the way he formulated his notes on the archives in 2014, writing, for example: 'There's a thread from ["England in October"], via the aborted "The Patron", the undeveloped "Service in Japan" and the TV play "Arthur Mason" to <u>The Remains of the Day</u>' (16.7). Other projects which only exist as notes, ideas, or outlines in varying degrees of development also bear some relation to *The Remains of the Day* and were placed in folders entitled 'Ideas for TV and film' dating from 1984 to 1986 (48.7–8) as well as 'Butler (notes & roughs), ca. 1985–1986' (17.1) and 'Butler – notes and ideas as they come' (17.3). Despite their provisional status, these documents deserve attention as manifestations of the creative directions Ishiguro was taking and the themes he was interested in at a time when he was also considering various options for a third novel. The most recurrent topics in the precursors, notes, and outlines relate to the 'missed-life' theme, the notion of a mythical vision of England, self-deception at the individual and national levels, the question of dignity, and the growth of racism and fascism in Britain.

Several critics have pointed to the prominent similarities between the butlers in *The Remains of the Day* and *A Profile of Arthur J. Mason*. The latter is a thirty-minute television film starring Bernard Hepton as a live-in butler who completed a novel several decades earlier that is suddenly rediscovered and published to international acclaim, prompting a television team to make a documentary profile about its author. Nagaoka-Kozaki has analysed the 'textual incorporation' and 'palimpsestuous rewriting' of the screenplay in the novel, while Barry Lewis has argued that '[t]he butler/writer and his relation to English values anticipate the concerns of *The Remains of the Day*', and Peter Sloane, in his contribution to this *Companion*, names Stevens Arthur Mason's 'progeny' and notes that screenplay and novel both raise questions of personal and professional regret.[19] On a note in the archives dated 2014, Ishiguro points out that the writing of this television film script was 'crucial in the evolution' of *The Remains of the Day*:

> This was my first outing with a butler character, and later, as I began work on <u>Remains</u>, I remember I saw in my mind for Stevens the face and manner of Bernard Hepton, the actor who portrayed Arthur Mason. The 'missed life' theme is here, also a tying of the butler's life to post-war upheavals in Britain. But the political themes are still underdeveloped, focusing rather crudely on trad. class issues rather than on the small man's relationship to big power, as it was in <u>Remains</u>. (16.4)

'The 'missed life' theme' is a recurrent topic in Ishiguro's published work and repeatedly appears in his unpublished material and in notes and ideas about future work. It features as early as Ishiguro's unpublished novel of the mid-1970s, *To Remember a Summer By*, in which a retired schoolmaster starts writing his first novel at the age of sixty and regrets having postponed it until it was too late, thereby having missed his chance of living the life of a writer (50.4). At the time of composition, Ishiguro summed up the theme of *A Profile of Arthur J. Mason* as follows: 'The film is about how easily someone's life can slip by, empty and unfulfilled. It also ponders the way social value is bestowed on people's lives and achievements. / The film should be comic, but finally the viewer should be left with a feeling of sadness and emptiness' (16.5) – a description which could apply, in part, to several of Ishiguro's published books.

As in *The Remains of the Day* and in other texts by Ishiguro, the theme of self-deception is central to the film as the butler hyperbolically insists that he is 'perfectly happy' with his life and has no regrets. As noted by the author, the film 'looks at how people deceive themselves when trying to come to terms with how they have spent their lives' and even makes the 'cynical suggestion that most chosen ways of life are empty and morally useless, and most of us only have varying degrees of self-deception to convince ourselves otherwise' (16.5). In the short story 'The Patron' (16.8), dating from around 1984, it is the fear of having wasted his life without having made any worthy contribution that encourages Sir Arnold Barraclough to donate a large sum of money to a charity that will build houses for the poor of London (16.8) – a scheme which actually never existed, Sir Arnold having been deceived by his own son. Sir Arnold's devoted butler, Carter, narrates the story in the first person and Ishiguro pointed out that the 'butler-master relationship is an earlier version of Stevens/Darlington, though the master here involves himself naively in <u>domestic</u> politics, not foreign affairs' (16.8). However, Ishiguro was dissatisfied with the 'uneven and unsteady' dimension of the relationship between butler and master, and wrote down in his notes that he 'didn't want it becoming too much like the Jeeves Wooster one' (the famous pair devised by P. G. Wodehouse), but that for the time being, it was 'too close perhaps to Jeeves relationship – upper class twit & clever, articulate butler' (16.8). He endeavoured to change the tone, which he judged too farcical, and aimed for 'a note of familiarity' which he thought Etsuko and Ogata-san 'hit just right' in *A Pale View of Hills* and which he hoped to emulate. He noted at the time of composition:

> ... it should be bantering, and quite competitive; the truth is, the two of them need each other and enjoy each other's company; they have been cooped up together for some time ..., and they are beginning to develop their own code about everything; an [*sic*] private, enclosed language; their intimacy however is restricted by the forms that need to be preserved, and in these, they adhere very well. (16.8)

In *The Remains of the Day*, Darlington and Stevens likewise share a private language but it does not include bantering, which is the new mode introduced by Stevens's American employer. In 2014, Ishiguro remarked that in 'The Patron', '[t]he butler's voice is quite close to that of Stevens' (16.8), a resemblance which may be perceived in the two characters' stiffness, formality, and indirectness, and their common use of the pronoun 'one' instead of 'I'. A few episodes in *The Remains of the Day* also find their origin in 'The Patron', as, for instance, the scene in the billiard room when Stevens is dusting portraits and Darlington apologizes for the humiliation he has just suffered because of Mr Spencer's questions of foreign policy, or the scene where Stevens and Miss Kenton observe the former's father walk up and down the steps where he had fallen some time earlier. Ishiguro's relentless revisions of these scenes point to his constant quest for the right tone, voice, word, and balance.

If 'The Patron' portrays Sir Arthur's despondency at the end of his life when he feels he has not made a lasting contribution to society and lets himself be deceived by his son, the unpublished short story 'England in October' likewise focuses on a case of (self-)deception. The story features a Japanese painter, Kenji, whose work, like Ono's in *An Artist of the Floating World*, was flawed by its propagandist and nationalistic dimension before and during the Second World War. In the early 1980s, Kenji's grandson cons him into donating money for his supposedly charitable organization in London (which turns out to be a terrorist group in Tokyo) by fuelling the painter's sentimental memories of a clichéd and fantasized England where he spent some ten years before the war, thereby kindling nostalgia for a place that never existed. Ishiguro identifies in this short story 'the first clear manifestation of ideas that later became The Remains of the Day', more specifically 'the idea of a mythical version of England and Englishness created for "nostalgia" and the consumption of foreign anglophiles' (16.7). Looking through his material from the early and mid-1980s, Ishiguro remembers that he was 'interested back then in a story that <u>literally</u> presented versions of a made-up England for the consumption of Anglophiles (Japanese, Irish) who had lost touch with the "real" England' (17.1). Such an interest finds an echo in *The Remains of the Day*, about which Ishiguro said that his purpose was to 'create a mythical England', or more precisely to 'rework a particular myth about a certain kind of mythical England' (*CKI* 73, 74).

A longing for an idealized England also characterizes two film projects, 'Tramps' (1984–6) and 'Tramps & Boxers' (1985), as well as notes for the 'East West Novel', which centre around the tendency of British people to deceive themselves in their perception of their country. One version of 'Tramps & Boxers' takes place in Ireland in the 1860s and features an English butler named Stephens, 'a comical Jeeves-type', noted 'for his behaving like a parody of the English butler in the presence of gentry, and his remarkable haughtiness when dealing with the "ordinary" Irish' (48.8). Stephens travels through the countryside to find a member of the Irish working class with whom his English master wants to organize a boxing match in order to show the Irish the English 'values of sportsmanship and gentlemanly conduct' and 'establish the chivalrous nature of the British character'. In the course of his trip, Stephens chooses to ignore the tales he hears and the evidence he sees about the culpability of the British in the Irish famine of 1845–52. Like Stevens and Lord Darlington in *The Remains of the Day*, both butler and master need to 'preserve a sense of pride in being British' and therefore 'ignore the evidence of the evils of British rule' (48.8).

The closest Ishiguro gets to *The Remains of the Day* is the outline for an unpublished and unfilmed television screenplay entitled 'Service in Japan' (1987), an 'off-beat comedy-thriller' featuring an English butler (Benson) and his master (Lord Gilbert) who travel to Tokyo in 1950 to take part in secret talks with Japanese and American representatives in order to lay the foundations of Japan's forthcoming Peace Treaty with the Allies. When Lord Gilbert mysteriously vanishes, his butler is asked to impersonate him (bringing to mind Stevens's assumed role on his expedition to the West Country when he is mistaken for a gentleman at the Taylors' in Moscombe) and he 'senses something personally crucial in this fleeting chance to occupy a key position in the world' (16.9). As noted by Ishiguro in 2014, '[t]he butler here resembles Stevens both in his "missed life" condition and his relationship to big power' (16.9). Earlier notes on another project entitled 'Butler in Japan' (1986) include some of the most important scenes and themes of *The Remains of the Day* but the main differences concern the Japanese dimension (the butler's new employer, Mr Farraday, takes him to Japan as a 'rest-cure' after a small mistake he has made) and the shared affections of Mary (later Miss Kenton) between the butler and a Japanese interpreter. However, Ishiguro's comments on the 'Butler projects' reveal his increasing hesitation as to the relevance of the Japanese side of the story, as suggested by the change of title to 'An English Butler' and 'A Butler in England', and the indication at the top of a page which lists the main episodes: 'Okay, so without Japan it looks like this' (17.3).

Letting go of the Japanese side may have seemed an important step to take after Ishiguro's first two novels, but the writer often said in interviews that he did not see his books as being 'about' a particular country or himself as having any 'clear role', 'society or country to speak for or write about' (*CKI* 58). In preliminary notes to *The Remains of the Day*, he pointed to the important notion of 'Britishness' but then added in longhand: 'Not so fond of "Britishness" being emphasised; no more reason why this should be <u>about</u>, Britain than Artist is <u>about</u> Japan...' (17.3). The analysis of the archives confirms that the setting or historical context are less important to Ishiguro than the main themes, as he told Eleanor Wachtel: 'My main purpose in writing these books wasn't to explain to readers what a specific point in history was like. I started off with the themes and the ideas and then thought, where could I set this particular story so that the themes and ideas came out powerfully?'[20] The archives reveal that Ishiguro's numerous projects, developed over the years, tend to focus on specific reflections and preoccupations (such as the 'missing life' theme) to which he keeps returning and that he keeps exploring further.

This selective view of Ishiguro's papers gives a first intimation of the richness of the material at hand and of the specificities of the author's meticulous method of planning and composition. The genetic dossier of *The Remains of the Day* is emblematic of this process as the novel grew out of a series of different projects and ideas until the author narrowed down his focus to produce the memorable butler in England. Such an example shows that access to the archives can inform a literary-critical perspective on published texts by bringing to the surface of the palimpsest layers that had been erased or hidden but that can still be recovered.

Notes

1 Vijay Mishra, *Salman Rushdie and the Genesis of Secrecy* (London: Bloomsbury, 2019), p.5.
2 Michel Contat, Denis Hollier, and Jacques Neefs, 'Editors' Preface', in Michel Contat, Denis Hollier, and Jacques Neefs, eds., *Drafts*, special issue of *Yale French*

Studies 89 (1996): 1–5 (2); Louis Hay, 'Does "Text" Exist?', trans. Matthew Jocelyn and Hans Walter, *Studies in Bibliography* 41 (1988): 64–76 (75).

3 Amy E. Armstrong, 'Kazuo Ishiguro : An Inventory of His Papers at the Harry Ransom Center' (accessed online at https://norman.hrc.utexas.edu/fasearch/findingAid.cfm?eadid=01143&kw=ishiguro). When quoting from Ishiguro's papers, the first figure refers to the box and the second to the folder (as in 1.1).

4 The following list indicates the number of paper folders (and floppy disks when applicable) relating to each book up to its publication (therefore excluding material about later film, radio, or theatrical adaptations): *A Pale View of Hills* (5), *An Artist of the Floating World* (13), *The Remains of the Day* (20), *The Unconsoled* (43, and 12 disks), *When We Were Orphans* (93, and 13 disks), *Nocturnes* (24, and 6 disks), *Never Let Me Go* (52, and 11 disks), *The Buried Giant* (1).

5 Although the concept of 'avant-texte' is not uniformly employed by geneticists, it 'carries with it the assumption that the material of textual genetics is not a given but rather a critical construction elaborated in relation to a postulated terminal – so-called definitive – state of the work' (Jed Depmann, Daniel Ferrer, and Michael Groden, eds., *Genetic Criticism: Texts and Avant-Textes* (Philadelphia: University of Pennsylvania Press, 2004), p.8).

6 'And Oh, in Berkeley', written in August 1974, and 'In Downtown San Francisco', written in October 1974 (51.6–8).

7 'Gundown in Dead City', written in the summer of 1975 (51.4).

8 The short film was shot on super 8mm film in and near Farnham in Surrey in the summer of 1975 (51.4).

9 'The Man with No Brain', performed on 15 April 1976 at the local hall in Ottershaw, Surrey (51.4).

10 Among them are the completed short stories 'Hitch-hiker', 'J and Mr Rogers', 'Double Agents', and 'Reinhart' dating from 1975 (51.4); 'The Cleaner and the Cat' from 1977–8 (51.4); 'The Playground' from 1979 (47.5)'; 'An Empty Flat' and 'A Bassline through the Ceiling' from 1980 (47.10–11); as well as a story identified as 'Experiment 4' (48.2), first written in 1991 and then revised in 1996 to be read at the Harbourfront Festival in Toronto, and 'Gershwin' (49.8), dating from 2008, which was originally part of *Nocturnes* but was not included because Ishiguro considered it 'not up to standard' (49.8).

11 *To Remember a Summer By*, written between 1975 and 1977 (50.2–4), submitted to and rejected by Duckworth, and *Sylvie*, written between 1977 and 1978 (50.5–7), which was not sent to any publisher.

12 '3rd novel', dating from 1978–9, which Ishiguro identified as the start to *A Pale View of Hills* (51.1), and *Flight from Nagasaki* (49.7), written from 1983 to 1986, which focuses on the effects of the Nagasaki bombing on a Japanese family and especially two sisters who are sent to a village in the hills, and is based on Ishiguro's mother's memories of the bombing.

13 'Potatoes and Lovers' written in 1978–9 (47.2).

14 Jacques Derrida, 'Archive Fever: A Freudian Impression', trans. Eric Prenowitz, *Diacritics* 25:2 (1995): 9–63 (9).

15 In her presentation of the archives, Amy Armstrong refers to Ishiguro's long 'contemplative, iterative technique focused on getting it just right' ('Kazuo Ishiguro: An Inventory'). This sometimes leads him to discard developments

which he had worked on for a long time, such as, for instance, the 'Coring Mystery', a parallel storyline meant for the third part of *When We Were Orphans*, which was eventually abandoned.

16 Louis Hay, *La Littérature des écrivains. Questions de critique génétique* (Paris: José Corti, 2002), pp.74–5, my translation.

17 In the presentation of the scope and contents of Ishiguro's archives, Armstrong writes: 'While preparing his papers, Ishiguro collected together several works that he refers to as "Run-up to The Remains of the Day"' ('Kazuo Ishiguro: An Inventory').

18 Michel Contat, 'Une idée fondamentale pour la génétique littéraire: l'intentionnalité', in Michel Contat and Daniel Ferrer, eds., *Pourquoi la critique génétique? Méthodes, théories* (Paris: CNRS Edition, 1998), pp.111–12. My translation.

19 Tomoko Nagaoka-Kozaki, '"Can't You See We're Eating?": Looking at the Textual Dietetics in Ishiguro's Butler Stories', *Reading* 24 (2003): 238–49 (238); Barry Lewis, *Kazuo Ishiguro* (Manchester: Manchester University Press, 2000), p. 77; Sloane, Chapter 10, in this volume.

20 Eleanor Wachtel, 'Kazuo Ishiguro' (1995), in *More Writers and Company: New Conversations with CBC Radio's Eleanor Wachtel* (1996; Toronto: Vintage, 1997), ebook, n.p.

7

ULRIKA MAUDE

The Unconsoled of *The Unconsoled*

Ishiguro and Modernism

The Unconsoled is Kazuo Ishiguro's great comic novel. Humour was on the author's mind in 1989 after publishing his 'breakthrough' novel, *The Remains of the Day*. Speaking to the Japanese novelist Kenzaburō Ōe during his first visit to his birth country as an adult, Ishiguro reflected on 'the kind of humor found in most of Western literature': 'Everything has this peculiar sense of humor', he explains, 'which is always on the verge of tragedy – a very dark humor' (*CKI* 55). In an interview with Maya Jaggi shortly after the publication of *The Unconsoled* in 1995, Ishiguro returned to the theme and revealed that he wrote the novel 'as a kind of comedy; not a ha ha ha falling about thing' but as a reflection on a 'whole world working in a darkly comic way' (*CKI* 113). Along with Kafka, he mentions Dostoevsky as an influence, commenting on the way that his four great novels build 'up to farce but with serious grand themes': resembling a 'low-comedy stage farce', different strands 'grow to hysterical pitch', producing a 'tone of hysteria' that Dostoevsky deploys 'to very serious ends' (*CKI* 114). *The Unconsoled* can be seen as similarly inducing a kind of dark hilarity in its readers, but in Ishiguro's case it is also one that involves an unstable blend of slapstick and what the modernist philosopher, Henri Bergson, refers to as 'a certain *mechanical inelasticity*' – a mechanical or inhuman quality that we might see as inherent in the comedic tragedy of both the modernist and the Ishigurian human subject.[1] Partly for this reason, perhaps, Ishiguro's fourth novel can also be considered by far his most experimental, and as the novel that most explicitly draws on, and even thematizes, modernist formal experimentation. By situating Ishiguro's lengthiest, most digressive, most formally challenging, and *funniest* novel within the European modernist tradition, I will analyse its marked formal experimentation in the light of its idiosyncratic and often highly disturbing blend of humour and mishap, of comedy and adversity. I want to propose that *The Unconsoled* can be considered not only Ishiguro's but also one of late modernism's great comic epics.

The Unconsoled focuses on Ryder, a concert pianist who has been invited to an unnamed central-European city as a kind of 'messiah figure' to solve the town's never-quite-articulated crisis.[2] During his two-and-a-half-day visit, Ryder takes part in the preparations for a concert at which he is to perform with the town's musicians, the 'disgraced, bibulous ex-conductor' Brodsky, and the hotel director's son and aspiring pianist, Stephan.[3] The purpose of the concert is no less than to resolve the unspecified crisis and the deep tensions that trouble and divide the town's inhabitants. From the outset, then, music in the novel is staged as a consolation and even as a medium capable of offering a resolution to an underlying communitarian crisis. The novel follows the various obstacles that get in the way of the grand event, which ultimately only part-takes-place in the form of Stephan's performance of 'Glass Passions', which on the first attempt and despite his talent, is taken by the audience merely as a 'testing out of the piano or else the amplification system' (*U* 477). Stephan's second, now-brilliant performance is followed by a calamitous orchestral recital conducted by Brodsky, while Ryder's planned Q&A session and his piano recital ultimately fail to materialize.

We get the first inkling of the novel's structure at a party Ryder attends at the Countess's house. He assumes that he will be the gathering's 'guest of honour ... the evening's great surprise' (*U* 125), but instead, and somewhat to his dismay, he goes unrecognized and even largely ignored by the other guests. Traversing the crowd in the company of his host, Ryder has 'the distinct impression we were walking around in slow circles', rather than towards 'a particular spot in the room or to a particular person', as he had at first assumed (125). In what one might call the novel's circular structural principle (it also *ends* with Ryder in a tram happily circling the town before his imminent departure for another engagement in Helsinki), *The Unconsoled* resonates, not least, with the post-war prose of Ishiguro's great modernist precursor, Samuel Beckett. In the interview with Jaggi, Ishiguro states that he 'read Samuel Beckett – mainly the prose' while composing the novel (*CKI* 114), and while critics have rightly pointed to the influence of Kafka on *The Unconsoled*, traces of Beckett are at least as prominent, including with respect to a kind of narrative circularity. As the first-person narrator of *Molloy* (1955) muses while crawling through a forest, 'when a man in a forest thinks he is going forward in a straight line, in reality he is going in a circle, I did my best to go in a circle, hoping in this way to go in a straight line'.[4] Other echoes of Beckett abound. Like Molloy, Ryder frequently finds himself lost or sidetracked, and both novels share an enigmatic setting, which is both 'strange, yet strangely familiar', as Cynthia Wong puts it: recognizable, bewildering, and disorienting at one and the same time.[5]

Both Molloy and Ryder suspect they may have a son – a motif in *The Unconsoled* that resonates with the prominent theme of the absent or distant parent in Ishiguro's wider body of work[6] – and both novels prominently feature the serio-comic tragedy of a dead dog. Perhaps most strikingly, the title of Ishiguro's novel resonates unmistakeably with the title of the third novel of Beckett's Trilogy, *The Unnamable* (1958). The titles of both novels consist of adjectives that, in a somewhat strained manner, become nouns by acquiring a definite article.[7] And both titles feature nouns that serve to negate what they name: somebody or something can't be named; somebody can't be consoled.

And then there are the details: in both novels, absurd particulars abound. In the fourth and final part of *The Unconsoled*, Brodsky appears with only one leg, which brings to mind the one-legged Mahood of *The Unnamable*, orbiting around his family. In Ishiguro's novel, Gustav – the existentialist porter of the hotel and, as it turns out, the father of Ryder's partner – narrates the story of Sophie's childhood hamster, Ulrich, which goes missing, much to the consternation of the young Sophie. Weeks later, Gustav hears 'very distraught sobbing – it went straight to the heart', he asserts. He hears Sophie call, 'I left Ulrich in the box! It was my fault! I forgot! I forgot!' as she remembers too late that she had placed her hamster in a 'little gift box' in order to take him out to '"show" him things' (*U* 84). Gustav, the father, fails to react to his daughter's anguish and distress, with devastating conse-quences for their relationship. In Beckett's hauntingly beautiful late prose work, *Company*, from 1980, a strikingly similar scene appears, only in Beckett's case featuring a hedgehog:

> You take pity on a hedgehog out in the cold and put it in an old hatbox with some worms. This box with the hog inside you then place in a disused hutch wedging the door open for the poor creature to come and go at will. . . . There then is the hedgehog in its box in the hutch with enough worms to tide it over. . . . The glow at your good deed is slower than usual to cool and fade. . . . Kneeling at your bedside you included it the hedgehog in your detailed prayer to God to bless all you loved. And tossing in your warm bed waiting for sleep to come you were still faintly glowing at the thought of what a fortunate hedgehog it was to have crossed your path as it did. . . . Now the next morning not only was the glow spent but great uneasiness had taken its place. A suspicion that all was perhaps not as it should be. That rather than do as you did you had perhaps better let good alone and the hedgehog pursue its way. Days if not weeks passed before you could bring yourself to return to the hutch. You have never forgotten what you found then. You are on your back in the dark and have never forgotten what you found then. The mush. The stench.[8]

The two scenes share more than the sum of their events: both feature a fall from innocence, and both raise stark ethical questions about the nature of good deeds, which in *The Unconsoled* repeatedly and near-consistently backfire. Almost every act of kindness that Ryder commits ends up only perpetuating the recipient's suffering. This is the case, for instance, with his childhood friend, Fiona Roberts, who has organized a party in his honour that Ryder fails to attend. Ryder subsequently lets her down a second time in his attempt to make amends by visiting her mocking and scornful friends. During the visit, he catches a glimpse of himself in the mirror: 'I saw that my face had become bright red and squashed into pig-like features, while my fists, clenched at chest level, were quivering along with the whole of my torso' (U 240). The scene of Ryder's pig-like, 'quivering' countenance recalls Gregor Samsa's predicament in Kafka's 'The Metamorphosis' (1915): finding himself transformed one morning into a beetle or a cockroach, Samsa observes '[h]is many legs, miserably thin in comparison with his size otherwise, flicker[ing] helplessly before his eyes'.[9] In both scenes, it is 'an overstepping between the limits of the animal and the human' that generates uneasy, disconcerting humour in the texts and that, in the case of Ryder, makes the often-conceited pianist for a moment doubt his own intentions.[10]

In his essay on laughter, Bergson proposes that 'the comic does not exist outside the pale of what is strictly HUMAN' and argues that one only laughs at an animal if one has 'detected in it some human attitude or expression'.[11] In *The Unconsoled*, however, Ryder is laughed at because he has the attitude and expression of a pig: pig-like and 'quivering', his humanity and dignity is comedically doubted. But the comedy is complicated and compromised. Is it even funny? Much as in Kafka's 'The Metamorphosis', which induces something closer to anxiety than hilarity in the reader, the laughter in *The Unconsoled* is choked by the motif of human animality. By the same token, while the tragic is usually conceived of as peculiarly human, Ishiguro's novel attributes the grand passions of tragedy more to Sophie's dead hamster (and later on to Brodsky's dead dog) than to people, just as in Beckett's *Company* it is the dead hedgehog that instigates in the young protagonist the tragic affects of guilt and regret. What is represented is the innocence and helplessness of the animal, while the human child undergoes a fall from such a state.

Unlike Sophie or Beckett's narrator, however, Ryder lacks the archetypally human capacity towards self-awareness, and therefore the ability fully to acknowledge the tragi-comic error of his ways. He spends his two-and-a-half days in the unnamed central-European city as a keen subject of flattery, and even while the thought of remorse flashes through his mind after he has half-unwittingly consented to being photographed in front of the controversial Sattler monument – another example of his loss of dignity in the townspeople's eyes – he mostly remains oblivious to the damage caused by his blundering good deeds. The Sattler monument, a building erected 'almost a century ago' (U 374) is considered by most of the townspeople too 'extreme' – too modernist, one might say – in its architectural design, standing as a trope for experimental artistic form that later turns out to epitomize the conflict the town is facing (375). It rests on a hill like 'a single turret ... removed from a medieval castle' (182), recalling in its design Kafka's last novel, *The Castle* (1926), which with its elaborate bureaucratic procedures also lends its mood of absurdity and banality to *The Unconsoled*.[12] And yet, despite his many failings and blunders, Ryder does not seem intentionally callous – he drifts from one situation to another and is often, comically, the victim of random circumstance or sheer, contingent bad luck.

In an interview with the German magazine, *Der Spiegel*, after the publication of *Never Let Me Go* in 2005, Ishiguro agrees that it is helpful to read his work in the context of Beckett and Kafka because, like theirs, his books should be read 'on a more metaphorical level': 'The setting of a novel for me is just a part of the technique', he continues, 'I choose it at the end.'[13] As Ryder rests in his hotel room, we get the first inkling of the spatial 'technique' (as Ishiguro calls it) of the novel:

> I went on scrutinising the ceiling for some time, then sat up on the bed and looked around, the sense of recognition growing stronger by the second. The room I was now in, I realised, was the very room that had served as my bedroom during the two years my parents and I lived at my aunt's house on the borders of England and Wales. (U 16)

Such stark heterotopic shifts in spatial configuration are not common in modernist writing, but they do feature prominently in Beckett's post-war prose, where, as in *The Unconsoled*, memory, perception, and imagination have a tendency to shift functions and merge into one. With its emphasis on memory, however, the scene also brings to mind the work of another key modernist writer, Marcel Proust. Speaking in 2001 about the first part of *Remembrance of Things Past*, Ishiguro observes that Proust made him realize that he could 'mimic the way memory rubs through someone's mind' (CKI 193). He elaborates on the idea by saying that 'a fragment of a scene [can be] dovetailed into a scene that takes place thirty years later', which is precisely what occurs in *The Unconsoled* (ibid.). Ishiguro comes back to this idea in his Nobel lecture when he says that Proust made him realize that he could 'compose in something like the way an abstract painter might choose to place shapes and colours around a canvas' (TCE 17). Proustian involuntary memory – which is triggered by sensory perceptions such as the taste of a madeleine dipped into a cup of tea or the musty odour of a public lavatory in the avenue of Champs-Elysées – has the power to bring back the entire structure of the past. But while drawing on Proust in terms of narrative structure and the representation of memory, *The Unconsoled* also stages something far more disconcerting, as Ryder's experience attests:

> I looked again around the room, then, lowering myself back down, stared once more at the ceiling. It had been recently re-plastered and re-painted, its dimensions had been enlarged, the cornices had been removed, the decorations around the light fitting had been entirely altered. But it was unmistakably the same ceiling I had so often stared up at from my narrow creaking bed of those days. (*U* 16)

The dimensions of the ceiling now differ from those of Ryder's aunt's house; there are no cornices and the ceiling rose has been altered. Yet, Ryder is convinced that he is 'unmistakably' in his aunt's house at the border of England and Wales. The ceiling, which isn't the same ceiling, is for Ryder the same ceiling. In other words, Ishiguro transforms Proustian involuntary memory into something far more disquieting: instead of reconnecting the narrator with his past selves and experiences, *The Unconsoled* stages memory as fundamentally unreliable and failing, as memory gone awry. Ryder experiences a form of cognitive dissonance in which the room is both the same and different from the bedroom in Ryder's aunt's house, and where a central-European hotel room morphs into a bedchamber that it never was in the Welsh borderlands of thirty years earlier. The dark turn on Proust, in other words, involves the involuntary memory of a character who misremembers or who is losing spatial orientation. The forgetful Ryder is a semi-amnesiac who frequently bumps into and recognizes people from his past, but who fails to remember or even at first to recognize Sophie and Boris, who turn out to be his partner and his adoptive son. And there's a weird contagion involved in this inverted Proustianism such that the novel not only represents but performs a kind of amnesia. By applying Ishiguro's spatial 'technique' and its concomitant temporal shifts, and by presenting the reader with a semi-amnesiac protagonist, the novel also performs what James Wood has called 'its amnesiac curse' on the reader. Writing twenty years after he read the novel, the exasperated Wood claims that he can remember 'almost nothing distinct' in its 'more than five hundred pages'.[14]

One of Ryder's dilemmas is that he has not received the schedule for his visit, which makes him feel doubly lost in the labyrinthine streets of the central-European town. Through social awkwardness, he fails to ask for a copy of the schedule, but later, in his hotel room, he suddenly remembers 'the long plane journey I had just completed': 'I had been sitting in the darkened cabin, the other passengers asleep around me, studying the schedule for this visit under the dim beam of the reading light', he comments, recalling 'the very texture of the thick grey paper on which the schedule had been typed, the dull yellow patch cast on it by the reading light, the drone of the plane's engines' even though, 'try as I might, I could remember nothing of what had been written on that sheet' (*U* 15). Ryder, in other words, has a tactile and a visual memory of the sheet of paper – recalled as 'thick' and 'grey' – and he also recalls the 'drone' of the aeroplane's engines, but the contents of the schedule are lost to him. This sets the scene for the novel's mood, which, with its enigmatic setting, is both alien and familiar, and which, with its strongly sensuous but cognitively disconcerting involuntary memories, resembles something like a Proustian nightmare.

The unidentified central-European city of *The Unconsoled* is itself both anywhere and everywhere and yet, by the same token, also nowhere. It remains unnameable, and is, as the author has stated, 'by and large a landscape of the imagination' or even a dreamscape: 'I started to ask myself, What is the grammar of dreams?'[15] When Ryder first encounters the city, on his long late-evening walk with Sophie and Boris, it appears remarkably if not uncannily empty. Sophie leads Ryder and Boris through dark, steep, and mysterious streets:

> Sophie had in fact turned down a side-alley, whose entrance was little more than a crack in the wall. It descended steeply and appeared so narrow it did not seem possible to go down it without scraping an elbow along one or the other of its rough walls to either side. The darkness was broken only by two street lamps, one half-way down, the other at the very bottom. (*U* 43)

If the scene is geographically and architecturally uncanny, it is also so, perhaps, in the echoes it evokes of other European texts, most prominently the work of Kafka, in the great European tradition of modernist writing to which Ishiguro so deftly and so disorientatingly gestures.

Inexplicably, Ryder encounters Geoffrey Saunders – an old schoolmate from his time in England – in the pool of light cast by one of the street lamps. Ryder is struck 'by how much he had aged' and by his 'overwhelmingly down-at-heel' appearance, but he nonetheless recognizes Saunders as the 'golden boy of our year' at school (*U* 44, 45). The chiaroscuro of the scene, as well as the labyrinthine and claustrophobic street, recall another modernist tradition, that of German Expressionist film, which favoured theatrical and unnaturalistic sets, while Geoffrey Saunders's sudden appearance in the pool of light brings to mind one of Expressionist film's favourite techniques, the lingering close-up of the human face.

As Ryder and Boris wait for a bus, Stephan Hoffman from the hotel randomly pulls up in his car. Part of the narrative weirdness of *The Unconsoled* is that buildings in the countryside suddenly morph into the hotel at which Ryder is staying, and mysterious portals open up in the buildings he visits only to lead him back to the hotel, the central hub of the novel's events, perhaps echoing Kafka's unfinished and posthumously published first novel from 1911–14, *Der Verschollene* (translated variously as *Lost in America*, *The Man who Disappeared*, and also simply as *Amerika*). Ishiguro has explicitly acknowledged Kafka as an influence on *The Unconsoled*, referring to the 'dream-like quality' of his work (*CKI* 114), and the traces are everywhere apparent. Richard Robinson has noted that the protagonist of *Amerika*, Karl Rossman, gets lost in the opening scene of the novel in the ocean liner's 'countless corridors', and that the experience is later repeated in the 'spacious upstate country house', where he 'runs into dead ends, and thinks he is going round in circles'. Rossman's predicament distinctly resembles the manner in which, in *The Unconsoled*, Ryder frequently finds himself lost or sidetracked in the streets and houses of the central-European town that he seems both to recognize and acknowledge, and of which he simultaneously seems to have no memory.[16] In the third part of the novel, Ryder finds himself disoriented anew, desperately trying to locate the concert hall, 'obviously lost and uncertain', and worrying about his dignity in the eyes of the townspeople, should they spot him: 'I found myself wandering from one tiny side-street to the next, quite possibly going in circles, the concert hall not visible anywhere' (*U* 386). His irritation mounting, he observes the '[u]tterly preposterous obstacles everywhere', including a random wall at the end of a street that has become a tourist attraction, and the 'network of narrow little alleys' that prevent him from finding his way (388, 389).[17]

Robinson has written about the influence on *The Unconsoled* of Josef von Sternberg's late-Expressionist film, *Der Blaue Engel* (1930), pointing out that a number of the place names and proper names in the novel originate in the film, including the 'Sternberg Garden', in which Brodsky and Miss Collins meet (*U* 146), and 'Horst Jennings, the city's most senior actor' (381), whose name originates in 'Erwin Jennings, the male lead' of *Der Blaue Engel*. Robinson identifies persuasive intertextual affinities between the focus on 'artistic performance' and the anxiety of 'public humiliation' in the film and in Ishiguro's novel,[18] but one can also find in *The Unconsoled* distinct echoes of earlier Expressionist films such as Robert Wiene's *Das Kabinet des Dr Caligari* (1920), which features a similar maze-like setting of dark, narrow, and unnaturalistic streets, and Robert Murnau's *Nosferatu* from 1922, in which yet another castle produces fear and uncertainty in its protagonist and shares affinities with the hotel and the Countess's house in *The Unconsoled*. Ishiguro's novel also chimes with Fritz Lang's Dr Mabuse films, in which Mabuse is a mesmerist or 'mind doctor' who manipulates people into acting to the dictates of his will, just as the hapless Ryder's actions seem to be directed by a host of townspeople who appear in the novel. All of these films contain prominent references to such disorders as amnesia, somnambulism, and hysteria, and one might see the perpetually exhausted and forgetful Ryder as a kind of somnambulist suffering from degrees of amnesia and perhaps even from a protracted mental breakdown. The novel's profoundly disconcerting instability of tone, intention, and seriousness, and Ryder's unstable mental condition are all part of the novel's modernist inheritance, then. Ryder experiences intense anxiety throughout the novel, one of his most pervasive worries being a concern over his parents' impending visit, and the 'arrangements' that may or may not have been made to accommodate them. He catastrophizes, believing that 'if things went very badly indeed, it was not impossible one or the other of them would suffer a seizure' (U 386), and we learn that medical and other arrangements have been put in place for their visit, almost as if some kind of a disaster is to be expected (512). Ryder's anxiety is ultimately wasted, however, for the visit, like so many other sources of consternation in the novel, fails to take place, even though he is certain that he has heard the arrival of his parents ('When I stopped the car in the woods, I could hear them coming, their horse and carriage' (ibid.)), in another example of the cognitive dissonance that characterizes both the novel and Ryder's state of mind.

German Expressionist films share a highly stylized performance style, often reminiscent of cabaret or music hall performances, which *Der Blaue Engel* in fact thematizes. *The Unconsoled*, too, is permeated with slapstick moments such as the scene of the impassioned, one-legged Brodsky fervently conducting an orchestra at the grand recital while using an ironing board as his crutch. The scene, however, is also at the same time a self-reflexive, parodic commentary on artistic production and performance itself:

> Brodsky swung his baton in a large arc, almost simultaneously punching the air with his other hand. As he did so, he appeared to become unstuck. He ascended a few inches into the air, then crashed down across the front of the stage, taking the podium rail, the ironing board, the score, the music stand, all with him. (U 496)

Music in *The Unconsoled* in fact acts as a trope for modernist literary experimentation, perhaps in recognition of the fact that it was the first medium to witness a break with classical form, rendering it the modernist forebear well before such formal shifts had manifested in literature or even in the visual arts. Music functions as an opportune figure for literary modernism, for as Tim Armstrong has observed, it is 'close to or "like" a language – a highly formal one with inbuilt codes and expectations'.[19] In Ishiguro's novel, Brodsky is staged as the formalist radical, so much so that the orchestra he is conducting begins to rebel and to perform in discord and dissonance against him since, for their liking, he has taken experimentation beyond its limits, far beyond the confines of popular taste – and consolation. This can be read as a kind of proleptic metatextual reference to *The Unconsoled* itself: on publication in 1995, many reviewers were enraged by the novel's baffling, form-shattering strategies after the 'formally cunning' perfection of Ishiguro's previous novel, *The Remains of the Day*.[20]

The (modernist) artist-figure at the centre of the novel is the pianist-genius Ryder. Renowned for his exceptional talent, however, Ryder is in every other way strikingly underwhelming, a characterological paradox or tension that constitutes the focal point of *The Unconsoled*. As Cynthia Wong has argued, Ryder is 'simultaneously at the centre and the periphery of what occurs in the novel'.[21] Nearly everyone Ryder encounters during the two-and-a-half days of the novel's span, expects a 'favour' from him, and elicits commitments that almost without exception fail miserably to have the desired effect or that Ryder neglects or is unable altogether to fulfil. The scrapbooks collected by the wife of the hotel manager Hoffman offer but one example. Hoffman has requested that Ryder view and sign his wife's scrapbooks, which are filled with newspaper cuttings charting Ryder's illustrious career over many years. But despite several reminders, this favour, too, fails to materialize, as the distracted Ryder is repeatedly and near-mechanically sidetracked from his intentions. In this, Ryder can be seen as the modernist anti-hero who is frequently humiliated, an uncomprehending outsider in the culturally and historically specific context of the unnamed European town, joining the ranks of Joyce's relatable Bloom (a cuckolded Everyman of Jewish heritage in Catholic Dublin), Kafka's neurotic K (an ethnically other Czech Jew in a distinctly Germanic village), and Beckett's cantankerous Molloy (a disorientated tramp in a place strangely reminiscent of, but not quite, rural Ireland). The recurring motif of Ryder's failure to fulfil the expectations that others have of him again recalls Kafka's novel, *The Castle*, in which K's ambition to enter the titular castle is repeatedly blocked by 'the most mundane of obstacles'.[22] What James Wood has described as 'the crushing procedural banality' represented in Kafka's novel also forms a central aspect of *The Unconsoled*, in which nearly every task carries with it an absurd set of elaborate instructions.[23] But in Ishiguro's novel, this functions as a source of comedic absurdity, not least in the extravagant procedure, devised by Hoffman for Ryder's Q&A session at the concert hall. Hoffman respectfully explains how the clunky electronic scoreboard will be used:

The first question will be announced, spelt out on the scoreboard, you will give your reply from the lectern, and, once you have finished, Horst will read out the next question and so on. The only thing we would ask, Mr Ryder, is that at the end of each reply, you leave the lectern and come to the edge of the stage and bow ... thus provoking inevitable applause .... Then, just as each round of applause is dying, Horst's voice and the scoreboard will announce the next question, giving you ample time to return to the lectern.   (U 382)

The arrangement conjures up a whole techno-bureaucracy that has comedically taken over the otherwise familiar and straightforward convention of a celebrity Q&A. The pedantic bureaucracy, the cumbersomely elaborate and awkward procedure that is exhaustively detailed brings to mind the digressive elaboration of the permutations that permeate Beckett's writing, such as the scene of the sucking stones in *Molloy*, in which the protagonist sucks a series of sixteen pebbles with obsessive mathematical precision, moving each pebble from one pocket to the next, making sure each and every one is sucked in turn. Gary Adelman has detected in *The Unconsoled* the distinct presence of Beckett 'behind the emphasis on details of elaborate (as if choreographed) routines',[24] while Michael Wood has argued that Ryder's 'life is overwhelmed by irrelevance, buried under pointless but irresistible demands' that we quickly realize he is going to fail to fulfil.[25] Writing eloquently about the digressions, absurd particulars, and banal distractions by which Ryder is endlessly beset – beginning with Gustav's unnecessarily lengthy and comically tedious disquisition on the portering code of conduct at the start of the novel (U 5–9) – Wood argues that *The Unconsoled* finally opens up to the reader 'Ishiguro's deepest subject: ... the comedy and the pathos and the sorrow of the stories we tell ourselves to keep other stories away'.[26] The Q&A scoreboard might itself be seen as a faultily technological distraction from the finally empty promises of Ryder's supposedly salvational presence in the town.

But the scene, like many others in the novel, also reveals Ryder's central dilemma as a maestro – and just indeed as a human being: his lack of agency, his passivity and inability to take charge of his own affairs, to decide, to act, on his own behalf. Indeed, this is a man who can't even seem to control himself, if it comes to it. His emotions quickly shift from compliance or mild compassion to irritation and anxiety, and comments on his 'intense annoyance', 'rising' anger, and feelings of being affronted abound (U 243, 91). Ryder lacks self-determination and intention, and his drifting demeanour casts the very notion of agency into doubt. The novel's other central artist-figure, Brodsky, is similarly non-agential: an alcoholic and notably pig-headed, he is nevertheless at the mercy of Miss Collins, the lover he has lost, and of the other townspeople, who are busy plotting his fate.

As if in step with the narrative arc of German Expressionist film, we might say, *The Unconsoled* refuses notions of consolation or redemption, and therefore parts company with classical (or Aristotelian) narrative structure. Classical tragedy moves from an initial state of equilibrium to a period of conflict, which is ultimately resolved when a new, now altered state of equilibrium is established. Aristotelian or classic models of tragedy, in other words, are ultimately affirmative, redemptive, or consolatory. Critics such as Simon Critchley have argued that tragedy 'is not tragic enough' for the modern age, and this might explain the salient and highly successful dark humour of Ishiguro's novel, for comedy, the so-called low genre, is 'more tragic than tragedy', precisely because of its generic disposition not to add up to grand meanings.[27]

Ishiguro does in fact make explicit reference in *The Unconsoled* to the search for 'consolation' when Brodsky states of his desire to reunite with Miss Collins that '[s]he'll be like the music. A consolation. A wonderful consolation' (*U* 313). And yet neither Miss Collins nor the novel itself finally come up with what Ryder and the reader (near homophones, although not as near as writer/Ryder) ultimately seek.[28] In one respect, we might say that some of the disappointed early reviewers of the novel may be correct in their assessment of the novel's tone and tenor, since it lacks the intellectually and affectively consoling qualities that readers and reviewers so often expect. But in this, Ishiguro is drawing out and developing a salient feature of modernist literature: its frequent and often stern refusal to console.

One final instance from the tradition with which Ishiguro's novel engages might help to establish the point. The resistance to consolation is prominently staged in Beckett's post-Second World War novella, 'The Calmative' (1946), with its titular foregrounding of precisely this question. In 'The Calmative', the first-person narrator decides to 'tell myself a story, I'll try and tell myself another story, to try and calm myself'.[29] He recalls a childhood memory:

> [T]his evening it has to be as in the story my father used to read to me, evening after evening, when I was small, and he had all his health, to calm me, evening after evening, year after year it seems to me this evening, which I don't remember much about, except that it was the adventures of one Joe Breem, or Breen, the son of a lighthouse-keeper, a strong muscular lad of fifteen, those were the words, who swam for miles in the night, a knife between his teeth, after a shark, I forget why, out of sheer heroism. He might have simply told me the story, he knew it by heart, so did I, but that wouldn't have calmed me, he had to read it to me, evening after evening, or pretend to read it to me, turning the pages and explaining the pictures that were of me already, evening after evening the same pictures till I dozed off on his shoulder.[30]

Like Beckett's novella, *The Unconsoled* takes care to present only minor miseries and mishaps: there is no major tragedy to endow the works with a grander 'meaning' – or, indeed, with the grandeur of meaning. For while these texts can be said to be performative, shifting rapidly, in the mode of late modernism, between effects of anxiety and comedy while opening themselves up to local points of analysis, they stubbornly refuse the hermeneutic urge to make such instances, or such affects, add up. Brodsky's radical performance at the concert hall itself fails to console, because it is precisely these consolatory gestures that are withdrawn from the formally disruptive works of modernism.[31] Literary modernism refuses in its content, and even more explicitly in its form, to withhold or to mask contingency: it purposively abandons, not least through its digressive comedic mishaps, what Frank Kermode called 'the power of form to console'.[32] In this, Ishiguro's novel performs that most difficult of tasks: it successfully resists the major consolation of meaning-making, parting company with narrative as a calmative and leaving behind the affirmations of consolation and solace.

And yet, while the influence of modernist writers such as Beckett, Kafka, Proust, and Dostoevsky is marked and distinctive in *The Unconsoled*, Ishiguro also, in important ways, parts company with each and every one of these writers. His work does not resonate with the intense linguistic experimentation of Beckett's, although his brilliantly unsettling blending of blandness with a kind of jagged formal and conceptual resistance to the insipid, banal, or conventional in *The Unconsoled* certainly owes something to his predecessor's work. While it looms prominently in the background, Kafka's writing lacks the distinctive hilarity of indignity and fallibility that *The Unconsoled* unpacks in such lucid and sometimes such excruciating detail. Dostoevsky's work, in turn, lends the dark air of farce, anxiety, and even hysteria to Ishiguro's novel, but *The Unconsoled* does not share any part of the predilection for transcendental spiritualism that permeates Dostoevsky's major works. Finally, while Proust offers a narrative model for writing about memory, Ishiguro's work lacks the affirmative overtones of Proustian involuntary memory. Indeed, *The Unconsoled* offers the reader darker, more disconcerting recollections that often resemble a radical form of amnesia or cognitive dissonance rather than the consoling recognition of a remembered and re-lived past. Ishiguro's brilliant late modernism is very much his own. While the author acknowledges his indebtedness to his great modernist predecessors, he also adds a distinctively stylized work to the modernist canon, rejigging it jaggedly into new and unsettling shapes, and in the process making us see the work of his modernist forebears in a new, now reconfigured and reimagined light.

Notes

1 Henri Bergson, *Laughter: An Essay on the Meaning of the Comic* (New York: Macmillan, 1921), p.10.
2 'Messiah figure' is Ishiguro's term for Ryder in the 1995 interview conducted by Maya Jaggi (*CKI* 115).
3 Wai-chew Sim, *Kazuo Ishiguro* (London: Routledge, 2010), p.56.
4 Samuel Beckett, *Molloy*, ed. Shane Weller (London: Faber, 2009), p.86.
5 Cynthia Wong, *Kazuo Ishiguro* (Liverpool: Liverpool University Press, 2004), p.73.
6 Compare Barry Lewis, *Kazuo Ishiguro* (Manchester: Manchester University Press, 2000), p.115.
7 'Unconsoled' is a past participle that functions as an adjective, which in turn becomes a noun by acquiring a definite article.
8 Samuel Beckett, *Company, Ill Seen Ill Said, Worstward Ho, Stirrings Still*, ed. Dirk Van Hulle (London: Faber, 2009), pp.18–19.
9 Franz Kafka, *The Metamorphosis and Other Stories*, ed. Joyce Crick (Oxford: Oxford University Press, 2009), p.29.
10 Simon Critchley, *On Humour* (London: Routledge, 2002), p.36.
11 Bergson, *Laughter*, pp.3–4.
12 See Tim Jarvis, '"Into Ever Stranger Territories": Kazuo Ishiguro's *The Unconsoled* and Minor Literature', in Sebastian Groes and Barry Lewis, eds., *Kazuo Ishiguro: New Critical Visions of the Novels* (Basingstoke: Palgrave Macmillan, 2011), p.158.
13 Kazuo Ishiguro, '*Spiegel* Interview with Kazuo Ishiguro: "I Remain Fascinated by Memory"', *Spiegel International*, 5 October 2005: n.p. (accessed online at www.spiegel.de/international/spiegel-interview-with-kazuo-ishiguro-i-remain-fascinated-by-memory-a-378173.html). See also *CKI* 58 for Ishiguro's comment on finding locations for his novels in 'the way that a film director might search for locations, for a script he has already written'.
14 James Wood, 'The Uses of Oblivion: Kazuo Ishiguro's *The Buried Giant*', *The New Yorker*, 16 March 2015.
15 Dylan Otto Krider, 'Rooted in a Small Place: An Interview with Kazuo Ishiguro', *Kenyon Review* 20:2 (1998): 146–54 (151); Susannah Hunnewell, 'Kazuo Ishiguro, The Art of Fiction No. 196', *The Paris Review* 184 (2008): n.p. (accessed online at www.theparisreview.org/interviews/5829/the-art-of-fiction-no-196-kazuo-ishiguro).
16 Richard Robinson, 'Nowhere, in Particular: Kazuo Ishiguro's *The Unconsoled* and Central Europe', *Critical Quarterly* 48:4 (2007): 156–78 (120).
17 This mood of anxiety, irritation, and disorientation embodied in the circular narrative logic of the novel, brings to mind Ishiguro's original, although subsequently much altered and revised script for *The Saddest Music in the World* (2003), further testifying to an interest he shares with other modernist writers in German Expressionist film.
18 Richard Robinson, '"To Give a Name, Is That Still to Give?" Footballers and Film Actors in *The Unconsoled*', in Sean Matthews and Sebastian Groes, eds., *Kazuo Ishiguro: Contemporary Critical Perspectives* (London: Continuum, 2009), p.70.

19 Tim Armstrong, 'Modernism and Music', in Ulrika Maude and Mark Nixon, eds., *The Bloomsbury Companion to Modernist Literature* (London: Bloomsbury Academic, 2018), p.120.

20 James Wood, 'Kazuo Ishiguro's (Mostly) Brilliant Blandness, *The Harvard Gazette*, 5 October 2017 (accessed online at https://news.harvard.edu/gazette/story/2017/10/harvards-james-wood-on-nobel-prize-for-kazuo-ishiguro/).

21 Wong, *Kazuo Ishiguro*, p.68.

22 Wood, 'Kazuo Ishiguro's (Mostly) Brilliant Blandness'.

23 Ibid.

24 Beckett, *Molloy*, pp.69–74; Gary Adelman, 'Doubles on the Rocks: Ishiguro's *The Unconsoled*', *Critique* 42:2 (2001): 166–79 (169).

25 Michael Wood, *Children of Silence: On Contemporary Fiction* (New York: Columbia University Press, 1998), p.176.

26 Ibid., p.177.

27 Simon Critchley, *Infinitely Demanding: Ethics of Commitment, Politics of Resistance* (London: Verso, 2012), p.79. See also Simon Critchley, *Very Little ... Almost Nothing: Death, Philosophy, Literature* (London: Routledge, 1997), pp.141–80.

28 See Natalie Reitano, 'The Good Wound: Memory and Community in *The Unconsoled*', *Texas Studies in Literature and Language* 49:4 (2007): 361–86 (382, n.22).

29 Beckett, *The Expelled, The Calmative, The End with First Love*, ed. Christopher Ricks (London: Faber, 2009), p.19.

30 Ibid., p.21.

31 For a monograph-length study on the topic, see Paul Sheehan, *Modernism, Narrative and Humanism* (Cambridge: Cambridge University Press, 2002).

32 Frank Kermode, *The Sense of an Ending: Studies in the Theory of Fiction* (New York: Oxford University Press, 1967), p.151.

8

PETER BOXALL

'A More Sophisticated Imitation'

Ishiguro and the Novel

There is a moment in Kazuo Ishiguro's 2021 novel *Klara and the Sun* that offers itself as a prism through which to read Ishiguro's long conversation with the novel form.

The moment comes in a scene, three quarters of the way through the novel, in which the protagonist and first-person narrator Klara makes a critical discovery about the nature of artistic representations. This discovery is intimately related to the various forms of artificial life with which the novel is centrally concerned. Klara is an automaton whose sole purpose in life is to act as an 'Artificial Friend' (or AF) to her owner, a teenaged girl named Josie. But if Klara is the most obviously artificial persona in this novel, she is part of an environment that has become more generally artificial, manufactured, and simulacral. Children need AFs in the world of the novel – an oddly skewed version of a North American suburb – because life has become so technologically mediated that there are few places left in which young people might socialize with each other, and so make real friends. Children do not go to school, but are educated at home on their mobile devices (in a somewhat eerie enactment of homeschooling during the 2020 pandemic). Their education and their social life are empty, a tinny replica of shared life, and the children themselves are biologically engineered, made in the laboratory. Wealthier families subject their children to a form of genetic enhancement known as 'lifting', which makes the enhanced students more readily able to learn the lessons given to them by their avatar professors. The genetically modified children learn in artificial educational environments from simulacral educators, and it is the job of AFs like Klara to assuage the loneliness and isolation that such radically alienating social engineering produces.

This biomedical adaptation of children like Josie to the artificial environment of the novel – reminiscent, of course, of Ishiguro's earlier novel *Never Let Me Go* – comes at a great cost. Being 'lifted', we learn, does not only render these children strangely evacuated and out of focus, but it is also dangerous. Josie had an older sister, named Sal, who died of the procedure.

Josie herself, from the beginning of the novel, is seriously and possibly terminally ill, also as a side effect of the lifting process. Josie is so weak that she is more or less housebound, but despite her illness she makes regular trips to the nearby city, where she visits the studio of a local artist named 'Mr Capaldi' in order to sit for a 'portrait'. There is something fishy both about this portrait, we are led to suspect, and about the portraitist, something obscurely connected to Josie's illness, and to her artificiality. Josie's boyfriend Rick (the only 'unlifted' child we meet) is suspicious of him. 'This guy,' Rick says, 'this artist person. Everything you say about him sounds, well, *creepy*' (KS 121). 'All he seems to do', he says, 'is take photos up close. This piece of you, that piece of you. Is that really what artists do?' (121). Josie's housekeeper Melania – a tough-talking immigrant worker of unspecified ethnicity – also expresses her distrust, perhaps more plainly. 'That Mr Capaldi', she says, is 'one creep son bitch.' Klara, confused by Melania's virulence, replies 'but housekeeper, isn't Mr Capaldi just wishing to paint Josie's portrait?', and Melania only intensifies her hostility: 'Paint portrait fuck. AF, you watch close Mr Son Bitch or something bad happen Miss Josie' (177).

It is when Klara and Josie, and Josie's mother and father, pay a visit to Mr Capaldi in his studio that the moment I am interested in here arrives. Klara's mother and Josie say to Mr Capaldi that they want to see the portrait he has made of her. 'It's kind of scary,' Josie says, 'but I'd like to take a peek.' Mr Capaldi, though, is a little reluctant. 'You must understand,' he says, 'it's still a work in progress. And it's not easy for a layperson to understand the way these things slowly take shape' (KS 196). Josie is forbidden to look at the portrait, but Klara, with Melania's emphatic instructions in her mind, breaks into the studio, to see it for herself:

> I turned the corner of the L and saw Josie there, suspended in the air. She wasn't very high – her feet were at the height of my shoulders – but because she was leaning forward, arms outstretched, fingers spread, she seemed to be frozen in the act of falling. Little beams illuminated her from various angles, forbidding her any refuge. (204)

The 'portrait' of Josie, we realize at this moment, isn't a portrait at all. Klara had already intuited this, she says to Mr Capaldi and to Josie's mother. 'I'd suspected for some time', she says, 'that Mr Capaldi's portrait wasn't a picture or a sculpture, but an AF' (207) – an automaton like Klara herself. Through all of Josie's trips to sit for Mr Capaldi, as he photographed the various disaggregated 'pieces' of her, Mr Capaldi had not been making a *representation*, but rather a new version of her, one that might take her place when she herself dies, a victim of her own genetic artificiality. As Mr Capaldi says, 'What you have to understand is this. The new Josie won't be an imitation. She *really will be Josie*. A *Continuation* of Josie' (208). Mr Capaldi has made a new automaton body to replace Josie's when she dies; and he explains that Klara too is part of the portrait that he is making, that Klara's own true purpose is to act as a replacement, a continuation, of Josie's mind, of her personality. 'That Josie you saw up there', Mr Capaldi says to Klara, 'is empty.' Klara must 'inhabit' her. 'We want you to inhabit that Josie up there with everything you've learned' (209). 'You're not being required simply to mimic Josie's outward behaviour. You're being asked to continue her' (210). 'The second Josie won't be a copy', Mr Capaldi says to Josie's mother. There's 'nothing inside Josie that's beyond the Klaras of this world to continue' (210). 'She'll be the exact same and you'll have every right to love her just as you love Josie now' (210).

This moment is the crux around which Ishiguro's novel turns, a moment that one can only begin to address by placing it in dialogue not only with Ishiguro's wider *oeuvre* but with the longer history of the novel form. Rebecca Walkowitz, in a seminal essay on Ishiguro published in 2001, before either *Klara and the Sun* or *Never Let Me Go* were written, might have been addressing this moment, *avant la lettre*, when she says that Ishiguro's novels 'register this dialectic, between the narratives that generate identities and the narratives that describe them'.[1] How, Ishiguro asks, are we to find or guard the line, in a fictional world, between an act of imitation and an act of creation – that is, between mimesis and prosthesis, between representing a missing thing, and being the thing that is missing? When Klara says, in her first-person narrative voice, that 'I saw Josie there, suspended in the air', how are we to read the referring power of the proper name 'Josie'? Do we sustain a difference, within the name itself, between the living child Josie and the prosthetic replacement of Josie that Mr Capaldi has made? I saw Josie there, Klara says, and we hear her saying that the doll Josie she saw was so like the real Josie, such a 'sophisticated imitation' of her, that it felt as if she was looking at Josie herself. Or do we hear, in that single name being used to refer at once to Josie and this imitation of her, this replacement, this *continuation*, the suggestion that there is no difference between the real Josie and the artificial Josie, that 'Josie' is artifice, is fiction, pure and simple, and so the distinctions between first-order and second-order versions of her collapse at the moment that her status as fiction, as an *effect* of fiction, is revealed?

Ishiguro asks this question at this moment in *Klara and the Sun*, and in asking it he poses a question about the nature and history of the novel form – a form he has always worked with in a highly self-conscious fashion, so that one never forgets, when reading Ishiguro, that he is working in the wake of a

crowded host of ancestors. Ishiguro's fiction is always haunted in this way –
he mobilizes multiple literary and national traditions with every stroke of his
pen – but this episode of the portrait is perhaps unusually rich in associations, unusually powerful in its evocation of the imaginative apparatus of
prose fiction itself. To place a character in a fiction in front of their represented likeness in order to ask whether the original or the copy has ontological primacy; this is to mobilize a tradition of fictional portraits that
reaches back through the history of the novel. It is to employ a device that
knows it is a device, and that knows that it is a device that has been
employed, at every key moment in the history of fictional representation,
to anatomize the texture and mimetic potency of the device itself. As Klara
stands in front of the portrait of Josie – as these different forms of artificial
life confront one another under the technological and political conditions
that determine representation in *Klara and the Sun* – we can feel Ishiguro
weighing the balance, in 2021, between prosthesis and mimesis, pressing at
the ways in which the technological, political, and material production of the
real is related to our capacity for crafting representations. And as we feel
Ishiguro approaching this difficult, shifting ground, we can see, ranged
behind this meeting between the portrait and its subject, earlier stagings of
this encounter, each of which speaks in its own terms of the relation between
the prosthetic and the mimetic, between life and the representation of life.

Take, for example, the centrality of the painted portrait to Thomas
Pynchon's 1965 novel *The Crying of Lot 49*. This work sits at a junction in
the history of prose fiction in part because it articulates the growing revolutionary power of the aesthetic representation to overcome that which is
represented. The novel's protagonist Oedipa Maas feels herself to be ensnared
in a series of interlocking representations that have no reality underpinning
them – to be trapped, as she sees it, in a simulacral tower – and the vertiginous
sense that Pynchon's novel is partaking itself of this representational ground-
lessness is concentrated in a moment at which Oedipa stands in front of a
painting that depicts other women, other Rapunzels, similarly trapped in their
own towers. The painting, *Embroidering Earth's Mantle* by Remedios Varo,
depicts a 'number of frail girls' locked in a tower, embroidering a tapestry that
spills out of its frame, so that 'all the waves, ships and forests of the earth were
contained in this tapestry, and the tapestry was the world'.[2] The imagined
portrait here bears the weight of an epistemological revolution – the revolution that came to be known as postmodernism – that tends to invert the
relationship between original and copy, between fiction and the real. To read
Ishiguro's portrait against Pynchon's (and Varo's) is to approach the balance
between the material and the informational, as this has shifted in the passage
from the later twentieth to the early twenty-first century, and from the

postmodern moment to whatever has come to replace it. And then behind Pynchon's portrait, we can see other portraits reaching back, to modernism, and then before that to nineteenth-century realism, and before that to the earliest manifestations of the modern novel form.

Take the moment in Edith Wharton's *The House of Mirth* (1905), when Wharton's protagonist Lily Bart feels herself to be a continuation of Joshua Reynolds's portrait of Mrs Lloyd. This scene follows closely the contours of the meeting between Josie and her portrait in *Klara and the Sun*, but in Wharton the meeting is given its epistemological weight by the tension, at the turn of the twentieth century, between a realist and a modernist world view. In Wharton's novel Lily Bart manifests her affinity with the Reynolds portrait, quite literally, when she poses as Mrs Lloyd during an evening of *tableaux vivants* – becoming a living picture, just as Josie's portrait is a living picture of Josie. 'She had shown her artistic intelligence', Wharton's narrator says of Lily's performance, 'in selecting a type so like her own that she could embody the person represented without ceasing to be herself. It was as though she had stepped, not out of, but into, Reynolds's canvas, banishing the phantom of his dead beauty by the beams of her living grace.'[3]

Lily is not an imitation of Mrs Lloyd, any more than Mrs Lloyd is an imitation of Lily. As Lily stands static on the stage, allowing her body to assume the posed attitude of Mrs Lloyd, the two are *continuations* of each other, sharing their being with each other, as Josie shares her being with her prosthetic twin. It is in becoming Mrs Lloyd, Lily's pseudo-lover Lawrence Selden thinks, that she becomes 'the real Lily Bart', 'the Lily we know'.[4] Lily's reality is enhanced, for Selden, by this intimately shared relation between being and representation; but in Wharton this struggle between life and artifice does not quite lead to the overcoming we see in Pynchon, but stages rather a fraught struggle between a modernist aestheticism and a real that it cannot fully either accommodate or eject. Wharton's modernism is materialized in this politically weighted encounter between a fictional character and a painted portrait; and one can see that this moment is itself staged as a corrective to or conversation with earlier such encounters. It is impossible not to see in Lily's affinity with Mrs Lloyd an after-image of Oscar Wilde's living picture in *The Picture of Dorian Gray* (1891). Dorian's portrait has what Wilde's narrator calls a 'strange affinity' with the life that it represents and substitutes, but Wilde imagines this affinity not as incipient modernism but rather as a late Gothicism, in which the spectacle of the living painting is altogether more ghoulish.[5] The eeriness of the bond between the portrait and its subject, that one can feel in Ishiguro and in Wharton, is given full rein in Wilde (and in a mass of nineteenth-century gothic works by Bram Stoker, Sheridan Lefanu, E. T. A. Hoffman, Edgar Allen Poe and others).

And it runs, too, throughout the realist tradition, where the capacities of the novel to depict life truly are insistently shadowed by a fascination with the painted portrait, its particular fidelities and duplicities. Think, for example, of the central episode of the portrait, earlier in the nineteenth century, in Jane Austen's *Emma* (1815). Emma adopts an artificial friend (an early version, perhaps, of Ishiguro's Klara) in the form of the cheerful Hartfield resident Harriet Smith. Emma has no real feeling for Harriet, the narrator suggests, and the manufactured friendship is a sign of Emma's faulty and partial understanding both of people around her and of herself. This gulf, between the novel's world and that world as Emma sees it, is given its most condensed form in the portrait that Emma decides to paint of Harriet, with the intention of dazzling the local vicar, Mr Elton, with Harriet's beauty. The delicious comedy of this episode turns around the fact that Harriet, focalized through Emma's own skewed forms of perception, is already an artificial figure, and so Emma's amateur and deliberately mistaken likeness of Harriet is not so much a bad portrait as it is another version of Harriet, a *continuation* of the ways in which the novel sees her (or fails to see her). Each of the central characters expresses a view on Emma's artistry, and in eliciting these critiques the portrait serves as an index of the novel's reality effect, a means of testing how ways of seeing, ways of representing, relate to a notional real Harriet, lying somewhere beyond the limits of the text. Emma's doting valetudinarian father Mr Woodhouse fails to understand that the painted Harriet is not susceptible to the common cold: 'The only thing I do not thoroughly like is, that she seems to be sitting out of doors, with only a little shawl over her shoulders.'[6] The schoolmasterly Mr Knightley simply refers Emma to the errors in her portrait: 'You have made her too tall, Emma'.[7] Mrs Weston sees the gap between Harriet and Emma's flattering portrait, but her love for Emma leads her, in Procrustean fashion, to blame the subject for failing to conform to the portrait, rather than the other way around. 'Miss Woodhouse has given her friend the only beauty she wanted', she says. 'The expression of the eye is most correct, but Miss Smith has not those eyebrows and eye-lashes. It is the fault of her face that she has them not'.[8] Mr Elton, of course, artificially in love with the painter of the portrait rather than its subject, is overflowing with feigned admiration for the picture: 'It appears to me a most perfect resemblance in every feature. I never saw such a likeness in my life …. Oh it is most admirable! I can't keep my eyes from it. I never saw such a likeness.'[9]

When Ishiguro imagines Klara standing in front of Mr Capaldi's prosthetic version of Josie – the artificial friend, the pasteboard puppet – he activates this novelistic tradition of portraiture, this long and variegated examination of the ways in which representations – likenesses – diverge from and unite with the people and things they represent. One can feel, at work in this triangular encounter between Josie, Klara, and Mr Capaldi's 'imitation' of Josie, a history of the novel's struggle to make of represented forms a new kind of reality. As Ishiguro asks how far contemporary forms of artificial life can replace or stand in for human life we can see behind this question the forms invented by Pynchon, by Wharton, by Wilde, by Austen – fictional forms that are a record of the material historical forces that determine both how our representations imitate the world, and how they serve to create it. In *Klara and the Sun*, and throughout his work, it is one of Ishiguro's singular gifts to create this effect, this sense that a given act of imagination comes about in a layered relation with the other imaginative acts that inform it, that enable it, that constrain it. From the early 'Japanese' works *A Pale View of Hills* and *An Artist of the Floating World*, through his intricate study of Englishness in *The Remains of the Day* and the dislocated dreamwork of *The Unconsoled*, to his skewed science fictions *Never Let Me Go* and *Klara and the Sun*, Ishiguro has worked this strange magic, this capacity at once to imagine, and to reveal the hidden historical determinants of the imagination, its richly embedded conditions of possibility.

Ishiguro's work is always attentive, in this way, to the history of form, always conscious of the histories and traditions that attend every act of imagination; and the most recurrent means by which he explores and articulates these histories is through his fictional recreation of the work of art itself. As *Klara and the Sun* is centrally interested in the capacity of the portrait both to represent and to create life, so his work more generally sets out to anatomize the machinery of the work of art, and to examine how the precise mechanics of aesthetic representation relate to the political and historical realities that the artwork witnesses. In the early 'Japanese' novel *An Artist of the Floating World*, for example, this exploration is conducted in relation to painting, and particularly in relation to the ways in which a painted canvas is bound up with the world that the canvas represents. The novel concerns the artist, Masuji Ono, whose paintings, it is suggested, served a propagandist function in the build-up to the Second World War. Ono is retired as the narrative begins in October 1948, and he spends the novel looking back on his career as an artist, and on the disastrous consequences of Japan's military intervention in the war (including the death of Ono's own son, who served as a combatant). As in so much of Ishiguro's fiction, Ono's reflections on the war, on his family, on his painting, are conducted through a kind of thick filter, an emotional stuntedness and a distorted perspective that makes it difficult to see clearly the world on which Ono reflects, and so to make accurate judgements about it. But the task and pleasure of reading the novel is to see through Ono's confusions and blindnesses, to understand what kind of reckoning he is trying to make – with his early political investment in Japanese nationalism, his estranged relation with his authoritarian father, and his own weaknesses and failures as a father to his dead son and living daughters. And at the heart of this reckoning is Ono's attempt to understand how his painting contributed to Japan's entry into the war. He painted a work named 'Eyes to the Horizon' in the thirties, he remembers, which featured a soldier who 'held out his sword, pointing the way west towards Asia', under the slogan 'Japan must go forward' (*AFW* 169). He fears that this painting, and others that he made in the thirties, had a material influence on the course of Japanese history, and the pathos of the novel is bound up with his slow and partial attempt to take responsibility for that influence, and to come to terms with his errors of political and aesthetic judgement. But what is so peculiar and haunting about Ono's reflection on his role in the escalation of Japanese militarism is that it cannot float free from his own inability to separate the aesthetic components of his artwork from the political ones. The novel's particular, enveloping sadness arises in large part from Ono's failure to measure or judge the relation between brute political reality and the intricacies of his work as an artist. His regret is not the regret of a propagandist – who necessarily paints in broad brush strokes – but of an artist still convinced that real material change might be brought about by his old teacher's determination to 'change fundamentally the identity of painting as practised in our city' (144), or to 'bring European influence into the Utamaro tradition' (202). It is hard for Ono to understand his failings as an artist, as a citizen, as a father, when he can't focus the relation between the artwork and the realities it reflects – when, as he himself puts it, he is prone to make 'a naïve mistake about what art can and cannot do' (172).

An Artist of the Floating World is centrally concerned with this question, with how to calibrate what it is that art does, how art relates to forces that are larger than it and beyond its control. In the Japanese novels, it is painting that is the focus of this question, and then as Ishiguro's work develops he expands to explore other artworks and other genres as they engage with the political contexts that determine them. In his 1995 novel *The Unconsoled* – perhaps the most sustained and powerful analysis of the political purchase of the artwork that he has made – the medium is not painting but music. The protagonist, Ryder, is a world-famous pianist, who has arrived in an unnamed Middle European city to give a recital that for opaque reasons is of crucial importance to the entire community. From the beginning, the narrative suffers that same miscalibration, that same derangement of scale, that we find in *An Artist of the Floating World*, but here it is much more extreme, as the fabric and texture of the fictional world becomes immeasurably more fissile, warped, subject to dreamlike transformations and incongruences.

The city itself is both entirely unknown to Ryder and some half-forgotten version of his childhood home; the people he encounters are both strangers and intimate friends. Two strangers he meets, a woman named Sophie and her child Boris, are his lover and his adopted son, even though they never cease, at the same time, to be strangers. The city swirls around Ryder in this confused amalgam of the familiar and the strange, and at the heart of the confusion, of the drastic lack of proper focus, is the question of Ryder's role as a musician, and the purpose that his upcoming recital should serve. Ono's teacher wants to 'change fundamentally the identity of painting as practised in our city'; Ryder's visit to the city of *The Unconsoled* is bound up with some obscure responsibility that he has to cure all of the community's ills – to heal a sickness that has infected the souls of the inhabitants – by bringing about some change to the identity of music as practised in *his* city. The leaders of the community, wildly improbably, are concerned not with parking restrictions or refuse collection or local taxation levels, but with the obscurer intricacies of contemporary musicology. The health or sickness of the community rests on the correct interpretation of the difficult music written by the novel's imaginary musical avant-garde – fictional composers such as 'Kazan', or 'Mullery'. The disgraced conductor and former head of the community Mr Christoff complains to Ryder that it is difficult to achieve progressive political change in the community, to bring the ailing city back to some semblance of order, when the musical literacy of the inhabitants has been allowed to fall so low. 'But the modern forms!', Christoff says, they're too difficult, too demanding for the person in the street to master. 'How can people like this, untrained, provincial people, how can they ever understand such things, however great a sense of duty they feel towards the community' (*U* 186). The confusion that attends Ryder's relation to his environment, that estranges him from his family and from himself, is part of some wider malaise, it is suggested, some failure of scale and relation that it is Ryder's task to correct, through his mere talent as a musician. He will take to the stage at the climax of his visit to the city, it is suggested. He will give a perfect rendition of one of the more demanding pieces by Kazan or Mullery, and the community will be magically healed, brought back to clarity, reality, legibility, by the sheer beauty of his 'crushed cadence', or his 'vented rest'.

Ishiguro's test of the function and purpose of art is almost always conducted through this failure of scale, this misreading or warping of the relation between art and reality. Music takes on an exaggerated or misconceived importance in *The Unconsoled*, as painting does in *An Artist of the Floating World*. The clones in *Never Let Me Go* have to demonstrate their capacity to 'be creative' in order to prove that they have souls, as the portrait in *Klara and the Sun* is required not to represent its subject but to become it

(*NLMG* 26). But if this is the case, perhaps the most singular characteristic of Ishiguro's work is that such misreadings do not produce a malfunction of the artwork itself – or do not *only* produce such a malfunction – but rather open onto an encounter with its very conditions of possibility. Ishiguro's fiction binds itself to other art forms in ways that distort and dismantle those forms, but he does so, always, in order to approach the difficult, vanishing space that underlies form itself, the space from which the possibility of the artwork arises, and into which it always threatens to disappear. In *The Unconsoled*, for example, the dreamlike ductility of the novel's architecture makes it feel always as if the scenery is about to come down, as if the reality effect is on the point of collapsing. The environment of this novel – modelled as it is with great intimacy on the dreamscapes of Kafka's fiction – feels too fitful, too prone to reversals and contradictions, to be sustainable. The landscape, furniture, and atmosphere of the novel is drawn directly from *The Trial* or *The Castle*, so directly that one never loses the feeling that we are inhabiting the inside of a Kafkan fiction. Ryder will have long conversations with community leaders in the darkened space of a cinema, while other patrons sit around playing cards; or doors will open that suddenly connect spaces that should be remote from one another; or strangers will turn out to be Ryder's old friends from school; and at every moment we know that we are in the fragmented, disarticulated space of a dream, and more precisely the dream as it is imagined in the world of Kafka's novels. Ishiguro casts us, with no guide, into this dismantled terrain, and does so, it seems, precisely in order to push the reality effect to breaking point, in order to take the narrative past the point at which it has any cohesion or integrity. Even the machinery of narrative perspective, the apparatus that situates and focalizes the narrative voice, is too dismantled, too dreamlike, too Kafkan, to sustain a coherent imagined world, to embed Ryder in his relation to himself and to others. Early in the novel, for example, Ryder drives a character named Stephan to a meeting with another character named Miss Collins. Ryder stays in the car, while he watches Stephan walk to the entrance of Miss Collins's house and press the doorbell. 'The door was opened by an elderly, silver haired woman' – Miss Collins herself. 'The door closed behind him', Ryder says, 'but by leaning right back in my seat I found I could still see the two of them clearly illuminated in the narrow pane to the side of the front door' (*U* 56). Ryder can still see Stephan and Miss Collins even though they are in the house; and when they start speaking, Ryder can somehow hear what it is that they are saying, through some strange and impossible narrative telepathy. And then, as they walk together further into the house, Ryder can follow them still, from his position in the car, his gaze effortlessly telescoping out, sliding beyond itself into the interior of the building:

'I watched her lead Stephan through a small and tidy front parlour, through a second doorway and down a shadowy corridor decorated on either side with little framed water colours. The corridor ended at Miss Collins's drawing room – a large L-shaped affair at the back of the building' (56–57).

Such disruptions in the narrative architecture of the novel should have the effect, as I say, of bringing the building of the narrative crashing down, reducing it to a pile of rubble. But it is the particular magic of Ishiguro's work, both in *The Unconsoled* and throughout his *oeuvre*, that it does not, that the distances, the failures of communication and relational orthodoxy that recur in all of his fictions, lead not to narrative malfunction, but to some contact with the substance of prose fiction itself, the space that the narrator of *The Unconsoled* shares so closely with Kafka's narrative voices. When Ryder's voice seems to float free from the bounds of his being – when he finds that he cannot focus or understand his relations with his son, or his lover, or his beloved parents who he believes are on their way to the city, even now, to watch him perform – this does not lead to a loss of narrative investment in those relations, but instead to a singular access to the foundational possibility of narrative relation at all, to the imagined grounds upon which such relations are built. It is this access that generates Ishiguro's pathos, his peculiarly intense uncovering of the terms in which we long for and relate to others. We never get to meet Ryder's parents, as we never fully understand the nature of Ryder's relation with Boris; but this dislocation does not prevent the narrative from producing an extraordinarily powerful sense of the keening loss that a father feels for a son with whom he cannot communicate, or the loss that a son feels for parents who are dead or otherwise out of reach. Ryder starts to realize, towards the end of the novel, that his parents are not going to attend his performance after all, that they are not going to watch him play or witness his talent, as he so longs for them to do. 'I was sure, this time, at last, that they would come', Ryder says. 'Surely it wasn't unreasonable of me to assume that they would come this time' (*U* 512). As he understands that they are not coming, that they will never come, he says, 'I collapsed into a nearby chair and realised I had started to sob' (512). This sobbing – like the overwhelming sadness that namelessly engulfs him as he stands before Boris, the simulacrum of a son, and knows that he can't reach him, can't feel for him, can't console him – this grief never finds a place within him, within an achieved narrative persona. He 'realised' he had started to sob, as if it were someone else doing the sobbing, not him. Not him. But it is the discovery of *The Unconsoled* that these emotive ties are not bound to subject positions, and do not require a reality effect to generate them, but are at work in the process of imagining itself, are there already in the undifferentiated stem cells of fictional life.

This access to the unmade ground of fiction, the place from which narrative being emerges, is Ishiguro's particular gift as a novelist, and it determines too his conversation with the novel as a form, the conversation I have been tracing here. When Ishiguro reanimates Kafka in *The Unconsoled*, or when he summons the ghost of fictional portraits past in *Klara and the Sun*, he draws our attention to the ways in which the novel form, over the course of its history, has negotiated the shifting terms of our relations to ourselves and to others. Ishiguro's conversation with Kafka in *The Unconsoled* is shaped by the material historical forces that bear differently, on Kafka and on Ishiguro, as both reach for an articulation of the narrative forces that bind us to the world. Similarly, *Klara and the Sun* enjoins us to reflect on how the relation between representation and life figures differently in the various portraits that it calls to thought, in Austen, in Wilde or Wharton or Pynchon. Both the evolving history of prose fiction, and the shifting political and technological conditions for the production and reproduction of life, are given a form of articulation in the dialogue that Ishiguro stages between Klara's artificiality and the artificiality at work in Wharton's Lily Bart, or Austen's Emma. But even as Ishiguro conducts this examination of the evolving historical conditions that determine our access to our artificial extensions, he opens this strange channel to the underworld of the novel itself, the space shared by Ryder and K, by Klara and Emma. Ryder remains at a distance from himself in *The Unconsoled*, just as Ono in *An Artist of the Floating World* cannot build a bridge between his post-war and his pre-war view of the world. For both Ryder and Ono their art – their music, their painting – is a mark of that estrangement. Music in *The Unconsoled* contains a fugitive form of life within it that cannot come to expression or taxonomy. Beneath the 'outer structure' of Ishiguro's music, Ryder says, there are 'peculiar life-forms hiding just under the shell' (*U* 492). These are the unspeciated life forms, the estranged 'imaginary animals' that are drawn by the clones of *Never Let Me Go* in order to prove to their creators that they have souls (*NLMG* 176). But if the imagined artwork in Ishiguro's fiction gives expression to this kind of alienation, this refusal of speciation, it also preserves, even in its dismantlement, an underlying logic of attachment, a particular bond between being and representation that is the common inheritance of the novel form.

It is at a climactic moment in *Klara and the Sun* that we can see this logic of attachment most clearly. As so often in Ishiguro's fiction, this is a climax that happens out of time, that happens too early, and in the wrong place. Josie's mother has planned to take Klara and Josie on an outing to see a nearby waterfall, but on the morning of the trip, 'the mother' (as Klara calls her) decides, tyrannically and cruelly, that Josie is too ill to leave the house, that she must be confined to her sickbed. In another twist of the cruel knife, the mother insists that she and Klara should take the trip regardless, as if Klara has already taken Josie's place, already become the mother's daughter. When the two arrive at the waterfall, as they are sitting together at a picnic table, the mother begins properly to explore this possibility for the first time, to ask herself if Klara might really be able to act as a prosthetic replacement of her daughter – as a *continuation* of her daughter. 'Okay, Klara', she says. 'Since Josie isn't here, I want *you* to be Josie' (*KS* 103). In one of the uncanniest moments in all of Ishiguro's fiction, Klara says that she will try, try to walk like her, talk like her, to 'give a more sophisticated imitation' of her (103). If Josie were sitting here instead of Klara, the mother says, 'how would she sit? I don't think she'd sit the way you're sitting.' No, Klara replies, 'Josie would be more ... like this.' 'That's good', the mother says. 'That's very good':

> 'But now I want you to move. Do something. Don't stop being Josie. Let me see you move a little.'

> I smiled in the way Josie would, settling into a slouching, informal posture.
> 'That's good. Now say something. Let me hear you speak.'
> 'I'm sorry. I'm not sure...'
> 'No. That's Klara. I want Josie.'
> 'Hi, Mom. Josie here.'
> 'Good. More. Come on.'
> 'Hi, Mom. Nothing to worry about, right? I got here and I'm fine.' (104)

This is a moment of intense proximity to what the novel does, to how it works, to its imitation of being that is also a continuation of being. Josie's mother, leaning forward – rapt and revealed, Klara thinks, so she 'can see the cheekbones of her face very pronounced beneath her skin' – exhibits a kind of dismantled grief that is Ishiguro's signature effect. This is the grief that Ryder feels, as he realizes he is sobbing for his dead parents, the grief that Ono feels for his son killed in the war. This is the grief of a mother for her dead daughter, Sal, and for her daughter, Josie, who is in the process of dying. In all its uncanny power, it is a wadded grief, wreathed about in artificiality, seen through the dark window of a mother's brutal willingness to replace the person she most longs to hold to her, to never let go. Ishiguro's novel gives us this artificiality in the most naked imaginable terms, an artificiality revealed not only at the level of the plot, but in the syntax, in the tinny affectlessness of the language. But, magically, almost miraculously, the artificiality opens onto something unguardedly, edgelessly real. 'Hi, Mom. Josie here.' This is Josie talking, insofar as Josie has ever talked. This is a voice back from the dead, back from the condition of never having been. This is a more sophisticated imitation, more sophisticated than any imitation has the right or the power to be, because it is not an imitation at all. There is no join, no seam, between Klara speaking and Josie speaking. As the mother leans forward, the mother who can't express her grief, who can't distinguish between the dead daughter and the living, who can't console Josie for the loss of her sister or for the loss of her own health; as the mother leans forward and speaks to Klara, she is speaking to Josie. She is not speaking to someone like Josie, or to an imitation of Josie, but to Josie. 'I'm sorry Josie', she says. 'I'm sorry I didn't bring you here today' (*KS* 105). The central questions that Ishiguro's novel asks – can Klara save Josie? can artificial forms save life rather than replace it or imitate it? – are answered here, too early and too late, as the novel voice speaks at once for Josie and Klara, for both the artificial and the real, the living and the non-living. The beauty of this moment is that Josie's mother is able to make the apology, the act of loving contrition for their distance and unreality that so many of Ishiguro's parents and lovers and children long to make. Its sadness lies in the fact that, in receiving that apology, in hearing and accepting it as she does, Josie can only conform to the artificiality for which it seeks to atone, can only demonstrate that none of us are quite at home in ourselves, or in each other.

It is at this moment, this moment when Ishiguro's embrace of artificiality touches most closely on his pathos, that we glimpse the ground of the novel form itself, the ground that Ishiguro unearths in his conversation with Kafka, with Wharton, with Austen. This is an oddly collapsing ground, made at once of the necessarily estranged difference between being and the forms in which it knows itself, and of the magical overcoming of such difference. The voice that speaks here is the voice of the novel, the voice that can reveal to us the terms in which we encounter ourselves, but only by installing a prosthetic distance at the heart of that self-encounter. 'Don't worry', the novel says to us here, speaking at once as Klara and as Josie. Don't worry, I can forgive you for your distance and your failure to be, and that forgiveness can be real. But the reality of such forgiveness relies on the revelation that the consolation it offers us is a fiction, a fiction deeply at work in the world, at work in all our perceived realities. 'Don't worry Mom', the daughter says from the other side of an impassable divide, 'I'm going to be fine' (*KS* 195).

Notes

1 Rebecca L. Walkowitz, 'Ishiguro's Floating Worlds', *ELH* 68:4 (2001): 1049–76 (1052).

2 Thomas Pynchon, *The Crying of Lot 49* (London: Vintage, 2000), p.10. For a reproduction of Varo's painting, see Janet A. Kaplan, *Unexpected Journeys: The Art and Life of Remedios Varo* (London: Vintage, 1988), p.21.

3 Edith Wharton, *The House of Mirth* (Oxford: Oxford University Press, 1999), p.132. For a reproduction of Reynolds's portrait, see Mark Hallett, *Reynolds: Portraiture in Action* (New Haven, CT: Yale University Press, 2014), p.263.
4 Wharton, *The House of Mirth*, p.133.
5 Oscar Wilde, *The Picture of Dorian Gray* (London: Penguin, 1985), p.136.
6 Jane Austen, *Emma* (London: Penguin, 1996), p.42.
7 Ibid., p.41.
8 Ibid.
9 Ibid., p.42.

9

DOUG BATTERSBY

Ishiguro and Genre Fiction

It would be difficult to convey the diversity and range of Kazuo Ishiguro's *oeuvre* without considering the way his novels imaginatively rework a whole host of literary and artistic genres. Ishiguro's debut, *A Pale View of Hills*, for instance, draws liberally on the gothic tradition, from the eerie mirroring of Etsuko's and Sachiko's stories to the phantasmic figure of '[t]he woman from across the river' (*PVH* 18) who only Mariko seems to be able to see.[1] The title of *An Artist of the Floating World* riffs on a literal translation of *ukiyo-e*, the popular genre of Japanese woodblock prints specializing in scenes from the pleasure districts of Edo (modern-day Tokyo) practised by Masuji Ono, the protagonist of this *Künstlerroman*, the subgenre of the *Bildungsroman* that deals with an artist's formative years. Ishiguro has acknowledged that not only P. G. Wodehouse's Jeeves but 'all the butler figures that walked on in the backgrounds of films' were a 'big influence' on *The Remains of the Day*, which one critic has described as a revivification of the 'dying genre' of the estate novel, which reads 'the fate of the nation through the condition of the English country estate'.[2] In this chapter, however, I want to explore the more specific way in which Ishiguro's four most recent novels engage with and exploit the norms and expectations of genre fiction, including the detective, dystopian, fantasy, and science-fiction novel.

One of the difficulties of discussing genre is that the term has been used variously to distinguish between basic literary modes (lyric, narrative, dramatic), forms (poetry, novels, plays), and subject matters (crime, possible scientific futures, alternative realities, and so on). Genre fiction, by contrast, refers specifically to works of prose fiction that are readily recognizable as belonging to a pre-existing genre by virtue of mobilizing customary narrative preoccupations, tropes, and character types.[3] For much of the post-war period, critics tended rather dismissively to characterize genre fiction as popular, accessible, and chiefly concerned with entertainment rather than aesthetic innovation, as opposed to 'literary' fiction, deemed by definition to be less formulaic, conventional, and predictable in both narrative and style.

This contradistinction has, however, been pervasively challenged in the wake of the so-called turn to genre in contemporary writing, already so widely discussed that observing it has become something of a cliché.[4] The turn to genre is defined, not by an increase in the production or consumption of genre fiction but, as Matthew Eatough puts it, by 'an elevation in [the] cultural status' of popular genres after 'middlebrow and highbrow authors have repurposed these once degraded forms and transformed them into material for so-called quality literature' – a rehabilitation signalled by the raft of major prizes awarded to writers such as Michael Chabon, Junot Díaz, Jennifer Egan, Cormac McCarthy, and Colson Whitehead for works clearly indebted to various popular genres.[5] As this account indicates, scholarly and public discussions of the turn have focused on questions of literary prestige – specifically, how in the wake of what China Miéville describes as the 'détente between litfic and its others' literary and genre fiction have come to be seen as less inimical to one another than they once were.[6]

In this chapter, my aim is not to affirm or contest assertions about aesthetic value but to examine Ishiguro's generative reworkings of popular genres. To do so, however, it is important to recognize how shifts in literary prestige have led contemporary novelists to invoke genre fiction in a very different spirit to that of modernist and postmodernist writers before them, as Theodore Martin explains:

> Whereas modernism is well known for its antipathy to genre, and postmodern culture is famously characterized by its pastiche of multiple genres at once . . ., authors and filmmakers have become increasingly interested in working within the constraints of popular genres . . . . The resulting works of art are not superficial pastiches of dead styles but earnest attempts to contribute to the history of a given genre.[7]

As we will see shortly, the earnestness or otherwise of Ishiguro's forays into a range of genres varies considerably across his *oeuvre*. In a published conversation with Neil Gaiman, Ishiguro recalls how he himself observed and was inspired by the 'change of climate in the mainstream literary world' that arose in the last decade of the twentieth century:

> [F]rom the Nineties onwards, I sensed that there was a whole generation of people emerging who had a very different attitude to sci-fi, and that there was a new force of energy and inspiration because of that. I may have had the crusty prejudices of somebody of my generation but I felt liberated by these younger writers. Now I feel fairly free to use almost anything.[8]

The most dramatic ramification of this change in attitude was on the final form of *Never Let Me Go*. In his conversation with Gaiman and elsewhere,

Ishiguro has described how he made two attempts to write the novel in the 1990s but abandoned both because he was dissatisfied with disease and contact with nuclear materials as justifications for why his young protagonists' lifespans were artificially contracted; only in 2001, thanks to the influence of David Mitchell and Alex Garland, did he hit upon the idea of making his characters clones.[9] Ishiguro's account of how he turned to science fiction so as to 'contrive' a narrative scenario is indicative both of the work genre does in his fiction and of the oddly equivocal relation to genre his novels often display.[10]

Indeed, Chris Holmes has gone so far as to suggest that a resistance to generic classification is precisely Ishiguro's goal:

> Ishiguro plays a keen game of genre Jenga: he aims to see how much architecture of novel-making you can remove, how much distance can you put between the character and their floating world and still have a standing, recognizable form. In short, what is the minimum number of recognizable structures of genre required to make a world? Why else would Ishiguro dirty his hands, as it were, with clones and giants if not simply to show a steady hand?[11]

This characterization of Ishiguro's intentions is notably at odds with the author's account of how he has turned to genres to engineer 'solutions' to problems in constructing specific narrative scenarios, as well as his evident impatience with taxonomic deliberations and genre gatekeeping.[12] By contrast, I follow John Frow in approaching literary works as 'performances of genre rather than reproductions of a class to which they belong'.[13] Such an approach allows us to redirect critical attention from often rather reductive questions about whether *x* novel 'counts' as *y* genre to more interesting ones about how thematic and rhetorical characteristics that recognizably draw on pre-existing fictional genres present 'cues' or 'metacommunications' that generate 'a set of expectations that guide our engagements with texts' – expectations that can, of course, be redirected, confounded, or satirized, as they frequently are in Ishiguro's fiction.[14]

Take the opening chapter of *When We Were Orphans*. When Banks tells us that he is among 'the most celebrated detectives of the day' (*WWWO* 12), readers are also being told that he exists in a world where detectives *are* celebrated and the genius of their exploits is a matter of public interest – that is, the world of the golden age detective story. The joke, in playing up to one of the more far-fetched assumptions of classic detective fiction, is not only on the genre but also, more significantly, on Banks himself, raising the possibility – which becomes increasingly likely as the narrative progresses – that such a world exists only in Banks's mind. What's more, however much it might present itself as detective fiction, the novel invariably passes over

Banks's deductions and working hypotheses, and even the basic facts of the case in question, an elision that leads Hélène Machinal to suggest that the 'narrative has all the décor of the celebrated detective story, but ... very little of the substance or internal logic'.[15] What the novel particularly omits is the performance of deductive brilliance that is a calling card of the genre, as when, in the opening of Arthur Conan Doyle's 'The Adventure of the Blue Carbuncle' (1892), Sherlock Holmes infers an unknown man's changed financial, moral, and romantic fortunes, among a plethora of other data, from nothing but his hat.[16] In the later sections of *When We Were Orphans* set in Shanghai, the few deductions Banks does make become increasingly unmoored from reality, culminating with his reckless mission into the war-torn slum where he believes his parents have been held for more than three decades. It is ultimately an accomplice to the crime, Uncle Philip, who has to explain to the detective just how profoundly he has misunderstood the events of his past. Ishiguro's revelation that abandoned early drafts of *When We Were Orphans* contained 'a genre novel within the novel' with Banks successfully 'solving another proper mystery in the Agatha Christie way' is in keeping with the way the novel adopts a protagonist from central casting whilst mischievously diverting the characteristic pleasures and expectations of the genre.[17]

The transformation of *When We Were Orphans* from a novel that conforms readily – indeed, perhaps *too* readily – to the detective genre to something approaching parody is both illustrated and prefigured by the changing depiction of Banks's magnifying glass, that stock prop of the golden-era detective novel. Banks recalls how he was given the magnifying glass as a birthday present from two friends at school:

> Its appearance has changed little over the years; it was on that afternoon already well travelled. I remember noting this, along with the fact that it was very powerful, surprisingly weighty, and that the ivory handle was chipped all down one side. I did not notice until later – one needs a second magnifying glass to read the engraving – that it was manufactured in Zurich in 1887. (*WWWO* 8)

The details of manufacture are no doubt a sly allusion to Holmes's first appearance in print in *A Study in Scarlett* (1887), as well as the hero's death at the Reichenbach Falls, not far from Zurich, in 'The Adventure of the Final Problem' (1893).[18] The association of the two detectives is reinforced by Banks's self-conscious performance of Holmesian observation, as he details the magnifying glass's age, efficacy, weight, materials, and condition. Yet the inspection of one glass by another also hints that processes of perception and inference are themselves under scrutiny here, leaving readers – like Banks's friends, who laugh as he unwraps the gift but become 'confused about their intentions' (*WWWO* 9) as he becomes engrossed in inspecting butter smeared on the tablecloth – unsure quite how seriously to take the scene.

As the novel takes a turn towards the surreal, Banks's recourse to his magnifying glass becomes both more comic and more disturbing, starting with his futile inspection of the wounds of the Japanese soldier he (almost certainly mistakenly) believes to be his childhood friend Akira (*WWWO* 254, 261), and coming to a head in the scene where he finally finds the house where he believes his parents are being held, only to be confronted with the mangled corpses of a family killed by a recent bombardment and a young girl who he ineffectually tries to reassure:

> 'I swear to you, whoever did all this, whoever did this ghastly thing, they won't escape justice. You may not know who I am, but as it happens, I'm ... well, I'm just the person you want. I'll see to it they don't get away. Don't you worry, I'll ... I'll ...' I had been fumbling about in my jacket, but I now found my magnifying glass and showed it to her. 'Look, you see?'
>
> I kicked aside a bird-cage in my path and went over to the mother. Then, perhaps out of habit as much as anything else, I bent down and began to examine her through the glass. Her stump looked peculiarly clean; the bone protruding out of the flesh was a shiny white, almost as though someone had been polishing it. (*WWWO* 272)

There is a certain pathos but also an absurdity to Banks's claim that he is 'just the person' the bereft girl needs – a claim that displays his creditable sense of ethical responsibility but also his delusional sense of his agency to shape events of a geopolitical magnitude. His pompous promise to bring the perpetrators to justice is similarly laughable, not only because the perpetrators are more or less already known, this being an active war zone, but also because he commits a kind of generic error in approaching societal calamity through the lens of individual criminal responsibility. That Banks lacks not so much the right tools or information as the right frame of analysis is brought home in the comically grotesque inspection of the protruding bone, as though any clues he might furnish could begin to redress the scale of suffering that surrounds him. By the end of the novel, the magnifying glass becomes emblematic, not of Banks's extraordinary powers of perception, but of his tragicomic propensity, like Stevens in *The Remains of the Day*, to scrutinize the wrong things in the wrong ways.

The almost automatic way in which Banks reaches for his magnifying glass in this scene also registers the extent to which being a detective is a kind of comforting performance that enables him to avoid confronting the reality of suffering and loss. This is a role he begins to play in childhood, when he and Akira act out 'dramas' from Conan Doyle's stories (*WWWO* 53) and later, more ominously, games in which they rescue Banks's missing father (106–12). Even in the first chapter, however, we have intimations that there is something oddly artificial or rehearsed to Banks's behaviour, for example when he counters Osbourne's recollection of him as an 'odd bird' at school with his own memories of how he 'blended perfectly into English school life' by 'reproducing' various 'gestures, turns of phrase and exclamations popular among [his] peers' (7).[19] In hindsight, the excessive affiliations to the detective genre appear to be the presentational choice of the narrator rather than only the author, while other characters' effusive genuflections to his brilliance raise the suspicion that *When We Were Orphans* presents 'a landscape that to some extent accommodates and bends to meet the irrational wishes and desires of the narrator', as Ishiguro puts it.[20] It is again left to Uncle Philip to pierce the illusion and force Banks to confront the possibility that his life as a detective is a kind of elaborate role play: 'A detective! What good is that to anyone? Stolen jewels, aristocrats murdered for their inheritance. Do you suppose that's all there is to contend with? Your mother, she wanted you to live in your enchanted world for ever. But it's impossible. In the end it has to shatter' (294).

The potential unreliability of Banks's narrative is similarly registered in the opening chapter through his and Osbourne's differing memories of the past. That Osbourne's might be the more accurate recollection is later intimated when another friend suggests that he and Banks were both 'loners' at school – a characterization Banks dismisses as 'simply a piece of self-delusion on Morgan's part – in all likelihood something he had invented years ago to make more palatable memories of an unhappy period' (*WWWO* 183–4). These subtle but persistent hints that Banks relates his past in ways that diminish its more distressing aspects works hand in hand with the detective story frame to solicit a suspicious response to Banks's narrative, encouraging us to parse it for signs of hidden or repressed meaning, just as Banks himself scrutinizes other people's words.[21] The novel notably ends with Banks rereading the letter sent to him by Sarah Hemmings ten years earlier, their first communication since Banks abruptly abandoned their planned elopement: 'There is something about these sections of her letter – and those last lines in particular – that never quite ring true. Some subtle note that runs throughout the letter – indeed, her very act of writing to me at that moment – feels at odds with her report of days filled with "happiness and companionship"' (*WWWO* 313). Such doubts encourage readers to wonder whether Banks's claim to 'own up to a certain contentment' in the next paragraph might likewise not quite ring true, and whether the very act of rereading Sarah's letter might indicate that he is more haunted by the path untaken than he is willing to acknowledge, even to himself.

Whether or not *When We Were Orphans*'s refusal to fulfil the expectations and anticipated pleasures of the detective story precludes it from being classified as 'belonging' to the genre is finally less important than how Ishiguro uses the genre to explore the cardinal concerns of his early work – the unreliability of our memories of the past, the authenticity of the emotions we think we feel, and the extent to which self-deception is simply necessary to make the losses of life bearable.

By contrast, the significance of a novel's exploitation of genre to its larger thematic preoccupations is much harder to chart in the case of *The Buried Giant*, perhaps Ishiguro's most critically elusive work since *The Unconsoled*. *The Buried Giant*'s Arthurian sources and depiction of a society governed by knightly codes of honour make plain its debt to medieval chivalric romance, and especially *Sir Gawain and the Green Knight*.[22] Just as conspicuous, however, is the debt to the genre of fantasy fiction, signalled by its quest narrative, regular scenes of single combat, and wide cast of magical creatures, from pixies to dragons. As with several of his other works, Ishiguro arrived at this generic setting relatively late in the composition process, having first considered Rwanda, Bosnia, and post-Vichy France as possible locales for a narrative about a society where 'an uneasy peace existed between two ethnic factions occupying the same territory' after a recent violent atrocity and where it is necessary '*not* to remember, as a society and as a nation, what happened a generation back' for that peace to hold.[23] Ishiguro ultimately opted for a 'mythical' setting because he wanted the book to be about, not a particular conflict, but 'a pattern that recurs throughout history'.[24] Given his explicit hope that *The Buried Giant* would be understood as a commentary on 'an eternal fact of the human condition', it is perhaps not surprising that it has frequently been described as an 'allegory' – a label that, in suggesting that its narrative meaning and significance is largely self-evident, risks misrepresenting this profoundly enigmatic novel.[25]

Central to the complexity of *The Buried Giant*'s use of stylistic and narrative elements drawn from fantasy fiction is the difficulty of knowing quite how seriously or otherwise they should be taken, precisely because of their suspiciously generic character. Indeed, Ishiguro has even worried that readers won't look *past* the novel's fantasy frame: 'Will they understand what I'm trying to do, or will they be prejudiced against the surface elements? Are they going to say this is fantasy?'[26] The aversion on display here prompted Ursula K. Le Guin, in a reprisal of her broadside against Margaret Atwood for expressing similar sentiments, to exclaim that '[n]o writer can successfully use the "surface elements" of a literary genre – far less its profound capacities – for a serious purpose, while despising it to the point of fearing identification with it'.[27] More interesting than the fairness or otherwise of this critique is its shedding light on the peculiar ambivalence with which *The Buried Giant* inhabits the fantasy genre, something especially apparent in the scenes of single combat. Ishiguro is clearly conscious of the distinctive ways combat is presented in different genres, recalling his bewilderment as a child when first encountering 'the Errol Flynn and Douglas Fairbanks universe', where combatants 'converse whilst they fence, going backwards and forwards around the castle, the tactic seeming to be to incrementally edge your opponent off the edge of a cliff or battlement', compared to depictions of sword fights between samurai, 'who quietly stare at each other for a long time – all the big emotions are there, that one will survive and the other will not – before there's an explosion of violence and it's all over'.[28] In both of *The Buried Giant*'s fight scenes (*BG* 128–40, 327–34), Axl observes the combatants as they approach one another with an expert appraisal of the relative advantages conferred by every minute movement, very much in the mode of the samurai comics and movies of Ishiguro's childhood.[29] Yet both scenes are also preceded by and intercut with protracted formal dialogues about the approaching 'contest', with each combatant emphasizing his respect for his opponent's honourable conduct, registering the extent to which these scenes closely conform to the generic conventions of the chivalric romance and its successors in medieval fantasy fiction.

The dialogue itself, meanwhile, is replete with the kind of self-consciously archaic turns of phrase found in much genre fiction, engendered by the deferral of objects, adverbs, and subordinate clauses to the ends of sentences, the use of obsolete meanings of words, and the elision of determinative pronouns and prepositions. Ishiguro's stated aim was for this 'stilted' prose to convey 'the sense that behind the English language being used there is an older, foreign language, the language of the Britons of that time' – in other words, to present the narrative, in Rebecca L. Walkowitz's terms, as 'born translated'.[30] While many of the verbal effects noted above are present in Ishiguro's early works, where he was attempting to write in a kind of 'translationese' (*CKI* 13), they are given a generically distinctive twist in *The Buried Giant* that is especially observable in the propensity of characters to continue calmly discoursing in the midst of grave danger or in the aftermath of some traumatic event. There is an inescapable bathos, even banality, to Beatrice's remark after Gawain, and with him the last of Arthur's knights, has been killed – 'He was the she-dragon's defender ... yet showered us with kindness. Who knows where we'd be now without him, Axl, and I'm sorry to see him fallen' (*WWWO* 333) – not only in the studious balance of the pronounced verdict on the dead knight, but in the affective flatness of its expression. As Gaiman points out, in *The Buried Giant*, '[t]here are adventures, sword fights, betrayals, armies, cunning stratagems and monsters killed, but these things are told distantly, without the book's pulse ever beating faster'.[31]

The larger ethical and political stakes of this tonal equivocation are brought into relief in the rare moments when the novel's deeper concern with questions about the historical legacies of traumatic violence come to the surface. As Axl, Beatrice, and Edwin flee the monastery via an underground tunnel, meeting Gawain who has come to protect them from the 'devil-dog' that resides there, Axl's innocent question about whether a mortal man can kill the beast unexpectedly enrages the old knight:

> What do you say, sir? I'm a mortal man, I don't deny it, but I'm a knight well trained and nurtured for long years of my youth by the great Arthur, who taught me to face all manner of challenge with gladness, even when fear seeps to the marrow, for if we're mortal let us at least shine handsomely in God's eyes while we walk this earth! Like all who stood with Arthur, sir, I've faced beelzebubs and monsters as well as the darkest intents of men, and always upheld my great king's example even in the midst of ferocious conflict. What is it you suggest, sir? How dare you? Were you there? I was there, sir, and saw all with these same eyes that fix you now! (*WWWO* 189–90)

On the one hand, this is the most explicit suggestion thus far that Gawain himself was involved in some kind of war-time atrocity. On the other, there is an unmistakable comedy to the self-important grandiloquence of his oration, the fragility of his ego, and how poorly disguised is the guilty conscience that leads him to misinterpret a pragmatic question as a potential slight on his honour. Axl and Beatrice's subsequent, similarly ingenuous observations about what they can see in the dimly lit tunnel prompt three further rants from Gawain, each more pugnacious and inadvertently revealing than the last, making it increasingly evident that the atrocity in question was the massacre of Saxon children, while maintaining the high temperature of the rhetoric: 'What is it you suggest, mistress? The skulls of babes? I've fought men, beelzebubs, dragons. But a slaughterer of infants? How dare you, mistress!' (*WWWO* 199). This is not ribald farce in the mode of *Monty Python and the Holy Grail* (1975) (though Ishiguro is clearly conscious of the dangers of such a likeness), but more tonally elusive writing, in which the generic quality of the prose is just a little too exaggerated to quite ring true while not being exaggerated enough to allow us to confidently label (and dismiss) it as straightforward pastiche.[32] Contra James Wood – who argues that 'in making literal and general what is implicit and personal in his best fiction' Ishiguro 'has written not a novel ... but an allegory' that aims 'to literalize and simplify' – it is precisely *The Buried Giant*'s unsettled tone that forecloses any pat translation of the novel's narrative into a consistent ethico-political stance concerning the commemoration and memorialization of historical violence, a resistance to peremptory resolution that has already elicited a startling array of diverse responses from readers, reviewers, and critics.[33]

The self-consciousness and ambivalence that marks Ishiguro's use of fantasy elements makes for a dramatic contrast with his most earnest forays into genre fiction, first in *Never Let Me Go* and more recently in *Klara and the Sun*. This contrast is similarly apparent from Ishiguro's remark to Gaiman that there is 'something reassuring' about the 'dystopian fiction' label, partly because 'there's always been this tradition of what you could call *Nineteen Eighty-Four* science fiction', and partly because the knowledge that 'it's going to be a commentary on our world' allays 'the fear of irrelevance' – the possibility that 'a writer is just weaving some sort of self-referential alternative world, that will not tell me anything emotionally or intellectually about the one I live in'.[34] The manner of that commentary in *Never Let Me Go* is not, however, to issue a warning about a possible future in the customary mode of dystopian narrative – an eschewal perhaps signalled by the decision to set the story in the past, in an alternative version of late-twentieth-century Britain. The novel likewise offers next to no details about the scientific or administrative practicalities of the cloning programme, nor does it seriously interrogate whether cloning might be ethically justified, giving a decidedly one-sided account that encourages readers to feel only outrage at the curtailment of the clones' lives for the benefit of others.[35] Rather, for Ishiguro, '[o]ne of the attractions about using clones is that it makes people ask immediately, What does it mean to be a human being? It's a secular route to the Dostoyevskian question, What is a soul?'[36] The novel's investment in this 'Dostoyevskian question' is made explicit in the scene that is in many ways the climax of the narrative, when Miss Emily reveals to Tommy and Kathy that the Guardians took the students' art, not to reveal the particularities of each individual soul, but 'to prove you had souls at all' (*NLMG* 255). By this point in the narrative, our intimacy with the intricacies of Kathy's emotional life places the notion that there might be some metaphysical difference between cloned and non-cloned persons beyond serious doubt; rather, Ishiguro's interest lies, not in questions about the distinctiveness of cloned life, but in using a narrative about cloning to explore questions about the distinctiveness of human life generally.

Klara and the Sun, described by Ishiguro as an 'emotional reply' to *Never Let Me Go*, marks a clear return to and intensification of that exploration, signalled with similar explicitness when Paul asks our eponymous android narrator: 'Do you believe in the human heart? I don't mean simply the organ, obviously. I'm speaking in the poetic sense. The human heart. Do you think there is such a thing? Something that makes each of us special and individual?' (*KS* 218).[37] Paul notably uncouples the 'human heart' from any organic site, leaving open the possibility, perhaps out of sensitivity for his interlocutor, that Klara might not be excluded from its ambit. Also like *Never Let Me Go*, *Klara and the Sun* leans heavily on the novel form's extraordinary capacity to place us in the mind of another person (or being), allowing us to recognize for ourselves the idiosyncrasies of Klara's mental life. In doing so, it quietly but insistently rebuffs any banally essentialist ideas about qualities deemed 'uniquely' human. Perhaps the most marked divergences between Klara's experience and those of ordinary humans are found in moments in the novel where excessive or complex visual stimuli trouble Klara's abilities to make sense of what she sees, as when, in the midst of a busy crowd, people appear to her as fragments of cones, cylinders, funnels, and other two-dimensional shapes (237). Yet the idea that this might in some way indicate a line that divides the human from the non-human is little more than a lure to repudiate lazily ableist assumptions about 'normal' ways of experiencing the world. Likewise, the observation that the android AFs – Artificial Friends – were 'swinging their legs freely as Manager had told them to do' (3) concisely raises the paradox of free will that animates the novel's reflections on artificial intelligence while according troublingly closely with the imitative character of so much human behaviour in Ishiguro's fiction, Banks's copying the mannerisms of his peers at school being a case in point.

Klara and the Sun gathers up ingredients from Ishiguro's most successful novels: the deft dramatization of the thoughts and feelings of a narrator who knows more than they are able to acknowledge in *The Remains of the Day*, the devastating acquiescence to one's own exploitation that is central to *Never Let Me Go*, and even, in Klara's struggles to comprehend the world around her, the evocation of profound disorientation found in his most formally challenging novel, *The Unconsoled*. What is distinctive, within the *oeuvre*, is the unprecedented ingenuousness with which it inhabits the genre of science fiction, chiefly because the genre is peculiarly well adapted to registering the philosophical questions that animate Ishiguro's later works about whether the qualities that make us human are unique, inimitable, or inalienable. Particularly marked is the contrast with *When We Were Orphans* and *The Buried Giant* – novels that cannot be identified as straightforwardly belonging to any one genre, but at the same time whose achievement is impossible to describe without some account of their relation to generic conventions, however sly, recalcitrant, parodic, or ambiguous that relation might be. Martin argues that '[g]enres lead distinctly double lives, with one foot in the past and the other in the present; they contain the entire abridged history of an aesthetic form while also staking a claim to the form's contemporary relevance'.[38] There is perhaps an assumption here that all writers of genre fiction aspire for innovation; the compulsive repetitiveness of Mills & Boon novels would be an obvious counter-example. Nevertheless, it is a characterization capable of encompassing the sheer diversity of Ishiguro's uses of genres across the course of his career, whether ironically surveying the psychologies of self-deception or earnestly interrogating the distinctiveness of human life.

Notes

1 See Jane Hu, 'Typical Japanese: Kazuo Ishiguro and the Asian Anglophone Historical Novel', *Modern Fiction Studies* 67:1 (2021): 123–48 (125, 129–32).
2 Susannah Hunnewell, 'Kazuo Ishiguro, The Art of Fiction No. 196', *The Paris Review* 184 (2008): n.p. (accessed online at www.theparisreview.org/interviews/5829/the-art-of-fiction-no-196-kazuo-ishiguro). John J. Su, 'Refiguring National Character: The Remains of the British Estate Novel', *Modern Fiction Studies* 48:3 (2002): 552–80 (552–3).
3 For representative definitions, see Chris Baldick, *The Oxford Dictionary of Literary Terms*, 4th ed. (Oxford: Oxford University Press, 2015), p.94.
4 China Miéville, 'The Autonovelator', in Jonathan Bastable and Hannah McGill, eds., *The 21st-Century Novel: Notes from the Edinburgh World Writers' Conference* (Edinburgh: Edinburgh University Press, 2014), p.42. Tim Lanzendörder suggests that the fact that 'genre poetics play an increasingly important role in contemporary literature' is by now simply 'taken for granted' ('Introduction: The Generic Turn? Toward a Poetics of Genre in the Contemporary Novel', in Lanzendörder, ed., *The Poetics of Genre in the Contemporary Novel* (Lanham, MD: Lexington Books, 2015), p.2.
5 Matthew Eatough, '"Are They Going to Say This Is Fantasy?": Kazuo Ishiguro, Untimely Genres, and the Making of Literary Prestige', *Modern Fiction Studies* 67:1 (2021): 40–66 (42). Theodore Martin, *Contemporary Drift: Genre, Historicism, and the Problem of the Present* (New York: Columbia University Press, 2017), p.8.
6 Miéville, 'The Autonovelator', p.42.
7 Martin, *Contemporary Drift*, pp.7–8.
8 Kazuo Ishiguro and Neil Gaiman, 'Let's Talk about Genre', *New Statesman*, 4 June 2015.
9 Hunnewell, 'Kazuo Ishiguro, The Art of Fiction No. 196'. Caryn James, 'Kazuo Ishiguro Returns to Literary Sci-Fi with "Klara and the Sun"', *WSJ Magazine*, 2 March 2021 (accessed online at www.wsj.com/articles/kazuo-ishiguru-klara-and-the-sun-new-book-interview-11614692315).
10 Ishiguro and Gaiman, 'Let's Talk about Genre'.
11 Chris Holmes, 'Kazuo Ishiguro's Thinking Novels', in Ken Seigneurie, ed., *A Companion to World Literature* (Chichester: Wiley Blackwell, 2020), p.5. Meghan Marie Hammond similarly argues that the slippage between genres in

The Remains of the Day is a calculated strategy to dramatize Stevens's failed attempts to find a narrative mode adequate to conveying and endowing with significance his life story ('"I Can't Even Say I Made My Own Mistakes": The Ethics of Genre in Kazuo Ishiguro's *The Remains of the Day*', in Sebastian Groes and Barry Lewis, eds., *Kazuo Ishiguro: New Critical Visions of the Novels* (Basingstoke: Palgrave Macmillan, 2011)).

12 Ishiguro and Gaiman, 'Let's Talk about Genre'.

13 John Frow, *Genre*, new edn. (London: Routledge, 2015), p.3.

14 Ibid., p.133.

15 Hélène Machinal, 'Kazuo Ishiguro's *When We Were Orphans*: Narration and Detection in the Case of Christopher Banks', in Sean Matthews and Sebastian Groes, eds., *Kazuo Ishiguro: Contemporary Critical Perspectives* (London: Continuum, 2009), p.84.

16 Arthur Conan Doyle, *The Complete Sherlock Holmes* (London: Penguin, 2009), pp.245–8.

17 Hunnewell, 'Kazuo Ishiguro, The Art of Fiction No. 196'.

18 I am grateful to Andrew Bennett for alerting me to these allusions.

19 For other scenes in which Banks emulates other people's habits and behaviours, see, for instance: *WWWO* 52–3, 56, 77.

20 Rick Kleffel, 'Interview with Kazuo Ishiguro', *Interzone* 198 (2005): 62–3.

21 See Doug Battersby, 'Reading Ishiguro Today: Suspicion and Form', *Modern Fiction Studies* 67:1 (2021): 67–88.

22 See Matthew Vernon and Margaret A. Miller, 'Navigating Wonder: The Medieval Geographies of Kazuo Ishiguro's *The Buried Giant*', *Arthuriana* 28:4 (2018): 68–89.

23 Rick Kleffel, Interview with Kazuo Ishiguro, *Bookotron*, 21 April 2015 (accessed online at http://bookotron.com/agony/audio/2015/2015-interviews/kazuo_ishi guro-2015.mp3).

24 Rebecca Rukeyser, 'Kazuo Ishiguro: Mythic Retreat', *Guernica*, 1 May 2015 (accessed online at www.guernicamag.com/mythic-retreat/).

25 Mike Doherty, 'Kazuo Ishiguro Goes Back in Time', *Maclean's*, 5 March 2015 (accessed online at www.macleans.ca/society/kazuo-ishiguro-goes-back-in-time/).

26 Alexandra Alter, 'For Kazuo Ishiguro, *The Buried Giant* Is a Departure', *The New York Times*, 19 February 2015 (accessed online at www.nytimes.com/2015/ 02/20/books/for-kazuo-ishiguro-the-buried-giant-is-a-departure.html).

27 Ursula K. Le Guin, 'Are They Going to Say This Is Fantasy?', *Book View Café*, 2 March 2015 (accessed online at https://bookviewcafe.com/blog/2015/03/02/ are-they-going-to-say-this-is-fantasy/).

28 Robert Pollie, 'Kazuo Ishiguro Radio Interview: "The Buried Giant"', *7th Avenue Project*, 12 April 2015 (accessed online at https://soundcloud.com/7th-avenue-project/kazuo-ishiguro-radio-interview-buried-giant).

29 Ishiguro and Gaiman, 'Let's Talk about Genre'.

30 Kleffel, Interview (2015); Rebecca L. Walkowitz, *Born Translated: The Contemporary Novel in an Age of World Literature* (New York: Columbia University Press, 2015).

31 Neil Gaiman, 'Here Be Dragons', *The New York Times*, 25 February 2015 (accessed online at www.nytimes.com/2015/03/01/books/review/kazuo-ishiguros-the-buried-giant.html).

32 Doherty, 'Kazuo Ishiguro Goes Back in Time'.
33 See James Wood, 'The Uses of Oblivion: Kazuo Ishiguro's *The Buried Giant*', *The New Yorker*, 16 March 2015 (accessed online at www.newyorker.com/magazine/2015/03/23/the-uses-of-oblivion).
34 Gaiman and Ishiguro, 'Let's Talk about Genre'.
35 Elsewhere, I have argued against the view, advanced by Nancy Armstrong and others, that the Hailsham students' humanity is really in question (Battersby, 'Reading Ishiguro Today', 78).
36 Hunnewell, 'Kazuo Ishiguro, The Art of Fiction No. 196'.
37 Brian Bethune, 'Kazuo Ishiguro's Newest Book Is an "Emotional Reply" to "Never Let Me Go"', *Maclean's*, 26 February 2021 (accessed online at www.macleans.ca/culture/books/kazuo-ishiguros-newest-book-is-an-emotional-reply-to-never-let-me-go/).
38 Martin, *Contemporary Drift*, p.6.

10

PETER SLOANE

Ishiguro's TV and Film Scripts

Recipient of numerous cultural and civic accolades, subject of international popular acclaim, at once (parodically) traditional yet delicately innovative, Kazuo Ishiguro is the consummate contemporary novelist. However, a career in literary fiction was not the 2017 Nobel Laureate's first or only artistic ambition. While discussing his most complex and arguably greatest work, *The Unconsoled*, Ishiguro confessed to Charlie Rose that in addition to harbouring lifelong ambitions of being a 'rock and roll star' he also 'wanted to be a filmmaker'.[1] His most conventionally 'realist' narratives, *The Remains of the Day* and *Never Let Me Go*, have been sympathetically adapted into commercially successful films respectively by the award-winning novelist and screenwriter Ruth Prawer Jhabvala, and by the author and director Alex Garland. Although these interpretations are only tenuously 'Ishiguro movies' (given that they were not adapted or written for the screen by him), he has also scripted several pieces intended for television and cinema. In Ishiguro's own estimation, however, the principal virtues of literature and film are somewhat at odds. In conversation with Linda Richards in 2000, he commented that the novel is 'able to explore people's inner worlds much more thoroughly and with much more subtlety' than film, which is predominantly 'a third person exterior form'.[2] He made a similar claim in conversation with Moira Macdonald in 2010, suggesting that the novel can follow 'thoughts and memories, something that I think is difficult to do on the screen', again because film is 'essentially a third-person medium'.[3] Ishiguro's distinction between introspective/subjective first person (text) and external/objective third person (screen), will be the primary focus of this chapter.

Ishiguro is an avid fan of world cinema, and film has had an indirect but pervasive influence on the psychological and emotional tenor of his writing.[4] In particular, as Rebecca Karni has suggested, the 'post-World-War I Japanese film aesthetic' may be said to have 'inspired the unique and subtle self-consciousness' that characterizes his fictions.[5] Anni Shen also focuses on the significant influence of Japanese cinema on Ishiguro's novels and the resulting 'amalgam of literary and cinematic techniques'.[6] More directly, and more broadly, the medium's perceived narratological distinctiveness (its 'specificity') inspired the evolution of the formal, structural, and thematic idiosyncrasies that characterize Ishiguro's writing. By his own account, after being 'offered work by the soon-to-be-launched Channel 4', the aspiring author 'rather obsessively' compared his draft teleplay for *A Profile of Arthur J. Mason* (1984) with his recently published debut novel, *A Pale View of Hills* (1982):

> Whole hunks of *A Pale View* looked to me awfully similar to a screenplay – dialogue followed by 'direction' followed by more dialogue. I began to feel deflated. Why bother to write a novel if it was going to offer more or less the same experience someone could have by turning on a television? ... I was determined that my new novel wouldn't be a 'prose screenplay'.[7]

As a response to his own disappointment, while composing his second novel, *An Artist of the Floating World*, Ishiguro 'entered an extended period of experimenting with different ways' to write what were ultimately 'unfilmable novels'.[8] What might an unfilmable novel look like? Presumably, action would be secondary to the compulsive iterative reflections that we see in Ishiguro's novels and short stories, and that tend to be prioritized over any interest in 'events' themselves. While endeavouring 'to find the territory that only a novel can offer', therefore, he also sought to develop a form of screenwriting that would 'work uniquely as a film'.[9] In film studies, so-called medium specificity theory holds that different art forms exploit unique qualities or attributes.[10] Although, as Kamilla Elliott reminds us, recent 'poststructuralist, postmodern, and posthuman theories have effectively dismantled' or at least undermined/destabilized this concept of discrete mediums, Ishiguro's insistence on foregrounding the most resonant distinctive elements of his given form invests his novels and screenplays with their peculiar aesthetic and affective power.[11]

This chapter will focus on Ishiguro's two short teleplays commissioned for Channel 4, *A Profile of Arthur J. Mason* (1984) and *The Gourmet* (1987), and on his feature-length screenplays for *The Saddest Music in the World* (screenplay 1987, film 2003) and the Merchant Ivory production *The White Countess* (2005).[12] I will argue that Ishiguro's films simultaneously highlight and exploit the incompatibility of his characteristic narrative style and the medium of film. Discarding the kind of intimate yet often misleading first-person narrator that works so effectively in his novels, Ishiguro allows concealed ethical and political themes to emerge not as a consequence of unreliable narration, as in the novels, but from disjunctions between moving images, lines of dialogue, and stage directions. His films also interrogate those aspects of experience that happen 'inside' the mind – specifically in relation to thoughts in *A Profile*, memories in *The Gourmet*, and imagination in *The White Countess*. By drawing attention to and manipulating film's singular qualities, Ishiguro's screenplays perform a metacommentary on or anatomy of the practice of film-making.

Television

A Profile of Arthur J. Mason

Although it has been critically neglected, Ishiguro's first screenplay has much merit. What is perhaps most striking is the TV play's anticipation of the central preoccupations of Ishiguro's later work: questions of romantic and vocational 'regret'; living a 'worthwhile and rewarding' life; and 'an artist's duty towards society' (*AJM* 31, 12).[13] Anticipating *The Remains of the Day* in some ways, *Arthur J. Mason* offers a faux documentary of the eponymous ageing live-in butler, who has been in the service of Sir James Reid for the past thirty-six years. In the public eye after his novel, *The August Passage* – written thirty-eight years previously and 'gathering dust in the drawer' since 1948 – has finally been published to international acclaim, Mason is interviewed by Anna, a 'late twenties, highly educated' aspiring journalist (*AJM* 2). Sir James and his household have suffered a change of fortune and are living as 'antiques, throwbacks' in a small cottage in a once rural but increasingly suburban town (29). A tragically overlooked 'major writer', according to his literary agent Mortimer Crane, Mason is little more than a general dogsbody, required to 'prepare meals, do a little cleaning, a little mending, see to the provisions' (30, 6).[14] Yet, as Barry Lewis has commented, although Mason seems unperturbed by his fortunes, in typical Ishiguro fashion, 'a different picture emerges from the extracts of the book he reads out'; that is to say, Mason's selection of passages from his own novel appears to hint towards various profound regrets for his perceived failures, and for the resulting breakdown of his marriage.[15] Like his literary heir Stevens, if Mason abandons his belief that service 'is no less worthy an activity than that of writing books', he would be admitting to having 'wasted [his] best years and talents' to following the wrong path (31).[16]

Mason's novel, *The August Passage*, appears to be autobiographical, with the protagonist Kathrine encouraging her lover to escape their life of 'daily toil' as servants just as Mason's wife Mary had tried to encourage him. As Mason recalls, Mary 'saw the book as a ticket to a new life – for us and for the children' (*AJM* 21–2). Sadly, after his manuscript was rejected 'by just about everybody' and he abandoned hope of publishing, Mary left with the children (22). Asked whether his fiction is 'Marxist', Mason equivocates, claiming that he fails to 'quite see it that way', only to admit later that the aftermath of the Second World War witnessed 'a lot of talk about a new egalitarianism' and about how 'people such as ourselves ... would run the country' (8, 25).[17] Much to Anna's frustration, she and we discover that the post-war 'revolutionary figure' Arthur J. Mason is not the subject of the interview at all; he is now simply the apolitical, unambitious, loyal 'Mason' (7). Indeed, he barely recognizes himself as the book's author; after reading a passage he seems perplexed when asked if he remembers writing it, replying unconvincingly 'I suppose I must have written this. Yes, I suppose I do' (12). Such subtle deformations of self constitute the corrosive tragedy of Ishigurian characters such as Etsuko in *A Pale View of Hills*, Ono in *An Artist of the Floating World*, and of course Stevens in *The Remains of the Day*, who recognize but valiantly resist confronting the changes they have undergone. This enables them to sustain some consolatory – if illusory – continuity in their being through time, and to obscure, however temporarily, personal and professional failures. Radical Arthur J.'s transfiguration into servile Mason, signified by the removal of 'Arthur J.' from his name, frustrates Anna's aspirations to make a film about 'an important man, one the public should be given an insight into' (*AJM* 15). Although that 'important man' no longer exists, in name or fact, Anna inadvertently provides insight into the subject of Mason's book – incremental self-erasure through passivity, self-abnegation through dedication to another's needs – but also the imperceptible yet irrevocable metamorphoses that result in the emergence of unfamiliar, often disappointing selves.

Perhaps his most overtly postmodern effort, Ishiguro's TV play is a faux documentary concerning a 'real' documentary that Anna is endeavouring to make. The opening production note specifies that 'the whole of what follows should actually LOOK like a documentary film (*a la* "The South Bank Show" or "Omnibus")' (*AJM*, cover). But if Ishiguro explores film's possibilities in his own first attempt, Anna, in her 'much longed for ... stab at making a documentary profile', seems not to have mastered the form's quasi-scientific objectivity. In one scene she describes Sir James's catatonic uncle, Lord Reid, but despite trying to 'produce the tone of a professional and objective narrator', she 'fails to keep the contempt from her voice' (19). In theory, Anna represents the disinterested external observer, which is typical of what Ishiguro describes as the 'third person exterior form'. However, she is unable to mask her own visceral responses to the inert object in front of the lens, and her presence, as a 'modern' woman perplexed, even outraged by Mason's archaic acquiescence, intercedes between camera and study. In the telling rhetoric of Ishiguro's stage directions, the camera is figured as itself disgusted, as it moves insect-like 'slowly all over LORD REID – over his feet, his hands, his neck, his face', representing a *formal* failure that mirrors Anna's *narratorial* failure (19). The scene reveals nothing of substance about the aged peer because the camera can do little more than scan the surface of the prone body, which remains impervious to the mechanical observer. But those figures that should be invisible to the camera, the author and documentary film-maker, *are* revealed.

Anna's primitive (by contemporary standards) television camera interferes with its subject merely by virtue of its sheer bulk, as well as by the way in which it creates unease in its unprepared subjects. In one farcical scene, Anna defies Sir James's injunctions against filming their private moments, bringing the camera into the dining room, to the discomfort of the self-conscious guests who look 'apprehensively at CAMERA' despite Anna's absurd plea that they 'just go on, just as normal. Just go on talking, don't look this way, just go on' (*AJM* 22–3). Anna's camera attempts to witness without interacting with or altering her subject, in the way that the traditional narrator might: Dickens, in the guise of the spectre-like omniscient narrator, can exploit the permeable textual boundaries between inside and outside to observe the most intimate moments, even thoughts, of his characters (an act of constructive observation masquerading as witnessing). Eventually the camera goes too far, trying not simply to observe *as if* it were a dinner guest, but to occupy the same spatial coordinates and point of view. Ultimately, in Heisenbergian fashion, the means of observation collides with its subject, but in so doing it not only *displays* but also *displaces* the very thing it seeks to reveal, jostling Lord Reid, who 'goes over stiffly and silently, like a manikin, his mouth remaining open' (23). Even were it able to occupy the same space, Ishiguro shows us, the camera would be unable to disclose the mind in the manner that a work of fiction can. As we see elsewhere in the play, Anna asks a question but must wait 'while ARTHUR silently follows his thoughts' (27). As the screenplay directs, in the film Anna simply sits opposite and watches a silent Arthur as he attends to his thoughts and memories, the contents of which are implied, or can be inferred, but which remain unexpressed within both the film and the screenplay. We might see here evidence for Ishiguro's suggestion that a work of fiction is able to follow 'thoughts and memories' in ways that are 'difficult to do on the screen'. In another scene, attempting to get a reaction from Lord Reid, Anna shouts at his unresponsive face, 'Lord Reid. Are you there somewhere?' (19). These confrontations with the limitations of vision and by implication the film medium, are structural to the form; as George Bluestone observes, film may be able to 'lead us to infer thought' but it 'cannot show us thought directly'.[18] Ishiguro's first screenplay, then, not only acts as a precursor to *The Remains of the Day*, but initiates his exploration of the possibilities of fiction and film. The screenplay amounts to a careful interrogation of the distinction between the forms. *A Profile* simply offers a profile, a partial (in both senses) rendering of depthless contours, of the exterior of its subject that also has implications for Ishiguro's later fiction and his often somewhat depthless narrators.

The Gourmet

First broadcast in 1986,[19] Ishiguro's second television commission earned the Chicago Film Festival's 'Golden Plaque for Best Short Film', while the screenplay was published in Granta's *Best of Young British Novelists 43*, because, according to the editors of that volume, 'it reads so effectively on the page'.[20] *The Gourmet* follows a celebrated but jaded epicurean who, having consumed everything (including human flesh), is on what we under-stand to be a career-capping quest to savour something *'not* of this earth' (*G* 106). We accompany him enduring an evening in a church with London's homeless, hungrily preparing for the arrival of his fantastic meal, the ghost of a murdered pauper.[21] With its focus on the homeless, *The Gourmet* is arguably Ishiguro's only explicit comment on his political present. As Sebastian Groes and Paul-Daniel Veyret remark, it as 'a politicized, tragi-comic gothic tale exposing the social and cultural catastrophe of Thatcherism'.[22] Although the play's political critique is undermined by its farcical concept, Wai-chew Sim reminds us that the absurdity also serves to illustrate that the 'non-realist features of *The Unconsoled* are not as atypical [of Ishiguro's writing] as they are often taken to be'.[23] Homelessness would have been fresh in Ishiguro's mind after his experiences as a community worker in Renfrew, Scotland in 1975, and with the West London Cyrenians between 1979 and 1981. In this discussion, however, I want to focus not so much on politics (which Groes and Veyret cover) as on unpicking the idea of Manley *devouring* and the camera *capturing* the intangible, considering it as a further interrogation of film's possibilities.

Manley's evening among those who come to the church for the more mundane sustenance of bread and beans foregrounds the play's central theme; as his destitute guide David remarks, 'I'm the ghost around here. Could vanish tonight, nobody would notice' (*G* 121). Indifferent to David's plight, Manley explains that in this very church, 'in nineteen hundred and four, a pauper was murdered [because] some human organs were needed for research' (120). A casualty of the economic inequalities which persist eighty years later, and already a victim of calculated corporeal violence, the ghost of the pauper is the intended object of another ethical transgression. The ghost duly arrives and through Manley's archaic ritual and televisual wizardry, is captured, cooked, and eaten. Manley's alchemical conversion of spirit into flesh in the sanctity of the vestry (into which he and David trespass) subverts the Catholic ceremony of the Eucharist, with its transubstantiation of wine and bread into Christ's blood and flesh. At the crucial moment when the ghost arrives, Manley initially mistakes the visitation for another vagrant, asking him 'kindly to remove yourself from that vicinity' (122). However, Manley and David quickly realize that they are in the presence of the anticipated ghost:

> For a fleeting moment, we glimpse the tramp's face, which has changed. It is the face of a dead man – staring, horror-struck, blood on the lips. We only catch this fleetingly, because we immediately cut to: Manley and David, utterly shocked. Manley comes to his senses first.

In this 'fleeting' instant, the tramp undergoes a metamorphosis, from the trespassing vagrant to not simply a ghost but a 'dead man' presumably in the moment immediately following his murder. After we witness and possibly share the shock of Manley and David at the gruesome transformation, Manley springs his trap, 'The net covers the camera' as proxy for the ghost before 'the screen goes black' (123). The screenplay reveals the ghost's spatio-temporally doubled reaction, firstly to the original act of violence in the church in 1904, and secondly to the present threat in 1984. Oddly, the expression of horror which is appropriate for both the past and present assault is different: in the first instance it is the reaction of a corporeal being to its violent death, in the second the echoes of the corporeal in the spiritual faced once more with a perhaps more permanent erasure.

Shortly after his gruesome feast, Manley stumbles from the church looking 'very ill ... clutching his stomach and breathing heavily' as he huddles around a fire with another 'Homeless Man' (in Ishiguro's script the vagrants are an unindividuated mass), who attempts to sympathize, asking '[o]verdid it, did we?':

> MANLEY: How could *you* ever understand the kind of hunger I suffer?
> HOMELESS MAN: Well. We all get hungry, don't we?
> Manley gives the homeless man another disparaging look.
> MANLEY: You have no idea what *real* hunger is.

Manley might be accused of cultural insensitivity: the homeless and destitute are perhaps the only ones in a 'wealthy' 'developed' nation to know 'real' hunger. Groes and Veyret view Manley as 'the embodiment of ruthless greed and selfishness, of decadence and excess, which make him blind to the implications of his taboo-breaking behaviour'.[24] But another reading might see Manley more positively. In his instructions for the scene in which the homeless are fed, Ishiguro directs that they should 'appear to be eating only because they know they should, without really caring if they do or not' (G 113). There are two interpretations of the listless appetite of the homeless: 1) their apparent lack of self-regard *results from* a lifetime of poverty and deprivation; or 2) in the screenplay's Thatcherite context, the homeless are perceived by some as lacking drive and motivation, and their indifference *results in* their poverty. For Manley, eating – as a metaphor for human desire broadly construed – is a sacred act, as he ponders despairingly and with a relevance beyond nutrition: 'Hunger. The lengths I've gone to satisfy it. Yet it always returns' (110). Although he performs an act of sacrilege, of desecration within a Christian ethos and site of worship, his own quasi-religious devotion to exotic food supersedes these concerns. In this sense, we might sympathize with his assumption that if all other food has left him *spiritually* undernourished, a spirit may indeed offer him sustenance. Indeed, the play opens with just such a suggestion, quoting Mathew 25:35: 'I was hungered and ye gave me meat / I was thirsty and ye gave me drink.' The Bible plays on an ambiguity of the spiritual and the bodily here that is also powerfully at work in the Eucharist itself. There is a sense in which Manley sacrifices his life to his pursuit, with a kind of stereotypical or even parodied machismo (he is manly, after all) that contrasts with the homeless David, who, although 'reluctant' to assist, acquiesces with little pressure. Unfortunately, the meal is '[n]ot quite as extraordinary as one may have expected ... A disappointment all in all' (G 126). After a life devoted to satisfying an unfathomable appetite, Manley comes to realize what he has always suspected, even feared: that his 'hunger' itself is 'not of this earth'.

In an important moment in *A Profile*, the camera, and the viewer, must simply wait for an answer to Anna's questions as Mason 'follows his thoughts'. Something similar occurs in *The Gourmet*; as night falls in the church and the hour of the ghost's arrival approaches, Manley seeks assistance from David, his temporary companion, in finding the vestry. Sated on bread and beans, David is sleeping in a dormitory bed when Manley wakes him. Confused that Manley has not accepted the meal proffered earlier because he was 'going to dine later', and by his odd insistence that food remains in the vestry, David initially 'turns over to go back to sleep' (G 115). However, he then 'remembers the times *he* has been hungry. Almost immediately, he looks up again at Manley, sighs and begins to get up' (115). We are invited here to ponder David's capacity for empathy, which is in stark contrast to Manley's 'taboo-breaking' narcissism. But David's memory, like Mason's 'thoughts', are not detectable by the camera, which cannot reveal 'people's inner worlds'.[25] Intriguingly, in these two examples we see that thoughts (Mason) and memories (David) are available to the page but not the screen. A text can expose us to the unedited processes of thought, whereas a camera can merely 'show us characters thinking' but 'cannot show us thought directly'.[26] We may be led by screenplay, direction, and performance to infer specific ideations or mental content, but this remains latent, gestural. This brings us to the paradoxical crux of the TV play itself, its conceit that some form of material nourishment might be gained from the immaterial, whether culinary or cultural.

Feature-Length Screenplays

The Saddest Music in the World

If the concerns of Ishiguro's short TV plays are UK-based and somewhat parochial, his later, longer works evidence more global ambitions. According to Groes and Veyret, both *The Saddest Music in the World* and *The White Countess* explore hypothetical utopian possibilities in which nations might coexist in harmony.[27] Investigations of this misguided and ultimately futile ambition occur again in *When We Were Orphans* and *The Unconsoled*. Originally written for Channel 4 in 1987 alongside *The Gourmet* and *A Profile*, Ishiguro later said that *The Saddest Music* became 'too big for T.V', so that it spent fifteen years circulating among directors and producers until it found its way to the celebrated Canadian writer and director Guy Maddin in 2002 (*CKI* 212). As Maddin relates, 'this poor thing had been passed around in the bushes like a big bottle of cheap wine, from Atom Egoyan [Ishiguro's preferred director] to Don McKellar to Bruce McDonald, and so forth'.[28] Maddin recalls that the original 'was set in London and in the present day, which was 1983, but its premise was very strong: that there was this contest co-sponsored by a CNN-like news thing and a distillery that would reward countries for singing the saddest song'.[29] Although Maddin liked the premise, he and Toles completely rewrote the script. As Gerry Smyth remarks, only the 'original idea remained: namely, the questions of music's ability to embody emotion and the central role it plays in people's emotional lives'.[30] Maddin and Ishiguro tell very different stories about the collaboration. Maddin remembers that 'right up until the moment before he gave permission, Ishiguro didn't like our treatment. He thought it was terrible.'[31] By contrast, Ishiguro remembers that he had 'never seen a filmmaker' like Maddin who was 'a demi-God in the world of avant-garde filmmaking', and was happy to become a script editor for his own script, which retained 'the very essence' of a story about countries competing to produce 'the saddest music in the world' (*CKI* 213). Maddin and Ishiguro agree, however, that all that remained in the film was the central premise of a brewery-sponsored sad music contest. Shot in black and white in Maddin's characteristic 'imitation of silent' cinema the final film bears little to no relation to the original script.[32] However, *The Saddest Music in the World* shares with Ishiguro's other works a fascination with the political and redemptive possibilities of art, and with the consolations potentially offered by music, which becomes the central motif of his most unfilmable novel, *The Unconsoled*.

The White Countess

Unlike *The Saddest Music in the World*, Ishiguro's second screenplay, for the Merchant and Ivory production *The White Countess*, was used essentially as he intended. Ismail Merchant and James Ivory, who successfully adapted *The Remains of the Day* as a feature film, are famous for the lavish production values of upper-middle-class period dramas often based on classic English novels such as *A Room with a View* and *Howard's End*. But *The White Countess* was poorly received by viewers and critics, and has even been considered a failure by some.[33] Perhaps this is because, as Justin Chang has remarked, 'Ishiguro's ambitious screenplay stalls in its attempts to blend the intimate and the historical on the same canvas' – a remarkable failure for an author whose novels so deftly interweave the personal and national.[34] Another shortcoming of *The White Countess* is that it is Ishiguro's most conventional story, lacking the technical strategies that make his work so distinctively powerful. Although crucial plot details are at first occluded before being gradually revealed (in a similar manner to his novels and short stories), and despite the recurrent intrusion of flashbacks and distorted memories so typical of Ishiguro's fictions, the narrative is linear, the relationships both uneventful and lacking the deeply divisive ambiguities facilitated by his complexly narrated fictions. This might be attributable to the fact that, as Ishiguro himself remarks, he was 'writing for a very specific director' (James Ivory), who has a very specific cinematic style and way of working, and felt there was 'no point my writing stuff that he's not going to do' (*CKI* 212). Critics have commented on the connections between *The White Countess* and Ishiguro's other works, noting the way the film returns to the late-1930s Shanghai of *When We Were Orphans*, and to a consideration of the consequences of the 1919 Treaty of Versailles in *The Remains of the Day*; and to its interest in multicultural microcosms of bars and cafes that is also evident in *The Unconsoled*. As Lisa Fluet suggests, the film 'invokes many character-types, plot situations, settings and conflicts developed in his novels ...

rearranges the remembered novelistic material in the same way that Ishiguro's protagonists rearrange material from their own pasts'.[35] The screenplay acts a bit like a photo album, parading Ishiguro's familiar themes before the camera. While these intertextual echoes are interesting, I want to consider the ways in which it manifests Ishiguro's engagement with film as form, by drawing attention to the screenplay's fascination with the senses, particularly sight and sound, and internal experience in the form of imagination.

The White Countess returns to a recurrent theme in Ishiguro's work: war and its aftermath. The script builds on *When We Were Orphans*, which Ishiguro had recently finished and for which he had a 'whole lot of research' he had not used (*CKI* 212). Like much of the early sections of *When We Were Orphans* in which Banks's childhood is conveyed, *The White Countess* takes place in Shanghai's International Settlement immediately prior to and during the beginning of the second Sino-Japanese War, which was instigated by the Japanese invasion of mainland China in 1937. As Ishiguro has remarked in an interview, 'that entire world stopped instantly when the Japanese moved in'.[36] Ishiguro has a personal connection with the city: his father was born in Shanghai after his grandfather was sent there to set up a Chinese branch of Toyota.[37] Unlike *When We Were Orphans*, which divides the action between China and London, very little of *The White Countess* takes place beyond the boundaries of the Settlement, which means, as Cheng remarks, that we see the 'foreignness of the Chinese city and the oddity of the Chinese people [presenting] a Western impression of pre-war Shanghai, in which the cityscape is lively and theatrical while Chinese natives seem inert and irrelevant'.[38] However, this outside perspective seems entirely suited to a film which explores colonialism, invasion, and cultural appropriation.

The film's plot is relatively straightforward: Todd Jackson, a 'distinguished American diplomatist' blinded in a terrorist attack which had killed his daughter (years after another had killed his wife and first child), lives in Shanghai in the late 1930s and creates the 'bar of [his] dreams' after a sizeable win at the racetrack (*WC* 00:13:38).[39] He headhunts his ideal staff, even security, because 'with a good team of bouncers ... you could conduct the place like an orchestra' (00:15:18–00:15:20). Most importantly, Jackson seeks a hostess, the titular 'White Countess', Russian émigré Countess Sofia Belinskaya, now a taxi dancer – a paid dance-partner employed to attract clientele – in a run-down club. Again, we see some problematic colonial politics, here, as Jackson works to create his colony (the bar) within the colony (the Settlement) and to port European royalty into an Oriental enclave secured by his 'bouncers'. His vision for the bar is a kind of settlement within the settlement, a further refined micro-instantiation of the ostensibly cosmopolitan international zone, but one over which he would exercise total control with the Countess as figurehead.

However, Jackson realizes that without 'political tension' his bar would be no more than 'confection'; so he and his mysterious acquaintance Matsuda, a 'much feared and loathed' Japanese military official (although Jackson is unaware of this), arrange to introduce 'Chinese Soldiers ... Japanese merchant sailors', along with businessmen, gangsters, and communists (WC 01:07:58–01:08:10). Like a diplomat, with echoes of Lord Darlington, Jackson assumes somewhat hubristically that he can manage these deep ideological divisions in the tightly controlled confines of the bar. His intentions, as Fluet argues, are seemingly altruistic, or at least benign: the bar is not an escape 'from the terror lurking outside – but rather a figure for, or a portal to, a world in which things might be repaired'.[40] One might indeed see such an endeavour as offering a model for larger spaces of reconciliation. But one might by contrast see a further example of interwar American geopolitical interference facilitated by wealth. Unfortunately, Matsuda has been in Shanghai preparing the way for an invasion. Shortly after *The White Countess* opens, the bombs fall and Jackson is forced to flee the city. The attack is figured in the script not simply as an assault on Shanghai, but on the possibility of a harmonious post-national or post-racial political space, and as such stands as an act of ideological violence.

As we have already noted, the distinction that Ishiguro draws between fiction (introspective) and film (external) is reducible to the fact that, as Bluestone puts it, 'the novel is a linguistic medium, the film essentially visual'.[41] Film relies on the senses, particularly sight and sound, and so its antitheses are blindness and deafness. *The White Countess* plays with the distinction between sight and vision, and the screenplay simply would not work with a sighted Jackson because it would not then be able to develop its central rhetorical conceit. Ishiguro and Ivory recall that the idea of a blind protagonist was added after the film had been cast and shooting had started. Either way, whether preconceived or developing organically, metaphors of vision and sightlessness come to play a prominent role in the symbolic infrastructure of the film. Interestingly, the screenplay was originally adapted from a novel by Junichiro Tanizaki, whose other notable works include the short story 'Moumoku Monogatari' ('A Blind Man's Tale', 1931), is narrated by a blind servant, and there is a possibility that Ishiguro creatively interwove fruitful elements from each work.[42] Although ocularly impaired, Jackson has a fascination with seeing things, with vision, and often remarks that things are inside his head, that he somehow sees things inside. Again, by constructing visual scenarios which involve the absence of mental images but the implication of ideations in the character's mind, Ishiguro draws our attention to the limits of film and to the unfilmable. If film can 'show us characters thinking' but not thought, here it can show us a character imagining things but not the thing imagined.[43] While reinforcing the ocular distinction between film and text, the scenario also enables a sustained interrogation of the idea of vision, of sight, foreground-ing the capacity of imagination to construct internal 'sights' even in the unsighted. However, where Jackson imagines rather than 'sees' his ideal nightclub in his mind, the viewer is encouraged also to share in Jackson's vision, and in this sense although Jackson's (implied) mental content cannot be visualized on screen, it evokes cognate images in the mind of the viewer.

In conversations with his colleague, Jackson also explores the difference between 'looking' and 'seeing', pointing out that the former may prevent an obstacle to the latter: 'You don't see any of This, do you, Thomas? I mean, you look at This and you see nothing. Nothing' (WC 01:20:30). In many ways this is an overused image, of the blind seer, dating back at least to Tiresias. In this scene, however, and in the film more generally, the implica-tion is that even if film can render something visually, there is something beyond show (Jackson's ideational deictic 'This') that can only ever be hinted at by the camera. In this sense, Jackson's ethical blindness to the corruption of the Settlement and his own complicity in it enables him imaginatively to sustain an idealized view of a pragmatically unsustainable space that, as Cheng remarks, is already segregated from the wider Chinese community in which the Settlement and the bar sit. Jackson unwittingly recreates the colonial enterprise which leads directly to the 'terror' of war which textures the work, as Japan seeks to expand into China. In this sense, Thomas, unable to imagine the micro-utopian space of Jackson's vision because it seems both unrealizable and untenable in the instability of the Settlement, has a form of sight that Jackson does not.

Jackson remains conceptually and morally 'blind' to the implications of his interference, and constructing these hypothetical political spaces in this and other works Ishiguro develops what Rebecca L. Walkowitz calls a 'critical cosmopolitanism', whereby comparisons are generated 'not to create equivalences but to notice continuities and mergings among different polit-ical circumstances'.[44] Walkowitz suggests that critical cosmopolitanism does not seek to flatten out difference by reducing political and national complex-ities, but rather to trace points of intersection and shared concerns. For Ishiguro, 1930s Shanghai was 'almost a prototype of the great multicultural cities that we find today: lots of different ethnic groups' and necessarily 'rivalries between outside powers, a great place for gangsters, a drug cul-ture'.[45] While the film examines the 'possibility of creating a utopia where harmony between nations might be established', it is also a failed project (again, not least because it is inherently exclusionary and colonialist in its ambitions). Ishiguro has commented that while researching When We Were

Orphans he had 'become interested in subjects like the Russians and the Jews' (*CKI* 212). This interest is foregrounded in the screenplay: while travelling through an area of deprivation to visit Sofia, Jackson hears someone shouting at her neighbour, Mr Samuel Feinstein, 'Jew! Dirty Jewish scum!' (*WC* 00:31:56). Jackson, a little naively shocked for a well-travelled diplomat, asks '[d]o you have to put up with a lot of that around here?' (01:34:05). Feinstein asks '[w]as someone shouting something bad? I didn't listen. Luckily, I'm hard of hearing …. That kind of thing … after what we've endured, what is it? Nothing. I don't hear it. The children don't hear it' (01:34:07–01:34:45). Like Jackson, Feinstein feels 'lucky' to not have the use of a sense which might impinge on the more inclusive world he constructs for himself and his children. But Feinstein is selectively deaf, and has become not literally unhearing but rather impervious to the anti-Semitism from which the Jewish inhabitants of the city had attempted to escape. In a foreshadowing of the theme of memory loss in *The Buried Giant*, Ishiguro seems to be suggesting that one way in which harmony can be achieved in multicultural and multi-ethnic spaces is for individuals to adapt to prejudice by electively and selectively editing sensory experience or even memories of past traumas. However, one might see this as simply a temporary illusion of harmony, a reading supported by the conclusion to *The Buried* Giant.

The White Countess, like *A Profile of Arthur J. Mason* and *The Gourmet*, plays with the senses most associated with film and that give it its 'medium specificity'. Sight and sound are crucial not only to film as an art, but to the possibilities it sustains in distinction to text. If film's strength over the novel is its capacity to not simply provide prompts for visualizations but to present scenes themselves, it is also its very reliance on spectacle and those things susceptible to display (objects, actions) which limits its capacity to examine qualia, memory. *The White Countess*, by repeatedly drawing attention to the distinction between ocular vision and vision more broadly construed, interrogates the limits of its own form, while also metaphorically gesturing towards the other varieties of blindness which inhabit the film.

Ishiguro's screenplays have not been met with the acclaim accorded to his literary fiction. His idiosyncratic style of incremental, almost accidental revelation, linguistic ambiguity, and repetition with subtle memory-distorted variation, shares more with the introspective possibilities offered by writing. Moreover, what distinguishes and even elevates Ishiguro's fiction writing is his development of a unique and uniquely peculiar narrative voice, one which relies upon varieties of evasion and (self-)deceit difficult to render on screen. Returning to his own taxonomy, the confessional stories he tells are more suited to a form that is 'able to explore people's inner worlds' than it is to one which exploits the 'exterior', 'third-person' world.[46] Although scholarship has been interested in finding connections with his fiction, his works for television and film have a significance beyond such references. His films tease out those things which are impervious to the camera but central to the page: internal states, 'qualia', in the form(lessness) of 'thoughts' (*A Profile of Arthur J. Mason*), 'memories' (*The Gourmet*), and 'imagination' (*The White Countess*). Most recently, Ishiguro has written the script for the Oliver Hermanus film *Living* (2022), an English-language adaptation of Akira Kurosawa's 1952 film *Ikiru*. Once more, Ishiguro returns to the Japanese cultural heritage which has had such an influence on his life and work. *Ikiru* has all the essential elements for an Ishiguro work, dwelling on personal and professional regrets, turning points missed, and wrong paths taken. Ishiguro has said that

> [t]he inner story [of *Ikiru*] suggests that it's the responsibility of each of us to bring meaning and satisfaction to our life. That even against the odds, we should try to find a way to be proud of, and happy with, the lives we lead [while] struggling to see what our individual contributions can possibly amount to within the broader picture.[47]

It is enlightening to see how Ishiguro has adapted such an iconic work of Japanese cinema to a British cast and setting, with Bill Nighy, stalwart of the quintessentially British cinema, starring as a terminally ill civil servant in post-war London, trying valiantly, like so many of Ishiguro's characters, to make a meaningful contribution to society – or to make amends for a life of inaction and servitude, before his death. Ishiguro's adaptation of the Japanese film, and its translation into a 1950s British setting, further illuminates both his engagement with film and his interest in drawing links between two distinct cultures. More, *Living* is evidence that Ishiguro's interest in film and film-as-form is not simply casual but has persisted from the earliest days of his career, and that his work with film and for television has been and continues to be a fruitful counterpoint to his other writing. Perhaps more scholarly attention should be paid to modes of writing that, while exploiting different techniques and sensory experiences, share a great deal with Ishiguro's celebrated novels.

Notes

1 Charlie Rose, 'Kazuo Ishiguro', 10 October 1995 (accessed online at https://charlierose.com/videos/18999).

2 Linda L. Richards, 'January Interview: Kazuo Ishiguro', *January Magazine*, October 2000 (accessed online at www.januarymagazine.com/profiles/ishiguro.html).

3 Moira Macdonald, 'Novelist Kazuo Ishiguro on the Film Adaptation of *Never Let Me Go*', *The Seattle Times*, 5 October 2010 (accessed online at www .seattletimes.com/entertainment/movies/novelist-kazuo-ishiguro-on-the-film-adap tation-of-never-let-me-go).

4 So devoted is he to film that he 'has a home cinema … with special seating and blackout blinds' in his London house (see Nicholas Wroe, 'Living Memories', *The Guardian*, 19 February 2005 (accessed online at www.theguardian.com/books/ 2005/feb/19/fiction.kazuoishiguro)).

5 Rebecca Karni, 'Made in Translation: Language, "Japaneseness", "Englishness", and "Global Culture" in Ishiguro', *Comparative Literature Studies* 52:2 (2015): 318–48 (328).

6 Anni Shen, 'Adapting Mizoguchi's *Ugetsu* in Kazuo Ishiguro's *The Buried Giant*', *Adaptation* 15:2 (2022): 207–22.

7 Kazuo Ishiguro, 'Thatcher's London and the Role of the Artist in a Time of Political Change', *The Guardian*, 24 June 2016 (accessed online at www.theguar dian.com/books/2016/jun/24/kazuo-ishiguro-my-turning-point-reading-proust-on-my-sickbed.

8 'An Interview with Kazuo Ishiguro', *Book Browse* (2005) (accessed online at www.bookbrowse.com/author_interviews/full/index.cfm/author_number/477/ kazuo-ishiguro).

9 Rose, 'Kazuo Ishiguro'; 'An Interview'.

10 See, for example, Berys Gaut's explanation that 'for a medium to constitute an art form it must instantiate artistic properties that are distinct from those that are instantiated in other media' (*A Philosophy of Cinematic Art* (Cambridge: Cambridge University Press, 2010), p.287).

11 Kamilla Elliott, 'Unfilmable Books', in Julie Grossman and R. Barton Palmer, eds., *Adaptation in Visual Culture: Images, Texts, and Their Multiple Worlds* (Cham: Palgrave Macmillan, 2017), p.21.

12 Michael Whyte, *The August Passage: A Profile of Arthur J. Mason* (Channel 4: 1984); Michael Whyte, *The Gourmet* (Channel 4: 1987). Kazuo Ishiguro, *The Saddest Music in the World* (1987 screenplay unpublished and unfilmed, but loosely adapted by Guy Maddin in 2003). James Ivory, *The White Countess* (Merchant Ivory Productions: 2005). Hereafter citations will be made parenthetically and abbreviated *AJM*, *G*, *SM*, and *WC* respectively. Many thanks to Paul McAllister at ScreenOcean for sending me the video of *A Profile of Arthur J. Mason* and of *The Gourmet* from the Channel 4 archive.

13 This trauma persists into *The Unconsoled*, as Hoffman lives in the perpetual (and ultimately groundless) fear that his wife will leave him when she discovers he is not a composer.

14 *A Profile* and *The Remains of the Day* share much: in her contribution to the present volume, Vanessa Guignery traces the connection through the Ishiguro archive, held at the Harry Ransom Center.

15 Barry Lewis, *Kazuo Ishiguro* (Manchester: Manchester University Press, 2000), p.76.

16 Ishiguro, 'Thatcher's London'.

17 As Setsuko does in *A Pale View of Hills*, Kathrine aspires to move because '[t]hings are different in America' (*AJM* 10).

18 George Bluestone, *Novels into Film: The Metamorphosis of Novels into Cinema* (Berkeley: University of California Press, 1968), p.48.

19 Some disagreement exists about the first broadcast, but the archived video dates the film to 1986.

20 Lewis, *Kazuo Ishiguro*, p.xii. Ishiguro, 'The Gourmet', *Granta: Best of Young British Novelists* 43 (1993), p.91.

21 Waiting for a ghost is also the subject of Ishiguro's short story 'Waiting for J.' (1981).

22 Sebastian Groes and Paul-Daniel Veyret, '"Like the Gateway to Another World": Kazuo Ishiguro's Screenwriting', in Sean Matthews and Sebastian Groes, eds., *Kazuo Ishiguro* (London: Continuum, 2009), p.38.

23 Wai-chew Sim, *Kazuo Ishiguro: A Routledge Guide* (Oxford: Routledge, 2010), p.101.

24 Groes and Veyret, 'Like the Gateway to Another World', p.38.

25 Richards, 'January Interview'.

26 Bluestone, *Novels into Film*, p.48.

27 Groes and Veyret, 'Like the Gateway to Another World', p.32.

28 Jonathan Ball, 'No Sob Story: Director Guy Maddin and Screenwriter George Toles on Collaboration *The Saddest Music in the World*' (2004) (accessed online at www.jonathanball.com/guy-maddin-and-george-toles-interview/).

29 Paula Bernstein, 'Guy Maddin on *The Saddest Music in The World* and His Interactive *Seances*', *Filmmaker*, 29 March 2016 (accessed online at https://filmmakermagazine.com/97888-guy-maddin-on-the-saddest-music-in-the-world-and-his-interactive-seances/#.YyRKvKSSmFQ).

30 Gerry Smyth, '"Waiting for the Performance to Begin": Kazuo Ishiguro's Musical Imagination, in *The Unconsoled* and *Nocturnes*', in Sebastian Groes and Barry Lewis, eds., *Kazuo Ishiguro: New Critical Visions of the Novels* (Basingstoke: Palgrave Macmillan, 2011), p.145.

31 Ball, 'Guy Maddin and George Toles'.

32 William Beard, *Into the Past: The Cinema of Guy Maddin* (Toronto: University of Toronto Press, 2010), p.20.

33 Chu-chueh Cheng, 'Reframing Ishiguro's Oeuvre through the Japanese Militarist in *The White Countess*', *Orbis Litterarum* 74:6 (2019): 381–91.

34 Justin Chang, 'Review: *The White Countess*', *Variety*, 27 November 2005 (accessed online at https://variety.com/2005/film/awards/the-white-countess-1200520062/).

35 Lisa Fluet, 'Introduction: Antisocial Goods', *Novel: A Forum on Fiction* 40:3 (2007): 207–15 (207–8).

36 Howard W. French, 'Searching for Scenes from Shanghai's Lost Past', *The New York Times*, 28 November 2004 (accessed online at www.nytimes.com/2004/11/28/movies/MoviesFeatures/searching-for-scenes-from-shanghais-lost-past.html).

37 Stuart Jeffries, 'Shanghai Surprise', *The Guardian*, 30 March 2006 (accessed online at www.theguardian.com/film/2006/mar/30/china).

38 Chu-chueh Cheng, 'Shanghai in *The White Countess*: Production and Consumption of an Oriental City through the Western Cinematic Gaze', in Lisa Bernstein and Cheng, eds., *Revealing/Reveiling Shanghai Cultural Representations from the Twentieth and Twenty-First Centuries* (New York: SUNY Press, 2020), p.163.

39 Andrew Bennett traces the figurative use of blinds and blindness in *When We Were Orphans* in Peter Sloane and Kristian Shaw, eds., *Kazuo Ishiguro: New Essays* (Manchester: Manchester University Press, 2023).

40 Fluet, 'Antisocial Gods', p.233.

41 Bluestone, *Novels into Film*, p.vii.

42 Junichiro Tanizaki, *Seven Japanese Tales*, trans. Howard Hibbett (London: Vintage International, 1997).

43 Ibid., p.48.

44 Rebecca L. Walkowitz, *Cosmopolitan Style: Modernism Beyond the Nation* (New York: Columbia University Press, 2006), p.109.

45 French, 'Searching for Scenes'.

46 Richards, 'January Interview'.

47 Andrea Wiseman, '"Living": Bill Nighy & Aimee Lou Wood to Star in Kazuo Ishiguro Adaptation of Kurosawa's "Ikiru" for "Carol" Producer Number 9 & Rocket Science', *Deadline*, 15 October 2020 (accessed online at https://deadline.com/2020/10/living-bill-nighy-aimee-lou-wood-to-star-in-kazuo-ishiguro-adaptation-of-kurosawas-ikiru-for-carol-producer-number-9-rocket-science-afm-1234597919/).

11

STEPHEN BENSON

'I'm a Songwriter at Heart, Even When I'm Writing Novels'

Ishiguro and Music

One of the more benign markers of mainstream public success, as that success is celebrated in the UK, is an invitation to appear on BBC Radio 4's venerable Desert Island Discs. The programme, rather than relying solely on a conventional confessional interview, employs a words-and-music model of autobiographical show-and-tell: an interview accompanied by a set of eight pieces of music chosen for the occasion by the guest. While both elements are broadly within the control of the interviewee, the music, how-ever knowingly stage-managed in advance, sounds in the moment as a shadow autobiography whose relation to the words it supplements has the potential for all manner of counterpoint, both consonant and otherwise.

Kazuo Ishiguro appeared on the programme in February 2002. His musical choices were noteworthy for all being songs – 'I have a problem with orchestras', he admitted – whether written and performed by notable singer-songwriters – Emmylou Harris, Gillian Welch, Bob Dylan, Leonard Cohen – or interpreted according to the conventions of a particular vocal genre: the folk-song tradition, in the shape of Dick Gaughan's rendition of 'Now Westlin Winds', and items from the Great American Songbook as performed respect-ively by Stacey Kent and, as instrumental jazz standard, Keith Jarrett.[1] The exception was Chopin's Nocturne Op. 27, No. 2; an exception that proved the rule insofar as it is one of the quintessentially songful melodies of Romantic piano literature, in keeping with the nineteenth-century piano nocturne as a genre characterized by an artfully song-like melody. Ishiguro's selection thus suggested a listener for whom song *is* music, a music whose ostensible simpli-city is the source of an enduringly elusive attraction.

The castaway's musical choices were on this occasion consonant with the official biography. Song and songwriting are two from a handful of struc-turing motifs in the Ishiguro story; indeed, song figures as the origin of the self-narrated story of Ishiguro the writer: from taking up the piano aged five and the guitar aged fifteen, through to the arrival of pop music around the age of eleven and a first encounter with Dylan (*John Wesley Harding*) at thirteen. Listening to Dylan and then Cohen was the spur to try songwriting, during a period, lasting well into his twenties, that Ishiguro refers to now as his 'apprenticeship'.[2] The practice of writing, according to the author's own much-repeated formulation, begins in song: 'Many of the things I do, still to this day as a writer, as a novelist, I think it [sic] has its foundations in what I discovered and the kind of place that I arrived at as a writer of songs'; and not only begins in song, but continues as an informing relation between one art and another: 'I realize, even now, new things about songs and the value system that counts when you try to write songs .... I now realize more and more as I get older how they define my decisions as a novelist.'[3]

Perhaps the most revealing version of this autobiographical topos was given by Ishiguro in an interview following the publication of *The Buried Giant* (a novel hardly notable for its music): 'I'm a songwriter at heart, even when I'm writing novels.'[4] There is something of the performative about this statement – something songlike, that is – in its being nonchalantly throwaway and yet rather extraordinary. How might it be understood by a reader? What evidence does the writing provide of the profound, and specifically heartfelt, importance of music in Ishiguro's work? The author himself is certainly an astute commentator on the sustaining appeal of the art of the song in particular, in ways clearly conceived in terms of a stated or implied relation to the formal and tonal properties of his writing. In the Desert Island Discs interview he speaks of the Chopin nocturne as having a 'simple, still surface' the effect of which is to suggest profound emotion (he agrees with the interviewer's interpretation of the latter in terms of yearning and nostalgia, especially for childhood). The attraction of song is characterized as an art of elusiveness, whether of the singing voice itself – 'There's something almost impossible to capture in words about the quality of a singing performance' – or the evocative undecidability of a lyric's meaning.[5] It is hardly a surprise to find Ishiguro, a novelist of lost things, drawn especially to songs 'where you can't figure out what it is they're missing'.[6]

Song thus deployed is both a redescription and explanation of a general aspect of Ishiguro's writing, following a conventional structure of interpretative relation between the two arts, the verbal and the musical. An inclination towards formal and thematic variations on a small number of elements is another such general aspect that might be understood according to this convention. And of course, two of Ishiguro's works, *The Unconsoled* and *Nocturnes: Five Stories of Music and Nightfall*, offer straightforwardly confirming evidence of music's continued importance to his work, as does his original screenplay for what became the Guy Maddin film, *The Saddest Music in the World*, and, more recently, his having written lyrics for the American singer Stacey Kent.[7]

Yet there remains the summative statement by which the author expresses the defining centrality of music to his work *in toto*: 'I'm a songwriter at heart, even when I'm writing novels.' Surveying the Ishiguro canon with this notion in mind, it is striking how little actual music there is in the fiction; and of that little, how much is elusive, fleeting, and, in writerly terms, apparently slight. A number of the major works contain no mention of music of any kind, whether alluded to, written, performed, or recalled. Ishiguro's novels, mined for musical materials and inflections, are notable for their seeming avoidance, in large part, of precisely those inherited formal, descriptive, and thematic modes by which writers have sought to conjure and employ music in fictional prose. References to music appear rarely as part of the descriptive texture of the writing, in keeping with a relatively plain prose register. Neither is Ishiguro drawn to the resonantly detailed musical intertext such as we find in Thomas Mann on Beethoven, in Proust's 'petit phrase', or variously in Milan Kundera. The film adaptation of *The Remains of the Day* includes a telling scene in which guests invited to an '"unofficial" international conference' at Darlington Hall in March 1923 – Lord Darlington wishes to discuss a 'relaxing of various aspects of the Versailles treaty' – gather round a piano to hear an impromptu performance of Schubert's song, 'Sei mir gegrüsst', D.741.[8] The viewer is clearly intended to register the historical poignancy of the moment: the complacency and ultimate complicity of those for whom high culture serves as a self-confirming guard against barbarism. Faith in music's ineffably humanizing nobility proves once again to be a sign of ill health rather than of general immunity. No doubt Ishiguro is broadly in agreement with the political implications of the song as used here, but no such scene of precisely pitched musical intertextuality appears in the original novel nor elsewhere in the majority of his fiction. The writing rarely if ever offers an opportunity for close reading such as might be prompted by 'Sei mir gegrüsst' as an intertext in the screen adaptation of the novel. There is certainly no extended musical ekphrasis in Ishiguro. Musical intertexts do appear, namely the invented contemporary composers, works, and musical idioms of *The Unconsoled* and those instances of the Great American Songbook mentioned in several of the *Nocturnes*; but again, the musical material here is lightly sketched and offers relatively little to the reader in terms of a reciprocally informing relation between specific aspects of the two arts.

If ekphrasis and intertextuality are the first two of the trio of standard translational strategies for the musically minded novelist, formal modelling is the third. Influential examples of this third mode include Joyce's fugal permutations in the Sirens episode of *Ulysses*, the disputational counterpointing of Thomas Bernhard, the long-form leitmotivic structuring of Mann, and the various registers of jazz-inflected improvisational development used by Toni Morrison and Ishmael Reed. Ishiguro has spoken of the 'symphonic style' of Dostoevsky as a presiding influence on his work, *The Unconsoled* in particular, and of the constituent stories of *Nocturnes* as having a set of interrelations akin to those we might expect to find in both a sonata (as he calls it) and a 'concept album'.[9] More specifically, the variational mode detectable in *Nocturnes* can be read as modelled after the interpretive tradition of the American Songbook, the life of which is sustained over generations by a collective project of creative reinterpretation similar in kind to that of individual folk-song traditions. Anne Whitehead frames Ishiguro's interest here in the American Songbook in terms of an idea of repertoire as opposed to archive – 'a system of performed, embodied, and iterative behaviours through which knowledge is transmitted' – although, as her essay indicates, this is more a matter of the conceptual and ethical concerns of the collection than of any substantially descriptive, formal or structural properties of the constituent stories.[10] Ishiguro himself has confessed to not liking 'musical analogies' of this kind; and at the risk of sounding underwhelmed at the prospect, it could be said that they offer relatively slim critical pickings for the reader concerned specifically with the music of Ishiguro, certainly as compared with those resonantly reciprocal relations of form attempted by the likes of Mann and Morrison.[11]

I say specifically concerned, because of course there are undoubtedly scenes of music in the novels and stories – scenes of listening, performing, discussing – just as there are scenes involving all sorts of other objects, arts, and activities, few of which would ever be judged by the reader or critic to warrant special attention. A number of these scenes, specifically in *Nocturnes*, are modest in musical terms, however else they may signify or provoke; modest to the extent that some mainstream reviews of the collection regard the subtitle – *Five Stories of Music and Nightfall* – as a red herring. The presence of music in a writer's work does not necessarily mean that the work or the writer must have something of note to say about music, or about the relation of music and literature. A novel about music, or a short story collection, is not necessarily *about* music. Aboutness, after all, is a rather slippery quality, never more so than when the object in question, at least as conventionally conceived, is already notoriously elusive. Indeed, we might say that the subject of music is something of a test case for novelistic aboutness. Ishiguro himself, speaking of *The Unconsoled*, his musically themed novel, suggests that 'music is there as a kind of metaphor', one that 'stands for politics . . . for economic arguments'. It is an authorial steer that appears to confirm Roland Barthes's proposition that 'the value of music' is 'to be a good metaphor'.[12] Does it not follow from this that the reader and critic should concentrate their attention on the tenor of the metaphor rather than the vehicle?

Again, the quality most striking about music in Ishiguro's fiction, relative to the author's avowed and presiding love for the art form, is not its prominence or density of presentation so much as its textural and descriptive lightness, and the relative infrequency of its appearance. Borrowing further from Barthes, a fellow lover of song, we might read this quality symptomatically as a desire to preserve the uniqueness of the love object; specifically, to keep the quiddity of music alive in the writing precisely by shielding it from the deadening effect of extended adjectival fixing: from description and related registers. The ready-made adjective, precisely in its being on hand as part of an existing 'image-repertoire', is the verbal response most likely to neutralize the very thing that has provoked the desire to respond or testify, or simply to investigate in writing.[13] Music, for self-declared lovers of the art such as Barthes, 'is what struggles with writing', not what comes easily.[14] The relative absence in Ishiguro of extended musical ekphrasis or formal modelling is thus significant for any account of music's meaning for the author and his works; and yet the nature of that significance can only be established when set alongside an account of the particular music that Ishiguro does conjure, however slight-seeming or ordinary it appears. This preliminary conjunction of two kinds of literary music, one absent, the other modestly present, is figured in the ambient encounter that opens *The Unconsoled*, as Ryder arrives at his hotel. Although 'reasonably spacious', the lobby has a sagging ceiling the effect of which, much like that of Ishiguro's writing generally, is 'a slightly claustrophobic mood'. The ambient acoustic quality of the mood emerges as Ryder becomes 'aware that a piano is being played somewhere in the building, just audible above the muffled noise of the traffic outside'. The music comes to colour the mood and, having noticed the effect, Ryder 'listens more closely' (*U* 3–4). Taking our cue from this scene, we can ask: what do we hear as we tune in to the quiet literary music of these prose works?

The most memorable passage occurs not in the short story collection dedicated to the art, nor in *The Unconsoled*, but in *Never Let Me Go*. The novel takes its title from a track that appears on *Songs after Dark*, an album from 1956 by the singer Judy Bridgewater. A cassette tape of the album is owned by Kathy, the novel's narrator. It is her 'favourite tape', 'one of [her] most precious possessions' (*NLMG* 64). The copy of the tape Kathy has at the time of narration was purchased as a replacement for the lost, or 'disappeared', original she happened across at school in one of the Sales. Kathy notes that the cover of the tape is likely a 'scaled-down version of the record sleeve' and offers a brief description of the scene depicted (67). Yet she admits to having little interest in the singer or the album, only in 'this one particular song: track number three, "Never Let Me Go"': 'It's slow and late night and American, and there's a bit that keeps coming round when Judy sings "Never let me go ... Oh baby, baby ... Never let me go ..."' (69). Kathy imagines for herself a scene to accompany the song in which a woman sings the words to the baby she was told she couldn't have, and which she now worries she will lose. The tape disappears sometime after an 'incident' in which Madame happens to witness Kathy acting out her fantasy scenario as the song plays: 'singing along softly each time those lines came around again' (71).

Kathy admits that her imagined interpretation '[doesn't] fit with the rest of the lyrics', but is unconcerned: 'The song was about what I said' (*NLMG* 70). Ishiguro has confessed to a not dissimilar response to the evocative undecidability of song lyrics, a quality he identifies as part of the defining character of popular music (hence his affection for those songs in which 'you can't figure out what it is they're missing').[15] The scene of Kathy's listening beautifully captures the effect of the pop refrain as what Peter Szendy calls a 'sonorous stereotype': 'that strange structure ... in which the cliché, in its interchangeable banality, is nonetheless *unique every time for each one of us*'.[16] Pop's address is '[e]specially for you', the you that is each of its listeners.[17] The pop moment as performed in *Never Let Me Go* is the quintessential art form of the clone; or at least, it is that art form in which the ethics of the singular copy – '[e]ach time unique, in the impossible' – can be most affectingly sounded.[18] The answer to the question Kathy imagines from her auditor – 'What was so special about the song?' – must be nothing: a precious nothing. Hence the chains of repetition that structure the moment: the song's constitutional unoriginality, both in its generic sound – 'she's one of those singers from her time, cocktail-bar stuff' (*NLMG* 69) – and the authentically 'interchangeable banality' of its lyrics;[19] the technological reproduction of the LP; the transporting of the song and its cover art via the new technology of the cassette, together with the copies of the lost original; and Kathy's creative misreading as itself a form of interpretive cloning. Pop song is the 'good metaphor' for cloning because the pop song is a copy, albeit without an original, and because it encapsulates the affective force of a uniqueness structured by programmed repetition. There is of course nothing special about novelized pop music in this regard. All such verbal artefacts, musical and otherwise, appear as potential figures within the symbolic weave of the novel – of all novels. As themselves, such artefacts are always also something else; the question is only how provokingly effective they are in their doublings.

The song and its singer in *Never Let Me Go* are fictional in the sense of not having referents in the world. Ishiguro imagined 'a torch singer from the '50s, someone like Julie London', which explains Kathy's account of the music as generic 'cocktail-bar stuff'.[20] And yet 'Never Let Me Go' sounds beyond the confines of this particular novel's coding in such a way as to suggest the significance of the song as music rather than, or as well as, figure. A song with this title and of the appropriate musical type does exist, as Ishiguro knew at the time and has subsequently acknowledged. It is a ballad written by Ray Evans and Jay Livingston for a 1956 film noir, *The Scarlet Hour*. Nat King Cole performs the song in the film and was the first to make a recording. It is one of what Robert G. Kaiser refers to as the 'cousins' of the American Songbook and, as such, has had a rich afterlife both as a song and an instrumental jazz standard.[21] One instance of this afterlife is the version performed by Stacey Kent on her 2007 album, *Breakfast on the Morning Tram*. That it should have been chosen by Kent might be explained by the fact that this is the album for which Ishiguro wrote lyrics for four songs. The collaboration followed after Kent heard the author pick her version of Gershwin's 'They Can't Take That Away from Me' for his fictional desert island. Ishiguro's lyrics, as suggested by their titles, are new Songbook cousins of their own: 'The Ice Hotel', 'I Wish I Could Go Travelling Again', 'Breakfast on the Morning Tram', and 'So Romantic'. Each sounds a modestly well-turned variation on the genre, with urbane rhymes telling wistfully of loves past and present, and of the romance of the elsewhere.[22]

'Never let me go / Love me much too much / If you let me go / Life would lose its touch': so implores the voice in the original copy of Ishiguro's song.[23] To ask never to be let go is to imply that in the present one is being held; that one's love for the other is experienced as a form of holding. In the moment of our listening – of Ishiguro's melophilic listening and writing specifically – it is the song itself by which we are addressed; the generic song which, in its being momentarily unique, conjures, indeed depends upon, a felt experience of the same for each of its listeners. The song holds us and, in so doing, has its being; and in our being interpellated by its address, its life is secured. For the song is sounding out itself, as if singing of its own condition. Pop's iterative constitution – '[A] song is always *the* song in general' – has the effect, frequently and somewhat ironically, of self-reflexivity, the apparent naivete of the lyric serving as cover for a sophisticated form of auto-address, what Szendy calls 'auto-positioning'.[24] This voice as heard in the extra-novelistic 'Never Let Me Go' is anxious, eagerly desirous of confirmation and fearful of abandonment, yet suggesting by implication its own continuance as dependant precisely on its *not* being fully and so finally reassured. To be faithful to that songfulness in writing, as that writing seeks silently to acknowledge its having been specially addressed, thus requires that the object and its affects be both held and relinquished; made present and yet somehow also let be or kept elsewhere. Faithfulness, for the melophilic novelist, involves a paradoxically confirming infidelity; and it is this double-ness, in various forms, that lies at the heart of Ishiguro's literary music insofar as that writing sounds something other than or in addition to music's figurative potential. Ample evidence of that potential is provided by the mise en abyme of 'Never Let Me Go' in *Never Let Me Go*, as a figure, both structural and affective, for the central ethical scenario of the drama. Yet wittingly or otherwise, Ishiguro scatters the object of the song both within and beyond the frame of the novel, beginning with the question of its identity and continuing through a series of playful feints and cousinings; of pre- and afterlives. The effect is of a song both there and not there; a song never straightforwardly present as an object in the novel in the way that drawings are, to cite the example of that other non-verbal art form used here and elsewhere by Ishiguro. It is a scenario representative of the most telling aspect of his written music, an aspect the effect of which is akin to equivoca-tion: music made *music-ish*.

The Unconsoled presents something of a test case for this proposition. It is Ishiguro's music novel, and one of the few major novels of recent decades to take contemporary art music as its subject. That Ishiguro should have chosen this particular tradition of practice is surprising given his stated preference for the popular song form, hence for music that tends traditionally to be made from relatively modest means. A bridge of sorts from novel back to song was subsequently offered by the author in the form of 'Breakfast on the Morning Tram', one of the song lyrics written by Ishiguro for Stacey Kent. The song offers 'a recreation of the ending' of the novel, but regardless of its merits, it only serves to underline the fact that *The Unconsoled* uses another musical tradition entirely – complex long-form composed music, its perform-ance and reception – as the occasion for its drama.[25] Beyond that drama, however, the question of the novel's being about music is moot, not only because, as Ishiguro has suggested, the music in question 'stands for polit-ics ... for economic arguments', but also because it features so infrequently. There can be few novels composed around music that have so little music in them – music of any kind, whether described in itself or in relation to aspects of its making, performance, or reception. Even Thomas Bernhard, a fierce sceptic regarding the significance conventionally accorded music in fiction, tends to incorporate in his work a reasonably substantial amount of musical detail. Ishiguro's novel, by comparison, is notable in musical terms primarily for its cast of fictional composers and their respective works: *Verticality*, *Epicycloid*, and *Ventilations* by Mullery, *Dahlia* by Jean-Louis La Roche, Yamanak's *Globe-Structures: Option II*, a number of pieces by Kazan – *Asbestos and Fibre*, *Wind Tunnels*, *Glass Passions*, and *Grotesqueries for Cello and Three Flutes* – and the names Yoshimoto and Grebel.

The composer Ned Rorem, a none-too-enamoured reader of *The Unconsoled*, refers to these titles as 'outré' and to the musical matter of the novel, such as it is, as 'oversimplified' and 'ultimately senseless'.[26] Rather than being outré, however, the titles suggest a now rather dated-sounding late modernism characterized by forbidding formalism and abstraction. This fictional contemporary music is set against a scattering of references to familiar composers of the European canon: to Bach, Beethoven, Mozart, Chopin and Tchaikovsky. 'Even the man in the street could make a reasoned guess' about the workings of this music, according to Christoff, one of the novel's musicians, whereas the sounds of the 'modern forms', being 'so complex now', are beyond the reach of even the 'trained musician' (U 185–6). And therein lies a central concern of *The Unconsoled* and the basis of the novel's thematic structure: the ostensibly competing claims of art music today – of serious music, so the novel implies – insofar as that music is felt to communicate with an audience and so, potentially, serve as the symbolic object around which the shared values and practices of a community might be confirmed and sustained. While the 'good metaphor' of music in *Never Let Me Go* is the vehicle for the ethics of the clone, here in *The Unconsoled* it is the vehicle for an ethics of community and, more broadly, all forms of relations with others, familial and romantic especially. The music of the novel may be 'oversimplified', as Rorem suggests – there is certainly very little by way of descriptive substance – but it certainly is not 'senseless'; it is, rather, as metaphor, only too sensible.

Ryder, Ishiguro's pianist, does not give his scheduled performance. Personal and collective reparation such as might be promised by music thus conceived, is largely withheld. We the readers, along with many of the characters, remain unconsoled – except, that is, insofar as the disputed significance of contemporary music as dramatized *in* the novel is resolved *by* it, in its thematic and symbolic patterning. The meaning of the fictional contemporary music is precisely its withheld meaningfulness as described in the text, a withholding the force of which is due in large part to an inherited conception of music as precisely the art of consolation (Schubert's 'An die Musik' is perhaps the most famous example of the topos). Frustrated or failed communication and the ramifications thereof are what *The Unconsoled* is about; that the reader should be given so little by way of musical substance is therefore only to be expected. When considered within the context of Ishiguro's *oeuvre*, however, this signal element of the novel sounds precisely as an instance of the paradoxical fidelity to its object that marks his literary music. Music's much-fabled consolations are withheld not only because the novel is concerned with the individual and communal predicament of such withholdings, but also because to make those consolations present in writing – to represent them for the reader according to the conventions for doing so – would be, paradoxically, a form of silencing. Peter Dayan, one of the few critics to have given sustained conceptual thought to the relation of music and literature, refers to a music that is 'actively un-spoken' in writing, a phrase that helps to get to the heart of the particular quality of music in Ishiguro's aesthetic.[27] A proper literary music that lives as music and is experienced as such will somehow 'refuse to be the object of a faithful image'.[28] A repertoire of such refusals and escapings constitutes the signature of each writer insofar as the writing works to be animatingly inadequate to its object. *The Unconsoled* works the 'good metaphor' of music just as carefully and affectingly as *Never Let Me Go*, but it is also a sustained performance of actively unspeaking music, albeit by different means. Where the latter works by dispersal and doubling – of holding close while also letting go – the former uses deferral and absence. Moreover, the longer novel has one of the qualities identified by Dayan as accompanying literary music's infidelity: 'a constant longing for fidelity'; for 'the inability to represent can only have value if we know the temptation to believe that we can represent'.[29] The temptation is akin to a longing for consolation; as such, it is not unrelated to the longings of Kathy, and of her and the novel's song. Rorem's composerly dismissal of *The Unconsoled* suggests an inability to conceive the failings of success as regards literature's claim on music, and concomitantly, an inability to imagine the achievement of a particular kind of representational withholding.[30]

Nocturnes, the third text of Ishiguro's that is of particular interest for the musically minded, is designated a set of stories *of music (and nightfall)*. The author's fondness for popular song, and for the Great American Songbook in particular, is evident, along with his abiding interest in the practicalities of musicianship – in practice, performance, and recording; in music as an occasion for romance, and in music's signature comforts. These materials furnish the dramatic and thematic matter, and to that extent the collection does bear out the promise of its subtitle. Yet according to the parallel conception of a literature of music being suggested here, the stories should also include something other; and so they do. It appears in 'Cellists', the final story of the five. Tibor, a young Hungarian cellist temporarily resident in Italy, is approached by an American tourist, Eloise McCormack. Eloise was in the audience for a recital given by Tibor. She was impressed by his playing, and as a self-professed cellist of note herself, recognizes something she calls *'potential'* (N 195). She offers, rather boldly, to help Tibor, and although initially affronted, he accepts. Thus begins a brief series of scenes of teaching in Eloise's hotel room, elliptically described by Ishiguro. Tibor plays – Britten is mentioned, and Rachmaninov – while Eloise listens and then responds verbally. She is frank in her judgement – 'It won't be easy, but you can do it' – but the details of her commentary and instruction are not given, only summarized in terms of their impact: 'Her words would always strike him initially as pretentious and far too abstract, but when he tried to accommodate their thrust into his playing, he was surprised by the effect' (201, 202). Her 'presence' alone, eyes closed and hands 'shadowing the movement' of the player, is enough to summon 'notes that held new depths, new suggestions' (201).

'Cellists' is the counterpart of 'Crooner', the first story in *Nocturnes*. Both are framed anecdotes of love's vicissitudes, melancholic in tone and related in their wistfully itinerant Europeanness to the lyrics Ishiguro wrote for Stacey Kent. Unlike 'Crooner', however, the crux of 'Cellists' involves another of the periodically telltale instances of ambivalence in the author's literary music. The mystery with Eloise the teacher is that she never plays herself. She senses Tibor's awareness of this fact one afternoon and suggests to him that it is on his mind. While she is correct in her intuition, Tibor demurs, saying he prefers their method: 'You suggest verbally, then I play. That way, it's not like I copy, copy, copy. Your words open windows for me. If you played yourself, the windows would not open. I'd only copy' (208). Yet a slight distance has been established and Eloise hears it in Tibor's playing. Her response is a confession of sorts in what is the longest passage of speech in the story. The motif word of the confession is recognition: Eloise's of Tibor's 'very special gift' and, so she believes, his of hers. The fact of their mutual acknowledgement – 'we recognise each other' – outweighs that of her not playing. Eloise, in her own words, is a 'virtuoso', but one 'yet to be *unwrapped*': 'Even as a small girl, I had this instinct. I knew I had to protect my gift against people who, however well-intentioned they were, could completely destroy it' (213). Hence her not having played since she was eleven so as to avoid the harmful influence of those '*professional*' teachers who 'talk so well'.

Confession made, the spell of the relation is broken and the story moves dutifully towards another quietly dying fall. Music has again served as the 'good metaphor', whether as figuring a fragility in the recognition of self and other or, equally conventionally, an ineffability at the heart of the aesthetic relation. Yet that figuring of music also involves a scene of non-communication; indeed, we might say this is the quintessential scene of Ishiguro's writing of music insofar as it can be read as an allegory for the very possibility of such writing (that is, as a figure for the possibility of figuration). Here we have music, in the shape of Tibor, and words, in the shape of Eloise.[31] Each is implicated in a scene of recognition: of knowing, or knowing again. The avoidance of a 'fake' kind of fidelity in the relation – the 'copy' suggested by Tibor, and by implication, the verbal fluency of the professional teacher – requires that literature does not play; that is, does not occupy the place of music, even, or especially, when that occupancy is in the service of music. True recognition involves also, not misrecognition, but a gap, slippage, equivocation, or moment of silence in recognition itself. These gaps and slippages, however fleeting or apparently inconsequential, are the very signature notes of Ishiguro's literary music.

None of which is to suggest that literature might or should relinquish any claim on music. The relation of one art to another persists: not only because literature is perennially desirous of music, but also because music needs literature, odd as that may sound. Conventional wisdom has it that literature is forever inadequate in its relation to music, hence a tendency to deferential idealization. Deference of this kind has certainly not been a hindrance to writing; indeed, many of the canonical works of musically minded literature have resulted from such an attitude. The amorous relation of one art to the other does not, however, require a melocentric hierarchy of word and tone; not if we acknowledge that music is in a sense always already literary. As Peter Szendy puts it, 'there is no music that produces itself as such, that appears as such without diverging from itself, without letting a gap open at its heart'.[32] The constitution and so hearing of music as music, rather than as undifferentiated sound, specifically requires an act of self-divergence – Szendy's 'gap' – that is made by and happens in language. Music in this sense depends upon the recognition of words, hence the poignancy of Eloise's time with Tibor. Literature about music, according to this alternative conception, is simply the artful working out of music's inherent wordfulness.

What distinguishes those singular forms of literary music, forms such as we find in Ishiguro, is the inclusion also of an analogous element of something other than recognition by means of which the constitutive gap at music's heart, rather than being simply filled in and so effectively disappeared, is sustained. To borrow again from Dayan, music, in order not to be entirely 'falsely answered' in literature, should include something by or through which it is 'actively un-spoken'.[33] Ishiguro's writing of music is characterized, not by virtuosic flourishes of description, analysis, intertextuality, or form, but largely modest representations of aspects of musical life and experience. As well as suggesting a series of good metaphors, so performing one of the conventional functions according to which literature speaks for music, they have enclosed within them, each differently, an element of equivocation, slippage, or silence. While the former – the modest representations and figurings – suggest an abiding love such that the music will never be let go, the latter admits the need also, always and each time anew, to do so. Never let me go / always let me go: therein happens the counterpoint through which Ishiguro performs his writerly relation to his beloved originary art.[34] Perhaps this is how we should understand his declaration of commitment: that he is 'a songwriter at heart, even when ... writing novels'. The novels in question are far from musical in any conventional sense, and certainly not songlike except in the broadest of terms. A love for the words-and-music of song is present, rather, in the precise way his words bring music into literary life while also keeping alive the promise of music's being elsewhere. Song's elusiveness, the quality so beloved of Ishiguro, thereby finds its affirming and sustaining echo in the 'enigmatic and musical artefact' of the writing.[35]

Notes

1 Ishiguro's appearance on Desert Island Discs is available at www.bbc.co.uk/programmes/p009482g.
2 Ishiguro has given various accounts of this stage of his life. See in particular his *Paris Review* interview with Susannah Hunnewell ('Kazuo Ishiguro, The Art of Fiction No. 196', *The Paris Review* 184 (2008): n.p. (accessed online at www.theparisreview.org/interviews/5829/the-art-of-fiction-no-196-kazuo-ishiguro)). The reference to songwriting as an 'apprenticeship' is taken from an interview with Nicholas Wroe ('Living Memories', *The Guardian*, 19 February 2005 (accessed online at www.theguardian.com/books/2005/feb/19/fiction.kazuoishiguro)).
3 Terry Gross, NPR interview, 'Kazuo Ishiguro Draws on His Songwriting Past to Write Novels about the Future', 17 March 2021 (accessed online at www.npr.org/2021/03/17/978138547/kazuo-ishiguro-draws-on-his-songwriting-past-to-write-novels-about-the-future?t=1625483331937).
4 From an interview given on BBC 6 Music (www.bbc.co.uk/sounds/play/p02mf8kf). While the date is not given, it is likely to have been 2015.
5 Terry Gross, NPR interview. In his Nobel lecture, Ishiguro characterizes his abiding love for song as an attraction 'less to the lyrics being sung, and more to the actual singing' (*TCE* 21).
6 Taken from Ishiguro's Desert Island Discs appearance.
7 The film has its origins in a screenplay by Ishiguro, but the final version as used by Maddin, although retaining the titular premise, was written by the director.
8 Quotations taken from the original novel (*RD* 75, 92).
9 The comment on 'symphonic style' is taken from a 2015 RTÉ Radio 1 interview with Sinéad Gleeson on the subject of music and writing (https://soundcloud.com/thebookshow/season-2-episode-32-the-book-show-season-final). Ishiguro suggests possible musical models for the form of *Nocturnes* in an interview with Decca Aitkenhead (*The Guardian*, 27 April 2009 (accessed online at www.theguardian.com/books/2009/apr/27/kazuo-ishiguro-interview-books)). Gerry Smyth identifies several 'common musical properties and effects' in the story collection: 'repetition with variation, evenness of tone, the manipulation of meaning at the material level of the signifier' ('"Waiting for the Performance to

Begin': Kazuo Ishiguro's Musical Imagination in *The Unconsoled* and *Nocturnes*', in Sebastian Groes and Barry Lewis, eds., *Kazuo Ishiguro: New Critical Visions of the Novels* (London: Macmillan, 2011), p.152).

10 Anne Whitehead, 'Kazuo Ishiguro's *Nocturnes*: Between Archive and Repertoire', *Modern Fiction Studies* 67 (2021): 20–39 (22).

11 Ishiguro expresses his dislike for 'musical analogies' in the *Guardian* interview with Decca Aitkenhead.

12 Roland Barthes, 'Music, Voice, Language', in *The Responsibility of Forms: Critical Essays on Music, Art, and Representation*, trans. Richard Howard (Berkeley: University of California Press, 1991), p.285.

13 Roland Barthes, 'The Grain of the Voice', in *Responsibility of Forms*, p.268.

14 Roland Barthes, 'Rasch', in *Responsibility of Forms*, p.308.

15 Ishiguro describes song in these terms during his Desert Island Discs interview.

16 Peter Szendy, *Hits: Philosophy in the Jukebox*, trans. Will Bishop (New York: Fordham University Press, 2012), p.28.

17 Ibid., p. 1.

18 Ibid., p. 29.

19 Ibid., p. 28.

20 Interview with Peter Howell, *Toronto Star*, 30 September 2010 (accessed online at www.thestar.com/entertainment/movies/2010/09/30/howell_the_hunt_for_the_elusive_judy_bridgewater.html)

21 Robert G. Kaiser, notes for Stacey Kent, *Breakfast on the Morning Tram* (Parlophone, 2007). It should go without saying, given the iterative life of pop, that there are other 'Never Let Me Go's in the world besides the one by Evans and Livingston.

22 Three more Ishiguro lyrics appear on Kent's 2013 album, *The Changing Lights*: the title track, 'The Summer We Crossed Europe in the Rain' and 'Waiter, Oh Waiter'. Music is once again supplied by Kent's chief collaborator, Jim Tomlinson.

23 For various renditions of the song, see http://livingstonandevans.com/never-let-me-go/.

24 Szendy, *Hits*, pp.6, 17.

25 Ishiguro commented on the relation of song to novel during a webchat hosted by *The Guardian* in January 2015 (accessed online at www.theguardian.com/books/live/2015/jan/16/kazuo-ishiguro-webchat-the-buried-giant-the-unconsoled).

26 Ned Rorem, 'Review of Kazuo Ishiguro, *The Unconsoled*', *Yale Review* 84:2 (1996): 154–9 (158).

27 Peter Dayan, *Music Writing Literature, from Sand via Debussy to Derrida* (Aldershot: Ashgate, 2006), p.126.

28 Ibid., p.132.

29 Ibid., p.133.

30 The majority of readings of *The Unconsoled* follow Ishiguro in conceiving the music of the novel in broadly symbolic terms. One notable exception is the account given by Peter Sloane in *Kazuo Ishiguro's Gestural Poetics* (London: Bloomsbury, 2021), pp.96–101.

31 Ishiguro's musical relationships, where an element of romantic attraction is involved, are exclusively between men and women.

32 Peter Szendy, '*Parole, Parole*: Tautegory and the Musicology of the (Pop) Song', in Keith Chapman and Andrew H. Clark, eds., *Speaking of Music: Addressing the Sonorous* (New York: Fordham University Press, 2013), p.189.

33 Dayan, *Music Writing Literature*, p.126.

34 *Always Let Me Go* is the title of a 2002 album by jazz pianist Keith Jarrett, one of whose performances (although not from this album) was selected by Ishiguro for his desert island. Jarrett, a noted interpreter of the American Songbook, has twice recorded the Evans and Livingston 'Never Let Me Go'. The title of his 2002 album was chosen to acknowledge the relation between the free improvisation which is that album's musical mode and the standards-based performance of pieces such as 'Never Let Me Go'. The suggested relation between a musical holding and relinquishing offers an appropriate parallel with the workings of Ishiguro's writing of music.

35 Dayan, *Music Writing Literature*, p.126.

PART III

Ethics, Affect, Agency, and Memory

12

ROBERT EAGLESTONE

Ethics and Agency in Ishiguro's Novels

'What are the things you hold on to, what are the things you want to set right before you go? What do you regret? What are the consolations? What are the things you feel you have to do before you go?' (*CKI* 197). Ishiguro asks these questions in an interview: they are the core concerns of his novels. The questions are about values and ethics but they are phrased in a language of action (holding, setting right, doing) and reflection on action (regret, consolation). That is to say, they are questions of ethics posed as questions about agency.

The idea of agency has a long philosophical and literary critical history. Roughly, 'agency' means the ability to make choices for oneself. However, I am going to turn to conceptions of agency and action developed by Hannah Arendt in *The Human Condition* (1958) where she argues that 'to act, in its most general sense, means to take an initiative, to begin ... to set something into motion'.[1] Her ideas on action throw useful light on Ishiguro's novels in five key ways.

First, for Arendt, action and speech are 'closely related because the primordial and specifically human act must at the same time contain the answer to the question ... "who are you?"'.[2] That is, both action and speech reveal character, in life as in fiction: often, what is revealed is not at all what the agent or speaker would wish, a tension Ishiguro frequently explores. It is through their actions that characters reveal *who* they are, which is why, as Aristotle observes of drama, there 'is no such thing' as 'speeches in which the speaker reveals no choice'.[3] Choosing not to do something is an action (and to state this is to disagree with the thrust of Maria Christou's perspicacious essay on Ishiguro and inaction).[4]

Second, for Arendt action always involves others, what she calls the 'web of human relationships'.[5] In this sense, I question Ishiguro's Nobel citation, which suggests that he uncovers the 'abyss beneath our *illusory* sense of connection with the world' (my italics): instead, I argue that his consideration of action and agency reveals our real and inextricable connections to the world and to others.[6]

Third, stemming from the 'web', are concerns about the 'chain' of actions and reactions. Arendt argues 'a doer', bound into the 'web' as we all are, is

> always and at the same time a sufferer. To do and to suffer are like opposite sides of the same coin, and the story that an act starts is composed of its consequent deeds and sufferings. These consequences are boundless, because ... every reaction becomes a chain reaction and ... every process is the cause of new processes.[7]

Ishiguro's characters are bound by their actions and the chain of reactions that follow, and this leads to attempted justifications, regrets, a desire for consolation, and forms of working-through or coming-to-terms, or the failure of these. In his later novels, as I'll show, this also leads to an interest in how to interrupt, break, or 'cure' the unpredictable and boundless chains of action and reaction, a 'cure' that parallels Arendt's ideas very interestingly.

Fourth, the representation of action, because it is interwoven with language, is inextricable from style and form: Ishiguro's writing style and form itself is a working-through of ideas about agency and action.

Finally, using these ideas about action allows us to trace significant changes over his eight novels. I suggest that Ishiguro's novels have three phases: the first three novels concern reflections on past actions (retrospection is 'rather useful ... for writing novels') (*CKI* 155). The second three more experimental novels explore different conditions of agency both in content and style. The two most recent novels deal with the impact and risks of the chain of actions and reactions, and explore how this chain might be ended. More, this concern for action also illuminates two recognizable literary devices across his novels: the way his characters 'project' themselves onto others (one aspect of what Peter Sloane calls his 'gestural poetics') and what Ishiguro calls the 'dream grammar' of some parts of his prose and plotting.[8]

Agency Reflected

Ishiguro has suggested that his first three novels were 'really attempts to write the same novel', and, indeed, they do share broad thematic similarities: each reflects on actions taken in the past and deals with their impact on the present (*CKI* 153). But from the point of view of action and ethics, each is slightly different.

Etsuko, the narrator and protagonist of *A Pale View of Hills*, is trapped in her life, trapped in her small, hot, box-like apartment close to a stinking 'wasteground' (*PVH* 99). This is one reason for the recurring images of ties (132), binding (41), and ropes (83). The 'pale outline of hills' (99) is her vision of freedom. Etsuko contemplates escape by projecting herself onto her friend Sachiko: as Ishiguro says, 'she sees in what happened to Sachiko something that happened to herself. For the purpose of this story she's telling, Sachiko represents herself' (*CKI* 99). Ishiguro will frequently reuse this 'character projection' device. Sachiko's life is one of escape: from her family, from the war, from her inconsiderate husband and her 'uncle', and finally from Japan with her unreliable America lover. Etsuko follows a similar (but perhaps more strategically considered) path to become Mrs Sherringham, an event which happens 'between the scenes' a couple of years after the time in which the main part of the novel is set.

Her father-in-law is Ogata-San, a retired headteacher who took Etsuko in 'long before' (*PVH* 28) when she was a 'mad person' (58). He will become almost a stock character for Ishiguro: a person who decided to act for a cause which has both failed and been revealed as wicked, in this case, Japanese militarism. Ogata is smarting from a denunciation in a magazine by one of his former protégés, Shigeo Matsuda. In their confrontation scene, Ogata is unrepentant ('we cared deeply for the country and worked hard to ensure the correct values were preserved and passed on' (147)), but Matsuda – while understanding ('you shouldn't be blamed for not realising the true consequences of your actions' (148)) – is firm: the actions of Ogata and people like him led Japan into 'the most evil disaster in her entire history' (147) because they 'taught lies' and did not teach children 'to see, to question' (147). Ogata effectively surrenders, as if he has lost at one of the games of chess he plays with his son, but does not appear to change his view. The consequence of his past action is his total loss of esteem, but there seems to be no profound impact on his character or view.

Interestingly, Etsuko calls Matsuda's argument 'vile nonsense' (*PVH* 149): this is because she and Ogata are linked thematically. Recounting this story of her past, Etsuko, now Mrs Sherringham, is looking back at a terrible, personality-shattering event, as Ogata is. Unlike Ogata, however, she bears a terrible guilt for the consequences of a past action. She feels that the suicide of her daughter is a reaction to her escape from Japan: more bluntly, she feels that she has murdered her daughter and cannot admit this. The events of the novel are retold through memory 'grown hazy with time' (41). Central to this haziness are the accounts, half-submerged, of child murders in Nagasaki: someone is strangling children, a girl is left 'hanging from a tree' (156). This is interwoven with the story of Etsuko and Sachiko and is the other reason for the references to ties, ropes, and binding: 'my daughter hanging in her room for days on end' (54). The 'murder plot' is the emergence in Etsuko/Mrs Sherringham's account of the past of her guilt as a kind of 'murderer'. In a peculiar and much-discussed scene, the narrative voice shifts, mixing persons and times in a piece of 'dream grammar' which looks forward stylistically to *The Unconsoled*. It is as if Etsuko is the murderer who, with a rope, is threatening to kill a little girl who is both Sachiko's daughter and her own first daughter. While the threatened girl escapes, this 'dream grammar' sequence is a manifestation of the guilt that Etsuko cannot explicitly admit. In an early example of the kind of condensed metaphor at which Ishiguro excels, Etsuko/Mrs Sherringham's recurring dream of the girl playing on a swing (47) is both the hanged daughter's death, the memory of her daughter's happier Japanese childhood (the 'pale view of hills'), and her surviving daughter's English childhood. Niki's friends think Etsuko is impressive: 'you ought to be proud of what you did with your life' (90). Almost, but not quite, there is a kind of forgiveness.

Both Ogata and Mrs Sherringham lay a path for Masuji Ono in *An Artist of the Floating World*, another story about agency. While Etsuko and Ogata's actions are 'off stage', we hear, recounted, Ono's moments of action and choice: these lead to the fulfilment, in part, of his artistic ambition and eventually to the ruination of his personal and nationalist political ambitions. Ambitious Ono leaves his first master for Mori-san and chooses to be drawn into Japanese militarism by Mr Matsuda. In the climactic scene of the novel, his new convictions lead him to leave Mori-san in order to become a propaganda artist: 'I cannot remain forever an artist of the floating world' (*AFW* 180). We see his increasing political radicalization as his artistic and political beliefs and ambitions become aligned. It seems to me that showing these moments of temptation and choice makes Ono a more sympathetic character.

Unlike Ogata and Etsuko, however, Ono reflects explicitly on his actions, and even, possibly, apologizes. After the war, his networks of patronage have become toxic and threaten the marriage of his daughter. At the meal intended to confirm his daughter's engagement, Ono makes an apology in this semi-public forum: 'I freely admit I made many mistakes. I accept that much of what I did was ultimately harmful to our nation' (*AFW* 123). Pressed further, Ono even surrenders 'my paintings, my teachings' (123). He says he was sincere in his beliefs, but that he was mistaken. It is hard to know how honest his apology is. In a typically deft Ishiguro phrase, Ono describes his interlocutor as 'watching me rather like a teacher waiting for a pupil to go on with a lesson he has learned by heart' (123), which suggests the apology is rote and not somehow authentic: but why should a planned apology be less sincere? Ono's reflection on this moment is also equivocal: the declaration was 'painful' but also prudent; it's important to take responsibility for 'past deeds' and come to terms 'with the mistakes one has made' yet there is 'no great shame in mistakes made in the best of faith' (124–5). Ishiguro suggests that he is interested in 'how people use the language of self-deception and self-protection' (*CKI* 5): but one reading is that Ono is messily human, accepting his guilt (and making a sincere apology) while at the same time denying it.

Ogata, Mrs Sherringham, and Ono all shape *The Remains of the Day*'s Stevens. He shares Ono's parochialism and limitation of vision and Ogata's and Mrs Sherringham's guilt, but there are also notable differences from the point of view of agency. Ogata and Ono sought to lead (Ono is called 'sensei' by his acolytes in the bar) and Stevens seeks only to follow; we are shown Ono's moments of seduction while Stevens's choice of 'dignity' occurs at some earlier unseen moment; Ono atones or gives the appearance of atonement and Ogata confronts his accuser whereas Stevens just develops his skills to include bantering, refusing to 'work through' his past. Where Ono changes, Stevens remains fixed.

The fixedness of Stevens tells us something important about the workings of agency and action. Appiah argues that Stevens has chosen his own life, and, while his values 'may not be values for us . . . they are values for him, given his plan of life' and we should respect them.[9] Although Ishiguro said in his Nobel lecture that *The Remains of the Day* concerns a man who 'has lived his life by the wrong values', Appiah's argument is, roughly, that they were at least *his* chosen values (*TCE* 19). Appiah suggests that Stevens has decided to be a butler, and so delimits his agency under that 'description' (i.e. at each moment of choice, he asks himself 'what would a perfect butler do?' and does that). This 'description' controls all parts of his life, as if his one fixed choice shapes everything else. Contrast this to Ono: his choices change in relation to the different roles he undertakes. He is an ambitious artist, then a Japanese nationalist, then a father and grandfather. Ono's agency responds to different ('floating') roles, and while these different roles allow his rise and fall, they also allow acknowledgement and something like coming to terms. Steven's self-description prevents this process. Perhaps then, we are not 'all butlers', as Ishiguro suggests (*CKI* 142). As if responding to this novelistic discovery that our self-descriptions shape our agency, Ishiguro's next three novels explore and play with precisely the conditions that shape our agency.

The Conditions of Agency

If the first three novels 'cover the same territory', *The Unconsoled* is an 'adventure in another country' (*CKI* 170, 210). That otherness lies principally in the structure and style, which in turn has profound implications for ideas about action and agency. Told in the 'language of dream' (*U* 128) and set in a 'landscape of the imagination', Ishiguro talks of using 'dream as a model' in which Ryder, the protagonist, wanders 'about in this dream world . . . bumps into earlier, or later, versions of himself': a boy in Boris, a young man in Stefan, an old, broken artist in Brodsky, all just as Etsuko projects herself onto Sashiko (*CKI* 128, 129, 114). This is the part of the dream grammar that allows *The Unconsoled* to break so many novelistic conventions: the novel has scenes the first-person narrator could not know or have seen, like the conversations between Brodsky and Miss Collins (*U* 319–27); significant but unexplained back stories like the Sattler monument; unresolved plots; slips in time and geography (*CKI* 209).

Even more significantly, the dream grammar marks a fundamental change in ideas about action and so about ethics. Ishiguro says that *The Unconsoled* is told as if you are in 'a completely dark room where someone moves along with a torch like this ... [he moves his head along the length of the coffee table as if reading with a magnifying glass]' (*CKI* 132). Life is not a clear path, lived under a description, nor planned out. Rather, the image of life in *The Unconsoled* is quite without agency. Ryder begins no actions and is just what his name suggests, a rider (not a driver) on the bus of life. He rarely seems to choose but is stopped, picked up, pulled along, prevented and so on. If Stevens is *too* beholden to his self-description as a butler, Ryder in his dreamworld is not at all beholden to any of his self-descriptions, as a son, father, husband, guest or even as a pianist. The grammar of dreams means we have no agency, we make no meaningful choices. If life is a 'dark room illumined by a torch' then many aspects of moral life traditionally understood – planning, making an agreement or promise, behaving consistently, regretting, and the agency that undertakes these – all seem meaningless. Without some degree of rootedness in ourselves and our agency, we are simply shallow, swept along by events. (It is a sign of Ishiguro's astonishing craft as a writer that he can turn this shallowness into a novel.) Ryder still feels responsible for the people he meets (son, wife, parents) but without agency and action that responsibility has no meaning, since any action is free of consequence. Removing the narrative condition of agency effectively removes both the meaning and impact of agency: under these conditions, no consolation is possible because, in effect, there is no self over time to be an agent.

If Ryder doesn't have enough agency, Ishiguro's next novel explores someone with too much: Christopher Banks in *When we Were Orphans* is *too* rooted in his self-description as a detective and too keen to make choices based on that self-description (in this way he echoes Stevens, too). For Banks is a detective not simply in terms of solving crimes but right down to his inner, irrational emotions. The novel imitates a detective story, and just as a detective choses to attempt to mend the breakages of the world, so Banks uses his agency to force the resisting world into the shape his need for consolation requires. Everything is seen, and acted upon, as if it were a detective mystery: he is a psychotic detective, in fact. To a man with a hammer, everything looks like a nail: to a psychotic detective, everything looks like an unsolved case.

If *The Unconsoled* explores a dreamworld beyond agency, and *When We Were Orphans* a world shaped by too much agency, *Never Let Me Go* investigates a world of the powerless, where any choices made are twisted in such a way as to work against the character's greater good (one of the most terrible facets of agency, well known to scholars of the Holocaust). The characters *of Never Let Me Go* are first denuded of agency and then deprived of the very capacity for it by being isolated. This is made clear through the form of the novel itself.

Never Let Me Go is in form an *anti-bildungsroman*. Kathy does not develop from a child's to an adult's world, but instead has her world incrementally stripped from her; rather than become integrated into a community, she becomes increasingly isolated, as her friends are murdered for their organs; instead of coming into agency, beginning action and speech, as Arendt suggests, the conditions for this, the presence of others, is taken from her. Arendt analysed this loneliness in *The Origins of Totalitarianism*: regimes based on terror isolate people, sever 'political contacts', which means that 'the human capacities for action and power are frustrated', just as Kathy is deprived of the capability for action.[10] Loneliness uproots people, which means, like the clones, they 'have no place in the world, recognised and guaranteed by others', which in turn leads to their being made 'superfluous ... not to belong to the world at all': here, to be harvested for organs.[11] One of Arendt's terms for the capacity to begin action anew is 'natality', action metaphorically summed up in the idea of birth: and, of course, Kathy is deprived of this actually and metaphorically, poignantly and painfully condensed in the image of the doll and the song that give the novel its title. Kathy is both the doll and, fighting off her isolation, making her lonely self a maternal dyad, mother to the doll.

The world in the novel is structured through global complicity with a public secret: everyone, including the clones themselves, knows they live only to be murdered. This public secret is enacted in the language Kathy and others use from the very first sentence: the sinister euphemisms of 'carer', 'donor', 'completed'. It is enforced by the freedom denied the clones: no right to privacy, money, or belongings. No friendship, just the isolation about which Kathy complains. Any contact the clones do have is clandestine, like camp inmates: Kathy sent a 'message ... through a contact' (*NLMG* 213); Ruth 'ran a few risks' (229) to get Madame's address; the final, climatic meeting is 'against regulations' (254). It is demonstrated, too, in the unbridgeable gap, when recognized, between the clones and 'normal humans': Madame's visceral fear when surrounded by the clones when children, 'afraid of us in the same way someone might be afraid of spiders' (35). The power of this society-structuring public secret which contorts agency resonates with what Primo Levi described as the Nazi's 'most demonic crime', the creation of the *Sonderkommando*, those prisoners forced to aid the perpetrators in the murder of Jews: the clones work as 'carers' for the donors before becoming 'donors' themselves. As Levi points out, the creation of the *Sonderkommando* was pragmatic, to reduce the work for the perpetrators, but it also shifted 'the burden of guilt on to others – specifically the victims – so that they were deprived of even the solace of innocence'.[12] The minimal scope for action given to the clones – as 'carers' – makes them complicit with the processes of their own destruction.

Forgetfulness, Forgiveness, and the Chains of Action

The questions of Ishiguro's two most recent novels return, in a way, to the earliest ones: the impact of action. However, unlike the first three, these two later novels are not just retrospective: they both pose the question of how the chain of actions and reactions can be broken. That is, they seem to seek more than consolation.

As Yugin Teo's book shows, memory has always been a crucial aspect of Ishiguro's novelistic thought and *The Buried Giant* explores the relationship between action, ethics, and memory: can forgetting be a way of breaking the chain of actions, for individuals or for communities?[13] Set in a version of 'dark ages' England, the characters inhabit a waste land, 'cursed with the mist of forgetfulness' (*BG* 48). This mist comes from the breath of a dragon, Querig, on which, many years before, Merlin had put a spell: the consequence is that the peoples of the land forgot a treaty-breaking genocide of Saxons committed by King Arthur and his Briton armies (311). The central characters are Axl and Beatrice, now 'two elderly Britons' (36) but once powerful nobles: Axl negotiated in good faith the treaty that Arthur broke.

These ideas about action and memory allows us to see how different *The Buried Giant* is from Ishiguro's previous novels. The most obvious differences are formal: the narration and the focalization. The main narrator is a weird undying Charon-like boatman, able to talk easily about 'those days' (*BG* 3): perhaps he was a child in the long-abandoned and ruined Roman villa (39); perhaps his parents died in the plague; perhaps the 'you' (291) he addresses, who have 'crude wooden crosses or painted rocks' (291) as monuments, are the murdered babies who haunt the novel (faces seen in the water; skulls trodden on in the escape from the monastery).[14] The novel is mainly focalized though Axl, but there are, for Ishiguro, unusual shifts: a boy, Edwin, becomes the focalizer for several chapters, and twice we have access to Gawain's reveries. This is the 'dream grammar' of *The Unconsoled* at work, just as the English 'mythical landscape' of *The Remains of the Day* is present here too (*CKI* 45). The 'dream grammar' which projects one identity not-quite onto another shapes many of the characters, not just the protagonist: Axl and Beatrice's story of adultery and betrayal echo Arthur and Guinevere's; Wistan, a Saxon bought up by a Briton, is almost a heroic cliché character (like Uthred from Bernard Cornwell's popular 'Last Kingdom' series, set in roughly the same period); and in returning with an arm torn from an ogre, Wistan echoes Beowulf; Jonus has 'his liver pecked' (184) like Prometheus.

Differences from his other novels appear in the plot, too. The story is full of decisive action as characters fight ogres, dragons, and each other, escape from burning towers, commit to final journeys: an adventure novel filled with agents. As the mist begins to clear in their minds, the characters recall things they have done wrong in the past and take action to address these. The strange device the monks use is to 'atone for crimes once committed in this country and long unpunished' (*BG* 165): uselessly, as it happens, since it offers no justice while another faction in the monastery argue that 'we must uncover what's been hidden and face the past' (166). Wistan tells Axl that '[j]ustice and vengeance await' (322). The characters predict, too, terrible future actions: Axl asks 'who knows what will come when quick-tongued men make ancient grievances rhyme with fresh desire for land and conquest' (323) and Wistan agrees: 'the giant, once well buried, now stirs' (324).

This is the core concern of the novel: the future impact of past actions. Does forgetfulness end the chain of action and reaction? In the novel, both amnesia and memory have baleful consequences on individuals and on communities.

Axl and Beatrice cannot recall their son, or their own lives or histories. Yet the slow return of memory brings back the couple's own 'dark things' (*BG* 307): infidelity on Beatrice's part and Axl's vengeance, forbidding her to visit their son's grave. Yet this is mediated by the role of religion in the novel. While Gawain claims to have been doing God's and Arthur's work by committing genocide, he admits that Axl's path was more 'godly' (294), recalling how Axl, in battle, stands unarmed and unafraid: 'if God chooses to direct an arrow this way ... I'll not impede it' (230). Throughout, Axl and Beatrice make choices shaped by Christianity: Beatrice shares her bread with the witch-like stranger, for example, and both believe 'the Lord's promise to walk beside us at all times' (16) in contrast to the amnesiac superstitions of the younger people in their village. When it is suggested that God might have forgotten them, Beatrice is incredulous since 'we're each of us his dear child. Would God really forget what we have done ...?' (70), although she admits he might be 'angry' or 'ashamed' of them (83). Axl says that God 'wouldn't allow' (49) their memories to go forever, letting their love fade, and indeed the narrative of the novel bears him out: their memories do come back, painful as well as loving. 'God will know the slow tread of an old couple's love for each other, and understand how black shadows make part of its whole' (341). It is through the action of personal forgiveness that this wound has been healed and properly mended. Memory, not forgetting, leads here to forgiveness.

The impact of the amnesiac fog and of the memories that it hides are not the same for communities, however. Forgetfulness destroys the communal. The Britons live in a kind of animalistic 'warren' (BG 5) 'on the edge of a vast bog' (4) (recalling Etsuko's house by a marshland) and can barely remember their own names, traditions, or religion, trapped as they are by forgetfulness. The Saxons, too, 'remember nothing of their orders or the reasons for them' and behave like 'crazed wolves' (64). Axl and Beatrice play a crucial role in the killing of the dragon by Wistan, which will lead to the return of memory, but this also brings destruction. Wistan speaks of the 'hated' (318) Arthur and tells of Saxon vengeance and justice: where now Briton and Saxon 'mingle village by village' (323), Wistan prophesies that 'the friendly bond between' Saxons and Britons 'will prove as knots young girls make with the stems of small flowers. Men will burn their neighbour's houses by night. Hang children from trees at dawn. The rivers will stink of corpses bloated from their days of voyaging' (324). Interestingly, Wistan forgives Axl for his unwitting treachery: 'I see today he may have acted without cunning, wishing well for his own kin and ours alike' (320) (does this 'good faith' defence absolve Ogata, Ono, and Stevens too? Etsuko? Ryder?). But if personal forgiveness can end the chain of actions between individuals, there seems no possibility of wider forgiveness, and to forget communally destroys communities.

Klara and the Sun continues this development in Ishiguro's novelistic thinking about agency, action, and forgiveness: the core moment of the novel, as I'll suggest, is an act of forgiveness that breaks a chain of actions, precisely the kind of forgiveness that Wistan denies in his vision of vengeance. And although that forgiveness is between two people, it spreads if not to the whole community, at least to the community of the novel.

Josie is ill, possibly dying from 'being lifted', that is, genetically enhanced. Her mother (who, like Etsuko/Mrs Sherringham has already lost a daughter because of the action she has taken) lashes out bitterly at Rick. But in response he passes on a message from Josie of love and of forgiveness. Josie loves her mother, and was happy to be lifted despite the risks ('she'd do exactly what you did and you'll always be the best mother she could have' (*KS* 282)). Josie forgives her mother's action and its chain of consequences. The Mother replies: '"That's some message", she said finally … "Jesus", the Mother said, and sighed quietly. "That's some message"' (282). The mother means 'Jesus' as a kind of expletive but we don't have to hear it that way. Arendt notes that the 'discoverer of the role of forgiveness in the realm of human affairs was Jesus of Nazareth. The fact that he made this discovery in a religious context and articulated it in religious language is no reason to take it any less seriously in a strictly secular sense.'[15] It is forgiveness that prevents endless bitterness and anger and is the resolution to the problem of the unpredictable consequences of sequences of action: 'forgiveness may be the necessary corrective for the inevitable damages resulting from action'.[16] Derrida's view of forgiveness echoes Arendt's: 'forgiveness is not, it *should not be*, normal, normative, normalising. It should remain exceptional and extraordinary … as if it interrupted the ordinary course of historical temporality.'[17] Forgiveness is not one more reaction in a chain of action and reaction but the interruption, the breakage of that chain. More, Derrida points out that for thinkers like Arendt, forgiveness is 'a human possibility'.[18]

The significance of this 'human possibility' is foregrounded in the novel precisely because the narrator is a machine that gives the illusion of having agency, but does not in fact possess it. Klara is programmed and so ultimately obeys her owner, Josie's mother, even when, chillingly, those commands seem to threaten Josie. Klara says that she 'believed it was my duty [i.e. programming] to save Josie, to make her well. But perhaps this is a better way' (*KS* 214). Klara can only follow an algorithm. Josie, however, is able to forgive and so break the chain of events and throw off the burden of the past. This is unlike any of Ishiguro's other characters: even Axl's forgiveness of Beatrice's affair leaves 'black shadows' as part of its whole. Josie's recovery may not stem from her forgiveness, but her physical recovery is almost secondary to the psychic one. More, this moment undoes the novel's knots and plots for everyone: Josie is free to live on; Rick is freed from his obligations to Josie and so any sense that he needs to be 'lifted'; the sinister plan with Mr Capaldi will come to nothing. The forgiveness begins the happy ending of the novel: Klara's 'slow fade' is no sadder than putting an old phone in a drawer.

Now a wild claim: *Klara and the Sun* retrospectively imagines this forgiveness across Ishiguro's whole *oeuvre*, using his now-recognizable 'dream grammar'. This is why *Klara and the Sun* is so full of powerful echoes from other Ishiguro novels. In each case, characters are redeemed from their actions. Coffee Cup Lady ('I estimated sixty-seven years old' (*KS* 19)) and her Raincoat Man ('I estimated seventy-one years old' (19)) are Beatrice and Axl, once sundered and now reunited: 'at special moments like that, people feel a pain alongside their happiness' (21). They are also Miss Kenton and Mr Stevens, spending not the remaining hours but the sunny day together: 'She and the man were holding each other so tightly they were like one large person, and the Sun, noticing, was pouring his nourishment on them' (20). The Mother and Miss Helen are echoes of Etsuko and Sachiko from *A Pale View of Hills*, right down to the are-they-aren't-they-involved in some kind of murder plot and the uncertainty about their degrees of mental stability: but nothing wicked comes, no kittens are drowned or children murdered. The Mother, too, with her 'Sal' doll (and potentially her Josie doll) hints at Kathy's dance in *Never Let Me Go*: but this mother has a real child. Josie and Rick parallel Kathy and Tommy, a couple who hope that their love will allow them something special. Rick, like Tommy, is kind of a failure (he has not been 'lifted') but has something special to show (his mechanical birds which will be used for surveillance, of what is past or passing or to come). Yet both grow out of their love in a healthy and human way. Klara is also like Kathy, with her naivety and her keen observation of others, but with her blindnesses, too: but Klara (unlike Kathy) is simply a machine, so we need feel no sorrow on her behalf. Klara is also like Stevens, with views on good household management and, much more significantly, abetting something wicked or questionable because she is told to by an authority: but she sacks no Jewish maids, nor does the plot for her to replace Josie come to anything. Klara is also teased by Josie's cronies in a way that clearly recalls Stevens's interrogation by Lord Darlington and his friends, in which Stevens has to act the role of 'the man on the street': but Klara does not feel shame, nor does she need to dissimulate. Even in terms of the style, the novel has sections which echo the oneiric quality of *The Unconsoled* (why, for example, are the shop's shelves complete with coffee cups in the barn?). However, in contrast to *The Unconsoled* we even see one of these dream scenes 'from the inside' where we and Klara understand what it means (the meaning is redeemed, as it were), while the interlocutor, Manager, does not: there's a version of the same bravura prose trick earlier in the novel too, in a conversation between Rick and Klara. All this is to say that Ishiguro has gone some way to answering the challenge made by Wistan in *The Buried Giant*: he has found, for an individual and a small community at least, a way of breaking the chains that lead from action to retribution. That is: forgiveness. 'That's some message.'

Conclusion

In the end, stories are about choices and actions, as Aristotle recognized, and it is in that, for him, that the ethics of poetry and drama lay. This chapter has argued that Ishiguro's novels approach issues of ethics not through, for example, long discussions (as a 'novel of ideas' might) nor through the play of sympathy or empathy, but through representing agency and action. Shaped by Arendt's discussion of action, I clustered Ishiguro's novels into three groups. The first three focus on a character looking back over a life, reflecting on the impact of action; the second three investigate what happens to agency under different conditions in fiction, either through the use of the agency-free language of dreams (*The Unconsoled*), the over-agential language of detection, or in the normal-seeming but murderous world of *Never Let Me Go*. The third group, his most recent two novels, explores the consequences of actions, but rather than looking back at them, they examine how the sequence of action and reaction can be stopped: they find that 'cure' in forgiveness, rather than in forgetting, first for individuals and then, with limitations, for small communities. This is not to argue that Ishiguro planned out his career: rather, it is to suggest that the novel, and Ishiguro's novels in particular, are a kind of laboratory for thinking in the profoundest way possible.

Notes

1 Hannah Arendt, *The Human Condition*, 2nd ed. (Chicago: University of Chicago Press, 1998), p.177.
2 Ibid., p.178.
3 Aristotle, *Poetics*, trans. Antony Kenny (Oxford: Oxford University Press, 2013), 1450b10–11.
4 Maria Christou, 'Kazuo Ishiguro's Non-Actors', *Novel* 53:3 (2020): 360–82.
5 Arendt, *The Human Condition*, p.184.
6 The Nobel Prize in Literature 2017: www.nobelprize.org/prizes/literature/2017/summary/.
7 Arendt, *The Human Condition*, p.191.
8 See Peter Sloane, *Kazuo Ishiguro's Gestural Poetics* (London: Bloomsbury Academic, 2021).
9 Kwame Anthony Appiah, 'Liberalism, Individuality, and Identity', *Critical Inquiry* 27:2 (2001): 305–32 (315).
10 Hannah Arendt, *The Origins of Totalitarianism* (London: Harvest, 1958), p.474.
11 Ibid., p.475.
12 Primo Levi, *The Drowned and the Saved*, trans. Raymond Rosenthal (London: Abacus, 1988), p.37.
13 See Teo Yugin, *Kazuo Ishiguro and Memory* (Basingstoke: Palgrave Macmillan, 2014); and see Ch.15, below.
14 I owe this idea about the boatman's audience to a conversation with Nicoleta Bechiă and Cosmina Hodoroagă.
15 Arendt, *The Human Condition*, p.238.
16 Ibid., p.239.
17 Jacques Derrida, *On Cosmopolitanism and Forgiveness*, trans. Mark Dooley and Michael Hughes (London: Routledge, 2001), p.32.
18 Ibid, p.37.

13

CYNTHIA F. WONG

'Emotional Upheaval' in *An Artist of the Floating World* and *The Buried Giant*

Ishiguro's Literary Landscape

On the surface, the second and seventh novels by Kazuo Ishiguro bear scant resemblance to one another in terms of their characters, plot, setting, or situation. *An Artist of the Floating World* has an ageing pro-nationalist Japanese painter tell his story over four diary-like entries covering a post-war period from October 1948 to June 1950. The narrator, Masuji Ono, attempts to reinterpret his vocational past in the post-war context to avoid compromising his second daughter's marriage prospects. The setting of *An Artist of the Floating World* in post-war Nagasaki contrasts strikingly with the post-Arthurian setting of *The Buried Giant*. The latter novel's mostly third-person narration includes two first-person reveries by an elderly Sir Gawain and one other first-person narration by a mysterious boatman at the novel's end. An elderly couple, Axl and Beatrice, encounter these figures as they make an arduous physical, emotional, and geopolitical journey to reunite with their son in the next village. The emotional experiences of the characters in these two novels invite readers to immerse in Ishiguro's affective worlds and examine the moral implications of his characters' tumultuous lives and loves.[1]

Ishiguro doesn't so much emphasize an explicit progression of plot, conflict, and resolution in these novels as focus on what he has termed the essential 'emotional upheaval' of his characters' lives (*CKI* 6). A violent or sudden change of emotions could presage turmoil, and a profound disruption could force a person to examine past and present situations. Ishiguro's novels have consistently explored contrasting emotions beneath the surface of characters' speech and actions in order to explore contradictions between them. The sub-textual emotions help readers to distinguish what characters say from what they do and also to establish mood and tone – often apprehensive, melancholic, even elegiac – within the narratives. Emotional upheavals are reflected in Ishiguro's literary language to explore his characters' conflicted situations as they strive to emerge from darkness to enlightenment, from confusion to a sense of calm and certainty, and from despair to some form of consolation. Notably, these 'emergences' also work in reverse as regressions, whereby characters may continue to hide their emotions despite a reckoning and therefore remain paralyzed. Whether from confrontations with the hidden and sequestered or from a hope of divesting from ineffable pain and suffering, Ishiguro's characters navigate their circumstances to reflect the author's sense of their affective struggles as they work, un-work, and rework their stories and strive to present a best self. A polarizing effect in relation to whether the narratives truthfully represent events or whether they are intended to present characters' fictionalization of those events hinges in particular on the emotions that come to the surface or remain buried. Crucially, Ishiguro gives as full a portrait as possible of positive and negative emotions affecting his characters but often leaves their effects unresolved.

Among the contrasting value systems that Ishiguro employs in *An Artist of the Floating World* and *The Buried Giant*, the dyads of surface and depth, as well as of youth and old age, are the most important for tracking emotions. Situations in the novels develop deeper emotional significance for the characters as the stories progress, with what a character says often not quite matching other details in the narration. In his historicist critique of *An Artist of the Floating World*, Timothy Wright identifies the misalignment as comprised of 'the rebarbative and conflictual elements' that are 'buried beneath its surfaces' concealing a character's negative emotions. Wright finds these elements to be 'the most distinctive characteristic of Ishiguro's work' in that a character's attempt at concealment hints at a 'conflict [that] must be *excavated by the reader*.'[2] In this sense, readers' responses to the novel's affective power might be determined by degrees of unreliability in the narrative point of view. How deeply must the reader go to locate the truth of the events narrated? Can those events be entirely free from the taint of a narrator's subverted emotions? Ono's relatively mild, genial tone throughout his diary-like narration might persuade a reader to accept at face value his memories and descriptions of events. But a reader might also consider that Ono's diaries are deeply personal and his private confessions are not intended as public proclamations. Taking Wright's advice to excavate conflict from deep within Ishiguro's novels, however, a reader might find Ono's polite demeanour and his self-proclaimed flawed memory to be veils for the shame and guilt that he tries to keep buried beneath a surface calm.

An examination of Ono's trait affectivity – such as politeness that shrouds arrogance, or memory failure that works as an evasion of truth – would disclose how he double-exposes his unwarranted self-importance as a nationalist painter before the war in order to appear as a devoted and caring father after the war. These reader's excavations of conflict also benefit *The Buried Giant*, where they are imagined by Ishiguro in an even more literalized way. Catherine Charlwood notes how Ishiguro's landscapes can be metaphors for detecting the characters' conflicting emotion: 'While the people may have forgotten their past, the land keeps memories in the form of physical remains.'³ For example, she comments that in *The Remains of the Day*, when Stevens tours a mythologized English landscape, he inevitably crosses emotionally into a past that contextualizes his personal wretchedness against interwar history.⁴ While Stevens tries to keep his memories repressed and unacknowledged, Beatrice and Axl have had their memories erased. And yet the couple conduct a journey similar to that of Stevens, in that a personal teleology is conflated with physical movement across a terrain that keeps its own catastrophic histories intact. Ivan Stacy notes that memory in *The Buried Giant* is at once 'the source of the familial bonds that Axl and Beatrice hope to repair' and 'the basis of the social identities that threaten to consume the land with violence'.⁵ At moments when an involuntary memory crops up for Axl, for instance, he unwittingly exposes his fragile defence against concealed conflicts, which then adds another layer of emotional dread that, to keep the peace in his marriage, he tries to subvert. These conflations – personal self with public lands; familial with national bonds – allow Ishiguro to explore the overlap between the characters' states of being and historical places, and to highlight the way cultural contexts involve or reflect their conflicting states. In both novels, characters' emotions can be explicit and accord with their situations, can be concealed or subverted to bury difficult or painful situations, and can be symbolically rendered to offer fascinating conflations of self, place, and history, as the characters manage their past alongside their present physical journeys.

Lost Bearings in *An Artist of the Floating World*

Ono tries to veil his agitation and deny his shameful past as he tries to repair any damage to his family's post-war reputation. Despite his attempts to keep now-disreputable aspects of the past hidden, we soon learn that he is not out to gain atonement for his assumed contributions to the war, which now threaten to ruin his daughter's marriage negotiations, but is instead attempting to appease his other daughter. He recalls his married daughter Setsuko urging him: "'I merely wished to say that it is perhaps wise if Father would take certain precautionary steps. To ensure misunderstandings do not arise"' (*AFW* 49). Ono immediately acts as if it is only his art career that presents impediments to smooth marriage negotiations for Noriko. In fact, he does not seem to believe that Setsuko's words refer to anything else but in fact that historical events ceased favouring him and his choices. Ono's pride and pragmatism compel him to adjust accordingly the public's perception to improve his family's situation. He may not be able to alter world history but he can try to direct the attitude of others more favourably towards him. But Ishiguro evokes a bitter rift with the younger generation represented by Ono's deceased son, son-in-law, and former pupils, and it is from accounts of his encounters with younger people from his past that readers might excavate Ono's inner turmoil.

To preserve his self-image, Ono often presents himself as a refined gentleman who is very attuned to the emotional sensations that he and others around him experience. But he just as easily glosses over or even pleads ignorance to the implications of the younger generation's hostility towards his generation when it benefits him and his own past choices. From the anecdote early on about his success in winning the purchase of the Sugimura's impressive estate, right to the novel's very end when he memorializes his conservative friend Matsuda, Ono's trait affectivity is to highlight what a conscientious person he is. Ono's facade of wisdom and of a person who cares about how other people feel, who deeply loves his family and yearns for their happiness and success, fractures quite soon, however, after he sets off from his prized home to make inquiries about the past.

An Artist of the Floating World is constructed by 'this rather enclosed narrator talking to somebody he imagined', as Ishiguro puts it, and represents Ono's thoughts about his daughters blended with meandering meditations on his past successes and self-proclaimed triumphs over disloyalty (*CKI* 150). While we label thoughts as 'inside' or 'unseen' unless articulated in speech or in writing, Ishiguro's novel places this character's thinking on the surface of the narrative to guide our understanding of moral character. Ono's explication of his memories is juxtaposed with an account of his activities such as taking his grandson around Nagasaki, making treks to homes of former students and friends to seek forms of appeasement, and undertaking domestic chores such as tending the garden. And yet the narrative actually moves in and around Ono's thoughts of the past, including successes such as the house purchase or winning art awards and gaining recognition, along with reminisces about his launch as a painter. And Ishiguro focuses in particular on the affective power of such memories. In the scene in which Ono's father requests a meeting with him to discuss the future, for example, Ono recalls a 'sense of shame' equal to 'a terrible fear' that caused him to live in constant 'dread' of such meetings (*AFW* 42). His excess of strong negative emotions helps him turn against his father, and he leaves to study under, and work for, two contrasting art teachers. He eventually abandons his teachers as well in order to lead his own art students in the decadent nightlife 'of pleasure, entertainment, and drink' of the 'floating world' (145). The victorious Ono in fact feels that he is strengthened by conflict with his father. 'The only thing Father's succeeded in kindling is my ambition', he tells his mother at one point (47). But in the narrative present, Ono takes precautions that on the surface strive for the happiness of his daughter, Noriko, without conceding to history's denunciation of men like him and Matsuda. Indeed, by the novel's end, a comfortable home, a professionally successful husband, and a child on the way all reflect Noriko's circumstances, which have been aided by Ono's ostensible taking of precautions. These surface achievements keep Ono's shame and guilt buried, and his minor triumphs reflect Ishiguro's sense that upheavals of human emotions bear witness to both personal and historical tides.

Ono's emotional dislocations are emphasized by his physical wanderings and by what Chu-chueh Cheng identifies as his sense of being '[l]ost amid signs of a drastically altered landscape', in a Japan that is now 'an unfamiliar locale from which he feels ineffably estranged'.[6] On his way to seek out Kuroda, a pupil he had earlier reported to authorities for being unpatriotic but whom he now needs to visit to ensure that no 'unnecessary misunderstandings ... arise' (AFW 85), Ono observes the 'little alleys filled with dilapidated lodging houses' by his apartment block (109). After meeting Kuroda's pupil Enchi, Ono resists 'the possibility that Kuroda was as hostile to my memory as Enchi had suggested' and emphasizes his real goal that afternoon, which was not absolution or forgiveness so much as his 'duty as a father to press on with the matter' of protecting his daughter's marriage prospects, 'unpleasant though it was' (114). Fortunately for Ono, his own estranged former teachers, Takeda and Mori-san have fallen upon their own hardships, about which Ono refrains from seeming smug. With reference to his own Shigeta Foundation Award, Ono seems to gloat over his teacher Mori-san, who by contrast has experienced 'the steady decline of his reputation in the city' and is even in the post-war period 'regarded as fundamentally unpatriotic' (202–3). In this moment of deflecting anxiety concerning his own situation onto his former, disgraced teacher, Ono points to his own career outcomes. It is only because Setsuko urges him to take precautions that Ono glimpses how his own youthful arrogance against his father can be replicated by the younger generation against him, and how his reputation has fallen under a disgrace similar to that of his own teachers.

During the evening of the *miai* – a cultural meeting of prospective families seeking betrothal – Ono continues to wave away his past misdeeds and highlights Noriko's nervousness instead. Critics gauge the evening's events as truly embarrassing for Ono, who believes he has been able to win the respect of the prospective groom's family but has in fact only done so, if at all, through some missteps.[7] Ono reminds his listener of his attentive skills at reading people's hidden feelings. Ono's 'suspicions about young Mitsuo', the brother of the prospective groom Taro Saito, 'were aroused as soon as I saw him' and he remembers growing increasingly sure of the young man's 'hostility and accusation' over the course of the evening (*AFW* 117). But Ono gets paranoid when he suspects that while the other family members were ostensibly cordial, they might well have been just as hostile and that it is only Mitsuo who is 'not as skilled in disguising it' (117). Ono's own guilty feelings allow him to suppose that others are, like himself, skilled at keeping unpleasantness beneath a veneer of apparent benevolence.

In both *An Artist of the Floating World* and *The Buried Giant*, characters are not always what they seem on the surface, especially when factoring in the way that they are also driven by the forces of their historical and cultural contexts. Both novels address the treacheries of nation-building and relate the particular sentiments of individuals towards their respective cultural affiliations, as well as the deliberate contributions made by individuals to support or resist such endeavours. The individual and national complexities of Ishiguro's novels have the potential to uphold conflicting interpretations, and it is in examining how emotions are suppressed or expressed that readers might gauge characters' moral choices. Ishiguro noted, 'I wanted a certain poignancy to emerge from [Ono's] sense that a man's life is only so long, while the life of a nation is so much longer' (*CKI* 170). Timothy Wright observes that Ishiguro neither favours nor endorses Ono's equivocating self-representations but instead constructs a complex character for our literary archaeology.[8] One kind of reading emphasizes the triumph of the personal and registers the marriage plot, which the family could salvage this second time around if only fathers like Ono had not lived and worked on the wrong side of history. An alternative reading would also register more difficult truths about nations, and would attend to concerns about the deadly nationalism of Japan leading to the Second World War – a war that Ono proudly and with great conviction remembers his artistic work as exhorting and propagating. At the novel's end, five years after the end of the Second World War, Ono and his conservative friend Matsuda feebly exonerate themselves for a lack of foresight, with the latter noting how they were merely 'ordinary men ... with no special gifts of insight. It was simply our misfortune to have been ordinary men during such times' (*AFW* 200). Wright assesses the oscillating perspectives that Ono and Matsuda never ceased hiding behind:

> While ostensibly concerned with humanistic themes such as the well-being of society, the dignity of the individual, and the difficulty of family relations,

[Ishiguro's novels] hint at a nightmare world through which human subjects grope in blind desperation. One senses that beneath the placid and banal surface of the everyday lies a horror too powerful to be viewed directly, a horror whose disclosure must proceed not by the presentation of events but by indirection, dissemblance, projection, concealment, silence, and anamorphosis.[9]

Wright's identification of narrative portents helps us to understand the characters' emotions as they strive for certainty against uncertainty, enlightenment against ignorance, bliss against dread, calm against horror, and purpose against chaos. And these kinds of emotional upheavals will cause disruptions and destabilize characters in Ishiguro's seventh novel in different but equally compelling ways.

Dread and Hatred in *The Buried Giant*

The Buried Giant presents similar narrative complications regarding the disruptions of time and memory as it explores character affect and historical effect: the couple's personal journey to reunite with their son resembles the marriage plot of *An Artist of the Floating World* at least with respect to the way that family discord requires mending. While Ono worries that the outcomes from his former occupation might now scar the family reputation, for the elderly couple in *The Buried Giant* a reunion with their son seems to be tied to resolving problems in their marriage. Should the mist of forgetfulness conjured by Merlin from Arthur's orders vanish, however, their memories would return and might expose the fact that much of their happy marriage has been illusory, even self-fictionalized.

Axl's past with Beatrice is complicated by his military duties, including his involvement in Arthur's treacherous campaign against the Saxons and the slaughter of 'innocents' (as recalled by Gawain) (*BG* 230–4), and Axl slowly aligns his growing horror about his vaguely remembered past to the reason why Wistan and Gawain find him disturbingly familiar (118, 230). The difficult physical demands of the couple's walking journey to the next village, where Wistan and Edwin join them, then on towards the monastery to see Father Jonus with Gawain, and finally at the novel's end to the two rivers, are all points on a journey that are tragically grounded in, and even directed by, the remains from malevolent events entombed beneath their feet. The mental strain of struggling to recall events is symbolized by the consistently difficult physical journey, one that is foreshadowed in the novel's opening description of 'miles of desolate, uncultivated land' and 'rough-hewn paths over craggy hills or bleak moorland' (3). Each character carries memories that are impossible to retrieve through the mist of forgetfulness – a mist that obliterates all but the fragments of memory that puncture it at unexpected moments. Forgetting is necessary to sustain King Arthur's tribal victories, and Ishiguro builds narrative suspense by leaving open the question of whether the dragon Querig will be destroyed and the mist dissipated. Bernadette Meyler observes that in the novel, any form of 'forgetting is not the work of a day but requires an ongoing labor of erasure' such as Querig's 'constant vigilance'.[10] Characters' suppressed memories cause deep uneasiness, requiring them to ignore some signs that emerge, or to work at retrieval, which exacerbates the hard peripatetic work of their physical journey.

Ishiguro further explores emotional effects through contrasts that drive character conflicts such as youth and old age, while those involving past events are seen to impact negatively upon present affairs reflecting divisions in time, space, and human relationships. Emotions at each end of a wide spectrum also guide the degree of narrative reliability in the novels and establish tonal shifts in Ishiguro's emotional discourse. Anxiety and relief, dread and calm, grief and joyfulness, desolation and gratification, and a host of other semi-articulated feelings can be gleaned from both novels to explore times when emotions disrupt the characters' well-being. With respect to affective possibilities, then, Ishiguro's novels are not the straightforward stories about individuals recalling and reconstructing the past for their forgiveness that they might seem to be. Just beyond the novel's literal surfaces and metaphorical aesthetic terrain, an entire subterranean world of affect and emotional consequence may be unearthed to explore the characters' self-equivocations.

In his study of whether Ishiguro argues for history as a constructed narrative or as an objective series of events to be retrieved, Ivan Stacy declares that the dominant tone of *The Buried Giant* is 'the sense of foreboding experienced by the protagonist Axl'.[11] In fact, however, foreboding is not only felt by Axl but is uniquely experienced by each of the wounded or debilitated characters as they forge their truths: Beatrice with the pain in her side and blood in her urine worrying that she will not be well enough to reach their son; the young boy Edwin, whose bite by 'a ferocious creature' causes a village to revolt (*BG* 98) and who hears his mother's voice urging him towards Querig; and Sir Gawain, limited by age-related deteriorations of his warrior's body, who has secretly been sent to guard Querig rather than destroy her. These characters suffer from their physical ailment but also from a worry that something terrible will thwart their quest. Apprehension hovers as the mist of forgetfulness deepens their dread – the harrowing feeling that drags one down to a bottomless pit – and takes root to morph into some physical manifestation at nearly every turn. Their state of mind and the associating emotions reflect their anxiety about whether they will ever be able to remember the past truthfully or attempt a feasible reconstruction that will alleviate their dread. As we will see, neither option will prove better than the other.

In Part One, Axl and Beatrice are ostracized by others, and their decision to leave the warren is rationalized by an urge to be with their son. Arriving at a ruined villa, they encounter 'a small, bird-like old woman' cradling a rabbit she might use as barter or could kill for dinner, and 'a thin, unusually tall man' (BG 36–7). The old couple discern that there is animosity between these two people and attempt to help the strangers make peace, but Axl has an ominous sensation that Beatrice immediately intuits. When Beatrice queries him, Axl hopes to diminish her anxiety by reassuring her: 'It's nothing, princess. When the man speaks of wars and burning houses, it's almost as if something comes back to me. From the days before I knew you, it must be' (45). The characters are set on high alert for potential danger. The personal journey by the elderly couple is framed by encounters with old women – particularly widows – and the boatman, who appear at both the beginning and the end of the novel.[12] When Beatrice questions the boatman about the strength of a couple's bond and whether what 'truly lies in people's hearts' can be so confidently discerned, the boatman assures her that indeed one can see through the deceptions since '[a]biding love that has endured the years – that we only see rarely' (47). The couple's journey is now compromised by a gnawing unease that a successful family reunion somehow depends upon the strength of their marriage bond. They attempt to recall simple details such as their son's physical appearance and chastise one another for this failed remembrance. Beatrice stresses blood ties to validate her maternal emotions, and she inverts the parent–child responsibility in her adamant point about their son's strength. But the boatman's test of a couple's true love troubles the couple, and their journey together soon exposes splinters in their relationship and indicates that they are among the majority of couples in not having a rare, abiding love.[13] After consulting with Father Jonus about her ailments and also receiving counsel about good and bad memories, Beatrice is determined to keep believing that their marriage, 'whatever its shape' is 'a thing dear to us' (172).

Solace for Beatrice is short-lived, as the couple and Edwin must escape soldiers invading the monastery. Beatrice is horrified but certain that she has stepped on the corpse of a dead child within the dark tunnel (BG 182), and later, near the novel's end, she insists sorrowfully that she has seen many dead babies in a pond (296). Her responses hint at her deeper misgivings regarding both her marriage and a sense of doom. Before they are reunited with the others, Axl and Beatrice travel towards Querig in two separate baskets, an anxious journey that permits them to question one another about the memory fragments now surfacing. Beatrice recalls Axl leaving her and their son (247), a painful time of betrayal which now foreshadows their imminent final separation: will one or the other become widowed? The basket journey is fateful in another way when Axl hears an indeterminable voice from a strange old woman they encounter in a boat: 'Leave her, stranger. Leave her to us' (252). Emotional complexity here intensifies from dread to terror, and the character's desire to know shifts towards the necessity to suppress memory and halt negative premonitions. Even as characters struggle to maintain reasonable demeanours towards other people, the ending of their journey stirs up many unresolvable emotions and portends negative consequences.

A pattern of tribal reunification underscores the novel, in which unlikely persons may actually have unseen ties or bonds, that can strengthen empathy and stave off uncertainties. This type of reunification also reflects Ishiguro's concerns with how personal and cultural memories are eventually linked in the novel to create its unsettling conclusion. Thus, for example, the allegorical situation of Beatrice the mother seeking her son is soon mirrored by sons who are missing their own mothers and seeking a way to return to them. In a moment of emotional empathy that establishes a vital link between the old and the young, Beatrice communicates with Edwin as if he could be her own son. After being bitten by the creature, Edwin begins to hear 'his real mother's voice' (BG 92), which will beckon him throughout the novel, and he believes that his journey with the old couple and the warrior Wistan is taken to reunite with her. Edwin believes that the bite on his chest will bring him to his real mother.[14] Edwin's memory of a young girl with her hands tied behind her back in an abandoned field, however, jogs a deeper understanding of what is likely to have happened to his real mother. He recalls thinking that the young girl 'was an apparition or a sprite', and as he reads the signs of her captivity he notes that her explanations do not accord with her 'lying on her back in the rough grass, her torso twisted to one side' (203). It dawns on Edwin that her captivity is much more sinister than she reports and that it could be similar to the fate of his real mother. This is confirmed when Wistan reveals to Edwin that his own mother was abducted when he, too, was a child. Like Edwin, Wistan had misread his mother's disappearance as a successful escape, not in terms of the sexual violation and bodily destruction that probably ensued:

> 'These were times of war, and in my foolishness, seeing how the men slaughtered and hanged so many, I rejoiced to see the way they smiled at her, believing that they meant to treat her with gentleness and favour. Perhaps it was this way for you too, Master Edwin, when you were young and still to know of men's ways.' (BG 263)

From the similarity of the trauma and of the pattern of abduction of women, Wistan conveys how war produces deep personal losses. There are some events that can find no resolution, even with the difficult and constant work of catharsis, even with the concerted effort of sublimation, and even when conscious memory is constrained by a 'mist of forgetfulness' (48). By sharing traumatic memories of the violent abductions of their mothers, Wistan first extracts from Edwin a confession about his deception in leading him to the dragon Querig (261–2) and then compels the young boy to promise to 'carry in your heart a hatred of Britons' (264), which augurs the possibility that vengeance will defeat pain.

> 'We've a duty to hate every man, woman and child of their blood. So promise me this. Should I fall before I pass to you my skills, promise me you'll tend well this hatred in your heart. And should it ever flicker or threaten to die, shield it with care till the flame takes hold again.' (BG 264)

Yiping Wang offers a compelling way to assess the legacy of Wistan's hatred: 'The challenge he offers humans is no longer concerning the individual pursuit of honour or honesty. His task is not to reveal the covered crimes, but to trigger the hatred. So his unveiling of the history represents evil and conspiracy as well as truth and justice.'[15] In this terrible continuity of devastation leading to hateful antagonisms across communities, Ishiguro explores the never-ending wretchedness of hatred and violence between communities in the context of a history that continually propels individuals towards 'this circle of slaughter' (BG 232).

But such acts and impulses of tribal vengeance are complicated by the dragon's breath and the forgetting that it instils in people. In addition to Querig's mist of forgetfulness affecting the memories of the elderly couple, it has undone the capacity of people serving their national cause to recall who were friends and who were foes. The symbolism of the gathering – the old Briton couple; the wounded Saxon boy Edwin trying to find his real mother; the Saxon warrior Wistan who had been trained to fight by Britons (BG 156) and is intent on veiling his deep-seated desire for vengeance; and an aged Gawain standing in for victorious Britons after Arthur's successful but vicious campaigns – is now evident. Whether they are each oppressed or each saved from forgetfulness, they will nevertheless journey to the destruction or salvation of Querig to discover their fates.

Eventually, the companions meet for one last time, with Wistan's destructions signalling the historical turn towards greater miseries and catastrophes. In a vein similar to Wright's ominous portents for *An Artist of the Floating World*, Charlwood asserts that in *The Buried Giant*, 'Ishiguro's text resists closure because there is no good answer ... [and] the novel offers little in the way of reconciling [opposing factions]'.[16] The final separation of Axl and Beatrice by the boatman is preceded by encounters with widows and by other unusual or supernatural creatures signifying despair and demise. Their mutual infidelities rise to their awareness around the same time that they come to a dreadful realization that their son has been dead these many years. The great sorrow of confronting self-failures and of causing disappointment and regret in themselves and in each other is the culmination of the characters' never-ending grief and the novel's undercurrent of incessant hatred.

Ishiguro's Profound Affects

In 1995, Ishiguro told Maya Jaggi, '[w]hen we're talking about things that go wrong fundamentally, at the heart of somebody's life, we are often talking about family and things early on – something crucial to do with emotional bereavement or emotional deprivation' (*CKI* 115). Ishiguro's narrative techniques and characterization have a powerful impact on the reader's own emotional responses to the characters and situations. His perceptive sense of how humans feel and act in relation to those feelings lies at the heart of the two novels discussed in this chapter, and are arguably prominent across all of his novels to date. In a 2006 interview, Ishiguro comments on his flawed characters and the 'bad news' that 'we already know about how we will all die someday'. When he talks about how a novel like *Never Let Me Go* 'really stresses the positive side of human nature' he could be speaking for any of his novels, but the comment particularly reflects the deeply sad ending of *The Buried Giant*: 'Humans are capable of caring deeply for one another, even though they make mistakes, because they are prey to human emotions such as jealousy, possessiveness, or anger. Ultimately, they are capable of being very decent. It was a kind of celebration, which could be seen in this bleak backdrop' (*CKI* 220). In *An Artist of the Floating World* and *The Buried Giant*, characters may act deplorably in certain circumstances, they might fall under violent and destructive emotions, or even irrevocably harm themselves and others. But it is through such unrelenting narratives of moral struggle that Ishiguro draws his readers in to attend to the profound affects that underscore and also cause upheavals in human lives.

Notes

1 In an interview from 1990, Ishiguro told Allan Vorda and Kim Herzinger that, chiming with his characters' view of their work and contribution to society, 'I write out of this fear that I, myself, will waste my talent. Not only waste my

talents, but indeed end up backing some cause that I actually disapprove of or one that could be disastrous' (*CKI* 87).

2 Timothy Wright, 'No Homelike Place: The Lesson of History in Kazuo Ishiguro's *An Artist of the Floating World*', *Contemporary Literature* 55:1 (2014): 58–88 (85–6).

3 Catherine Charlwood, 'National Identities, Personal Crises: Amnesia in Kazuo Ishiguro's *The Buried Giant*', *Open Cultural Studies* 2:1 (2018): 25–38 (31).

4 Ibid., 29.

5 Ivan Stacy, 'Looking Out into the Fog: Narrative, Historical Responsibility, and the Problem of Freedom in Kazuo Ishiguro's *The Buried Giant*', *Textual Practice* 35: 1 (2021): 109–28 (110).

6 Chu-chueh Cheng, 'Cosmopolitan Alterity: America as a Mutual Alien of Britain and Japan in Kazuo Ishiguro's Novels', *Journal of Commonwealth Literature* 45: 2 (2010): 227–44 (231).

7 See, for example, Barry Lewis, *Kazuo Ishiguro* (Manchester: Manchester University Press, 2000), p.61.

8 Wright, 'No Homelike Place', 85–6.

9 Ibid., 61.

10 Bernadette Meyler, 'Aesthetic Historiography: Allegory, Monument, and Oblivion in Kazuo Ishiguro's *The Buried Giant*', *Critical Analysis of Law* 2 (2018): 250, 252.

11 Stacy, 'Looking Out into the Fog', 109.

12 Shen argues that the 'three seemingly different women are actually the same ghost [woman] encountered by [Beatrice and Axl] at three separate times' (Anni Shen, 'Adapting Mizoguchi's *Ugestsu* in Kazuo Ishiguro's *The Buried Giant*', *Adaptations* 10:1 (2021): 1–21 (2)).

13 That couples truly in love get the best deal in life and beyond is an echo of the wishful thinking that clone-couples in *Never Let Me Go* rely on to defer their completion.

14 Physical and emotional wounds are symbols in *A Pale View of Hills* (1982) and *The Unconsoled* (1995) and are used to signify the irreducible hurt that people endure from their trauma. Etsuko in the former and Brodsky in the latter each carries wounds on their bodies. Etsuko notes, 'it is possible to develop an intimacy with the most disturbing of things', which seems to be true for Edwin, too (*APV* 54).

15 Yiping Wang, 'Ethnic War and the Collective Memory in Kazuo Ishiguro's *The Buried Giant*', *English Studies* 102:2 (2021): 227–42 (235).

16 Charlwood, 'National Identities, Personal Crises', 37.

14

LAURA COLOMBINO

Ishiguro and Love

The representation of love in Kazuo Ishiguro's work most commonly involves both loss and longing. Lovers and married couples feature in his fiction as bound by intense but vulnerable relationships that are constantly threatened by the possibility of separation. Equally touching is Ishiguro's depiction of mothers whose bond with their children has been, or may be, severed, if not precluded altogether. The scene in which a melancholy Kathy dances to the fictional singer Judy Bridgewater's song in *Never Let Me Go* is exemplary in this regard, conflating as it does romantic and motherly love: the song lyrics refer to a woman who is afraid of losing her lover, but Kathy takes the word 'baby' in the song literally, instinctively associating it with a mother who holds her baby tenderly to her breast, fearing they might be separated (*NLMG* 266). The pathos of this scene speaks of the way Ishiguro's characters typically '[try] to hold off sorrow, to lose themselves for a moment in the fleeting joys of life', as he explains in the sleeve notes to a music CD, 'while never being able quite to forget its shortness and fragility'.[1] His lovers' yearning is often so intense that its frustration is too much to bear: at the end of *The Remains of the Day*, for example, when love finally disarms Stevens's strong emotional defences, he recognizes that his 'heart was breaking' (*RD* 252).

In Ishiguro's fiction, love is both unfulfilled promise and consolation, the wound and the balm. Above all, it ranges widely: from the difficult, guilt-ridden love of Etsuko for her suicided daughter in *A Pale View of Hills*, through Stevens's barely acknowledged and unrequited love for Miss Kenton in *The Remains of the Day*, to the frustrated belief in romantic love's redemptive power in *Never Let Me Go*, and, finally, the long-standing but fragile and doomed conjugal love of Axl and Beatrice in *The Buried Giant*. In a sense, Ishiguro's latest novel, *Klara and the Sun*, circles back to the beginning of his career: once more, the theme of the remorseful mother facing the experience of the (possible) death of her child comes centre stage, but the compulsive return of the unmastered past found in Etsuko's reminiscences morphs into Chrissie's anxiety about the fateful consequences of her decision to subject her daughter to what we can assume is a form of gene editing.

However, before trying to understand the place of love in Ishiguro's writing, we need to consider love as a concept. Love has been a mainstay in philosophy since the ancient world and more recently also in psychoanalysis. A range of theories have been produced in order to grasp its complex and elusive nature, which wavers between the sensible and the ineffable – between the embodied and instinctual, on the one hand, and the intellectual or even the spiritual, on the other. The *Oxford English Dictionary* has an extensive record for the word – including but not limited to sexual desire, lust, deep affection, fondness, strong emotional attachment, sympathy, benevolence towards a group, category of people or one's country, amicable or peaceable settlement, and charity.[2] The slippery nature of the concept and the ensuing problems of definition can be resolved partly by reference to the Greek terms *eros, philia,* and *agape.*

In the *Symposium*, the initiating and most influential text on love in the Western tradition, Plato introduces the idea that human beings were at one time two people conjoined and that love is the desire we have to find the other half, in order to become whole again.[3] He also characterizes *eros* as a 'ladder' in which physical love is superseded in turn by love for the soul, for the law, for the institutions created by beautiful souls, and, finally, for the Form of Beauty that bounds all things beautiful and corresponds to the Good.[4] Plato has Socrates praise *eros*, but in the *Republic* he also foregrounds the idea that, like poetry, love speaks the language of the gods and therefore transgresses logic and rationality, such that it must be kept at bay in order to build the ideal city.[5] In *Civilization and Its Discontents*, Sigmund Freud similarly argues that erotic energies must be repressed for civilization to develop.[6] By contrast with the desiring and passionate yearning of *eros, philia* entails a brotherly fondness and appreciation of the other. In *Nicomachean Ethics*, Aristotle gives examples of *philia* incorporating young lovers, lifelong friends, parents, children as well as one's community or *polis*, and suggests that it is generally based on a certain mutuality.[7] Finally, Christianity introduces the concept of *agape* (charity), the unlimited love that Jesus felt, as a man, for humanity, when he allowed himself to be crucified.[8] In its broadest sense, the term designates a form of unconditional love that acts regardless of changing circumstances and that is directed towards the well-being of any human being rather than just towards the happiness of the nearest and dearest or even towards one's own good. The universalism of *agape* contradicts the partiality of Aristotle, who argues that '[t]o be friends with many people, in the sense of perfect friendship, is impossible'.[9] The concept of universal love, of loving all equally, poses a variety of ethical questions, among them the impracticability, and possibly the ultimate emptiness, of such love. Nevertheless, *agape* is close in some respects to the contemporary conception of ethics developed by Emmanuel Levinas, which is based on the recognition of our common vulnerability and the sense of our infinite responsibility towards other human beings.[10]

Each of these traditions in the conception of love is touched on and developed in Ishiguro's work. The theme is inscribed in Ishiguro's larger investigation of the human search for meaning within a context of professional and parental obligations, on the one hand, and the inexorable passing of time, on the other. Labouring under the delusion that he can contribute to the good of humanity through his all-absorbing devotion to butlering, Stevens denies himself romantic love and, at the end of the novel, comes to a belated, poignant realization of his mistake. Apparently attuned to the Freudian idea that *eros* must be sacrificed to the construction of civilization, in *The Remains of the Day* Stevens fittingly renounces love for the higher good of Lord Darlington's deludedly idealistic conception of international politics. It is paradoxical that *The Remains of the Day*, a novel about a love story that never quite takes place, is the work by Ishiguro which has been most frequently associated with *eros*. In this respect, it has been repeatedly argued that Stevens's erotically unconsummated affection for Miss Kenton is the repressed unconscious desire at the core of the novel.[11] Ishiguro's language certainly gestures towards such a Freudian reading, not least when he has the butler '*diagnose*' self-deludedly his small errors in the carrying out of his duties, 'as *symptoms* of nothing more than a straightforward staff shortage' that could easily be resolved if Miss Kenton were to return to Darlington Hall (*RD* 51, my italics).[12] Tellingly, Miss Kenton is also the object of a Freudian slip on Stevens's part when, explaining to Mr Farraday the reasons for choosing the West Country for his motoring trip, he reveals inadvertently that 'a former housekeeper of Darlington Hall was resident in that region' (*RD* 14) – a momentous failure for a man who strives to be in perfect control of his language. Renata Salecl's Lacanian reading of the novel, however, diverges from the usual interpretation of Miss Kenton as the object of Stevens's desire, which he renounces in the name of professionalism. In Salecl's view, the relationship between the two colleagues exemplifies a form of love that is identified with or directed towards the 'ego-ideal', which in this case is embodied in the professional roles of the butler or housekeeper: 'all of his love is in the rituals. Inasmuch as it can be said that he loves Miss Kenton, he loves her from the perspective of submission to the codes of their profession.'[13]

The tension between the pursuit of a higher objective in life – which may be of importance to humanity – and the emotional stability found in love and intimacy ('something warm and sheltering, something I can turn to, regardless of what I do, regardless of who I become' (*WWWO* 251)) also remains unresolved for characters such as Ryder in *The Unconsoled* and Christopher Banks in *When We Were Orphans*. The former's ambition to make a difference in the world of music for the benefit of an entire community is at cross-purposes with his personal duty towards Sophie and Boris (who are, with varying degrees of certainty at different points, identified as his wife and his child). But he remains unable to solve the conundrum, entertaining the illusion that, after all, he may have time to fulfil both obligations (*U* 217–18). Yet readers feel that his failure is utter and complete: he betrays his nearest and dearest, while also demonstrating the impracticability of benevolence and charitable agency on a large social scale involving an entire community or even more than one.[14] In a similar vein, *When We Were Orphans* illustrates the ineffectiveness of political agency based on *agape*, as illustrated in Diana's well-intentioned but unsuccessful efforts to halt the opium trade: Christopher bitterly concludes that 'communism has been able to achieve in a handful of years what philanthropy and ardent campaigning could not in decades' (*WWWO* 352). As for his quixotic aspiration to redress the evils besetting both his family and the whole world on the brink of the Second World War, its inadequacy is made all the more evident by his unconscious complicity with such evils: not only is Christopher's quest to save his parents revealed as an entirely futile endeavour, but it also betrays his blindness to the suffering that has been inflicted on his loved mother, who, in exchange for the provision of his education, has endured sexual enslavement to the warlord Wang Ku.[15]

Motherly love holds a special place in Ishiguro's novels. In *A Pale View of Hills*, maternal love occurs in the context of a crisis in which the mother is torn between survival from and surrender to war ('You were very shocked .... We were all shocked, those of us who were left', Ogata-San says to Etsuko (*PVH* 58)). The latter is embodied by the woman Mariko sees in Tokyo, who has the unseeing eyes of depression: this archetypal figure is crystallized in our imagination in the uncannily ambivalent act of holding her baby in her arms to drown it, a caring gesture that turns into a murderous one (74). In Ishiguro's fiction, the relationship of a mother to her child is so intense that it can continue at a phantasmal level beyond the child's death: Etsuko is troubled by visions of her suicided daughter, while in *Klara and the Sun* new and developing technologies seem to offer Chrissie a way to 'continue Josie' (*KS* 210), if the latter should die. Ishiguro's mothers are often haunted by the ghost of their offspring and unable to undergo a process of mourning that Freud argues is necessary to form stable long-term memories of the loved child and to carry on without them.[16] *The Buried Giant* is exemplary in this regard, as Beatrice has not been able to come to terms with the trauma of the loss of her son, who is only ambiguously lost and who still lives in her (as well as his father's) imaginings.

Christopher Banks's mother is a figure of survival and resilience. She combines in herself archetypical elements of both humanitarian idealism and selfless love for her child: she is pure in her mission against the opium trade but also in her unconditional sacrifice, for the sake of her child, to men who sadistically abuse her either directly, as the warlord does, or indirectly, in the case of Uncle Philip. As such, she constitutes a kind of holy grail of Christopher's filial quest. Her motherly heroism finds a reprise in *Klara and the Sun*: as an Artificial Friend, Klara is manufactured to provide only friendship but ends up being a mother-figure to Josie; furthermore, her relationship of *philia* towards the girl acquires elements of *agape*, as she gives all of herself not just to another (Josie) but to all others who may need her (complying with the requests of Chrissie, Helen, the Father, and even Capaldi), without expecting anything in return. Above all, Klara believes idealistically in the fundamental goodness of all human beings. In interviews to mark the publication of the novel, Ishiguro reports his wife saying that Klara resembles his mother Shizuko, who gave up her career as a teacher to devote herself entirely to her family: 'everything she thought and did seemed to have this goal at the back of it .... Every small decision had behind it this big question: would it further the good of my children? ... In that sense she was almost like a programmed AI!'[17]

If fathers and sons negotiate historical crises in terms of which set of values should be embraced (as exemplified by *An Artist of the Floating World* and *The Remains of the Day*), mothers seem to symbolize nothing less than the survival of humanity. In *A Pale View of Hills*, Mrs Fujiwara exhorts Etsuko to 'keep [her] mind on happy things', as 'she needs a positive attitude to bring up a child' and to think ahead beyond personal and historical traumas (*PVH* 24, 25). In his brief 2017 Nobel Banquet Speech, Ishiguro recalled the time when, back in the days when his family was still living in Nagasaki, his mother showed him the picture of Alfred Nobel: 'she told the story about a man who'd invented dynamite, then concerned about its applications, had created the *Nobel Sho* – I first heard of it by its Japanese name ... to promote *heiwa* – meaning peace or harmony ... and young as I was, I knew *heiwa* was something important; that without it fearful things might invade my world'.[18] It is motherhood and motherly love rather than professional idealism that seem capable of connecting the individual to the collective level: however ineffectual on the political plane, *agape* can work on our conscience at the emotional level in enigmatic and unpredictable ways, nurturing our soul and making us more human.

The most common conception of love – as sexual love, *eros* – is only occasionally explored in Ishiguro's fiction. When it is, its treatment seems both to respond and often give the lie to the logic of the genre. In *The Remains of the Day*, the satirical vein that runs through the novel demands that sex (or, rather, its evasion) inspires one of the novel's most humorous scenes, when the impeccable Stevens awkwardly resorts to metaphors drawn from 'the glories of nature' (*RD* 94), in order to teach Darlington's godson, Reginald Cardinal, the basics of human sexuality. In *The Unconsoled*, sex is explored, just like everything else in the novel, in connection with the sense that time is running out. Brodsky's description of his attempt to reconquer Miss Collins as the 'last mission' (*U* 311) for his withered sexual organ has a humorous ring to it, but what he hopes to achieve is fully decent: still a few years of consoling affection and intimacy. Physical decay in association with sex is intended to produce a comic effect while also eliciting compassion: love is a 'consolation' (*U* 313) tinged with regret for the time that has been wasted. The same note is struck in *Never Let Me Go*, where *eros* is a balm for the clones' woundedness: the scar left on Tommy's body by the first donation accompanies his first sexual intercourse with Kathy. 'That first time, we still had stitches to worry about' (*NLMG* 234), she reminisces, adding that 'there was something in Tommy's manner that was tinged with sadness and that seemed to say: "Yes, we're doing this now and I'm glad we're doing it now. But what a pity we left it so late"' (235). In this novel, mortality has taken centre stage, expunging all residue of humour, as shown by Miss Emily's 'sex lectures' at Hailsham (82), a revisitation of Stevens's understated lesson on the mechanics of reproduction but purged of any comic intention: Miss Emily's use of 'a life-size skeleton from the biology class to demonstrate how it was done' is a grotesque, chilling conception, which transmogrifies *eros* into a sort of Dance of Death and an omen of the bleak future lying in store for the clones (82). Finally, *When We Were Orphans* is a case apart, as under the highly distortive, oneiric lens of the novel, sex acquires the perverse form of sadism and sexual abuse.

It is well known that Ishiguro 'sets up and then thwarts the reader's expectations' concerning genre and literary conventions more generally.[19] For example, in *A Pale View of Hills*, he 'appropriates the *Madame Butterfly* story ... and gives it a twist', by deviating from the tragic relationship between the American sailor and the Japanese girl, and focusing instead on the relationship between mother and child.[20] In *When We Were Orphans*, a distorted reflection of escapist romance can be found in the awkwardness of Sarah's romantic moment with Christopher Banks in the record shop:

'Then we were kissing – just like, I suppose, a couple on the cinema screen. It was almost exactly as I had always imagined it would be, except there was something oddly inelegant about our embrace, and I tried more than once to adjust my posture' (*WWWO* 262). Another case in point is the treatment of love in *Never Let Me Go*. In contrast to major science-fiction and dystopian novels such as *Nineteen Eighty-Four* and *Brave New World*, where romantic or sexual love inspires acts of subversion that threaten the stability of the system, the clones of *Never Let Me Go* do not rebel against the established order and their love in fact serves to support their subservience to an exploitative system. Finally, in *The Buried Giant* the transcendent courtly love of knights and damsels (which was not to be consummated but actively pursued in chivalric deeds) is turned into the more humane, ordinary love of an old couple: in place of the purity and delayed fulfilment of desire characteristic of this genre, we are confronted with the strenuous, poignant effort to preserve a long-standing relationship. It is also worth noting, in relation to genre, that many novels by Ishiguro share the motif of the quest for a loved one: someone who has been long absent (Miss Kenton in *The Remain of the Day* and Diana in *When We Were Orphans*); whose separation is approaching (Beatrice in *The Buried Giant*), so that the quest is about the impossible attempt to pre-empt parting and achieve the perfection of an eternal union; or else, whose loss is suspended in the limbo of forgetfulness (Axl and Beatrice's dead son).

The theme of love extends to Ishiguro's short stories and song lyrics. '[T]hough seemingly full of romantic yearning', as the musical genre evoked by the title suggests, his *Nocturnes* 'are never without the anticipation of disappointment'.[21] Where Ishiguro's late fiction privileges sustained, gravely serious treatments of love, these shorter works can touch on more light-hearted and even humorous tones, even while the prevalent mood is that of a melancholy irony. In 'Crooner', for example, Ishiguro contrasts Janeck's mother's unrequited love in a communist country with the affair between Linda and the singer Tony Gardner against the backdrop of the American jet-set; the mother's doomed but dignified existence in a country in which, sadly, she dies before it turns into a democracy, is set against the couple's shallow dream of social climbing, to which they sacrifice their love for each other. But it is not only through this cultural clash that Ishiguro wrings out sad ironies. He also explodes our unthinking belief in the truthfulness of love songs, as Gardner's opportunism gives the lie to the emotion he sells: his popular music, capable of eliciting an emotional response across national and ideological borders and making life more bearable for Janeck's mother, is revealed as a form of stylization at best and manipulation at worst. Nonetheless, the conclusion we draw is that the power of love songs is indeed authentic, even though the intention behind it may not be so. Love is a noble and universal streak in our otherwise flawed and fallible human nature.

Ishiguro's late songwriting activity is also worth considering in connection with the theme of love. In his lyrics for jazz singer Stacey Kent written since 2006, the limits of the medium, which reduces the narrative possibilities, impede the careful unfolding of human relationships characteristic of Ishiguro's fiction. The medium calls instead for unelaborated scenarios of crisis in non-places of transition and anonymity. Nondescript restaurants ('Waiter, Oh Waiter'), holiday resorts ('The Ice Hotel'), and means of transport ('Breakfast on the Morning Tram') are the settings for stories of disappointed love, where puzzled or deserted lovers '[go] over the broken pieces of [their] life, trying to coax from somewhere a little courage and perspective'.[22] Exploding once more a conventional view of love, 'The Ice Hotel' evokes stereotypical geographies of passion and romance such as Verona and Paris or tropical Barbados and Tahiti, only to suggest that they may be dangerously illusionary destinations for the two wary, puzzled lovers who opt instead for a cooler location suited to their tepid passion. But Ishiguro is never downright sardonic, seeming to believe that there is always decency and hope in love and human companionship. So, the icy atmosphere between the two is saved by light humour: there is hope for their love to be still alive tomorrow, provided they make it through a night spent sleeping on a block of ice.[23]

Ishiguro's most recent 'trilogy' of novels *Never Let Me Go*, *The Buried Giant*, and *Klara and the Sun* engages more directly with love in, respectively, an alternative present, a half-historical half-mythological past, and a near-future. The theme is explored in relation both to our mortal condition and to the evils besetting our societies and communities: marginalization; conflict and ethnic cleansing; new forms of fascism and the consequences of scientific and technological developments. The centrality of death in each of these works, combined with Ishiguro's interest in idealism, naturally calls for the interrogation of the idea of the eternity of the soul and the examination of the nature of love, which, in the Platonic conception, is its noblest part as well as something between the mortal and the immortal.[24]

In his more recent works, the ineffable quality of the soul comes under scrutiny to the extent that its very existence is problematized: *Klara and the Sun*, for example, examines the possibility that AI will reveal that the long-standing idea of a spiritual element in us that seems to guarantee our uniqueness as individuals may be only a consoling superstition. The conclusion that Klara draws at the end of the novel seems to be that Josie's soul (and, by extension everyone else's) is, in fact, not reproducible, because what is 'special' about it 'wasn't inside Josie' but rather 'inside those who loved her'

(KS 306). In *Never Let Me Go*, Kathy and Tommy feel they should demon-strate their love (which is synonymous with demonstrating they have a refined, authentic soul) through their drawings: interestingly, Ishiguro's use of love and art to interrogate the nature of our souls is found also in Plato's *Symposium*, which permits love to be understood only by those who are initiated into its comprehension through dialectical philosophy and artistic creativity, while the non-initiated can feel only physical desire. In their visit to Madame's house, Kathy and Tommy come to realize that the 'deferral' of 'donations' for couples who can demonstrate their love for each other is no more than a myth or superstition: the idea of romantic love as a higher truth which conquers all, death included, is a mere delusion. But what remains true is the beauty and meaningfulness of love as a form of consolation – not only under the guise of *eros* but also in Kathy's care (*philia*) towards friends and her unflagging devotion to the whole suffering community of the donors (*agape*).

The episode of the visit inaugurates the motif of the love test, which is further developed in *The Buried Giant*. Axl and Beatrice submit to the questions of the boatman in order to obtain the special dispensation to travel together to the island of afterlife that, they believe, is granted to couples with a strong bond of love – a trope that surely alludes to ancient Greek figures such as Achilles and Medea being sent to the Islands of the Blest, often as couples.[25] In *Klara and the Sun*, the motif of the test finds a necessarily minor reprise, because the love between Josie and Rick is as unstable and in flux as anything else in the novel. In a world where interchangeability triumphs in human relationships as much as between the humans and their artificial simulacra, the synthetic Klara becomes paradoxically the guarantor of the couple's love, which she considers a precondition to intercede with the Sun to cure the severely ill Josie.

Against the backdrop of a bare landscape, *The Buried Giant* explores the hardships of the lifelong journey of an elderly couple and shows how hard they 'have to battle to keep that flame alive', because of 'all the bad weather that threatens to blow the thing out'.[26] Above all, the novel engages with the merits and shortcomings of forgetfulness and memory in long-term love relationships by posing a series of questions. Should Axl and Beatrice hold on fast to their residual affection by allowing the mist of forgetfulness to linger in their minds, or should they probe into the dark passages of their past and run the risk of losing each other? This dilemma combines with another, which torments Axl as the end of Beatrice's life draws near: should he cling to what remains of their life together, however painful it may be for her, or would it be more considerate to overcome the dread of separation and let her go for her own good? Might death be a compassionate act and holding someone back for oneself a torture? As Anne Whitehead argues, 'caught between our desire to hold on and an ability to let go; we should care, but perhaps not too possessively or too exclusively'.[27] In *Never Let Me Go*, which also explores this theme not least in its telling title, the 'most unselfish act in the novel'[28] is Tommy's refusal to have Kathy nurse him at the end of his life: 'I don't want to be that way in front of you', he tells her (*NLMG* 257).

While Axl is tormented by the prospect of losing Beatrice, the latter in turn is haunted by the possibility that their love may be drained of substance and authenticity. Without a shared past, she wonders, can their affection last? Her doubt is encapsulated in one of the most lyrical images of the novel, when the elderly couple are sheltering under a tree: some raindrops are still falling on them, but the sky is clearing up. Are their emotions, like those raindrops, simply a residue of their past love that will also dry up (*BG* 49)? As for Axl's doubt about whether he should hold on to Beatrice or let her go, this is beautifully conveyed by the image of the couple floating down the river, each one in a large basket, tied to the other by a rope, symbolizing the fear that their bond may be severed. Other images point to love as the aspiration of two souls to become one, as when Axl and Beatrice find shelter under 'the twin rocks', sitting 'close against one another, as if in imitation of the stones above them' (265). The hardships of travel in the bare landscape of Arthurian England offer Ishiguro the occasion for splendid metaphors, nodes of emotional complexities that condense the couple's predicament.

In *Klara and the Sun*, the theme of loneliness is more central than in any other Ishiguro novel and investigated in a more fundamental way – not as concerning a time in our life but as constitutive of our being. Klara navigates a sea of human solitude, where the desire to love and be loved is forever frustrated and no relationship, be it amorous, professional, or friendly, seems permanent – or particularly intense. This existential loneliness leads Ishiguro to follow the trajectory of human desire: in their yearning for companionship and a sense of completion, the characters of *Klara and the Sun* are always projected towards others, whether humans or Artificial Friends. This characterization of the individual is reminiscent of Jacques Lacan's idea that lack is constitutive of our psyche such that, for this reason, we are constantly in search of something that may appease our desire for completeness; except that, being infinite, this desire can never be fully satisfied. Lacan sees love as something that seems to quench this need by deluding us into thinking we can be less lonely: in Ashley T. Shelden's clear synthesis of Lacan's concept, '[f]antasy ensures that the lovers never have to encounter the insurmountable chasm that separates them from each other ... by presenting the illusion of union'.[29]

'Each person is so complex that it is hard to build bridges between them', states Ishiguro in an interview.[30] The cartoon-drawing 'bubble game'

(*KS* 119) that Josie and Rick play, is precisely a figure of this difficulty and of the fragility of human bonds, especially of an amorous nature. If the aspiration that two may become one is only a comforting mirage for Lacan, for the Ishiguro of *Klara and the Sun* it is, less dramatically, an uncertain and impermanent conquest. The idyllic image of the drawings Josie lets float from her bed down to Rick, and that he passes back to her once he has filled in the bubbles with words, gestures towards the idea of two halves that try to reconstruct a whole: the image and the text are indispensable to each other to release the meaning, just as Josie and Rick seem indissolubly connected by shared memories, games, and mutual affection. And yet, as the name suggests, the bubble game is ephemeral: unlike the rope that ties Axl and Beatrice and that resists the powerful current of the river, the thread of this connection is so flimsy that a mere breath of air would be enough to tear it off. At the end of the novel, Klara still nurtures the hope that one day Josie and Rick may be reunited and look back with greater awareness at those precious moments together in their thoughtless youth, when life just ran through their fingers without them noticing.

But Josie and Rick are not alone in their untimeliness, as Ishiguro's characters always seem out of sync with their love: they recognize it (Stevens) or come to appreciate it (Kathy) only once it is too late; or else, they are suspended between the fear of losing it and the doubt about the reality of what they possess (Axl and Beatrice). Sexual or romantic love is most commonly compromised or undermined in Ishiguro's fiction. Often, it is ethical dilemmas that prevent his characters from embracing it: the infinite responsibility towards a community may appear to them as more honourable than private affection, as the latter entails the singling out of certain individuals as more deserving of attention than others (an idea thoroughly explored in *The Unconsoled* but still troubling Klara, when, pleading with the Sun for Josie's recovery, she wonders whether her appeal might imply a deplorable form of 'favouritism' (*KS* 276)). Over time, Ishiguro has shifted from the characterization of isolated individuals such as Ono, Stevens, and Christopher Banks, who vainly attempt to come to grips with the larger forces of history and politics, to the description of relationships, most often of love and friendship. A combination of *philia* and *agape*, the latter based on real human relationships and concrete acts of care rather than narcissistic ideals of professional excellence, features prominently in his last three novels, where love becomes almost synonymous with the soul. Both concepts are revealed as uncertain realities: no more perhaps than superstitions in the face of the inevitability of death; or else, in the age of AI that promises to conquer mortality, as possibly anachronistic ideas of the uniqueness of the human heart, that ancient and cherished notion which, we fear, we may have to let go.

Notes

1 Kazuo Ishiguro, 'Note by Kazuo Ishiguro', liner notes to Chopin: Favourite Piano Works CD, performed by Vladimir Ashkenazy (Penguin Classics, 1998), p.4.

2 'Love', *Oxford English Dictionary*, online (Oxford University Press, 2021) (accessed online at www.oed.com/).

3 Plato, *Symposium*, trans. Robin Waterfield (Oxford: Oxford University Press, 1998), p.47.

4 Ibid., p.55.

5 Plato, *The Republic*, trans. Robin Waterfield (Oxford: Oxford University Press, 2008), pp.360 (606d) and 362 (607e–608b).

6 Sigmund Freud, *Civilization and Its Discontents*, trans. James Strachey (New York: Norton, 1961), p.51.

7 Aristotle, *Nicomachean Ethics*, trans. Martin Ostwald (Indianapolis: Bobbs-Merrill, 1962), pp.218–44 (1156a–1163b).

8 Thomas Sheldon Green, *A Greek-English Lexicon to the New Testament* (Frankfurt am Main: Outlook Verlag, 2020), pp.5–6.

9 Aristotle, *Nicomachean Ethics*, p.225 (1158a).

10 Emmanuel Levinas, 'Philosophy, Justice, and Love', in *Entre-Nous: On Thinking-of-the-Other*, trans. Michael A. Smith and Barbara Harshav (New York: Columbia University Press, 1998), p.113.

11 See, for example, Adam Parkes, *Kazuo Ishiguro's 'The Remains of the Day': A Reader's Guide* (London: Continuum, 2001), p.45.

12 Kazuo Ishiguro claims that when he was writing *The Remains of the Day*, he 'imbibed a lot of reflexes from those loosely Freudian ideas' (Sean Matthews, '"I'm Sorry I Can't Say More": An Interview with Kazuo Ishiguro', in Sean Matthews and Sebastian Groes, eds., *Kazuo Ishiguro: Contemporary Perspectives* (London: Bloomsbury, 2009), p.120.

13 Renata Salecl, 'I Can't Love You Unless I Give You Up', in Renata Salecl and Slavoj Zizek, eds., *Gaze and Voice as Love Objects* (Durham, NC: Duke University Press, 1996), p.185.

14 See Lisa Fluet, 'Immaterial Labors: Ishiguro, Class, and Affect', *Novel* 40:3 (2007): 265–88 (275–6). In his discussion of *The Unconsoled*, Bruce Robbins defends Ishiguro's depiction of the 'compassion fatigue' of his cosmopolitan protagonist against Louis Menand's accusation that Ishiguro is offering only the banal piece of wisdom that 'people need love but continually spoil their chances of getting it' (Bruce Robbins, 'Very Busy Just Now: Globalization and Hurriedness in Ishiguro's *The Unconsoled*', *Comparative Literature* 53:4 (2001): 426–41 (437); Louis Menand, 'Anxious in Dreamland', *New York Times Book Review*, 15 October 1995, p.7. Robbins's urge to defend Ishiguro from Menand's criticism gives us a clue as to why scholars have been reluctant to engage the theme of love in Ishiguro: love carries with it notions of sentimentalism and idealism that seem suspiciously ideological to the materialist and historicist views that have shaped criticism in the late twentieth and early twenty-first century.

15 We might speculate that Ishiguro's exploration of unconditional motherly love and filial self-reproach is his indirect tribute, as a post-war child, to his less fortunate mother, who was exposed to radiation from the Nagasaki atomic bomb a mere fourteen years before he was born. It may have to do, in other words, with

the sense of guilt for not having been there to help and for having been spared by history.

16 Sigmund Freud, 'Mourning and Melancholia', trans. Shaun Whiteside, in *The Penguin Freud Reader*, ed. Adam Phillips (London: Penguin, 2006).

17 Seán Rocks, 'Nobel and Booker Winner Kazuo Ishiguro Talks to RTÉ Arena', 3 March 2021 (accessed online at www.rte.ie/culture/2021/0303/1200801-nobel-and-booker-winner-kazuo-ishiguro-talks-to-rte-arena/).

18 Kazuo Ishiguro, Nobel Prize Banquet Speech, 10 December 2017 (accessed online at www.nobelprize.org/prizes/literature/2017/ishiguro/speech/).

19 Cynthia F. Wong, *Kazuo Ishiguro*, 3rd ed. (Liverpool: Northcote House, 2019), p.134.

20 Wai-chew Sim, *Kazuo Ishiguro* (London: Routledge, 2010), p.34.

21 These are the words Ishiguro uses to describe Chopin's 'wonderful nocturnes' in 'Note', p.4.

22 Kazuo Ishiguro, liner note for Stacey Kent's *In Love Again* CD (Candid Productions, 2003) (accessed online at https://staceykent.com/liner-notes/).

23 Kazuo Ishiguro, 'The Ice Hotel' and 'Breakfast on the Morning Tram' for Stacey Kent's *Breakfast on the Morning Tram* CD (Token Productions, 2009); 'Waiter, Oh Waiter' for Stacey Kent's *The Changing Lights* CD (Token Productions, 2013). 'The Ice Hotel'.

24 Plato, *Symposium*, p.49.

25 Compare Laura Colombino, 'Transmodern Mythopoesis in Kazuo Ishiguro's *The Buried Giant*', in Susana Onega and Jean-Michel Ganteau, eds., *Transcending the Postmodern: The Singular Response of Literature to the Transmodern Paradigm* (London: Routledge, 2020), p.146.

26 Andy Kahan, 'Kazuo Ishiguro, The Buried Giant: Interview', Free Library of Philadelphia at the Central Library, 20 March 2015 (accessed online at libwww .freelibrary.org/podcast/episode/1339).

27 Anne Whitehead, 'Writing with Care: Kazuo Ishiguro's *Never Let Me Go*', *Contemporary Literature* 52:1 (2011): 54–83 (81).

28 Ibid., p.78.

29 Ashley T. Shelden, 'Introduction: Unmaking Love', in Shelden, ed., *Unmaking Love: The Contemporary Novel and the Impossibility of Union* (New York: Columbia University Press, 2017), p.8.

30 Anne McElvoy, '*The Economist* Asks: Sir Kazuo Ishiguro. Is AI Capable of Falling in Love?' 4 March 2021 (accessed online at www.economist.com/pod casts/2021/03/04/is-ai-capable-of-falling-in-love).

15

YUGIN TEO

Memory and Understanding in Ishiguro

Addressing what he saw as his next challenge in his considerations of memory soon after the publication of *Never Let Me Go* in 2005, Ishiguro commented that he was still 'fascinated by memory': 'What I would like to tackle next', he remarks, 'is how a whole society or nation remembers or forgets. When is it healthy to remember, and when is it healthy to forget?'[1] To date, a majority of Ishiguro's novels are narrated in the first person by someone remembering the past. And in each of these cases, the individual is afflicted by crucial lapses in memory or by a failure to understand the things remembered. The fundamental condition of narrating – that the narrator knows something that the reader or interlocutor does not – is therefore compromised by narrators who do not fully know or understand their own stories. A key exception is Ishiguro's 2015 novel *The Buried Giant* – a predominantly third-person narrative about a community afflicted by a supernatural mist of memory loss. Ishiguro's work is profoundly concerned with the fact that we account for ourselves in ways that are compromised by the fallibility of memory and understanding, and it is focused on the fact that individuals and communities sometimes need to forget. With a focus on *The Buried Giant*, this chapter explores the implications and ramifications of this critical question in Ishiguro's work.

Memory Work

Ishiguro's writing has been concerned with the complexities of memory and the failure of the individual to understand both past and present circumstances. All of the novels in his first trilogy, *A Pale View of Hills*, *An Artist of the Floating World*, and *The Remains of the Day*, are based on similar themes and feature older first-person narrators as protagonists reflecting on their lives, achievements, and choices. These characters seek out meaning and 'wholeness' by trying to understand their life stories and the circumstances that surround their past decisions.[2] The theme of neglect pervades *A Pale View of Hills* as Etsuko revisits both her past in Nagasaki and her estranged relationship with her late daughter Keiko. In *An Artist of the Floating World*, Noriko's *miai* and her marriage prospects account for some of the triggers of Masuji Ono's return to his life as a painter, and to the way he conducted his relationships with his former teacher and his students in Imperial Japan. Stevens's impending reunion with Miss Kenton (Mrs Benn) provides the impetus for him to take stock of his time at Darlington Hall, whilst being confronted with the missed opportunities of engaging with his father and Miss Kenton in *The Remains of the Day*. In what has been described as his 'Bewilderment Trilogy', Ishiguro's next three novels experiment with narrative structure, form, and genre, finding innovative ways of meditating on issues of identity and memory.[3] Instead of a retrospective point of view, *The Unconsoled* experiments with a protagonist narrating in the present, conveying a sense of being in the midst of the narrative's events, as Ryder struggles to remember and understand his relationship with the city's past. The unusual narrative form of *When We Were Orphans* offers a predominantly retrospective account of Christopher Banks's life in the first half of the novel, followed by a more immediate sense of being grounded in present events for most of the second half. This change in narrative perspective marks a heightened sense of unreliability with regard to Banks's claims about his intentions, and is indicative of his growing self-delusion and failure to reconcile with his past. The act of retrospection and testimony that governs the novel is given a science-fiction twist in 2005's *Never Let Me Go*, where the narrator and protagonist Kathy is revealed to be a clone, created for the purpose of organ harvesting. The foreshortened lifespan of clones in the novel alters the perception of what a typical lifespan for a human is, and enables Ishiguro to crystallize lived experience and to bring an intensified focus on the human condition.

The publication of *The Buried Giant* in 2015 constituted the fulfilment a decade later of Ishiguro's declaration (quoted at the beginning of this chapter) of his interest in exploring more explicitly the relationship between memory at the communal as well as at the individual level. Ishiguro's earlier meditations on testimony, understanding, and the complexities of memory are expanded beyond the individual realm, and this is facilitated by the use of a third-person narrator for the majority of the novel. This particular orientation of the narrative voice generates a greater sense of distance between the reader and the key characters, whilst simultaneously conveying the impression of a world in which the secrets of its past remain hidden just below the level of consciousness.

Giving an Account of Ourselves

Set in a post-Arthurian Britain, *The Buried Giant* depicts the journey of an elderly couple, Axl and Beatrice, as they leave their community in search of their estranged son. The land is surrounded by a mist of forgetting that is powered by the dragon Querig's breath and Merlin's spell, and instigated by Arthur in order to enforce a state of collective amnesia that covers up his war crimes.

Ishiguro's turn to communal experiences allows for an orientation in the novel towards individuals who are caught up in key events and transitional periods within a nation's tumultuous history. He has previously engaged with this theme from a first-person narrative position with protagonists such as Ono, Stevens, and Banks in *An Artist of the Floating World*, *The Remains of the Day*, and *When We Were Orphans*. These character-narrators provided subjective experiences of self-deception and hindsight when it comes to evaluating the past against the backdrop of the Second World War. *The Buried Giant* takes a significantly different perspective, utilizing the third-person narrative voice to explore experiences from a distance and from multiple viewpoints. Axl and Beatrice make for a good initial focal point in this area of enquiry. Their quest to reunite with their son at his village is a courageous, affecting, and deeply personal endeavour as they brave the unknown beyond their community's 'sprawling' hillside warren (*BG* 4). As the journey sees the pair joined on their travels by the warrior Wistan and the boy Edwin, both Saxons, and the old knight Gawain, their end-goal begins to change to encompass a more politically charged objective, which is to see the end of Querig and the mist of forgetting. As their journey progresses, they become more aware of how much they have forgotten as fragments return to them, strengthening their urge to remember what happened to their son and how things were before the mist descended. They are unable to perceive the larger consequences of the mission that they are eventually involved in – awakening the memories of genocide for the Saxons, and the widespread release of the anguish of loss and injustice. Axl and Beatrice initially hoped that the strength of their relationship would allow them to overcome whatever the past would reveal once the mist had gone. After Wistan slays Querig, Axl begins to realize the magnitude of the consequences of their actions in the removal of the mist by comparison with the relative insignificance of their own personal interests. Following Wistan's comment about the coming 'justice and vengeance' from the Saxons, Axl says to Beatrice '[y]ou and I longed for Querig's end, thinking only of our own dear memories. Yet who knows what old hatreds will loosen across the land now?' (323). Axl and Beatrice's focus on removing the mist denies them the wider perspective on what might lie beneath.

In *The Sense of an Ending*, Frank Kermode describes, in the context of fictional narrative, the human predicament of being 'stranded in the middle' between beginnings and ends, and the desire for meaning between those two points.[4] Being stranded in the middle means that it is often difficult to gain any kind of wider perspective or understanding on where one is during a period of change. As they get caught up in the search for their son while under the long-term influence of Merlin's spell, Axl and Beatrice are unable to sense the wider implications of their actions. According to Kermode, we are unable to observe the structure of our life stories from 'our spot of time in the middle', and instead find meaning from 'fictive concords' with our origins and ends.[5] Axl and Beatrice set out initially to find their son, but this intention gets muddled with other objectives that are uncovered along the way. In a ruined villa not long after they begin their journey, their encounter with an old woman and a boatman reveals Beatrice's personal interest in the story of an island to which people go to live out the rest of their lives, with the condition that they are unlikely to be with their partners. Beatrice's earlier encounter with a woman by the old hawthorn tree tells a similar story about this island of forgetting and of the sorrow of those left behind unable to be with their partners. Beatrice's curiosity, as well as her fear, about this island attracts her to its mythology and magical qualities, and just as Querig's voice calls to Edwin later in the novel, the island seems to call to Beatrice. Despite Axl's assurances that they have 'no plans to go to any such island', at the very end of the novel, when Beatrice is keen on letting the boatman ferry her to that location, she seems to have forgotten her earlier fear of being separated from Axl (*BG* 48). When Axl reminds her of the 'sly tricks' which these boatmen have been known to resort to, she insists on placing her trust in the boatman's promise of their 'time together on the island' (344). The couple, situated as they are in their spot of time between the end of Arthur's reign and the ascendancy of the Saxons, are unable to gain a wider perspective on their lives, and this is further complicated by the mist of forgetting that prevents them from accessing their memories. Both Axl and Beatrice try to look towards the future and find meaningful ends to their lives. As the mist begins to dissipate following the death of Querig, we find that the two characters have quite different thoughts about their future together. It turns out that Axl and Beatrice's relationship has actually been strengthened during the time of memory loss generated by the mist. Axl realizes that, with the imminent return of their memories, old hatreds might tear them apart again.

In *The Course of Recognition*, Paul Ricoeur theorizes the figure of what he terms the 'capable human being', comprising the ability to speak, to act, to narrate, and to give an account of one's own actions.[6] This represents the phenomenology of an individual subject who is 'capable' of these different accomplishments. However, this act of self-recognition also requires 'the help of others' at each step.[7] The enforced amnesia achieved by Arthur and Merlin's mist of forgetting questions and problematizes the ability of individuals to narrate and understand how their stories relate to those of others within their social environment. Following on from the community dispute about the use of a candle, as Axl comforts Beatrice she brings up the idea of going to the village of their estranged son and asks if this time Axl would permit them to travel to see him. Shocked by this question and the suggestion that he might have forbidden them to see their son in the past, Axl struggles to remember: 'many fragments of memories tugged at [his] mind', to the extent that he feels 'almost faint' and tries to recover his balance (*BG* 25). As characters no longer remember even the most significant and personal events, their ability to narrate their lives or orient themselves within their own life stories is rendered ineffectual. Ishiguro's interest in examining the dependency of couples on shared memories is demonstrated in the form of Beatrice, who fears that the love that she and Axl have for each other will disappear if they cannot remember their shared past. She likens their present feelings for each other to the raindrops still falling from the leaves of the tree they are sheltering under despite the rain having stopped, believing that their love will eventually 'fade and die' when there are no more shared memories (48–9). A person's ability to narrate their life story sometimes requires the help of others, as Ricoeur suggests, and this is achieved through shared memories that attest and affirm a relationship. Ishiguro utilizes the fantasy genre to create the murky backdrop of a mist that negatively affects people's ability to remember (although the mist seems to affect people to different degrees, and in the case of the warriors Gawain and Wistan, there seems to be hardly any effect at all). Edwin's memory of his mother, who was taken by Britons when his village was invaded, seems to persist, and it fuels his determination to 'one day bring her back' from captivity (262). Despite being able to remember his mother's kidnapping, Edwin's memory of her is clouded by another act of magic; in this instance it is a dragon's bite on his body creating a line of communication between him and Querig that manifests itself as his mother's voice. Edwin's role as a witness to the kidnapping, and his ability to narrate the crime, are negatively affected by the bite, as we see when he confuses Querig's voice with that of his mother.

The Buried Giant challenges the work of memory, exemplified in Ishiguro's earlier novels, and its function to 'overcome obstacles of forgetting'.[8] Ishiguro's previous novels acknowledge how dependent we are on others to remember our life stories, and how in being witnesses we 'affirm the memories of people, places and events that are important to us'.[9]

Ishiguro's post-Arthurian tale, however, makes the case that it is not always possible to remember and bear witness. The complexities of individual and collective memory have previously been acknowledged in novels such as *An Artist of the Floating World* and *Never Let Me Go*, for example when Ono expressed regret for his past involvement in Japan's war effort as a way of dealing with his guilt, and to secure his daughter Noriko's future through marriage, and in the shared memories of the former Hailsham students as they encounter one another as carers and donors towards the end of their foreshortened lives. In contrast to this, the people in *The Buried Giant* suffer from a number of years of enforced amnesia, and the process of remembering and cathartic release associated with the work of memory cannot take place for many individuals and communities. The human capacity to narrate and give an account of one's actions are heavily impeded by a lack of memory, at least for the Saxons and the Britons who live side by side. Ricoeur uses the term 'imputability' when discussing a person's ability to give an account of themselves, and how individuals can 'impute' (or ascribe) their own acts to themselves.[10] With the agency of imputability withheld from remembering subjects, the cathartic work of memory evident in earlier Ishiguro narratives is rendered ineffectual in *The Buried Giant*.

These considerations point to the inherent difficulty in understanding one's memories, and to the fact that even with the revelation of returned memories it is a challenge to understand the past and work out a suitable path for the future. As memories of his painful past with Beatrice return, Axl seems to bid a sad farewell to Beatrice, asking to 'hold [her] once more' as she prepares to be rowed first by the boatman to the island of forgetting (*BG* 345). The revelation of unresolved guilt, hurt, and anger over the death of their son might have influenced the boatman's decision to ferry the couple across separately, indicating the possibility that they will be apart indefinitely. While Ishiguro leaves the ending ambiguous, there is a palpable sense of conflict in Axl: would he be willing to live on the island with Beatrice whilst having no memory of her and no awareness of her presence, or would it be better to say goodbye to Beatrice and still have his memories of her? Even if they were allowed to retain their full memories whilst living on the island, the pain from the past might be too difficult for Axl to bear. It was not too long before they first set out on their epic journey that Axl woke up one early spring morning to discover that 'the last of the darkness' of their feud had left him (341). Their old wounds had 'healed slowly', but this has only been rendered possible because of the mist (341). Wounds that might otherwise have healed over a longer passage of time have been superficially patched up through magic and an enforced amnesia. Now, with the weight of their memories returning to them, the spectre of unforgiveness and guilt hover close by.

There are wider implications involved in the failure to understand memories and life stories. I discussed earlier the experience of subjects caught up in the middle of historical events being unable at the time to perceive the significance of things happening around them, an experience that applies both to individuals and to groups. In his consideration of microhistory, Ricoeur describes how historians are able to observe the unperceived connections within 'a village, a group of families, an individual caught up in the social fabric'.[11] Finding themselves 'stranded in the middle' of time, as Kermode has it, individuals and communities attempt to 'make sense' of their worlds and lives, and locate themselves within significant events.[12] This therefore necessitates the consideration of multiple mnemonic viewpoints. Michael Rothberg describes the ethical dimension of multidirectional memory as constituting acts that uncover existing and unresolved 'hidden histories, traumas, and social divisions'.[13] Ishiguro's innovative novel and his predominant use of the third-person narrative voice allows for a range of memory perspectives, comprising intergenerational and multi-ethnic groups. This creates in the narrative a sense of unease and instability concerning the past, whether it is Wistan informing Axl of the suffering endured by the Saxons at the hands of the Britons, the similarity of Edwin's and Wistan's traumatic childhoods, or the gradual revelation of Axl's historical role in the conflict between the Saxons and Britons. Axl, as a chief negotiator for Arthur, is gradually understood to have been instrumental in brokering a landmark peace treaty with the Saxons. Gawain defends his uncle Arthur's subsequent decision to breach the treaty and kill the Saxons in the villages as a just cause to end the 'circle of slaughter' and deliver a longer-lasting peace (BG 232). Gawain's (and Arthur's) politically motivated and rationalized view of the killings is very different to that of Axl, who has built a strong relationship with the Saxon communities as their 'Knight of Peace', and for him the betrayal and genocide concretizes a 'circle of hate' that will bear consequences, as it does towards the end of the novel (232–3). The different perspectives on war and war crimes are just one of the ways in which Ishiguro considers the complexities of narratives of conflict. Ishiguro's depiction of the acts of Arthur as King presents a revision of the popular notions of this quasi-historical and mythological figure from British history. *The Buried Giant* presents the heroic and legendary figure as a calculating and murderous autocrat, whose instigation of genocide goes against the grain of a popular national narrative. This portrayal of Arthur, with its allusions to the famed 'Battle of Mount Badon' where Arthur was victorious against the Saxons, represents Ishiguro's meditation and critique on the accuracy of the historical record.[14] Utilizing the fantasy genre to experiment with 'notions of reality and history' and subvert the Arthurian myth, Ishiguro's text questions the formation of national myths and traditional depictions of Arthur as the heroic leader against Saxon invaders.[15]

The Buried Giant represents Ishiguro's assessment on war and its relationship to nationhood. The novel bears witness to Ricoeur's argument that 'there exists no historical community that has not been born out of a relation that can, without hesitation, best be likened to war'.[16] In the novel, Arthur's solution for peace is a brutal eradication of several generations of witnesses, followed by the instigation of an enforced forgetting. If each civilization's peace has its origins in war and is sustained by collective forgetting, this would suggest that peace and forgetting are inseparable at both individual and collective levels. The constant threat of memory returning, of a reigniting of painful memories, means that peace is often tenuous and fragile. Both Gawain and Axl seem to recognize the cyclical nature of repressed hatred and the 'lust for vengeance' (*BG* 232). They both find themselves stranded in the middle of key events are and both manipulated by highly influential leaders, in a similar vein to Stevens in *The Remains of the Day*, all the while lacking in perspective and understanding as they try their best to 'perform [their] duty to the end' (234).

The Complexities of Communal Memory

Ishiguro's meditations on national memory and enforced amnesia constitute an enquiry into the complexities of communal and intergenerational memory, areas that have been highlighted by the work of theorists such as Marianne Hirsch. In her account of 'postmemory', Hirsch considers the intergenerational nature of traumatic memories, in which the legacy of trauma can be keenly felt by the next generation even if they have had no direct experience of the original events. The 'stories, images, and behaviors' conveyed to the next generation in their growing-up years can be so deeply transmitted as to '*seem* to constitute memories in their own right'.[17] Hirsch suggests that postmemory is less about recall than it is about 'imaginative investment, projection and creation' in its connection to the past.[18] Wistan, who as a child directly experienced the trauma of his mother's abduction by Britons, expects the lifting of the mist following Querig's death to unleash 'anger and thirst for vengeance' among the 'strong men and growing boys' within Saxon communities across the land (*BG* 263–4; 323–4). As the memory of genocide by the Britons returns, 'overwhelming inherited memories' of trauma will begin to shape the lives of the next generation of Saxons.[19]

The landscape covered by the mist includes sites of memory such as ancient burial grounds, hostile Saxon villages, and forgotten battlegrounds.

These sites constitute traces of distant traumatic events. With recall just out of reach of one's consciousness due to the effects of the mist, the ability to narrate the past and impute major crimes to specific groups is undermined. Rothberg's work on multidirectional memory highlights the multifaceted and interrelated nature of collective memory, and points to the necessity for multiple viewpoints of remembering in order to overcome historical inaccuracies. More recently, he has built on this analysis of the connections between history and memory to investigate 'the implication of those proximate to power' and the importance of collective responsibility for crimes committed in the distant past.[20] Ishiguro's earlier novels depict narratives that initially conceal the protagonists' culpability and guilt in relation to war and collective trauma. Ono's role as a propaganda artist in Japan's imperialist war effort, as well as his actions in undermining his former student Kuroda's career and livelihood are in stark contrast to the more benign portrait of a retired artist and grandfather in the first part of the novel. The first-person narration depicting Stevens's unflinching loyalty to Lord Darlington, and his misplaced trust in Darlington's judgement, is thrown into sharp relief by Mr Cardinal's explanation to Stevens of how Darlington is being manipulated by the Nazis. The first-person point of view of Ishiguro's earlier novels focuses the narrative onto the protagonists and their culpability concerning past events. In the case of Stevens, while he might not be directly involved in Darlington's political plans, his work has enabled those plans to proceed, and as his moment of being erroneously recognized as a gentleman will attest, he has, in Rothberg's words, 'benefited from privileged positions'.[21]

In *The Unconsoled*, Ishiguro expands his enquiry beyond Ryder, the protagonist, to incorporate the unnamed city's inhabitants. He makes an implicit comment on the beneficiaries and implicated subjects of war in *When We Were Orphans*, when Christopher Banks expresses his disdain for the opulent social event he attends in Shanghai, commenting on the 'denial of responsibility' and 'pompous defensiveness' among society's elite (*WWWO* 162). Ishiguro continues developing this theme of implication and responsibility in *The Buried Giant*, where it seems no one is innocent of the wars and atrocities that ravaged the landscape. I will focus below on both Axl (an individual) and the monastery (a collective). Axl, we learn, is renowned among the Saxon community for his role as the broker of the peace treaty named 'The Law of the Innocents', which is described as 'bring [ing] men closer to God' (*BG* 233). The treaty was intended to protect women, children, and the elderly living in the Saxon villages. Wistan remembers Axl from that time as the 'gentle Briton' whom he 'adored from afar' as a young boy, and who moved through his Saxon village 'like a wise prince' inspiring the villagers to 'dream' of the possibility of protecting the innocent from war (319–20). Arthur's eventual betrayal of Axl and the peace treaty, by slaughtering the innocents while they were unprotected in their villages, made Axl out to be 'a liar and a butcher' and placed him at odds with Arthur and Gawain.

The event of the mass slaughter of the innocents represents one of the novel's titular buried giants, involving the concept of multidirectional memory whereby the reader experiences the event recounted from the viewpoints of both the Britons and Saxons. Axl recognizes that he is implicated in the genocide, even though he did not participate directly in the atrocity. With the memory loss caused by the mist, Axl, formerly known as 'Axelum or Axelus' within Arthur's inner circle, cannot remember the betrayal and the slaughter (*BG* 233). Instead, we have Wistan and Gawain functioning as alternative witnesses to these horrific events.[22] Wistan's childhood memory of Axl is revealed through his observations of and questions to Axl over the course of the novel, whilst Gawain's memory of Axl is conveyed through the first-person narrative voice in his Reveries, which punctuate the text. Both of these voices demonstrate Ricoeur's concept of the human ability to narrate as well as to be accountable for one's actions. By allowing key characters to bear witness to Axl's past, Ishiguro's writing suggests that it is possible to find 'a different way of narrating' loss when the pain of loss can be a hindrance to remembering.[23] The complex nature of his past relationship with the Britons and Saxons taints Axl's legacy as a broker of peace. Having been betrayed by Arthur during his time as the Saxons' Knight of Peace, Axl will experience another betrayal, this time by Beatrice, leading to his fateful decision not to allow Beatrice the chance to visit their son's grave soon after his death, further complicating the way readers judge his past actions.

In Chapter Six of *The Buried Giant*, it quickly becomes evident that the monastery and its community harbour many secrets that are tied to a conspiracy of silence concerning past atrocities. Despite being able to seek temporary refuge and rest in the monastery, the motley crew of Axl, Beatrice, Wistan, and Edwin are not safe within its walls. It soon becomes noticeable that there is activity taking place to which the group are not privy. Axl recalls Wistan's keen observations of the monastery's architectural history, noting features that betray its origins as a Saxon hill fort, and one that likely saw the mass slaughter of Saxons by an invading army. In addition to the grounds bearing witness of mass bloodshed, Edwin also reports his discovery of a large iron cage and mask that Wistan surmises has been used by the monks as an instrument of penance through the mutilation of their bodies by wild birds – a self-inflicted penalty to atone for 'crimes once committed in this country and long unpunished', and a further indication of hidden atrocities (*BG* 165). Father Jonus, a senior monk who is sought by Beatrice, bears traces of such mutilations on his face when the group are taken to see him in his living quarters. The group are subsequently hunted down by soldiers called in by the abbot, with orders to kill both Wistan and Edwin. While soldiers pursue Wistan up the tower, Axl, Beatrice, and Edwin are tricked into going down an underground passageway that leads to a confrontation with 'the beast', a creature used by the monks to dispose of 'those they wish dead' (179). Religious establishments are not safe havens in *The Buried Giant*. The initial sense of refuge for the travellers quickly gives way to betrayal and mortal danger; the narrative even reveals the grounds of a religious establishment to be a site of war atrocities and unpunished crimes. The actions of the monks, both in their pursuit of atonement through the self-imposed mutilation of their bodies by wild birds, and in the practice of the brutal erasure of lives they wish to forget, are indicative of the complexities of national memory in relation to war crimes. The attempts at making reparations for past crimes acknowledge the sense of collective responsibility shared by those who, in Rothberg's terms, are implicated by their proximity to the event. But such attempts also evidence the levels of guilt experienced by those who seek atonement. As demonstrated by the monks' controversial (and criminal) actions, the collective pursuit of expiation frequently obscures the line between justice and forgetting.

Forgetting

The Buried Giant marks a tonal shift in how the theme of forgetting is approached and contrasts sharply with how it is handled in Ishiguro's earlier novels. The novels prior to *The Buried Giant* demonstrate some evidence of a profound forgetting, leading, in many cases, to a sense of possible catharsis for the characters. Here, forgetting is used as a form of weaponry to incapacitate the Saxons and to enforce an artificial peace between old enemies. There is, however, another dimension to forgetting to which the novel draws attention, and that is its complex relationship with memory. As we have seen, Ricoeur argues that being able to remember means that a person is empowered to narrate and give an account of or impute their own actions. Equally, forgetting allows for old feuds to be put aside to allow for a period of healing, as exemplified in the case of Axl and Beatrice. On a national level, it allows for a break in a cycle of violence and retribution between warring factions. As we have seen, such a peace is often tenuous and fragile and can be broken by the return of an unresolved past.

In his book *In Praise of Forgetting*, David Rieff argues that on occasions when collective memory causes all communities to feel 'the pain of their historical wounds', 'it is not the duty to remember but a duty to forget' that should be the focus.[24] Rieff discusses the cycle of oppression, citing the Rwandan genocide as an example of how quickly the role of oppressor 'can flip and how easily yesterday's victimizers become today's victims'.[25] Rieff, in a similar vein to Ishiguro, suggests that it might not be good to keep holding on to painful memories if doing so holds the subject captive to the past. Elsewhere, I have suggested that the concept of forgetting is utilized in *The Buried Giant* as 'a challenge to the sacralisation of memory', representing Ishiguro's critique of established pathways of amnesty and remembrance.[26] The novel engages directly with the question of forgetting (or erasure) as a fundamental element of peace. When Axl relates to the boatman that early spring morning and how 'the last of the darkness' had left him and the old wounds from his past with Beatrice had healed, we are aware that this is only possible because of the enforced forgetting provided by the mist (*BG* 341). What is also being addressed here is the nature of repressed memories and old resentments, and the idea that in this case some measure of forgetting is needed in order for peace to return.

The mysterious island, with the boatman as the gatekeeper, is a place of solitude as well as a place of forgetting. Alluded to from Chapter Two onwards, the boatman and the island appear to be some kind of final destination, a euphemism for death via an undisguised allusion to the Greek mythological figure of Charon, who ferries the dead over the Styx and Acheron rivers. The island is said to be 'full of gentle woods and streams', yet retains some 'strange qualities' where, for those who dwell there, it is as if they walk the island 'alone' with their neighbours being 'unseen and unheard' (*BG* 334). In order to be on the island, one must accept being alone indefinitely. Like Kathy and Tommy in *Never Let Me Go*, Beatrice and Axl seek a rumoured exception, whereby, if they were able to prove their genuine and deep love for one another, they would be permitted to live on the island as a couple and not be forever separated. In his First Reverie, Gawain claims to look forward to 'greet[ing] the boatman' when his time comes and entering his boat to be taken to the island (*BG* 233). The island represents the only place, once the mist is fully lifted, to which one could travel in order to forget. The symbols of the boatman and the island represent some of the dilemmas concerning memory and forgetting: if Beatrice and Axl wish for the mist to be lifted and for memories to return, they must be prepared for the return of painful memories. If they choose not to have their memories return, they will not be able to answer the boatman's questions in their attempt to remain unseparated. In the moment of his final farewell to Beatrice, the reader is left to wonder if Axl has in fact chosen to hold on to the happier memories of their relationship – a distortion of memory facilitated by the mist – rather than to live on the island either separated from Beatrice or having to face the complete return of painful memories. There are suggestions that Beatrice has also begun to remember some of the most painful moments of their marriage, but she seems to be more at peace with the past and ready to move on to the island than Axl is. Perhaps the guilt of denying Beatrice's wish to see their son's grave continues to weigh heavily on him, even after all this time, as does the realization that his real motives for doing so continue to perpetuate cycles of 'vengeance' (340). Beatrice and Axl seem to be going their separate ways in terms of how they choose to deal with their returning memories and their immediate futures.

The question of the importance of forgetting in how we deal with painful or traumatic memories is examined at both individual and collective levels in *The Buried Giant*. At an individual level, forgetting represents a paradox, according to Ricoeur. Citing Augustine's *Confessions*, Ricoeur describes forgetting's ability to destroy memory, whilst also providing moments of recognition when the forgotten object is 'rediscovered' later on.[27] When Axl and Beatrice visit the Saxon village in the neighbouring country in Chapter Three, Axl experiences a 'startle[d]' moment of recognition in identifying Wistan's bearing as being suited to combat, suggesting some prior knowledge that he has forgotten (*BG* 57). This indicates that perhaps that item of knowledge was never truly forgotten in the first place, but rather 'mislaid somewhere', especially if the remembering subject is able to recognize it (49). On the night of their visit to the Saxon village, the Britons Ivor and Axl discuss the 'strange forgetfulness' that pervades the village, soon after the couple were accosted by a hostile group of villagers and had to be rescued by Ivor (64). The mist of forgetfulness appears not only to have robbed the villagers of their memories, but some element of their true selves as well. The village, according to Beatrice who has visited before, is 'eerily still' (54). The strange atmosphere acts as a metaphor for the costs of an enforced forgetting on a collective or national scale, namely the threat to selfhood and identity, creating an atmosphere of fear and suspicion and resulting in the loss of humanity. The suggestion here is that whilst forgetting is a key component of peace, enforcing it at a collective level is too dangerous and destructive. Forgetting needs to occur in ways that are not regulated by the state or by an autocrat, but in ways that are mediated by the passage of time and a keen awareness of the full implications and responsibilities that are entailed by the groups that are both directly and indirectly linked to traumatic memories. Through a critical enquiry into the ways in which we account for our decisions, our failures in understanding, and the complexities of forgetting, *The Buried Giant* represents Ishiguro's most direct and sustained engagement thus far with the theme of collective and national memory.

Notes

1 Michael Scott Moore and Michael Sontheimer, '"I Remain Fascinated by Memory": Spiegel Interview with Kazuo Ishiguro', *Spiegel Online International*, 5 October 2005 (accessed online at www.spiegel.de/international/ spiegel-interview-with-kazuo-ishiguro-i-remain-fascinated-by-memory-a-378173 .html).

2 Yugin Teo, *Kazuo Ishiguro and Memory* (Basingstoke: Palgrave Macmillan, 2014), p.112.

3 Peter Kemp, 'Enigma Variation' (review of *Never Let Me Go*), *Sunday Times*, 20 February 2005.

4 Frank Kermode, *The Sense of an Ending: Studies in the Theory of Fiction with a New Epilogue* (Oxford: Oxford University Press, 2000), p.190.

5 Ibid., pp.7–8.

6 Paul Ricoeur, *The Course of Recognition*, trans. David Pellauer (Cambridge, MA: Harvard University Press, 2005), p.252.

7 Ibid., p.69.

8 Teo, *Kazuo Ishiguro and Memory*, p.151.

9 Ibid., p.156.

10 Ricoeur, *The Course of Recognition*, p.105.

11 Paul Ricoeur, *Memory, History, Forgetting*, trans. Kathleen Blamey and David Pellauer (Chicago: University of Chicago Press, 2004), p.210.

12 Kermode, *The Sense of an Ending*, p.190.

13 Michael Rothberg, *Multidirectional Memory: Remembering the Holocaust in the Age of Decolonization* (Stanford, CA: Stanford University Press, 2009), p.272.

14 Alan Lupack, review of *The Buried Giant*, *Arthuriana* 25:3 (2015): 118–20.

15 Deimantas Valančiūnas, 'Forgetting or Making to Forget: Memory, Trauma and Identity in Kazuo Ishiguro's *The Buried Giant*', in Regina Rudaitytė, ed., *History, Memory and Nostalgia in Literature and Culture* (Newcastle: Cambridge Scholars, 2018), p.222.

16 Ricoeur, *Memory, History, Forgetting*, p.79.

17 Marianne Hirsch, 'The Generation of Postmemory', *Poetics Today* 29:1 (2008): 103–28 (106–7).

18 Ibid., p.107.

19 Ibid.

20 Michael Rothberg, *The Implicated Subject: Beyond Victims and Perpetrators* (Stanford, CA: Stanford University Press, 2019), p.212, n.48.

21 Ibid., p.21.

22 See Yugin Teo, 'Monuments, Unreal Spaces and National Forgetting: Kazuo Ishiguro's *The Buried Giant* and the Abyss of Memory', *Textual Practice* (published online 18 May 2022).

23 Teo, *Kazuo Ishiguro and Memory*, p.95.

24 David Rieff, *In Praise of Forgetting: Historical Memory and Its Ironies* (New Haven, CT: Yale University Press, 2016), p.121.

25 Ibid.

26 Teo, 'Monuments, Unreal Spaces and National Forgetting'.

27 Ricoeur, *The Course of Recognition*, p.119.

16

IVAN STACY

Ishiguro's Irresolution

Resolution can refer to a consequential decision, to determination and firmness of purpose, or to the ending of a story. In Ishiguro's writing, all of these meanings of resolution are related in complex and often ambiguous ways. Many of his characters are defined by resolutions in the form of their decisions and determinations, yet their life-changing choices (think of Masuji Ono in *An Artist of the Floating World*) or firmness to the point of rigidity (Stevens in *The Remains of the Day*) are generally shown to bring disastrous consequences. Moreover, the narrators' ambivalent relationships with resolution are embedded in the narrative form of Ishiguro's novels. As Mark Currie notes, the term 'teleological retrospect' is sometimes used to describe narration from the position of 'looking back from an endpoint',[1] and this is an apt description of the way Ishiguro's narrators reflect on the consequences of their actions. At the same time, however, they also look forwards in the 'anticipation of retrospection',[2] and their narratives betray a need to justify their decisions and determinations. For this reason, the novels are driven by a tension between the narrators' struggles to provide their lives with meaningful and positive form, and our awareness that this desire often produces a self-serving and sometimes self-deceiving manipulation of narrative.

A further tension central to Ishiguro's work is the way that resolution rarely delivers that which it seems to offer. As Chris Holmes and Kelly Mee Rich argue, 'historical trauma weighs heavily on Ishiguro's characters, but following the promise of an artifact or recollection rarely if ever leads to clarity or resolution',[3] and this situation traps his protagonists – and by extension his readers – on the horns of a dilemma: it appears that resolution will provide a route to closure and meaning, a means of making sense of life, but it is precisely this impulse that leads the characters to make decisions and determinations based on an imperfect understanding of the world, the consequences of which they must later reckon with. Ishiguro's novels therefore present irresolution as possessing ethical value in the sense that it is preferable to misguided certainty. They also embody irresolution through their formal properties, however, and do so specifically through their refusal of closure in terms of the characters' relationships with the events that they recall. Ishiguro's equivocation with regard to the value of resolution is thus transferred to the reader: accepting the narrative resolutions offered to us by the likes of Ono, Stevens, and Banks (in *When We Were Orphans*) may be an oversimplification of the issues raised in the foregoing text, or worse, a form of complicity with the attempts by these first-person narrators to condone their own mistakes.

This chapter examines these tensions across three broad phases of Ishiguro's career. In the first phase, up to *The Remains of the Day*, resolutions in the form of decisions (represented as 'turning points') and determinations are emphasized. The second section addresses a transitional period encompassing *The Unconsoled* and *When We Were Orphans*, in which the narrators find themselves lacking the teleological drive towards an endpoint that the earlier narrators seemed to have. These texts thus represent irresolution as a kind of ontological drift that may be preferable to the firm resolutions of the earlier novels. The final section discusses Ishiguro's three most recent novels, *Never Let Me Go*, *The Buried Giant*, and *Klara and the Sun*, in all of which the protagonists are caught between the desire to make sense of their lives through clear resolutions, and to defer such endings in order to perpetuate a state of irresolution.

In each of these sections, the final text (*The Remains of the Day*, *When We Were Orphans*, and *Klara and the Sun*) is examined in detail, with the others addressed more briefly. Each section begins with a discussion of the ways in which (ir)resolution works thematically – that is, as a concern and guiding principle for the characters. The second part of each section then addresses the way that irresolution is also a formal property of the novels, and thus pertains to how the texts can be read, primarily through a discussion of their endings.

Turning Points

A Pale View of Hills, *An Artist of the Floating World*, and *The Remains of the Day* present protagonists who are grappling with the negative consequences of misguided decisions and determinations. While this fact implies that irresolution may be preferable to the sense of certainty that led the characters to face such reckonings, there is also a pervasive sense in the texts, sometimes articulated explicitly, that lives lived without courage or commitment may be shapeless and unfulfilled.

The narrators' efforts to come to terms with earlier decisions and their effects is complicated by the fact that these contingencies are shown to be opaque or even unknowable. For example, *A Pale View of Hills* is built around the absence created by a terrible resolution, namely the decision of the narrator's daughter, Keiko, to commit suicide. In the opening sentence of the novel, Etsuko introduces this event indirectly, stating that her youngest daughter, Niki, 'did not mention Keiko until the second day' of her visit (*PVH* 9). Doug Battersby argues that moments such as this opening 'conspicuously draw attention to the fact that something is being concealed, not only inciting readers' suspicions, but also encouraging us to cling to them by leaving them unresolved'.[4] Such absences are a central characteristic of the novel, and in this case are suggestive of irresolution functioning as a means of avoiding direct confrontation with a traumatic past.

In the following two novels, however, the narrators are impelled to address the consequences of their decisions more squarely. *An Artist of the Floating World* begins with the notion of irresolution through its reference to 'the Bridge of Hesitation' (*AFW* 7), so called, according to Ono, because 'until not so long ago, crossing it would have taken you into our pleasure district, and conscience-troubled men – so it was said – were to be seen hovering there, caught between seeking an evening's entertainment and returning home to their wives' (99). Ono's qualifying 'so it was said' implies that he does not count himself among these 'conscience-troubled men', but as regret and guilt begin to insinuate themselves into his narrative, it becomes clear that through his resolutions – the key decisions of his life – he may have been complicit with other decisions that have led to dire consequences for Japan, and have led directly to negative outcomes for the individuals around him. However, *An Artist of the Floating World* reverses the relationship between clarity and recollection seen in *A Pale View of Hills* with the consequences rather than the actions that caused these being subject to doubt and conjecture. As a result, the novel signals the difficulty of grasping the relationship between decisions and their later results, thus suggesting that a teleological endpoint does not necessarily provide a clear lens through which to interpret the events of the past.

In this phase of Ishiguro's career, the interplay between decisions and determinations is at its most complex in *The Remains of the Day*. The novel is structurally similar to *An Artist of the Floating World*, with the narrator trying to justify the resolutions that have defined his life. Peter Sloane suggests that in Ishiguro's writing lives are defined 'not by those occasional incidents in which we try to make or imagine that we have made a "contribution to the course of history" ... but by the slow synthetic accretion of the stratified minutiae that constitute the geology of our unremarkable, undocumented private lives'.[5] This description fits Stevens well, because his career and personal life are characterized not by discrete and momentous decisions but by his determination to live and act in a particular way. The key concept of 'dignity' that he tries, but never quite manages, to fully elucidate underpins a lifetime's work: it is 'something one can meaningfully strive for throughout one's career' (*RD* 34), and is an ideal to which Stevens attempts to adhere even as it is tested by external circumstances such as obnoxious guests and the temptations of romantic relationships.

While this type of resolution may look like passivity, it is in fact revealed to be a more active stance than it first appears. Stevens is determined not to make decisions beyond the scope of his professional role and consequently finds himself trapped by these self-imposed constraints, even when the situation calls upon him to seize the moment. Yet an unwillingness to make decisions does not result in a life free of consequences, and through the teleological retrospective mode of the novel, Stevens is shown reflecting on the results of his resolve. The novel again shifts the emphasis in the relationship between actions and their effects as previously explored in *A Pale View of Hills* and *An Artist of the Floating World*, and in this case Stevens is aware of the consequences of his actions, but only belatedly so, and he emphasizes the fact that he could not foresee these effects at the time the decision was made. The most notable instance of this is when he relates how his decision to end his one-on-one meetings with Miss Kenton was a 'turning point' in their relationship that destroyed the possibility of any future intimacy. He reflects that 'one can surely only recognize such moments in retrospect' and his tragedy is that he assumed that there still lay ahead of him 'an infinite number of opportunities in which to remedy the effect of this or that misunderstanding' (*RD* 188) when in fact the moment to act had already passed.

The personal consequences of Stevens's unwillingness to act decisively are shown most clearly during his recollection of a moment when he suspects Miss Kenton to be crying behind a closed door, and finds himself 'transfixed with indecision' (*RD* 222) regarding whether to comfort her. He fails to act, and loses Miss Kenton as a result. At first sight, this episode appears to suggest that irresolution can lead just as surely to tragedy and loss as the misguided decisions made by Ono. However, this decision is not so much the result of momentary indecision as it is the continuation of a lifetime's habits, themselves the product of his misguided resolve. Indeed, as the political ramifications of Stevens's inability to act outside the boundaries of his limited but voluntarily adopted role are fed into the narrative, the inflexible nature of his resolution emerges as a form of culpability. This is nowhere better illustrated than when Reginald Cardinal raises his concerns about Lord Darlington's relationship with the Nazis. Unable to influence the discussions taking place in the house, Cardinal finally vents his frustration on Stevens, asking: 'aren't you struck by even the remotest possibility that

I am correct? Are you not, at least, *curious* about what I am saying?' When Stevens replies 'I'm sorry, sir, but I have to say that I have every trust in his lordship's good judgement' (236), it becomes clear that Stevens's determination to avoid making decisions is one that he actively and consciously maintains. For these reasons, resolution in the form of both decisions and determinations, and in the way that these become conflated (Stevens, in effect, has decided not to decide) is shown to be personally disastrous and ethically suspect.

In terms of its form, *The Remains of the Day* is structured around the desire for resolution, with Stevens setting off for Cornwall in the hope of mending his professional and personal relationship with Miss Kenton (now Mrs Benn). The journey thus builds towards their meeting and the novel does, in this case, provide a clear resolution in terms of its plot when Stevens's hopes are crushed, and he is left to reckon with the consequences of 'turning points' that he failed to recognize and the decisions that he failed to make. In being denied the resolution that he hoped for, Stevens is impelled to reshape his story in order to accommodate these unwelcome developments while still providing a satisfactory narrative arc.

Stevens is unable, however, finally to resolve the central question of whether it is worth risking decisive action that may prove to be misguided, or to limit one's decisions to a more modest scope. Near the end of the novel, he initially suggests that Darlington's decisiveness was preferable to his own lack of action, claiming that the former 'chose a certain path in life, it proved to be a misguided one, but there, he chose it, he can say that at least'. He then proceeds to acknowledge 'I can't even say I made my own mistakes ... what dignity is there in that?' (*RD* 255–6). Yet he quickly retreats from this idea as it pertains to himself, telling his interlocutor that, 'for the likes of you and me, there is little choice other than to leave our fate, ultimately, in the hands of those great gentlemen at the hub of this world who employ our services' and asking 'what is the point in worrying oneself too much about what one could or could not have done to control the course one's life took?' (257).

While Stevens addresses these remarks to another professional servant on Weymouth Pier, throughout the novel there is a sense that the reader he addresses is also someone who shares his professional background. For all of Stevens's stiffness, then, there is embedded in the novel's mode of address an appeal to empathy, and this reaches its peak as he is finally forced to acknowledge his mistakes. However, the potential for empathic engagement with Stevens largely arises from the way that he is seen labouring to construct a happy ending from the ruins of his personal and professional life, and herein lies a suggestion that resolution may mask failings that ought to be recognized. The ethical question at stake here is whether the pathos of an ending in which Stevens both emphasizes his own lack of autonomy and almost acknowledges a broken heart downplays or excuses his complicity in Darlington's Nazi collusion and anti-Semitism. In this sense, *The Remains of the Day* may be said to perform its own form of irresolution: it implies that irresolution might be preferable to the kind of determination that results in blind adherence to social structures, while at the same time it critiques Stevens's imposition of a consoling narrative of irresolution to justify his own culpability. And yet the sympathy we are encouraged to feel towards Stevens as he gropes for solace nevertheless indicates that the desire for resolution exerts a powerful affective pull.

Drifting

Sloane suggests that 'the Ishiguro character is above all limited existentially, ontologically, and epistemologically' and that 'the worlds of Ishiguro's imagination remain opaque to his characters'.[6] This opacity leads the two protagonists of *The Unconsoled* and *When We Were Orphans* continually – and at times catastrophically – to misapprehend the world. Moreover, while Ishiguro's first three novels show their protagonists coming to terms with their own position in the narrative present of the novels, in *The Unconsoled* and *When We Were Orphans* the protagonists are comparatively unmoored, finding themselves unsure of the end point towards which earlier events have led. This ontological uncertainty is presented as a kind of drifting, a form of irresolution that permits a degree of freedom and optimism while also creating the risk of becoming lost.

As the many frustrated readers of *The Unconsoled* are only too aware, the temporal and spatial disjunctions created by the dream logic of the novel are disorienting. One of its signature features is the way that Ryder is repeatedly diverted by chance encounters and digressions, which he then belatedly reconfigures in his narrative as planned and meaningful events. The sense of resolution he creates is thus shown to be a retrospective imposition of form on the incoherence of life. Yet the illusion that one may strive towards meaningful endings remains seductive, as is suggested by Mrs Hoffman when she speaks of the 'lovely dreams in the early morning' (*U* 417) that evaporate as the day takes shape. It is between these two poles that the novel ends, as Ryder prepares to leave for Helsinki with little having been resolved either for the disappointed citizens of the unnamed city, or for Ryder himself, but with the promise of the next part of the story sufficient for him to maintain a sense of optimism and confidence in his professional abilities.

Disorientation is also central to Ishiguro's next novel, *When We Were Orphans*. This is, paradoxically, in part because Christopher Banks has in mind a clearer ending for his story than Ishiguro's other narrators, referring on a number of occasions to his 'mission'. Moreover, when he states of his return to Shanghai in order to solve the case of his parents' disappearance that 'I left England only once I'd formed a clear view of this case ... my arrival here isn't a starting point, but the culmination of many years' work' (WWWO 155), he envisages the different meanings of resolution outlined in the introduction of this chapter coming together: his decision to rescue his parents and his determination to persist with the case will produce a sense of closure. It is precisely for this reason, however, that his utter failure to resolve his parents' case leaves him, by contrast with earlier characters, only able to console himself with the thought that he has achieved 'a certain contentment' even while 'a sort of emptiness' sometimes seems to 'fill' his hours (313).

As the narrators in earlier novels do, Banks makes the key decisions of his life under the mistaken belief that he has grasped the complexities of the world. That this impression of mastery is a dangerous illusion is shown through the epistemological folly of Banks using a magnifying glass as his primary means of gathering evidence. In employing a tool designed to bring the microscopic world into clarity, Banks neglects the larger picture, and is unable to ascertain his own position within events of global scale. This is part of the novel's broader critique of Western failures to recognize the experiences and suffering of other ethnic groups, and suggests that, in the context of an over-reliance on the apparent certainties of empirical evidence and rationality, irresolution may be a positive value as a kind of ontological principle by which life may be lived.

The novel posits irresolution, in the form of 'drifting', as an alternative to the sense of mission that drives Banks. He uses this term a striking number of times throughout his narrative to describe his own and others' movements.[7] At several critical junctures, this idea is presented in positive terms, evoking a life unburdened by the teleological drive imposed by the need for resolution. For example, when Sarah Hemmings proposes that Banks abandon his mission in Shanghai and that they 'just drift around the South China Sea for a while' (WWWO 212), he feels 'an almost tangible sense of relief' (212), and 'as though a heavy burden had been removed' (215).

As is typical of an Ishiguro character, Banks finds himself caught between these two options, and while he initially agrees to Sarah's suggestion, he cannot completely abandon the idea of resolving his parents' case. As a result, in a section of the novel that makes Ryder's schedule look positively relaxed, he attempts to fulfil all of his remaining commitments in the city – including finding his parents – in a single morning. Indeed, from this point onwards, the idea of drifting begins to be refigured as a dangerous form of disorientation. For example, when Banks has entered the Warren, he is warned by Lieutenant Chow that attempting to navigate it at night will 'be like drifting through one's worst nightmares' (*WWWO* 212), and it is not long before he finds himself lost, with an 'impression of drifting further and further off my route' (247). In earlier Ishiguro novels, resolution is presented as seductive but unable to deliver on its promises; in *When We Were Orphans*, irresolution in the form of drifting is presented as an alluring alternative, but one that holds its own dangers.

Again, irresolution is built into the form of the novel through its final equivocation on the question of drifting. When Banks states that London 'has come to be' his home (*WWWO* 313), it appears that his situation at the end of the novel is less the result of clear resolutions than the product of chance and circumstance. Moreover, his life is defined by a lack of direction at this point, as shown when he describes himself as having 'drifted through these grey days in London, wandering about Kensington Garden' (310). He concludes his narrative undecided as to whether to accept Jennifer's invitation to live with her, and at peace with this issue remaining unresolved: 'I do not wish to appear smug; but drifting through my days here in London, I believe I can indeed own up to a certain contentment' (313).

While Banks thus appears to be at ease in this state of irresolution, particularly when contrasted with his earlier, manic behaviour, he cannot quite let go of the need for the sense of an ending. This internal sense of conflict is indicated by the peculiar formulation of the novel's title, which seems to suggest that orphanhood is a contingent and temporary state from which one may emerge – and from which the speaker has in fact emerged. Given that Banks believes himself finally to have located his mother, the title could be said to apply to his situation at the end of the novel. However, the consolation that he takes from their meeting results from him imposing the narrative that he wishes upon their conversation rather than from anything his mother – now senile – actually says. Moreover, as Dominic Dean argues, it is possible, and even probable, that the woman Banks meets in Hong Kong is not actually his mother.[8] This ironic distance created by these aspects of the narrative mean that we cannot help but treat Banks's professed satisfaction with some scepticism.

If the phrasing of the title is somewhat awkward, Banks's language in the closing passages also reveals that he occupies a conflicted position between resolution and irresolution. For example, he remarks of Jennifer's own mental health problems, which remain largely unelaborated, that 'there is every reason to believe that she has now come through the dark tunnel of her life and emerged at the other end' (*WWWO* 310). Tellingly, the way that Banks's metaphor fails to quite cohere betrays both his desire for, and the impossibility of finding, certain endings. Banks's figuration of depression as a 'dark tunnel' from which Jennifer has 'emerged' initially seems to make sense. However, he refers to the 'tunnel of her life', which she is of course still in the process of living and from which she cannot, therefore, have yet emerged. Similarly, he reflects of himself and Sarah that 'for those like us, our fate is to face the world as orphans, chasing through long years the shadows of vanished parents. There is nothing for it but to try and see through our missions to the end, as best we can, for until we do so, we will be permitted no calm' (313). Again, Banks's figurative language points to the way he is trapped between resolution and irresolution: if his parents have 'vanished', the shadows that he chases surely cannot be found, yet he cannot let go of the idea of completing his 'mission'. These contradictions indicate a fundamental problem with the search for resolution in the form of endings, particularly insofar as these are constructed through narrative: endings are the artificial imposition of form on lives even as life itself continues to unfold.

Deferrals

Late in *Never Let Me Go*, Kathy describes how Tommy enjoys reading paperbacks during his convalescence. She mentions by name *The Odyssey* and *One Thousand and One Nights*, the former a quest narrative with a desired end point, the latter a story about, and structured by, the perpetual deferral of resolution (*NLMG* 233). The contrast between the two stories echoes a central dilemma in Ishiguro's later work. In *Never Let Me Go*, *The Buried Giant*, and *Klara and the Sun*, the presence of impending death places the protagonists under pressure to achieve resolution in the sense of creating a satisfactory ending that provides meaning and coherence. At the same time, however, these texts exhibit a sense that such resolutions may not deliver what they promise, and may in fact show the characters unwelcome truths about their lives. For this reason, the narrators find themselves unsure as to whether to seek a definite ending in the mode of Odysseus or, like Scheherazade, to sustain a state of irresolution through a process of deferral.

Never Let Me Go represents irresolution both as a source of comfort for the clones and as a form of complicity with atrocity. As Currie notes, the title can be read as 'a request for everlasting captivity',[9] and throughout the novel, the deferral of resolution can be contrasted with unsettling moments of clarity in which the implications of the clones' status are revealed to them. Denied the rights and freedoms available to the normal population, the clones use irresolution to avoid conflict, and to define their own collective as a way of giving meaning to their lives. Ultimately, however, this avoidance of resolving difficult questions constitutes a failure to challenge the atrocity that will eventually kill them. When they do finally seek resolutions to the questions regarding their own status and options, Kathy and Tommy's efforts are directed not towards challenging the injustice of a system in which they are condemned to die early for the benefit of others (so-called normals) but towards marking themselves out as special in order to seek a 'deferral' of their own deaths – itself a kind of irresolution, but one that, it turns out, was never available to them in the first place.

The collective amnesia central to *The Buried Giant* effectively results in a deferral of violence – but a deferral that is doomed to fail, at which point revenge based on 'ancient grievances' (*BG* 323) will seem to offer a clearer and more definite resolution for rival ethnic groups. Uniquely among Ishiguro's novels, *The Buried Giant* is primarily narrated in the third person, and this means that Axl and Beatrice possess less narrative agency than other Ishiguro characters in terms of constructing the ending for which they hope. In one sense, this reinforces the general pessimism of the novel, but at the same time it means that narrative resolutions can no longer conceal larger problems.

Towards the end of the novel, Wistan's imagery of Saxon retribution as 'a ball of fire' rolling over the Britons represents retributive genocide as inevitable (*BG* 324). The only hope that this may be avoided is embodied in the hesitation of the young warrior Edwin to carry out this revenge. Following Wistan's predictions of bloodletting, there is a short section focalized through Edwin in which he recalls the promise he had made to Wistan that he would 'hate all Britons'. His relationship with Axl and Beatrice gives him pause, and he states: 'surely Wistan had not meant to include this gentle couple' (328). His equivocation at this point means that of all of Ishiguro's novels, *The Buried Giant* makes the strongest argument for the ethical value of irresolution.

In *Klara and the Sun*, a hyper-competitive society has created a market for risky genetic engineering. This situation, in turn, drives research into methods for deferring death, notably Henry Capaldi's idea of Josie 'inhabiting' another, artificial body that he is painstakingly constructing. Within this pessimistic premise, however, the novel leaves room for optimism in the way that what appear to be endings do not necessarily resolve an individual's life as might be anticipated. *Klara and the Sun* is a novel of second chances, and instead of having to live with the consequences of bad decisions or else slide into an aimless ontological drift, key turning points present the characters with opportunities to reconfigure their priorities and to address the world anew.

Near the end of the novel, Klara believes that she has identified the point at which the Sun ends its daily journey. However, the encounter does not take the form that she expects:

> I was surprised to see that the Sun himself, far from leaving, had come right within Mr McBain's barn and installed himself, almost at floor level, between the front alcove and the barn's front opening . . .. For a brief moment I was in danger of becoming disoriented. Then my vision readjusted, and ordering my mind, I realized the Sun wasn't really in the barn at all, but that something reflective had been left there by chance and was now catching his reflection during the last moments of his descent. (KS 276–7)

This experience initially threatens to produce disorientation, but instead Klara accepts it as an opportunity to recognize that she has not been apprehending the world accurately, and to reconfigure her understanding of that which she perceives. This moment in fact embodies three important features of (ir)resolution as it is represented in the novel. The first is that endings cannot be pinpointed in temporal terms. The second is that, similarly, their locus cannot be identified in spatial terms. The third is that resolutions can only ever be arrived at relationally, rather than through the desires or actions of any single individual.

Klara's epiphanic moment in the barn is the culmination of her attempts to find the spatial location at which the Sun ends its journey. When her experience of the world is limited to the store, she believes that the Sun sets behind the RPO building, but Josie's promise that from her bedroom 'you can see exactly where the Sun goes down' (KS 12) causes Klara to revise her understanding of the world, and of her position in it. At this point, she still remains unaware that locating the spot 'exactly' where the Sun goes down is a task that will, by its nature, be infinitely deferred, and a further revision of her understanding when she finally visits Mr McBain's barn seems inevitable. This revision is not the one we might expect, however, and rather than being disappointed at the realization that the Sun will always end its journey at the next horizon, Klara's description emphasizes her experience of the moment rather than attempting to place the event within a teleological narrative, as most of Ishiguro's other narrators would have done.

In temporal terms, events that appear to be resolutions in *Klara and the Sun* lack the same sense of finality as corresponding events in the earlier novels. Notably, Josie's recovery from a point of apparently terminal decline suggests that endings and resolutions do not always come in the place and form that we expect them to, and by contrast with other Ishiguro characters, she has the time and opportunity to reshape her life as a result of this second chance. In addition, whereas Kathy and Tommy, and Axl and Beatrice attempt definitively to settle or resolve their relationships, Rick reflects that his earlier promise that his and Josie's love for each other was 'genuine and forever' (*KS* 270) no longer holds, and states that this 'was the truth at the time' (292). Rather than regarding romantic love as a final resolution, Rick sees it as part of an ongoing process, a relationship that shapes both of their lives in positive ways by enabling them to learn from the experience.

Finally, and most interestingly, the novel proposes that resolutions are provisional and relational. What Klara sees in the barn is not the 'unified image' that she takes it to be, but in fact a composite of the Sun's reflection on several sheets of glass. Sloane argues that the desperation of Ishiguro's characters 'to fix some objective semblance of a self from the details of lives through recollection is, inevitably, fruitless, partially because that essence does not inhere or lie within these things (if it lies anywhere at all)',[10] and Klara's failure to find the place where the Sun sets, combined with the fact that she finally experiences it as a multiplicity of different images, supports this assertion.

These observations also echo Capaldi's argument with regard to human identity that there is nothing 'unique' and 'unreachable' inside of, and defining, each individual (*KS* 210). Klara later attempts to refute Capaldi, claiming that 'there *was* something very special, but it wasn't inside Josie. It was inside those who loved her' (306). Klara's and Capaldi's views are not incompatible, however, as both are premised on a lack of any inherent essence of the self. Where they differ is that, in contrast to Capaldi's nihilism and despite the somewhat sentimental tone of her insistence on the 'special-ness' of Josie, there is something valuable in Klara's relational approach to identity. As in Mr McBain's barn, Klara accepts the image that presents itself, while recognizing that this appearance is the product of a number of perspectives, all reflected and mediated rather than existing purely in the object itself. Meanings cannot, therefore, be fixed in temporal and spatial terms. In a similar way, by suggesting that resolutions are provisional, the product of a complex of subject positions and relationships that can, by their very nature, be revised, *Klara and the Sun* opens up the possibility of second chances and positive change – indeed, of irresolution.

Despite the opportunities presented by this form of irresolution, even Klara finds herself trapped by the same paradox as Ishiguro's other narrators. While her goal in narrating her own life appears to be relatively modest, and while she occupies herself in her 'slow fade' with 'memories to go through and place in the right order' (*KS* 306), she narrates for herself a satisfactory ending based on the belief that the Sun's 'special nourishment' healed Josie (292), and by clinging to her hopes for a happy ending to Josie and Rick's relationship. These beliefs and hopes are more obviously a fiction than the consolations fashioned by narrators such as Stevens and Ryder. In particular, Klara's quasi-religious relationship with the Sun places some distance between her and the other characters (as well as the reader), a point made by her refusal to provide Rick with details of her conversation with the Sun, and by the way that Manager is left perplexed, in the closing passages of the book, by Klara's claim that the Sun was particularly 'kind' to her (307). There is a sense, then, that Klara's desire for resolution in her own story is achieved only because she never leaves it open to contradiction by sharing it. This refusal runs counter to her own view of meaning as being constructed relationally, and for this reason Klara allows herself to be seduced by the possibility of narrating endings in a way that accords with her own desires.

Klara and the Sun thus offers a clear and positive role for irresolution, in that it permits a recognition of the way meaning can be created through provisional and relational resolutions without being beholden to these as definitive and conclusive. Yet Klara's own need to narrate a satisfactory ending for the story of herself, Josie, and Rick, indicates that the idea of resolution continues to exert a powerful hold on those who tell their stories.

Conclusion

The various overlapping forms of resolution discussed in this chapter – decisions, determinations, and endings – can all lead to misadventure and tragedy. Yet the difficulty faced by Ishiguro's characters (and, by extension, his readers) is that all of these forms of resolution are needed to make life meaningful and worthwhile. Ishiguro's novels themselves refuse to resolve this issue. They tend to end on a note of irresolution, leaving the reader also suspended between the desire for firm decisions and clear endings, and the sense that it is precisely this wish that has led his characters into positions where they are left wrestling with regret and attempting to eke out some consolation from their mistakes.

Given the central role that the need for resolution plays in the determination of his characters' motivations and decisions – including Ono's contribution to imperialism, Stevens's complicity with Nazism, and Wistan's fixation on genocide – Ishiguro's fictions suggest that learning to live with a state of irresolution is a less dangerous option, in ethical terms, than acting with a misguided sense of conviction. More recently, however, rather than simply framing it as the absence of a negative, Ishiguro has asserted a more positive role for irresolution. Moving away from plots that show the dangers of resolution, *Klara and the Sun* instead suggests that what we might perceive as resolutions are provisional, part of an evolving process of understanding self and world, rather than as twists in the plot on the way towards the kind of definitive resolutions that exist only within the self-deceiving fictions that his narrators construct for and about themselves.

Notes

1 Mark Currie, *About Time: Narrative, Fiction and the Philosophy of Time* (Edinburgh: Edinburgh University Press, 2007), p.33.
2 Ibid., p.30.
3 Chris Holmes and Kelly Mee Rich, 'On Rereading Kazuo Ishiguro', *Modern Fiction Studies* 67:1 (2021): 1–19 (8).
4 Doug Battersby, 'Reading Ishiguro Today: Suspicion and Form', *Modern Fiction Studies* 67:1 (2021): 67–88 (72).
5 Peter Sloane, *Kazuo Ishiguro's Gestural Poetics* (London: Bloomsbury, 2021), p.4.
6 Ibid., p.7.
7 'Drifting' is used to describe physical movements over twenty times in the whole novel as well as evoking mental processes on a number of other occasions.
8 Dominic Dean, 'Ishiguro and the Abandoned Child: The Parody of International Crisis and Representation in *When We Were Orphans*', *The Journal of Commonwealth Literature* 56:1 (2021): 150–67 (163).
9 Mark Currie, 'Controlling Time: Kazuo Ishiguro's *Never Let Me Go*', in Sean Matthews and Sebastian Groes, eds., *Kazuo Ishiguro: Contemporary Critical Perspectives* (London: Continuum, 2009), p.91.
10 Sloane, *Poetics*, p.8.

GUIDE TO FURTHER READING

Primary Works

Novels and Short Story Collections

A Pale View of Hills. London: Faber & Faber, 1982.
An Artist of the Floating World. London: Faber & Faber, 1986.
The Remains of the Day. London: Faber & Faber, 1989.
The Unconsoled. London: Faber & Faber, 1995.
When We Were Orphans. London: Faber & Faber, 2000.
Never Let Me Go. London: Faber & Faber, 2005.
Nocturnes: Five Stories of Music and Nightfall. London: Faber & Faber, 2009.
The Buried Giant. London: Faber & Faber, 2015.
Klara and the Sun. London: Faber & Faber, 2021.

Uncollected Short Stories

'A Strange and Sometimes Sadness'. *Bananas* (June 1980). Reprinted in *Introduction 7: Stories by New Writers*. London: Faber & Faber, 1981. 13–27.
'Getting Poisoned'. *Introduction 7: Stories by New Writers*. London: Faber & Faber, 1981. 38–51.
'Waiting for J'. *Introduction 7: Stories by New Writers*. London: Faber & Faber, 1981. 28–37.
'A Family Supper'. *Firebird 2: Writing Today*. Ed. T. J. Binding. Harmondsworth: Penguin, 1983. 121–31. Reprinted in *The Penguin Book of Modern Short Stories*. Ed. Malcolm Bradbury. Harmondsworth: Penguin, 1988. 434–42.
'Summer after the War'. *Granta* 7 (1983): 121–37.
'October, 1948'. *Granta* 17 (1985): 177–85.
'The Gourmet'. *Granta* 43 (1993): 89–127.
'A Village after Dark'. *The New Yorker*, 14 May 2001. Online: www.newyorker.com/magazine/2001/05/21/a-village-after-dark.

Screenplays

A Profile of Arthur J. Mason. Unpublished manuscript. Dir. Michael Whyte. First broadcast: Channel 4, 18 October 1984.
'The Gourmet'. *Granta* 43 (1993): 89–127. Dir. Michael Whyte. First broadcast: Channel 4, 8 May 1986.

The Saddest Music in the World. Unpublished manuscript. Dir. Guy Maddin. Released in the UK, 25 October 2003.

The White Countess. Unpublished manuscript. Dir. James Ivory. Released 21 December 2005.

Song Lyrics

'The Ice Hotel', 'I Wish I Could Go Travelling Again', 'Breakfast on the Morning Tram', 'So Romantic'. Stacey Kent, *Breakfast on the Morning Tram* (CD, 2007).

'Postcard Lovers'. Stacey Kent, *Dreamer in Concert* (CD, 2011).

'The Summer We Crossed Europe in the Rain', 'Waiter, Oh Waiter', 'The Changing Lights'. Stacey Kent, *The Changing Lights* (CD, 2013).

'Bullet Train'. Stacey Kent, *I Know I Dream* (CD, 2017).

'I Wish I Could Go Travelling Again', 'Craigie Burn', 'Tango in Macao'. Stacey Kent, *Songs from Other Places* (CD, 2021).

Miscellaneous Writings

'Introduction'. In Yasunari Kawabata, *Snow Country and Thousand Cranes*. Trans. Edward G. Seidensticker. London: Penguin, 1986.

'Letter to Salman Rushdie'. In *The Rushdie Letters: Freedom to Speak, Freedom to Write*. Ed. Steve MacDonogh. London: Brandon, 1993. 79–80.

Liner notes to Stacey Kent's *In Love Again* (CD, 2003).

My Twentieth-Century Evening and Other Small Breakthroughs: London: Faber & Faber, 2017.

Liner notes to *Chopin: Favourite Piano Works* CD, performed by Vladimir Ashkenazy (CD, 1998).

Interviews

Shaffer, Brian W. and Cynthia F. Wong. Eds. *Conversations with Kazuo Ishiguro*. Jackson: University Press of Mississippi, 2008.

Unpublished Works

For a summary of drafted but unpublished works in the Ishiguro Archive at the Harry Ransom Center in Austin, Texas, see Vanessa Guignery, 'The Ishiguro Archive' (Chapter 6, above), p.93 and nn. 6–13.

Selected Criticism

Books

Beedham, Matthew. *The Novels of Kazuo Ishiguro*. London: Palgrave Macmillan, 2010.

Cheng, Chu-chueh. *The Margin without Centre: Kazuo Ishiguro*. Oxford: Peter Lang, 2010.

Drag, Wojciech. *Revisiting Loss: Memory, Trauma and Nostalgia in the Novels of Kazuo Ishiguro*. Newcastle: Cambridge Scholars Press, 2014.

Lewis, Barry. *Kazuo Ishiguro*. Manchester: Manchester University Press, 2000.

Shaffer, Brian W. *Understanding Kazuo Ishiguro*. Durham: University of South Carolina Press, 1998.

Sim, Wai-chew. *Kazuo Ishiguro*. Abingdon: Routledge, 2010.

Sloane, Peter. *Kazuo Ishiguro's Gestural Poetics*. London: Bloomsbury, 2021.

Suter, Rebecca. *Two-World Literature: Kazuo Ishiguro's Early Novels*. Honolulu: University of Hawai'i Press, 2020.

Teo, Yugin. *Kazuo Ishiguro and Memory*. London: Palgrave Macmillan, 2014.

Wang, Ching-chih. *Homeless Strangers in the Novels of Kazuo Ishiguro: Floating Characters in a Floating World*. New York: Edwin Mellen, 2008.

Wong, Cynthia F. *Kazuo Ishiguro*. 2nd ed. Tavistock: Northcote House, 2005.

Collections of Essays

Groes, Sebastian and Barry Lewis, eds. *Kazuo Ishiguro: New Critical Visions of the Novels*. London: Palgrave Macmillan, 2011.

Holmes, Chris and Kelly Mee Rich, eds. Special Issue: Ishiguro after the Nobel. *MFS: Modern Fiction Studies* 67:1 (2021).

Matthews, Sean and Sebastian Groes, eds. *Kazuo Ishiguro: Contemporary Critical Perspectives*. London: Continuum, 2009₁

Matthews, Sean and Alexandra Mitrea, eds. Special Issue: Kazuo Ishiguro. *American, British and Canadian Studies* 31 (2018).

Shaw, Kristian and Peter Sloane, eds. *Kazuo Ishiguro: New Insights*. Manchester: Manchester University Press, 2022.

Wong, Cynthia F., Hülya Yildiz, and Rebecca L. Walkowitz, eds. *Kazuo Ishiguro in a Global Context*. Burlington, VT: Ashgate, 2015.

Chapters in Books

Bedggood, Daniel. 'Kazuo Ishiguro: Alternate Histories'. *The Contemporary British Novel since 2000*. Ed. James Acheson. Edinburgh: Edinburgh University Press, 2017. 109–18.

Colombino, Laura. 'Idealism, Farce and International Heterotopias: Aristocracy in Kazuo Ishiguro's *The Remains of the Day*'. *The British Aristocracy in Popular Culture: Essays on 200 Years of Representations*. Eds. Stefania Michelucci, Ian Duncan, and Luisa Villa. Jefferson, NC: McFarland, 2020. 185–99.

Holmes, Frederick M. 'Realism, Dreams and the Unconscious in the Novels of Kazuo Ishiguro'. *The Contemporary British Novel*. Eds. James Acheson and Sarah Ross. Edinburgh: Edinburgh University Press, 2005. 11–22.

Horton, Emily. 'Shifting Perspectives and Alternate Landscapes: Culture and Cultural Politics in the Fiction of Kazuo Ishiguro'. *Contemporary Crisis Fictions: Affect and Ethics in the Modern British Novel*. Basingstoke: Palgrave Macmillan, 2014. 159–216.

James, David. 'Apprehensive Alleviation'. *Discrepant Solace: Contemporary Literature and the Work of Consolation*. Oxford: Oxford University Press, 2019. 175–92.

Ostrovskaya, Maria. 'Reframing the Nonhuman: Grievability and the Value of Life in Kazuo Ishiguro's *Never Let Me Go*'. *Nonhuman Agencies in the Twenty-First-Century Anglophone Novel*. Eds. Yvonne Liebermann, Judith Rahn, and Bettina Burger. London: Palgrave Macmillan, 2021. 129–45.

Rushdie, Salman. 'Kazuo Ishiguro'. *Imaginary Homelands: Essays and Criticism, 1981–1991*. London: Viking, 1991. 244–6.
Sim, Wai-chew. 'Aesthetic Innovation and Radical Nostalgia in Kazuo Ishiguro's *When We Were Orphans*'. *British Asian Fiction: Framing the Contemporary*. Eds. Neil Murphy and Wai-chew Sim. Amherst, NY: Cambria Press, 2008. 329–49.

Journal Articles

Adelman, Gary. 'Doubles on the Rocks: Ishiguro's *The Unconsoled*'. *Critique: Studies in Contemporary Fiction* 42:2 (2001): 166–79.
Bain, Alexander M. 'International Settlements: Ishiguro, Shanghai, Humanitarianism'. *Novel: A Forum on Fiction* 40:3 (2007): 240–64.
Battersby, Doug. 'Reading Ishiguro Today: Suspicion and Form'. *Modern Fiction Studies* 67:1 (2021): 67–88.
Black, Shameem. 'Ishiguro's Inhuman Aesthetics'. *Modern Fiction Studies* 55:4 (2009): 785–807.
Cheng, Chu-chueh. 'Cosmopolitan Alterity: America as the Mutual Alien of Britain and Japan in Kazuo Ishiguro's Novels'. *The Journal of Commonwealth Literature* 45:2 (2010): 227–44.
Christou, Maria. 'Kazuo Ishiguro's Nonactors'. *Novel: A Forum on Fiction* 53:3 (2020): 360–82.
Dean, Dominic. 'Violent Authenticity: The Politics of Objects and Images in Ishiguro'. *Textual Practice* 35:1 (2021): 129–51.
Eatough, Matthew. 'The Time That Remains: Organ Donation, Temporal Duration, and *Bildung* in Kazuo Ishiguro's *Never Let Me Go*'. *Literature and Medicine* 29:1 (2011): 132–60.
'"Are They Going to Say This Is Fantasy?": Kazuo Ishiguro, Untimely Genres, and the Making of Literary Prestige'. *Modern Fiction Studies* 67:1 (2021): 40–66.
Fairbanks, A. Harris. 'Ontology and Narrative Technique in Kazuo Ishiguro's *The Unconsoled*'. *Studies in the Novel* 45:4 (2013): 603–19.
Furst, Lilian R. 'Memory's Fragile Power in Kazuo Ishiguro's *Remains of the Day* and W. G. Sebald's *Max Ferber*'. *Contemporary Literature* 48:4 (2007): 530–53.
Garland-Thomson, Rosemarie. 'Eugenic World Building and Disability: The Strange World of Kazuo Ishiguro's *Never Let Me Go*'. *Journal of Medical Humanities* 38:2 (2017): 133–45.
Garrido Castellano, Carlos. 'Ryder Meets Bourriaud: Kazuo Ishiguro's *The Unconsoled* and the Contradictions of "Creative Capitalism"'. *Critique: Studies in Contemporary Fiction* 61:2 (2020): 236–47.
Gehlawat, Monika. 'Myth and Mimetic Failure in *The Remains of the Day*'. *Contemporary Literature* 54:3 (2013): 491–519.
Gill, Josie. 'Written on the Face: Race and Expression in Kazuo Ishiguro's *Never Let Me Go*'. *Modern Fiction Studies* 60:4 (2014): 844–62.
Griffin, Gabriele. 'Science and the Cultural Imaginary: The Case of Kazuo Ishiguro's *Never Let Me Go*'. *Textual Practice* 23:4 (2009): 645–63.
Guth, Deborah. 'Submerged Narratives in Kazuo Ishiguro's *The Remains of the Day*'. *Forum for Modern Language Studies* 35:2 (1999): 126–37.

Holmes, Chris. 'Ishiguro at the Limit: The Corporation and the Novel'. *Novel: A Forum on Fiction* 52:3 (2019): 386–405.

Howard, Ben. 'A Civil Tongue: The Voice of Kazuo Ishiguro'. *Sewanee Review* 109:3 (2001): 398–417.

Hu, Jane. 'Typical Japanese: Kazuo Ishiguro and the Asian Anglophone Historical Novel'. *Modern Fiction Studies* 67:1 (2021): 123–48.

Johansen, Emily. 'Bureaucracy and Narrative Possibilities in Kazuo Ishiguro's *Never Let Me Go*'. *Journal of Commonwealth Literature* 51:3 (2016): 416–31.

Kanyusik, Will. 'Eugenic Nostalgia: Self-Narration and Internalized Ableism in Kazuo Ishiguro's *Never Let Me Go*'. *Journal of Literary and Cultural Disability Studies* 14:4 (2020): 437–52.

Lang, James M. 'Public Memory, Private History: Kazuo Ishiguro's *The Remains of the Day*'. *CLIO* 29:2 (2000): 143–65.

Lee, Ji Eun. 'Norfolk and the Sense of Loss: The Bildungsroman and Colonial Subjectivity in Kazuo Ishiguro's *Never Let Me Go*'. *Texas Studies in Literature and Language* 61:3 (2019): 270–90.

Lessinger, Enora. 'Genesis of a Self-Translation: Inside the Archive of Kazuo Ishiguro's *A Pale View of Hills*'. *Palimpsestes: Revue de Traduction* 34 (2020): 84–100.

McCombe, John P. 'The End of (Anthony) Eden: Ishiguro's *The Remains of the Day* and Midcentury Anglo-American Tensions'. *Twentieth Century Literature* 48:1 (2002): 77–99.

McDonald, Keith. 'Days of Past Futures: Kazuo Ishiguro's *Never Let Me Go* as "Speculative Memoir"'. *Biography* 30:1 (2007): 74–83.

Mazullo, Mark. 'Alone: Kazuo Ishiguro and the Problem of Musical Empathy'. *Yale Review* 100:2 (2012): 78–98.

Mead, Matthew. 'Caressing the Wound: Modalities of Trauma in Kazuo Ishiguro's *The Unconsoled*'. *Textual Practice* 28:3 (2014): 501–20.

Mickalites, Carey, 'Kazuo Ishiguro and the Remains of Empire'. *Critique: Studies in Contemporary Fiction* 60:1 (2019): 111–24.

Molino, Michael R. 'Traumatic Memory and Narrative Isolation in Ishiguro's *A Pale View of Hills*'. *Critique: Studies in Contemporary Fiction* 53:4 (2012): 322–36.

Ng, Lynda. 'Fixing to Die: Kazuo Ishiguro's Reinvention of the Bildungsroman'. *Textual Practice* 34:12 (2020): 2167–83.

O'Brien, Susie. 'Serving a New World Order: Postcolonial Politics in Kazuo Ishiguro's *The Remains of the Day*'. *Modern Fiction Studies* 42:4 (1996): 787–806.

Parkes, Adam. 'Ishiguro's "Rubbish": Style and Sympathy in *Never Let Me Go*'. *Modern Fiction Studies* 67:1 (2021): 171–204.

Quarrie, Cynthia. 'Impossible Inheritance: Filiation and Patrimony in Kazuo Ishiguro's *The Unconsoled*'. *Critique: Studies in Contemporary Fiction* 55:2 (2014): 138–51.

Query, Patrick R. '*Never Let Me Go* and the Horizons of the Novel'. *Critique: Studies in Contemporary Fiction* 56:2 (2015): 155–72.

Rajiva, Jay. 'Never Let Me Finish: Ishiguro's Interruptions'. *Studies in the Novel* 52:1 (2020): 75–93.

Reitano, Natalie. 'The Good Wound: Memory and Community in *The Unconsoled*'. *Texas Studies in Literature and Language* 49:4 (2007): 361–86.

Robbins, Bruce. 'Very Busy Just Now: Globalization and Harriedness in Ishiguro's *The Unconsoled*'. *Comparative Literature* 53:4 (2001): 426–41.

'Cruelty Is Bad: Banality and Proximity in *Never Let Me Go*'. *Novel: A Forum on Fiction* 40:3 (2007): 289–302.

Robinson, Richard. 'Nowhere, in Particular: Kazuo Ishiguro's *The Unconsoled* and Central Europe'. *Critical Quarterly* 48:4 (2006): 107–30.

Russell, Richard Rankin. 'Monsters of Anti-Semitism in Ishiguro's Rural English Landscape: Re-reading *The Remains of the Day* as Ethical Fantasy Novel'. *Critique: Studies in Contemporary Fiction* 61:4 (2020): 440–52.

Sloane, Peter. 'Literatures of Resistance under US "Cultural Siege": Kazuo Ishiguro's Narratives of Occupation'. *Critique: Studies in Contemporary Fiction* 59:2 (2018): 154–67.

Stacy, Ivan. 'Looking Out into the Fog: Narrative, Historical Responsibility, and the Problem of Freedom in Kazuo Ishiguro's *The Buried Giant*'. *Textual Practice* 35:1 (2021): 109–28.

Tamaya, Meera. 'Ishiguro's *Remains of the Day*: The Empire Strikes Back'. *Modern Language Studies* 22:2 (1992): 45–56.

Tan, Jerrine. 'Screening Japan: Kazuo Ishiguro's Early Japan Novels and the Way We Read World Literature'. *Modern Fiction Studies* 67:1 (2021): 89–122.

Tsao, Tiffany. 'The Tyranny of Purpose: Religion and Biotechnology in Ishiguro's *Never Let Me Go*'. *Literature and Theology* 26:2 (2012): 214–32.

Vernon, Matthew and Margaret A. Miller. 'Navigating Wonder: The Medieval Geographies of Kazuo Ishiguro's *The Buried Giant*'. *Arthuriana* 28:4 (2018): 68–89.

Walkowitz, Rebecca. 'Ishiguro's Floating Worlds'. *ELH* 68:4 (2001): 1049–76.

'Unimaginable Largeness: Kazuo Ishiguro, Translation, and the New World Literature'. *Novel: A Forum on Fiction* 40:3 (2007): 216–39.

Watson, George. 'The Silence of the Servants'. *Sewanee Review* 103:3 (1995): 480–6.

Westerman, Molly. 'Is the Butler Home? Narrative and the Split Subject in *The Remains of the Day*'. *Mosaic* 37:3 (2004): 157–70.

Weston, Elizabeth. 'Commitment Rooted in Loss: Kazuo Ishiguro's *When We Were Orphans*'. *Critique: Studies in Contemporary Fiction* 53:4 (2012): 337–54.

Whitehead, Anne. 'Writing with Care: Kazuo Ishiguro's *Never Let Me Go*'. *Contemporary Literature* 52:1 (2011): 54–83.

'Kazuo Ishiguro's *Nocturnes*: Between Archive and Repertoire'. *Modern Fiction Studies* 67:1 (2021): 20–39.

Wright, Timothy. 'No Homelike Place: The Lesson of History in Kazuo Ishiguro's *An Artist of the Floating World*'. *Contemporary Literature* 55:1 (2014): 58–88.

Yiping, Wang. 'Ethnic War and the Collective Memory in Kazuo Ishiguro's *The Buried Giant*'. *English Studies* 102:2 (2021): 227–42.

INDEX

Cambridge Companions To ...

AUTHORS

TOPICS